Trade and Empire in Muscat and Zanzibar

This book looks at the role of Oman in the Indian Ocean prior to British domination of the region. Omani merchant communities played a crucial part in the development of commercial activity throughout the territories they held by Oman in the eighteenth and nineteenth centuries, especially between Muscat and Zanzibar, using long-established trade networks. They were also largely responsible for the integration of the commerce of the Indian Ocean into the nascent global capitalist system.

M. Reda Bhacker, himself a member of a long established Omani merchant family, looks in detail at the complex relationship between the merchant community and Oman's rulers, first the Ya'ariba and then the Albusaidis. He analyses the tribal and religious dynamics of Omani politics both in Arabia, where he looks especially at the Wahhabi/Saudi threat, and in Oman's sprawling 'empire', with particular reference to Zanzibar where Omani ruler Sa'îd b Sulṭân had his court from the 1830s. His aim is to consider all Oman's overseas territories as a single entity, eschewing the conventional but misleading compartmentalisation of African and Arabian history.

Dr Bhacker finds that, despite their prestige and influence in the region, neither the merchant communities nor the Omani ruling classes were able to respond to Britain's determined onslaught. He traces the local and regional factors that allowed Britain to destroy Oman's, largely commercial, challenge to its hegemony and to emerge by the end of the nineteenth century as the commercially and politically dominant power in the region.

This book will appeal to students and scholars of history, economics and politics, especially those with interests in the economic development of the eighteenth and nineteenth centuries, in Middle Eastern, Indian and East African history, and in the growth of the British Empire.

Exeter Arabic and Islamic series

General Editor: Aziz al-Azmeh

Trade and Empire in Muscat and Zanzibar

Roots of British domination

M. Reda Bhacker

London and New York

First published 1992
by Routledge
11 New Fetter Lane, London EC4P 4EE

Simultaneously published in the USA and Canada
by Routledge
a division of Routledge, Chapman and Hall, Inc.
29 West 35th Street, New York, NY 10001

© 1992 M. Reda Bhacker

Typeset in 10/12pt Times by
Ponting-Green Publishing Services, Sunninghill, Berkshire
Printed and bound in Great Britain by
Mackays of Chatham PLC, Chatham, Kent

British Library Cataloguing in Publication Data
A catalogue record for this book is available from the British Library

ISBN 0–415–07997–7

Library of Congress Cataloging-in-Publication Data
Bhacker, M. Reda (Mohmed Reda), 1955–
    Trade and empire in Muscat and Zanzibar : roots of British
domination / M. Reda Bhacker.
        p.   cm. – (Exeter Arabic and Islamic series)
    Includes bibliographical references.
    ISBN 0–415–07997–7
    1. Oman–Commerce–History. 2. Oman–Foreign economic relations–
Great Britain. 3. Great Britain–Foreign economic relations–Oman.
I. Title. II. Series.
HF3765.B43   1992
337.4105353–dc20   91–47666
                                                              CIP

Dedicated with love and gratitude to Batool A. Ali Salman and Bhacker Habib Murad, my parents, first among my teachers.

Contents

Figures, Maps and Tables

Preface

One of the main objects of this book is to examine how and why the Omani international port of Muscat, which during the eighteenth century had dominated the commercial activity of the western Indian Ocean region, reverted to a forgotten backwater by the middle of the twentieth. In doing so, two interrelated topics are considered: the role of Muscati rulers and of various mercantile communities in Oman's commercial expansion at Zanzibar during the nineteenth century; and the factors that led to the initial rise of the Albusaidis in East Africa followed by the causes of their decline as a result of the interplay of internal Omani politics and external pressures.

The extent to which British policy was responsible for turning the once powerful rulers of Oman into proxies dependent on Britain by the last decades of the nineteenth century is analysed. This is reviewed against the backdrop of internal Omani politics and regional factors, the most important of which was the Wahhabi/Saudi threat not only to Oman but to all tribal principalities of the Arabian Peninsula. The book also accounts for the fortunes of the Ya'ariba (the ruling Dynasty in Oman before the Albusaid) in Albusaidi times, a topic hitherto sorely neglected by most modern Western writers and Arab historians.

The loss of influence by Omani rulers by the end of the nineteenth century has been conventionally interpreted as coinciding with the decline of commercial activities at Muscat. This study adduces contrary evidence to show that these activities continued throughout the nineteenth century in Muscat and, initially, were crucial in providing the impetus for the phenomenal commercial expansion at Zanzibar. Even before the British-sponsored dismemberment of the 'Omani State' in 1861, it was Muscati rulers who had lost any influence that they may previously have held in the regional Indian Ocean trade. That influence had, in any event, derived from their intimate links with members of mercantile communities from India who had been long-time residents of Muscat. As Britain intervened more and more in Omani affairs, these 'Omanis', for long active in Oman's regional commercial activities, were replaced by other traders who, although again from India, were now associated solely with British rather than Omani interests.

Historical studies on nineteenth century East Africa and Oman have tended, in their rigid compartmentalisation of reserving East Africa for Africanists and Oman for Arabists, to give a distorted picture and an often incomplete interpretation of the connections between the two. As a result of the failure to appreciate the effective integration of the two areas in a single entity, and the need to study events contemporaneously and concomitantly, the rise of Zanzibar has been attributed to the 'far-sighted policies' of the Omani ruler Sa'îd b Sultân (r.1806–56). Moreover, the transfer of Said's court to Zanzibar in the 1830s is frequently characterised as a move from a position of strength after the Omani ruler had allegedly consolidated his power in the Gulf.

In fact, Said's reign, throughout its duration, was plagued with dissensions among Omani and Swahili communities in East Africa as well as among the tribes in Oman. And contrary to what has been alleged, his move to Zanzibar, far from being part of a grand design seeking to establish an Omani 'empire', was a desperate attempt to save what commercial links remained to Muscat not only in East Africa but in the Indian Ocean region as a whole. In the final analysis, the move was the inevitable consequence of the seizure by Britain during the time of his father, Sultân b Ahmad (r. 1793–1804), of considerable powers and privileges that Muscat had previously enjoyed in India. By 1840, the need to shift the focus to Zanzibar had become urgent when the gaze of both Britain and France, hungry for new conquests, fell upon those territories in Africa which the Omani ruler had hitherto perceived to be under his suzerainty.

Besides attempting to give a more complete portrayal of the Omani–African links, firstly through an historical overview, and secondly by a study of internal events and dynamics taking place coterminously in Oman and East Africa, this book also analyses the underlying reasons for the inability of Muscati rulers to resist the external British challenge and their ensuing dependency upon Britain. The way the afore-mentioned factors were to affect the subsequent development of Oman is shown to have derived from the economic, political and social dislocations which emanated as much from the subordination of Muscati rulers to the British, aggravated by a lack of viable Omani institutions, as from the personal ambitions of Omani tribal and religious leaders.

Apart from Arab geographers' and historians' accounts, extensive use and reinterpretation of Omani chronicles and *dîwâns* (poetical compilations, correctly *dawâwîn*) have been made throughout the study. Contemporary narratives of travellers to Oman and East Africa have also been widely cited. The main archival sources consulted are the Zanzibar Archives in Tanzania, the India Office and Public Records Office in London and the United States Archives published in book form or on microfilm. In addition, information obtained in fieldwork by gathering oral traditions and conducting numerous interviews in East Africa, Oman and India between 1981 and 1989 has also been incorporated.

Acknowledgements

Although they cannot all be listed, it is a pleasure to acknowledge the many individuals whose advice, assistance and criticism have made this study possible. First and foremost, I wish to extend my thanks to the Government of Oman for giving me leave to pursue my studies and for funding part of my research. Without the backing of H.E. Yusuf b Alawi and H.H. Sayyid Haitham b Tariq, Minister and Undersecretary of the Omani Ministry of Foreign Affairs respectively, this book could not have been completed. My thanks to both of them for their understanding and support.

I would like to record here the debt I owe to the late Professor Tom Johnstone who, as a teacher and personal friend, encouraged me during my last year at the London School of Oriental and African Studies in 1980 to embark upon a doctorate project. Although I started my research in 1981, by the time work obligations in Oman permitted me to return to study at Oxford, Professor Johnstone had unfortunately passed away, a great loss to all who knew him and to the field of Omani studies.

I am grateful to all my three supervisors who, at various times, guided my research at Oxford: to Dr Roger Owen, a fellow old Bryanstonian, for 'launching me on my career' at St Antony's College, and to Professor Wilfred Madelung, especially for his insights on the Shi'i and Isma'ili aspects of my work. My special thanks and appreciation go to my main supervisor, Dr John Wilkinson, for his constant encouragement, invaluable advice and guidance.

Numerous teachers, colleagues and friends have contributed their constructive criticisms and useful suggestions throughout my research. Of these I would like to make a special mention of the following: Professors Charles Beckingham, Malcolm Yapp, K.N. Chaudhuri, Jawad b Jafar al-Khaburi; Drs Calvin Allen, Christine Nicholls and Garang Mehta; and Albert Hourani, Mustafa Muhammad Said, Abdul

Rahman Siddique, Eugenie Lucas, Chizuko Tominaga and my wife Bernadette who, despite her many domestic and professional duties, found the time to undertake the enormous task of proofreading and editing.

I also wish to express my appreciation to the many librarians, archivists and officers whose institutions are mentioned in the Bibliography, for their help and assistance in locating and obtaining often obscure material. Deserving of a special mention are Rosamund Campbell, Gillian Grant and Diana Ring of St Antony's College.

Finally, for the warm hospitality and friendship extended to me during my trip to East Africa, I am grateful to Ali b Nasir al-Ma'wali; Hammadi Omar, Director of the Zanzibar Archives; Abdul Rahman Muhammad Juma of the Zanzibari Ministry of Information, Culture and Sport; and Shaykh Salih b Salim al-Hadrami of Pemba.

Conventions and abbreviations

CONVENTIONS

A standard transliteration system is used for Arabic, Omani, Swahili, Persian and Indian words (Ar., Om., Sw., Per., In., respectively) which are set in italics, but, like names, are transliterated only when they first appear in the text. The transliteration is based on the system used by the *Encyclopaedia of Islam* except for jîm and qâf which are denoted by j and q respectively. In addition, no italics have been used to show double-letter transliterations (e.g. gh and not *gh* for Ghayn). Elongated vowels are shown by [^]. Hamza is shown by [`] and is usually not transliterated when coming at the beginning of a word. 'Ayn is denoted by ['] or ['']. Ta marbuta is indicated after a long alif (e.g. salât) and sometimes, for better reading, when followed by an alif lâm (e.g. al-Qasîdat al-Qudsîya). Alif maqsûra at the end of a word is not shown (e.g. Nizwa and not Nizwâ). Spellings given reflect local usages. English spelling is used for those proper names that have a recognised standard English (thus Sohar and not Suhâr). A for Abu (father of), b for ibn (son of) and B for Bani or Banu (sons of, in a tribal sense) are used in construction with proper names. Recognised plural forms such as 'ulama are used but more frequently plurals are indicated by the addition of s to the singular (e.g. Shaykhs and not Shuyûkh). 'The Gulf' is used for the Perso-Arabic, Arabian or Persian Gulf. 'Sayyid' is not used as a title before names and 'Sultan' describes the post-1861 rulers when the term officially came into use. Both terms are explained in the text and in the Glossary.

   Maria Theresa Dollar (MT$) a silver coin also known as the Austrian Crown, *thaler*, *Qirsh* or *Riyal*, was current in the Indian Ocean trading area throughout the nineteenth century. In Oman it was used, together with the Indian Rupee, as recently as the early 1970's when it was replaced by the Omani Riyal. Its value at different times is explained in the Notes.

ABBREVIATIONS

See the Bibliography for details on Omani and Archival works.

al-Adnaniya	'Al-Ṣaḥîfat al-'Adnânîya', Ibn Ruzaiq, 1258/ 1842, BL Or. 6569
AHS	*African Historical Studies*
Anon. MS.	'Anonymous Titleless History of Oman', MS BL Add. 23,343
BL	British Library
BM	British Museum
BS	'Selections from the Records of the Bombay Government', at IO
BSOAS	*Bulletin of the School of Oriental and African Studies*
Dissn	Dissertation
EALB	East African Literature Bureau
EAPH	East Africa Publishing House
EI2	*Encyclopaedia of Islam* (2nd edn)
EIHC	Essex Institute Historical Collections
al-Fath	'Al-fatḥ al-mubîn fî sîrat al-sâdat âl-bû-sa'îd-iyîn', MS Cambridge Uni. Lib. Add. 2892; tr. Badger G.P., 1871
FO	Foreign Office Records at PRO
FOCP	Foreign Office Confidential Print at PRO
Foster-Factories	'The English Factories in India', 1906–27
Guillain-Documents	'Documents sur l'histoire, la géographie et le commerce de l'Afrique Orientale', Guillain C., 1856
IJAHS	*International Journal of African Historical Studies*
IJMES	*International Journal of Middle Eastern Studies*
Int.	Interview with
IO	India Office, London
IOR	India Office Records, London
JAH	*Journal of African History*
JOS	*Journal of Oman Studies*
JRAS	*Journal of the Royal Asiatic Society*
JRGS	*Journal of the Royal Geographical Society*
Juhaina	'Juhainat al-akhbâr fî ta`rîkh Zanjbâr', al-Mughairî, 1979

Kashf	'Kashf al-Ghumma al-jâmi' li akhbâr al-`umma', attributed to its copier Sirhân al-Izkawî, BL Ms. Or. 8076.
Khabari Lamu	'Khabari Lamu', Shaykh Faraji al-Lamuy, ed. Hichens W., 1938, 'Lamu Chronicle'
Kitab al-Zunuj	'Kitâb al-Zunûj', text and Italian tr., Cerulli E., 1957
Lib.	Library
lit.	literally
al-Murjibi-	'Maisha ya Hamed bin Muhammed el Murjebi yaani Tippu Tip...', tr. Brode H., 1907; tr. and ed. Whiteley W.H., 1959; tr. and ed. Bontinck F., 1974
MES	*Middle East Studies*
MNHC	Ministry of National Heritage and Culture, Muscat
Morice-Projet	'Projet d'un Etablissement sur la côte orientale d'Afrique', 1777, tr. Freeman-Grenville G.S.P., 1965, 'The French at Kilwa Island'
Nahda	[in the main text] = Ibadi reform or revival movement
	[in the Notes] = 'Nahdat al-a'yân bi hurrîyat 'Umân', al-Sâlimî, Muhammad
NEMA	'New England Merchants in Africa', eds Bennett N.R. and Brooks G.E., 1965
Or.	Oriental
PAM	Political Agent, Muscat
PAZ	Political Agent, Zanzibar
Pr.	Press
PRO	Public Record Office, London
PRPG	Political Resident/Residency in the Persian Gulf
al-Qahtaniya	'Al-Sahîfat al-Qahtânîya', Ibn Ruzaiq, 1269/1852, Rhodes House MS Afr. S.3.
Qisas	'Qisas wa Akhbâr jarat bi 'Umân', al-Ma'walî, BM Ms Or. 6568
al-Qudsiya	'Al-Qasîdat al-Qudsîya al-nûrânîya fî al-manâqib al-'Adnânîya', Ibn Ruzaiq, BM Ms Or. 6565, vol. 2
r.	Reigned
RC	*Revue Coloniale*
SD	'The East African Coast: Select Documents', ed. Freeman-Grenville, G.S.P., 1962a

al-Shua'a	'Al-Shu'â' al-shâ`i' bi al-lam'ân fî dhikr A`immat 'Umân', Ibn Ruzaiq, Cambridge Uni. Lib. Ms
Tarikh al-Mazari'	'Ta`rîkh wilâyat al-Mazâri'a fî Ifrîqîya al-sharqîya', al-Mazrû'î, Amîn b 'Alî, n.d.
TBGS	*Transactions of the Bombay Geographical Society*
th.	thesis
TLSB	*Transactions of the Literary Society of Bombay*
TNR	*Tanzania (formerly Tanganyika) Notes and Records*
Tuhfa	'Tuhfat al-a'ayân bi sîrat ahl 'Umân', 'Abd-allâh al-Sâlimî, 1927
Uni.	University
US/Arch	US Archives (published or on microfilm)
Waqayi'	'Waqâ`i'-i manâzil-i Rûm', Abdul Qadir, Khwaja, tr. and ed. Hasan M., 1968, 'A Diary of a Journey to Constantinople'
ZA	Zanzibar Archives, Zanzibar

Table 1 The Albusaidi and other rulers of Oman and Zanzibar, 1749–1970

Oman	Zanzibar
Im. Aḥmad b Sa'îd (1749–83)	
Im. Sa'îd b Aḥmad (1783–89)	
Ḥamad b Sa'îd (1789–92)	
Sulṭân b Aḥmad (1792–1804)	
Badr b Sayf (1804–6)	
Sa'îd b Sulṭân (1806–56)	
Thuwaynî b Sa'îd (1856–66)	Mâjid b Sa'îd (1856–70)
Sâlim b Thuwaynî (1866–8)	
Im. 'Azzân b Qays (1868–71)	
Turkî b Sa'îd (1871–88)	Barghash b Sa'îd (1870–88)
Fayṣal b Turkî (1888–1913)	Khalîfa b Sa'îd
	(March 1888–February 1890)
	'Alî b Sa'îd
	(February 1890–March 1893)
	Ḥamad b Thuwaynî
	(March 1893–August 1896)
	Ḥamûd b Muḥammad
	(August 1896–July 1902)
	'Alî b Ḥamûd
	(July 1902–December 1911)
	Khalîfa b Ḥârib
	(December 1911–October 1960)
Taymûr b Fayṣal (1913–32)	
& Im. Sâlim b Râshid al-Kharûṣî	
(1913–20)	
Sa'îd b Taymûr (1932–70)	
& Im. Muḥammad b 'Abdallâh al-Khalîlî	
(1920–54)	
& Im. Ghâlib b 'Alî al-Hinâ`î	
(1954–5)	'Abdallâh b Khalîfa
	(October 1960–July 1963)
	Jamshîd b 'Abdallâh
	(July 1963–January 1964)
Qâbûs b Sa'îd (1970–)	

Notes: Im. = Imam; all rulers are Albusaidis except where indicated
Sources: Anon. Ms, 165–71; Kashf, 155; Juhaina, 136–8 and 260–480; IOR/P/381/33, Seton to Bombay, 9 July 1802; IOR/15/6/437–540 and IOR/15/1/719/3–6 and IOR/15/1/720–1 for Administration Reports, 1873–1947; ZA/*Zanzibar Gazette* and British Colonial Reports; ZA/AA1–5 series; Bathurst R.D., 1967, 323–5; Beckingham C.F., 1941, 257–60

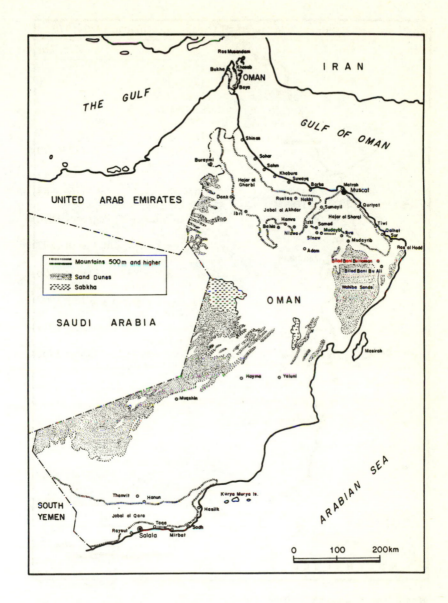

Map 1 The modern Sultanate of Oman

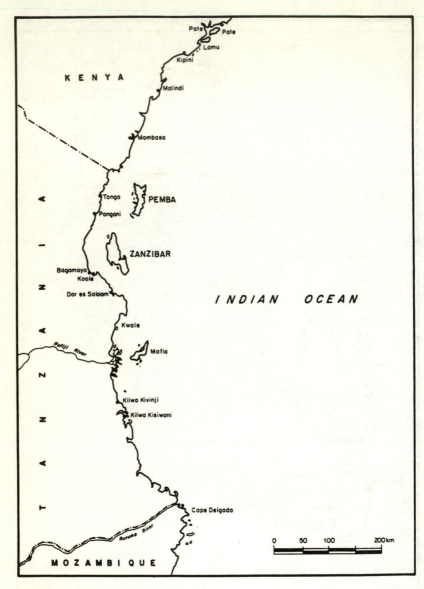

Map 2 The modern East African coast

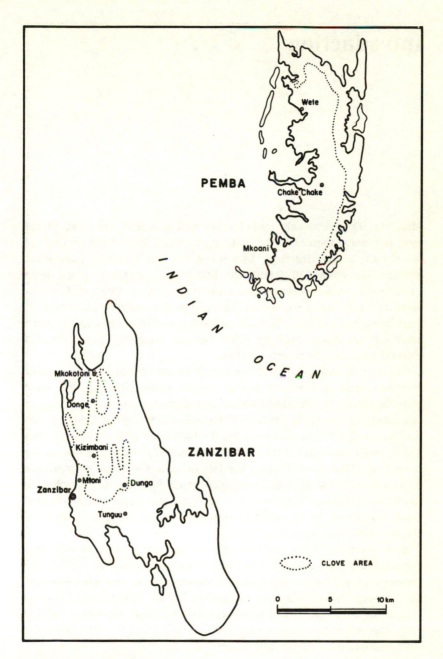

Map 3 Zanzibar and Pemba

Introduction

Maritime trade, Imamate Government and tribalism are three of the most pervasive themes in the history of Oman. Whilst the outlines of the Omani tribal structure, like those of long-distance commerce, antedate the advent of Islam, the final form of tribalism has been strongly influenced by the political dimensions of the Imamate Government following the rise of Islam. Thus, of the three above-cited themes, maritime trade has been the most persistent and resilient and has had a more lasting impact than the other two as a unifying economic and cultural force for the people of Oman.

Recent archaeological evidence puts back the origins of the impact of maritime trade on Oman to as early as the sixth millenium BC when parts of Oman are thought to have established commercial exchange links with the coastal inhabitants of the area known by the Greeks as the Erythraean Sea.[1] This area included the borderlands of the Arabian Sea and its two extensions of the Red Sea and the Gulf which penetrate the Afro-Asian land mass. During the Islamic era, the effect of maritime trade was such that the Ibadi religious-cum-tribal structure which gave rise to the Imamate Government could not have implanted its roots in Oman had it not, in its initial phases, received financial support from Oman's mercantile communities.

Being by nature a long-distance phenomenon, maritime trade bridges geographical and cultural boundaries and criss-crosses established commercial networks and political frontiers. In this phenomenon, Omani ports, forming part of the Indian Ocean region, have played a fluctuating commercial and political role on a local, regional or global scale depending on Oman's own political condition and its interaction with internal and external influences.

Although the Indian Ocean region has always been characterised as having culturally distinct entities – Perso-Arabic/Islamic Near and Middle Eastern, Hindu and Muslim Indian, and Chinese – underlying this there has also always been an inherent impression that the Indian Ocean has an independent and coherent force giving it a distinct sense of identity and sphere of influence. Parallels to the Braudelian conception of the Mediterranean Sea here are only too obvious.[2] From a 'longue durée' Braudelian perspective, before the introduction of mechanised maritime transport in the Indian Ocean in the late nineteenth century, this sense of identity was further reinforced by climatic conditions, most notable among which was the influence of a single global variable, the wind system known as *mawsims* (monsoons). The sailing pattern and consequently the trading seasons of the region were fixed with fine precision to coincide with the prevailing winds which could be gauged with remarkable accuracy by contemporary sailors and navigators.

It is as part of this Indian Ocean regional system that Omani commerce, having undergone a considerable development at Muscat, branched out during the second half of the eighteenth century to reap its share from the East African trade expansion which from that time was converging on to Zanzibar. That this East African commerce was to reach its zenith in the late 1870s and early 1880s was not solely due to the 'far-sighted' policies of Zanzibari merchants or Muscati rulers.[3] Nor was it a consequence of an active or deliberate 'African policy' pursued by Oman's mercantile or political leaders.[4] It was the result of a complex concatenation of geographical conditions, historical developments, religious considerations and economic factors. Among these, as the substance of this study will show, the economic and political situation of Oman combined with the increasing involvement of West European nations and the United States of America in the affairs of the Indian Ocean were to play a major part.

The legacy to which the Albusaidi rulers of the nineteenth century acceded can be traced back to the foundation of the Portuguese seaborne empire in the Indian Ocean in the early sixteenth century. One of the most important elements introduced by the Portuguese was their practice of conducting trade by warfare while controlling maritime commercial routes through the use of force. Among the ports involved in the Indian Ocean trade at that time, only Muscat, which by the end of the sixteenth century had become a prosperous commercial town,[5] together with a number of ports in Imperial China, had sufficient resources to construct defences in order to withstand Portuguese assaults.[6] With the rise of the Ya'ariba Dynasty in Oman and the expulsion of the Portuguese from Muscat by Sultân b Sayf al-Ya'rubî on 23 January 1650,[7] Oman was to enter a period of more than a century of maritime expansion, at the expense of the Portuguese, in India as well as in East Africa. In the same way as the Portuguese were driven out of Muscat with the collaboration of Banyan merchants resident at that port, so it was the continuation of similar cooperation between Muscat's rulers and merchants hailing from India that was responsible for the nineteenth century commercial development of both Muscat and Zanzibar.

In the pre-nineteenth century commercial field, as the monopoly over the protective costs of the Portuguese perfected 'peddling' trade, to use Steensgaard's terminology, was being supplemented by the newly introduced structure of the 'company' trade by the European East India Companies,[8] the Ya'ariba rulers of Oman, in the political sphere, were receiving positive assistance from Omani and Indian residents of East Africa in their joint struggle against the Portuguese.[9] Following the undermining of Portuguese influence, the eighteenth century Albu-saidis (correctly `Âlbûsa'îdîyûn` or collectively *al-`Âlbûsa'îd*) continued the practice adopted by the Ya'ariba of using both systems of trade. During the nineteenth century it was the English East India Company that took it upon itself, as it did in many other aspects affecting Omani commerce, to force Omani merchants to abandon the protective costs system by describing it as 'piracy'.

Close links between Oman and communities originating in Oman, which had a long history of settlement on the East African coast, can be traced back centuries before the advent of the sixteenth century to at least as far as the first century AD.[10] But it is important to bear in mind, in the context of an organisational backdrop of Omani society, that these communities, once settled in East Africa, continued to function within the familiar Omani tribal structure safeguarding their administrative and judicial independence. As in Oman, these communal or tribal groupings settled their own disputes and had a consensus that the *tamîma* or leader of each tribe or group should be their representative and spokesman before the ruler of the time whether he happened to be an Imam or a Sultan.

Such an essentially Omani tribal system was organised on the basis of regions of influence (*dâr*; pl. *diyâr*) for each tribe or group whose territorial limits were recognised and respected by all others. In such a system, the notion of a central government was non-existent. Thus, throughout Oman's history, one encounters ethnic-cum-religious groups within the Omani population, such as the Baluchi mercenaries, the Makrani Zadgalis, the Lawatiya, Banyan, Khoja and 'Ajam (Persian) merchants, the imported slaves, or more recently the Dhofaris, the Jibbalis and the Zanzibaris, originating from communities which did not belong to the so-called 'core' tribes. But like these tribes, each community had its own recognised quarters and administered its own affairs on quasi-tribal lines. Although these communities are now more intermingled, they continue to the present day to safeguard jealously their distinct identities. On the other hand, some of their members, having been subjected to massive acculturation processes such as uniform school curricula or political trends such as Arabism, have recently joined the older established tribes in their search to give a more 'Arabised' camouflage to their existence in the historically cosmopolitan world of Oman. However, even among those who have chosen to adhere to their former loyalties, some have been obliged to describe themselves in a tribal fashion, thus giving rise to *nisbas* (clan or locality affiliative name; correctly `*ansâb*) like al-Bulûshî or al-Lawâtâ.

By functioning on the principle of *'aṣabîya* (tribal or group cohesion), each tribe or group could theoretically change its allegiance as it best suited its interests at a particular point in time. During the periods of Ibadi Imamate governments, the Imam derived his authority as leader ideologically from the constitutional powers of the *sharî'a* (Islamic Law) while in practice he relied for his financial and physical support on his tribal and communal followers. Such a system of government perpetuated the tribal system of organisation in which the Imam assumed the role of a *tamima* and was thus no more than a 'primus inter pares'.[11] In the more recent era of the Sultanates, though the position of the rulers lacked a *sharia*-based complexion, the Sultans were nevertheless, like the Imams, totally dependent internally on their tribal and communal following. However, whether under Imamate or Sultanate rule, mercantile communities, including non-Muslim ones, lived and conducted their commercial activities in Oman's international ports, based successively at Sohar, Qalhat and Muscat, throughout the Islamic period. Even during Imamate times, the *mushrikûn* (polytheists) among these communities, such as the Hindu Banyans, were tolerated at these international ports where reciprocal taxation arrangements applied to them under `*amân* (protection) agreements in the same way as they theoretically affected Omanis living abroad.[12]

It will be quickly deduced from the preceding account that, at least from the early Islamic times, Oman has never been a monolithic Arab tribal entity. If the core of Omani 'nationality', as some writers would argue, has been the Ibadi-cum-tribal identity of the *dâkhilîya* (interior),[13] then the peripheral plural society on the Omani coast involved in maritime trade cannot be regarded as less 'Omani'. Throughout Oman's history, the coast and the interior have always been interdependent for their very survival. Indeed, as far as tribalism is concerned, the tribal system, as Khazanov has shown, can never be regarded as a pre-state formation but a final form having no potential by itself for further development.[14] For the Omani 'national' system, maritime trade, at times accompanied by foreign conquest, has been an integral part without which Oman as a 'state' could never have existed.

From a demographic angle, only about 55 per cent of Oman's population is said to be Ibadi.[15] Therefore, nearly half the number of Oman's people adhere to religions or other Islamic groups that are allegedly not part of the strict *dakhiliya* definition of Omani 'nationality'. This religious or cultural plurality of Omani society has hitherto not received the attention it deserves primarily because Omani history has been written from a *dakhiliya* point of view using predominantly Ibadi works. Written sources for a coastal perspective of Omani history are unfortunately non-existent. But there is a considerable amount of evidence, albeit fragmentary, for at least the commercial aspects of the coast in travellers' narratives which, when added to a careful sifting of oral traditions, give us a reasonable picture of Oman's ethnic-cum-religious communities that make up the coastal component of Oman's population. As far as oral traditions are concerned, as Spear has pointed out, 'no serious history can ignore local peoples' own perceptions of their past'[16] nor indeed the 'national state' to which they feel they belong.

Notwithstanding the exaggerated emphasis by historians placed upon the Arab tribal aspect of Oman's culture, the few anthropological studies so far carried out in Oman have come up, not surprisingly, with the conclusion that 'Oman is an internally varied and highly complex culture area...[where] cultural pluralism is today very marked...[and where] cultural traditions persist [not] because of ignorance of alternatives [but] because people believe in them and obtain satisfaction from them'.[17] This insight from a non-historical discipline into contemporary Omani society has application nonetheless in an historical perspective.

As the central theme of this study will make clear, it was this age-old plurality in Oman's coastal culture engendering a tolerant attitude among the various communities of the cosmopolitan Omani society, whether in Arabia, India or Africa, that was behind the nineteenth century commercial expansion of Oman. It will be shown that it was the relationship of Muscati rulers with certain prominent Banyan and other Indian merchants resident at Muscat and regarded as 'Omani', which was primarily responsible for the phenomenal rise in commercial activity at both Muscat and Zanzibar. Indeed, if we invoke the core and periphery theory describing Oman's 'national' identity, then the nineteenth century development at Muscat followed by the move to Zanzibar was no less than a revolution in that the so-called traditional core was pushed back to the peripheral boundary of the newly established centres.

As Omani commerce developed it received a boost at the beginning of the nineteenth century paradoxically from the suppression of the European slave trade. The surplus slave labour and Oman's own tribal and communal workers were both exploited for agricultural and commercial purposes such as the cultivation of cloves in East Africa and dates in Oman, the gathering of highly sought-after commodities such as ivory, pearls and cowries or the production of textiles. With the rise in demand for Omani-produced commodities and a corresponding decline in the cost of manufactured goods imported through Omani ports, the dynamics of a profitable development of commercial or commercially oriented manufactured products and agricultural activities were set in motion in Omani-controlled territories in Arabia as well as in Africa. The result was a multiplication of the existing trade routes and the introduction of new ones. As the Omani economy as a whole was progressively absorbed into the world economy, the frontiers of Zanzibari-controlled trade extended to regions as far apart as present-day Somalia to the north, Zaire to the west and Cape Delgado to the south while local African and Swahili leaders recognised Albusaidi suzerainty in parts of Kenya, mainland Tanzania, Uganda and even in certain areas of the Comoro Islands.

Nonetheless, once Oman had entered into treaty relations with Western powers, such as the United States of America, which were regarded by Britain as rivals, and once Oman's commercial development came to be perceived as a threat to the British position in the Indian Ocean, British authorities naturally responded unequivocally. The methods Britain used to curb the Omani challenge were based partly on the intensification of the British antislavery crusade coupled with the manipulation by British officials of the 'Indian' associates of Muscat's rulers. But these external reasons influencing the eventual subordination of Oman were bolstered to a considerable extent by domestic and regional factors which rendered Omani leaders incapable of resisting what was effectively a British threat to their own sovereignty and independence. Prominent among these more localised factors were the Wahhabi/Saudi incursions in Oman; the internal opposition to Albusaidi rule; the quarrels among the Albusaidis themselves; the lack of transformation in Oman's own institutions in order to meet the new challenges; and the personal ambitions of certain Omani political and religious leaders.

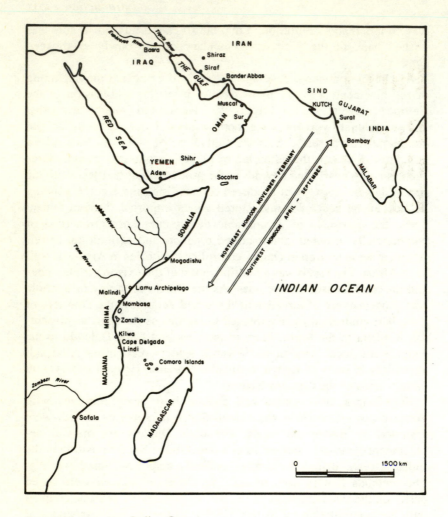

Map 4 The western Indian Ocean

Part I

Prelude to the rise of the Albusaidi dynasty in East Africa

1 Oman's links with India and East Africa

Historical problems and perspectives

'It was the Slave Trade which was originally responsible for generating the increased economic interest of the Omanis in the Swahili Coast'.[1] This quotation is a more recent example of the widely accepted view regarding the nineteenth century Omani expansion in East Africa. First of all, slavery as an institution was a centuries-old phenomenon admitted by Omanis themselves, during the nineteenth century, to have existed 'since the days of [Prophet] Noah'.[2] Secondly, the theory that the above statement seeks to propound is ill-supported by the available evidence, not least the facts that Oman's links with East Africa were well established by the nineteenth century and slaves did not constitute the foremost trading commodity in East African markets at the beginning of that century.

Leaving aside the very early links between Omanis and the inhabitants of the East African coast,[3] Omani political and economic interests in East Africa were widespread and recognised, as Bathurst has shown, from the mid-seventeenth century under the Ya'ariba.[4] While Omani rulers, since that time, appointed *wâlîs* (governors) to various principalities in East Africa, they did not establish any centralised political authority over them. Such a relatively modern European-originated concept of central government did not in fact impinge in any way upon their attitudes of thought nor upon their socio-economic infrastructure which was based on tribalism. Thus, as there never was an extensive and grandiose East African 'empire' in the heyday of Kilwa in the thirteenth century, despite the insistence of some early writers on popularising such romantic myths.[5] Similarly, there was no Ya'rubi nor indeed an Albusaidi 'empire' with viable institutions enabling Omani rulers to exercise centralised authority in territories in East Africa, even in those areas where they exercised some degree of control. That control, motivated primarily by the desire to protect trade and to collect duties, was derived from tribal allegiances, political alliances with local rulers and long-established commercial relationships.

Following the demise of the Ya'ariba, various factors combined to undermine the control and debilitate the power base from which the Albusaidis would ordinarily have expected to benefit by virtue of Oman's tribal system. Prominent among these factors were the turmoil which afflicted Oman during the civil wars of 1719–49; the Persian invasions; the squabbles between members of the newly established Albusaidi Dynasty and between the Albusaidi rulers and other dominant Omani groups both in Oman and overseas; the Omani struggle against European powers and its competition for trade in previously Omani-dominated commercial outlets in India, Africa and the Gulf region and the Omani conflict with the Wahhabis. Against such a multi-faceted economic and political edifice, it is a constant source of wonder that historians attach so much importance to the trading activities at Zanzibar in the nineteenth century and persist in treating them in isolation without the most cursory examination of trade in the Indian Ocean region as a whole in the seventeenth and eighteenth centuries. These earlier commercial activities were the precursors and the catalysts that were to trigger the later rise of the Omani-generated East African commerce. To disregard this crucial aspect is a fundamentally flawed assumption. And while it is true that the increasing European and American incursions and commercial interests in East Africa did give an unprecedented importance to Zanzibar from the third decade of the nineteenth century, it was the ability of the old commercial system in East Africa to fuel these new trends that gave an impetus to the burgeoning and progressively internationalised Indian Ocean economy.

Omani and Indian contributions to Swahili culture

In discussing the rise of Zanzibar in the nineteenth century, the picture most historians present is that 'following the stabilization of political affairs in Oman under the new Bu Saidi Dynasty',[6] Said b Sultan

> saw more clearly than his Portuguese counterparts had that his own people possessed neither the skills nor the capital to finance and develop the trading economy of East Africa....As the power of the Omani state increased in the Persian Gulf, he [Said b Sultan] did everything in his power to attract Asian merchants to Masqat[7]

to finance the trade of his so called 'empire'. This picture does not withstand closer analysis. As it will be shown below, Asian merchants were involved in Omani commerce since the beginning of the Islamic era. Moreover, it is incontrovertible that the Albusaidi Dynasty, from its very beginnings and throughout the eighteenth and nineteenth centuries, had been plagued with dissension and opposition. Said b Sultan's reign enjoyed nothing approaching even a semblance of 'stabilization of political affairs' internally, let alone creating a climate conducive to expansion externally in the Gulf region.

In addition, it is necessary to identify and distinguish those groups which are sweepingly referred to as 'Asians' from those alleged to be 'Said's own people'. Here we are forced to return to the vexed and convoluted question of the relatively recently introduced European concept of 'nationality' discussed in the Introduction. In the above-described view of the rise of Zanzibar, it is generally accepted that Omanis and Asians, relying on Asian capital to finance the slave trade, used slave labour and Swahili intermediaries to develop their clove plantation economy. This is thought to have brought about the prosperity of Zanzibar whose markets, from the beginning of the nineteenth century, were being linked to the world economy. In such a portrayal, it is extremely difficult to distinguish between the 'Omanis', the 'Swahilis', the 'Africans' or the 'Indians'. Given the long-established historical contacts between Oman, India and the East African coast, and the settlement of groups originating from Oman on this coast, especially during the Ya'rubi period, there must have been elements among the late eighteenth century 'Swahilis' which had as impressive Omani credentials as the Albusaidi rulers themselves. In fact, before the spread of the Swahili language and its extensive usage during the twentieth century, these early 'Swahilis' may be regarded as more Omani than, say, the Zanzibaris returning to Oman in the 1970s or, for that matter, the Dhofaris who have only recently started to participate in the mainstream of Oman's socio-economic system. For although these latter 'Omani' groups obtained Omani passports without too much difficulty, in the era of re-emergent Arabism of the 1970s many of them could be considered as less 'Omani' since they could hardly conduct a conversation in Arabic.

MIGRATIONS AND THE INTERACTION OF COMMERCE AND RELIGION IN OMANI AND SWAHILI CULTURES

Leaving aside the disputes still preoccupying historians as to the original birthplace of the 'Swahili' civilisation,[8] it is generally agreed by most East Africanists that Swahili history and civilisation have for the most part developed from a series of interactions which took place initially on some part of the East African coast or its islands. These interactions are thought to have derived from the responses of indigenous African development in parallel with imported notions from other parts of Africa, from the Middle East, especially from Oman and Yemen in Arabia and from Shiraz in Persia. Although modern East African scholars do make references to Daybul (a port in Sind) and include *Wâdebûlî* (people from Daybul) among the various Swahili groups,[9] most of them stop short of actually giving an explicit recognition to any Indian or Asian element within the Swahili culture, despite the fact that 'it is an established historical fact that Indians were carrying on a prosperous trade with East Africa in the century in which Jesus Christ was born'.[10] Since that time, there have been continuous infiltrations and migratory waves in all directions to and from India, East Africa and Oman.

Moreover, the historical evolution of the religious aspects of Swahili culture has been sorely neglected having been accorded at most a sidelong glance with undue emphasis having been placed on commercial and strategic interests. In general, research on the way heterodox Islamic movements may have affected Swahili civilisation has been inadequate.[11] This is not altogether surprising given the preoccupation of Western academia with a preconceived Sunni Islamic orthodoxy, and the tendency of the former to be led by this so-called orthodoxy to reject all other movements as heresies. Western academia has only just begun to move towards a better understanding of Shi'ism and Ibadism, two of the main historical rivals of the self-defined Sunni 'orthodoxy'. There is thus much ground to be covered before anything approaching a comprehension of the multitude of other bands that make up the spectrum of Islam can be grasped, let alone determine how these affected and provoked the emergence of various splinter groups which rapidly dispersed far and wide to the Atlantic and the Indus and beyond, from the first century of Islam.

In the East African context, the Julanda rulers of interior Oman, unable to resist the invasion of the armies of al-Ḥajjâj b Yûsuf al-Thaqafî, the <u>wali</u> of Iraq under the Umayyad Caliph 'Abd al-Malik b Marwân (AH 65–99 = AD 685–717), fled to East Africa (*Bilâd al-Zinj*) sometime between the years 700 and 705 (AH 81–6).[12] This was apparently 'a considerable migration, more than a group of entrepreneurs or dissidents'.[13] As it has been pointed out in 'Juhaina', for the Julanda to choose the East African coast indicates that they must have had strong connections there before the time of their migration:

'It does not make sense that rulers of Oman, Sulaymân and Sa'îd, sons of 'Abd al-Julanda, should escape with their families, their supporters and followers to a country or a land devoid of any Omani presence where they could not have had a guarantee for the security of their lives and the safeguarding of their religious beliefs'.[14]

Following this migration, there is a long gap of four centuries during which occasional references in the sources are made to some sort of Shi'i and Qarmati influence affecting Swahili culture,[15] while migrations to the coast from the Indian Ocean region at large continued throughout this period.[16]

With the establishment of the '*Shîrâzî*' Dynasty in Kilwa probably at the end of the twelfth century, Kilwa was to reach new heights as it began to wrest from Mogadishu the control of the gold trade of Sofala which served as a coastal entrepôt for the gold, ivory and probably slaves of Great Zimbabwe and Mozambique.[17] It has been suggested that the founding members of the Kilwa Dynasty were Shî'î in religion.[18] Nonetheless, although there were without doubt strong Shi'i influences in Kilwa in the early period, more recent research has shown that the Kilwa Dynasty was in fact Ibadi in origin having close links with Oman.[19] Having said that, we must hasten to add that there is no concrete evidence enabling it to be conclusively determined whether or not there existed a link between these Ibadis and the early eighth century migrants from Oman. Within this religious framework, another important Islamic element, also hitherto neglected, must be analysed: that of the Isma'ili *d'awa* (literally 'call') which appeared in the ninth century and has given rise to recurrent manifestations in the Indian Ocean region since that time and up to the present day.

Apart from commerce, another important reason why these various Islamic movements chose to migrate to East Africa was religious persecution from which these groups fled, as in the case of the Ibadi forerunner, in order to safeguard their own version of Islamic beliefs away from the centre of the expanding Muslim realm.[20] The Ismaili movement, from its inception, and throughout most of its history, like many other so-called 'heterodox' Islamic movements, is a salient example of how these movements suffered from such persecution, except of course in those times when they themselves had the upper hand, as the Ismailis did, in the era of the Fatimids.

According to Ismaili sources the Ismaili movement, from its beginnings in the year 808, was largely engaged in the establishment of a remarkable network of emissaries who came to constitute the *da'wa*, often inadequately rendered into English as 'mission' or 'propaganda'.[21] Having both religious and political motives the various officials called *du'ât* (sing. *dâ'î*), in the ranks of the *da'wa*, were carefully selected and subjected to rigorous training and discipline before being assigned for work in various geographical divisions known as *jazâ'ir* (sing. *jazîra*). In the beginning, the main *jazair* of the *da'wa* were Yemen, Oman and Sind in northern India. Indeed, it is maintained that 'Oman was one of the main objectives of the da'wa...and may well have served as a stepping-stone for spreading Ismaili influences'.[22]

With regard to the activity of opposition groups to the early rule of the Umayyads, there is evidence that Ibadis with centres of influence at Basra in Iraq and in parts of Oman and Yemen managed to establish an ephemeral principality in the Yemen between 747 and 750.[23] There is no mention, however, in Omani chronicles of any contemporary Ismaili activity in Oman. The absence of any such reference is not in itself altogether surprising since Omani chronicles were written exclusively by Ibadis with whose doctrines Ismailism at that time would have been competing for the purpose not only of gaining adherents but also of maintaining commercial links with mercantile communities. For without the active financial assistance of merchants, neither Ibadism nor Ismailism would have ever gained ground.[24] What is important to bear in mind is that the Banû Sâma b Lu'ayy, rulers of Multan in Sind who had originated from Oman and who had been in the forefront of the Islamic armies conquering India, had been converted by the tenth century, to the Ismaili cause at a time when the Ismaili Imams operating from Salmiya in Syria were preparing the way for the Fatimid Caliphate in North Africa.[25] The linkages between Oman and Sind, which had been so strong in pre-Islamic times, continued to remain so in the Islamic era.[26] One of the most prominent of Oman's Ibadi chroniclers, 'Abd-allâh al-Sâlimî, informs us that during the eleventh century the Ibadi Imam Sa'îd b Râshid al-Yahmadî attempted to convert the people of the Sindi town of Mansura to Ibadism.[27]

There is no doubt that the developments described above were motivated as much by commercial considerations as by religious factors. Indeed, the emergence of the Fatimid Caliphate, principally as a result of the successes of *du'at* operating from the Arabian Peninsula, in that part of North Africa nearest to the commercial city states of Italy (Amalfi and later Genoa), was a political product of the general revival of Mediterranean commerce from the tenth century onwards. It was also commerce that was the principal factor behind the subsequent expansion of the Fatimids eastwards in their attempt to wrest the control of trade with India from the Abbasids after conquering Egypt in 973.[28] Similarly, trade had previously been a major factor in the Islamic conquests in the east. In India, these conquests had been engendered to a large extent by the piratical attacks of Sindi merchants using *bawârij* (sing. *bârija* = battleship) to attack Omani trade-carrying ships in the Gulf.[29]

Maritime commercial traditions of Oman and the western Indian Ocean

Inheriting the pre-Islamic Sasanid mercantile organisation, which stretched from the south Arabian coast to both shores of the Gulf and then eastwards along the Makran coast to Sind, Omanis, in the early Islamic period, had played an active role in the general expansion of commercial activity in the Indian Ocean from their international entrepôt of Sohar.[30] By the mid-ninth century, Omani mercantile communities had emerged in Basra, Siraf, Daybul and Aden while merchants resident in Omani ports traded not only with those of East Africa and India but with others as far afield as Canton in China until its sack in 878.[31] Omani merchants, the 'original boat people', unlike their landward-based Meccan contemporaries who were too apprehensive to venture the risks of the high seas, were able navigators and proficient sailors.[32] This fact undoubtedly helped them to achieve a pre-eminence as traders and as carriers of commercial commodities from these early times. Regarding Oman's earlier links with India, so strong was the connection between Oman and Sind that as early as the eighth century Indian Muslims had been enlisted to man garrisons in Oman.[33] Some Omanis, as already noted, were to become rulers of parts of Sind in the tenth century, accepting Ismailism as their creed in the course of time. As far as the slave trade was concerned, Omanis did not take slaves only from Africa. In 1694, for example, during a raid on Salsette, an island adjoining Bombay, Omanis are said to have 'carried 1400 captives into irredeemable slavery'.[34]

Migratory movements and settlements were not solely one way but were matched by the reciprocal contraflow of communities and bodies of ideas, the residual effects of which are imprinted upon a number of Indian Ocean cultures in a variety of facets up to the present day. One has only to look at the faces of modern-day Omanis, Zanzibaris, Kenyans, or Tanzanians among other nationalities to see instantly the Indian origins of some, or the Arab, African or mixed roots of others.

Migratory movements from Africa to India also took place outside the context of the Slave Trade. Between the fourteenth and the nineteenth centuries, African mercenaries played a major role in the development of some south-central kingdoms of India. Often, these African mercenaries became rulers or regents themselves in these areas.[35] In the same period, some Africans were employed by Indian Muslim merchants for the protection of their cargo-laden ships against pirates.[36]

From the African angle, a number of 'Swahilis' (described by the Portuguese and later by other Europeans as Moors) were involved in direct trading with India. Tom Pires, visiting India in c.1511, had this to say about the trading partners of the Gujaratis, based in the north of the country:

> To Melacca, merchants of the following nations used to accompany the Gujeratis there in their ships and some of them used to settle in the place...they were from Cairo, many Arabs chiefly from Aden, Abyssinians and people from Ormuz, Kilwa, Malindi, Mogadishu and Mombasa, Persians to wit, Rumes, Turkomans, Armenians, Guilans, Khorasans and men of Shiraz.[37]

In East Africa itself, the Portuguese, on their arrival, encountered 'heathen and Muslim Indian traders' in all East African harbours north of Mozambique.[38] This is hardly surprising since 'the Turkish conquest of Gujarat [1303–4], the most active maritime province of India, coincided with renewed migrations to East Africa'.[39]

By the eighteenth century, African communities were reportedly well ensconced in areas south of Bombay, after being joined by more recent migrators to India.[40] Some of these Africans are said to have been promoted by the Mughal rulers of India to the important position of Admirals in their fleets.[41] Additionally, the coast of Oman, until Ya'ariba times, was governed by a series of foreign or foreign-dominated dynasties of various religious persuasions (Shi'i Buwayhids, Sunni Saljuqs, Christian Portuguese), and the western coast of India, especially Gujarat, 'the most cosmopolitan area of India',[42] was ruled by a succession of ever-changing dynasties.[43] In this context then, it is no great quantum leap to envisage that the impact of Indian or Asian influences on the 'Swahili' communities of East Africa was more or less comparable to its impact on 'Omani' communities whether resident in Oman, East Africa or elsewhere in the Indian Ocean. It is virtually inconceivable that this trans-cultural exchange had no lasting influence upon the various communities of the Indian Ocean region, including the 'Swahilis', engaged as they all were in daily intercourse with the mercantile and ruling classes of the region at large.

According to Swahili traditions, the Wadebuli Swahilis are people originating from Daybul which, on its occupation by the Muslim armies in 712, was a great commercial port in western India[44] and which was to maintain commercial links with Oman well into the twelfth century.[45] If these Wadebulis really did come from Daybul, it is interesting at least to speculate as to whether they made their way to Africa directly or after a period of residence in Oman. It would be equally illuminating to discover as to which religious persuasion they adhered at the time of their migration. Lack of evidence may never enable us to answer such questions but it is more than feasible, given the richly textured panoply of migrations, that the very name Wadebuli, as that of many other communities, was a descriptive nomenclature identifying their origins. More importantly, a detailed scrutiny of migratory patterns such as this enables us to dispel once and for all views, still surprisingly held by some modern historians, that people from Gujarat 'had no previous contact with East Africa' before the late nineteenth century.[46] Furthermore, without unravelling the complex threads of this backcloth, it is impossible to account for the existence, in the various trading outlets of the nineteenth century Indian Ocean region, of Hindu Banyans, Nizari Ismaili Khojas, Musta'lian Bohras, Sunni Memons and Sonaras, Parsi Wadias, and Sunni, Shi'i, Sufi and Ibadi Arabs, Persians and Lawatiyas and others who conducted age-old practices of commercial exchange with 'Swahili' people calling themselves Washirazi, Wadiba, Wadebuli, Waarabu, Washihri among other names, and with numerous groups of African and Western trading communities.[47]

Nonetheless, the paucity of sources, though enabling a tantalising outline to be etched, does not allow a more comprehensive picture to be filled in. Unfortunately, neither is such a task facilitated by the apparent lack of any records relating to the ubiquitous Gujarati merchants themselves. Most historical information about the Gujaratis has come so far in accounts obtained from non-Gujarati sources. It seems that the Gujaratis, encompassing a number of ethnic origins and a multitude of religious beliefs both in pure and adulterated form, have preferred to remain faceless. Their family histories and even those of entire communities remain to a great extent guarded secrets.[48] It must be pointed out, however, that this obscurity is not due to any lack of literate qualities for Gujaratis have been in constant touch with distant markets via correspondence, and have allegedly kept highly professional account books. Furthermore, when the need arose, they have also been known to have directed their energies to mastering new languages for the purpose of trade. During the course of the seventeenth century, for example, Portuguese and English were gradually added to their stock of languages used for trade.[49] Rather, their preference for anonymity, in the absence of contrary evidence, can be seen only as an expression of a deliberate policy of self-effacement whether for political, economic or cultural reasons. Despite this, their dominant position in the Indian Ocean trade, as will be examined below, is a fact that cannot be disputed.

THE PROMINENCE OF THE BANYANS IN INDIAN OCEAN COMMERCE

One of the most interesting questions occupying the thoughts of East African historians is why, among the motley collection of mercantile communities discussed above, it was the Banyans[50] who achieved such an undisputed pre-eminence in the Omani trade centred on Zanzibar during the nineteenth century.[51] The answer lies partly in the commercial regulations enforced by the Portuguese while subduing the Indian Ocean, and partly in the commercial methods employed by the Banyans themselves. Both will be explained in their appropriate places below.[52]

In their world view that a perpetual war between Islam and Christendom was inevitable, the Portuguese from the start set out, with their sword and cannon, to eliminate whatever influence Muslim communities may have exerted in Indian Ocean commerce. Such was their hatred for Islam that they could not bear seeing Muslim communities prosper through trade. They often forcibly expelled prominent Muslim merchants from their conquered territories in India as well as in East Africa,[53] preferring instead to have closer dealings with the non-Muslim Hindu Banyans. In return for giving these Banyans active protection, the Portuguese were able to use them as their proxies in order to protect their own multifarious interests.[54] Consequently, the Banyans emerged as having the sole prerogative of acting as intermediaries in the regional trade at first for the Portuguese and later for the European East India Companies which could not ignore the enormous influence the Banyans already exercised at the time of their arrival.[55]

It is not surprising, in these circumstances, that Omani rulers, in their trade wars against the Portuguese, held on to what contacts they already had with certain Banyans and started seeking new alliances with others.[56] It was through such alliances that the Portuguese were finally expelled from Muscat with the help of a Banyan called Narutem who was a resident of Muscat in the seventeenth century. Although Narutem may have concurred in the Portuguese strategy that crippled the trading activities of his Muslim competitors, he could not bear the thought of giving his beautiful daughter in marriage to the insistent Portuguese commander of Muscat.[57] Thus, he enlisted the support of the Ya'ariba, by then established in the *dakhiliya*, and with their backing masterminded a plot to eject the Portuguese from Muscat once and for all. The outcome of this unlikely alliance was that Narutem, his associates and his descendants were granted an exemption from paying any taxes to Omani rulers as a concession for not only ridding them of their foes but also enabling them to recapture Muscat.[58]

With the subsequent expansion of the Ya'ariba in East Africa, Banyan merchants continued to trade with the Swahilis, the Africans and the Omanis in East Africa, despite Portuguese protestations.[59] During the course of the eighteenth century, it was the capital provided by Banyan merchants that nurtured not only the Portuguese trade at Mozambique but also the Swahili/Omani trade at Kilwa.[60] Another important development in this trade mechanism, especially during the latter part of the century, was the reliance of Banyan merchants on Swahili and Omani intermediaries to carry out trading activities on their behalf with Africans on the mainland. The policies pursued by Portuguese officials only served to accelerate these agency-type arrangements. Portuguese commanders at Mozambique, themselves heavily reliant upon East African commerce, and witnessing with some trepidation the Banyans' encroachments on their traditional commercial spheres, started to impose swingeing taxes on the trading activities of the Banyans in order to discourage them. As a counter-measure, the Banyans soon started to consign their merchandise to Omani and Swahili agents living on the mainland who in turn brought African goods back for them, thus twice avoiding the necesssity of having to pay tax to the Portuguese authorities.[61]

Throughout this period, as commercial contacts were being strengthened between the Banyans and the Omani/Swahili merchants, Omani rulers found it expedient to continue to maintain their own close links with the Banyans and other mercantile communities. There is no doubt that the commercial rise of Oman in the nineteenth century, both at Muscat and at Zanzibar, owed a great deal to the already-established network of relationships between mercantile communities and Omani rulers. Sa'îd b Ahmad Âlbûsa'îdî, father of the founder of the Dynasty, was himself a coffee merchant at Sohar before his son, by force of circumstances, as we shall have cause to examine in greater detail below, came to power.[62] Ahmad b Said himself and his successors were heavily involved in trade. The far-reaching effect of the interaction between merchants and the Omani ruling elite, beyond mere commercial aspects, is exemplified by the importance that the Albusaidis attached to these merchants and the cooperation they received as a result when in need of assistance. In the 1720s, during the civil wars that brought the Albusaid to power, Ahmad b Said, seeking to establish his authority in East Africa, sent Omani reinforcements on ships 'borrowed from the Banyan merchants'.[63] In the same period, Ahmad is said to have used the services of a resident Shi'i merchant, one Muhammad b Mashriq, as his spokesman to the Persian garrison occupying Muscat before he treacherously annihilated its members at Barka.[64]

We also have evidence from a 1673 Dutch report that Shi'is, Sunnis and Ibadis at that time lived amicably in Muscat trading with Banyans and Jews.[65] Commenting on these Islamic sects, this report states that 'although they hold different opinions, they do not hate one another or dispute among themselves [but during their debates] each in his turn reads something more to edify than to effect dispute'.[66]

As for external links between rulers and merchants, Sultan b Ahmad (r.1793–1804), besides having intimate relations with the rulers of Mysore and Sind,[67] regularly appointed 'Indian' agents to represent his own trading interests in Bombay.[68] This was by no means a new phenomenon introduced by the Albusaid but a continuation of the practice adopted in Ya'ariba times. Sultân b Sayf I al-Ya'rubî (r.1649–79) had 'Indian' agents in Gujarat in order 'to supply the demands of the Musulmans [in India] for horses [exported from Oman]'.[69] A staggering number of 10,000 horses, valued at some 2,200,000 dinars, was apparently being imported at that time through the port of Ma'bar alone in southern India.[70] Muscat then is said to have controlled the whole of the Malabar trade and a major part of the Gulf trade, the latter being in the hands of Gujarati Banyans.[71]

As a result of the developments discussed above, the predominance of the Banyans and the continued importance of relationships between Omani rulers meant that the Banyans and other mercantile communities were well established and recognised in Omani dominions at the turn of the nineteenth century. And it was as a result of such relationships that Oman was to undergo a remarkable commercial expansion both at Zanzibar and Muscat in the course of the nineteenth century.

2 The importance of commerce to the early Albusaidi rulers

From the mid-seventeenth century onwards, the Ya'ariba rulers of Oman performed a political balancing act in the administration of the territories under their control. They increasingly directed their efforts towards consolidating their overseas possessions in East Africa by appointing *walis* and establishing garrisons in key towns like Mombasa, Zanzibar, Pemba and Kilwa[1] while they themselves remained in their capital in Rustaq, thereby keeping a firm grip on the tribal situation in Oman.[2] Since that time leaders of communal groups in East Africa became increasingly caught up in the political vicissitudes that were to affect Oman. Thus, from the time of the civil wars that plagued Oman from 1719 until the election of Aḥmad b Sa'îd Âlbûsa'îdî to the Imamate in 1749,[3] tribal allegiances in both Oman and Africa faced a need for re-adjustment with the change of leadership.[4]

ROLE OF COMMERCE IN THE EMERGENCE OF THE ALBUSAIDI

To maintain his position, Ahmad b Said could not rely on the insignificant power that his own tribe of the Albusaid could muster within the Omani tribal/communal configurations at the time of his election.[5] That he was elected Imam owed nothing either to his piety or indeed to his attainment in Ibadi theological tenets[6] but may be attributed to a number of other factors. Firstly, Ahmad had displayed to good effect his military prowess by overcoming the Persian army of Nadir Shah which had invaded Oman during the civil wars.[7] Secondly, he had killed the last of the Ya'rubi pretenders, Bil'arab b Ḥimyar, in battle, during the later stages of the wars.[8] Thirdly and more significantly, his influence and local support was derived from and swelled as a result of his commercial activities.

As already noted, Ahmad b Said's father was a coffee merchant in

Sohar. Ahmad's own connections with the Ya'ariba started when, on his way for commercial dealings in Muscat, he met with Sayf b Sultân II al-Ya'rubî (r.1728–32)[9] in what was then a village at Ruwi.[10] During this encounter Sayf persuaded Ahmad to go on a trading mission on his behalf to Hasa. After the success of the mission and the increased commercial relationships between the Ya'rubi and the Albusaidi, the latter not only married a *sayyida* from the ruling Ya'ariba family[11] but was also soon appointed as the Ya'rubi *wali* in Sohar.[12] Nevertheless, when Ahmad's fame spread and his reputation began to rival that of his ruler as a result of his integrity and impeccable propriety in commercial practices, Sayf looked for ways to rid himself of the Albusaidi and even instigated an unsuccessful plot to have his own *wali* assassinated.[13]

During the civil wars when his position as ruler came under threat, Sayf more than once turned to the ambitious Nadir Shah for succour, thus qualifying himself for the *laqab* (sobriquet) of *al-Jâ`ir* (tyrant) in Omani annals as a result of inviting a foreign power to meddle in Omani affairs.[14] At the beginning of 1743, the invading Persians under Taqi Khan managed to seize Muscat and, following a battle in which they lost 3,000 men, also captured Sohar.[15] But so powerful had the influence of the Albusaidi become by then among Oman's mercantile communities that traders from Muscat and Matrah apparently 'flocked to Barka' where Ahmad had established his headquarters.[16] After the expulsion of the Persians from Oman and his election to the Imamate, the Albusaidi, not surprisingly, relied heavily upon his mercantile and maritime resources to establish his influence both in Oman and in East Africa[17]:

> Ahmad, though indifferently supported by his subjects on various occasions, enjoyed their respect and esteem in a high degree and [had] not an unmerited reputation for justice and liberality.... Full religious liberty was allowed by Ahmad, even to Hindus; and security of the person and property of foreigners at Masqat was ensured by an efficient police. Ahmad affected greater state than previous Imams. He surrounded himself with a court in which not only political personages but also literati and men of the law held an honoured place; and he was a patron of poets'.[18]

But if he had the backing of Oman's mercantile communities, the Albusaidi rule, emerging as it did from a turbulent tribal background, was to be dogged by dissension, opposition and intrigue as members of the ruling family and *tamimas* of the major tribes jostled for pre-eminence and conspired to widen their own spheres of influence.

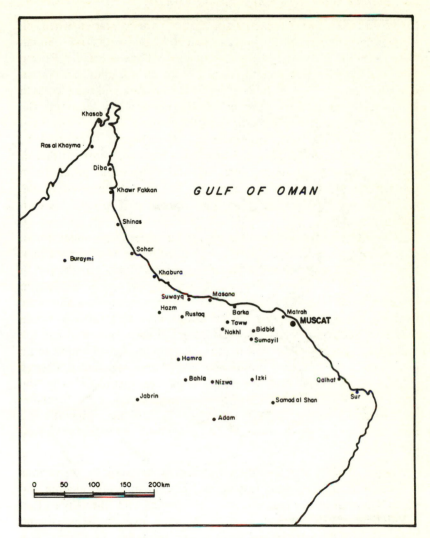

Map 5 Central and northern Oman: towns and villages

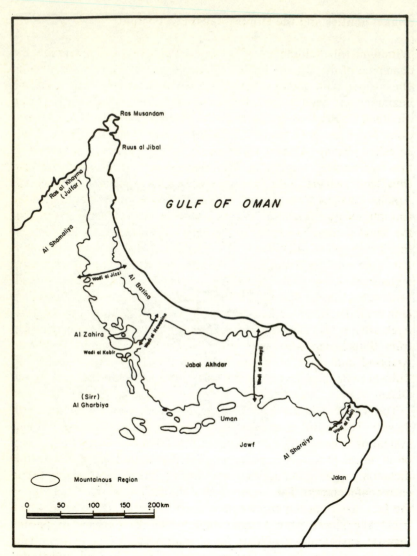

Map 6 Central and northern Oman: district names and main wadi passes

Omani politics and the Hinâwî–Ghâfirî dichotomy

Within the tribal alignment of Oman Ahmad b Said was essentially the champion of the Hinawi faction. During the civil wars, most tribes in Oman sided with one or other of the two major tribes which from the beginning had been in the forefront of the fighting, the Banû Hina and the Banû Ghâfir, thus giving rise to the Hinawi and Ghafiri confederations. Much has been made in both Arabic and Western sources of this so-called 'Hinawi-Ghafiri Dichotomy'.[19] The commonly held view is that the Hinawis, originating from Yemeni or Qahtani south Arabian tribal stock, adhere to the Ibadi creed while the 'Adnani or Nizari north Arabian Ghafiris are supposedly Sunnis. These simplistic delimitations and religious qualifications do not, however, account satisfactorily for the tribal pattern in Oman as the tribes, on closer examination, are found to be of mixed orthodoxy throughout.[20] The Ghafiri confederation often numbers Ibadis among its ranks while the Hinawis frequently include those who claim to be Sunnis or followers of other non-Ibadi *madhhabs* (Islamic School of Law). To complicate the situation further, both confederations include members who do not belong to the original Arab tribal stock. The Hinawis, for example, have members originating from Baluchistan who, with time, have become completely Omani Arabised and some of whom have adopted their own *nisba* of al-Bulushi to distinguish them from other groups in the tribal *mélange* of Oman.

The widely held view of the dichotomy then seems to be seriously flawed. The point to emphasise is that in the tribal-cum-religious system of Oman, religious affiliations and dubious genealogies based on mythical ancestors have never played as significant a role in this dichotomy as have the political ambitions of the major *tamimas* within each confederation. The importance of the dichotomy for Oman lay in the fact that from the eighteenth century onwards, the way in which tribal allegiances were formed, mainly for the purpose of putting forward a particular candidate for election to the office of the Imam, was governed by the imperatives of the Ghafiri-Hinawi dichotomy, which in time evolved into an intricate series of balance-of-power systems. Henceforth no *tamima* could have his candidate for the Imamate elected unless leaders of the opposite faction agreed to it, a process which effectively created a power of veto exercisable by either confederation.

In addition to the backing of the Hinawis, Ahmad b Said after his election on 10 June 1749[21] also received some support from a number of Ghafiris, although the powerful 'Aṭṭâbî Ghafiri shaykhs continued to control their formerly held territories of Jabrin, Bahla, Sumayil and al-Aynayn.[22] Despite this somewhat wavering support, opposition to Ahmad's rule very soon surfaced and gathered momentum both in Oman and in East Africa. In Oman, Ahmad came to be totally rejected in al-Zahira, the heart of the Ghafiri territory, and in Nakhl and Hazm which remained as centres of Ya'rubi influence.[23] Lacking the formidable naval fleet that the Ya'ariba had once possessed,[24] Ahmad set out, from the beginning, to rectify this situation. According to an eyewitness account, the Omani ruler's navy in 1756 could boast only two ships and a couple of gallivats.[25] By 1775, his fleet had undergone an enormous expansion reaching proportions and capabilities comparable to those of the Ya'ariba and having, in addition, the distinct advantage of bigger-sized ships.[26] As another contemporary report relates, the Albusaidi navy, by the 1770s, comprised four ships of forty guns each; twenty-five locally built ketches and gallivats of eight to fourteen guns each and a large unspecified number of dhows and trankies.[27]

In addition to the navy, and perhaps as a result of having an insecure and vacillating tribal base, Ahmad b Said found it necessary also to recruit a mercenary army of Baluchis, Zadgalis and African slaves to maintain his sway internally, especially when his own sons, whom he had appointed to the strategic posts of *walis* of important towns, started to conspire against him motivated by commercial reasons.[28] What residual control the founder of the Albusaidi Dynasty ultimately exercised in Oman became limited to the area around his capital Rustaq, in parts of the Batina and in the commercial outlets of Matrah and Muscat. As early as 1756, Niebuhr on his visit to Oman described the country as '[being] possessed by a number of petty Sovereigns, the most considerable of whom is the Imam of Oman or Maskat'.[29]

The reaction of Omani settlers in East Africa to the rise of the Albusaid

While opposition to Ahmad b Said's rule continued in Oman, Omani settlers in East Africa began to assert their independence from the mother country. Leaders of these settlers had been able to gain much ground between 1737 and 1744 when the attention and the energies of the people in Oman had been diverted by the Persian invasions. As early as 1739, the Mazari'a tribe of Mombasa, which at the time was the most important Omani base in East Africa, opposed the rise of the Albusaidis even before Ahmad b Said's election as Imam.[30] Ten years later, Muḥammad b 'Uthmân al-Mazrû'î, the *wali* of Mombasa appointed to that post during the Ya'ariba period,[31] had this to say, according to the Frenchman Guillain, on hearing the news of Ahmad b Said's election:

> 'Mohamed-ben-Osman said that 'Ahmed-ben-Said was not from the hereditary family, that he was his equal, that he had no right over Oman let alone Mombasa; and that since the former governor of Sohhar had usurped the sovereignty of Oman, he himself as governor of Mombasa could, with equal rights, declare himself sovereign of that island'.[32]

Besides Mombasa, all the other Omani principalities in East Africa governed by Ghafiri *walis* refused to give their allegiance to Ahmad b Said. Only Zanzibar, where the settlers were of predominantly Hinawi persuasion, accepted Albusaidi rule.[33]

As a matter of political expediency, the Mazaria rapidly forged alliances with rulers of the Lamu Archipelago (Lamu, Manda, Pate and other smaller islands), especially with the Banu Nabhan of Pate, in order to resist the Albusaid.[34] Thus started a period of nearly a century during which different Omani groups residing in both Oman and East Africa found themselves in recurrent conflict with each other in their struggle to gain the upper hand. East Africa also became a centre of opposition to which disaffected members of the Albusaidis themselves gravitated. In 1783, when Sa'īd b Ahmad, in accordance with his father's wishes, was 'elected' Imam in Oman, his younger brother Sayf disputed the succession.[35] After failing to elicit support in Oman, Sayf in 1785 sailed to East Africa where he initially succeeded in obtaining a degree of backing for his claims from a number of Omani settlers. However, an army dispatched from Oman soon persuaded him as to the wisdom of retiring to Lamu where, by way of compensation, his son 'Ali was appointed as the Omani *wali*.[36]

In this way, the fortunes of Oman and East Africa became inextricably intertwined. It is against such an intricate backcloth of conflicting interests and allegiances coupled with a closer examination of contemporaneous events in Oman and East Africa that the nineteenth century rise of Zanzibar, on the coat tails of Muscat, must be viewed. Historical studies on the nineteenth century connections between Oman and East Africa have so far veered towards rigid compartmentalisation with the Africanists claiming ascendancy for Africa and the Arabists according the pivotal role to Oman. These studies, although providing a wealth of finer detail, have led to an unjustifiable degree of specialisation within these two areas of learning. In the case of Oman's links with Africa, they have resulted in a distorted isolationist perspective marginalising the complementary interaction of Omani communities resident in both East Africa and Oman. For without integrating the two areas into a single Omani entity, how could one begin to explain why an established ruler in Oman should choose to move his court, most of his family and even items of his furniture from Oman to a small island some 2,200 miles away in East Africa, as did Said b Sultan during his reign? Together with this idea of a sprawling Omani 'State', we must always keep in view the commercial development of the Indian Ocean region as a whole for, as already explained, it was this dynamic force that provided more than any other factor the major impetus and catalyst for the historical development of both Oman and East Africa.

THE EMERGENCE OF MUSCAT AS A POLITICAL–COMMERCIAL CENTRE

The expulsion of the Portuguese from Muscat in 1650 set the mercantile and tribal communities of Oman on the path of political and economic transformation building Oman into a commercial and maritime 'State' despite opposition and intrigue at times against Omani rulers. Yet by the late eighteenth century, there was no noticeable evidence of any Omani, that is to say Albusaidi, political domination of East Africa, one of the main traditional destinations of migrants from Oman. That there was no attempt at a systematic conquest or the establishment of an effective administration apparatus in East Africa was doubtlessly due to the intertribal conflict in Oman itself which has been elucidated above. In fact, as a result of this conflict, by the latter part of the eighteenth century, the ruling branch of the Albusaidis had lost more ground at home, let alone having the will or the resources to consolidate its position overseas.

Ahmad b Said died on 14 December 1783,[37] and after 1785 when his successor Imam Said b Ahmad (r.1783–9) virtually retired from politics and resided in Rustaq allowing his son Hamad to take control of the affairs of Muscat, different members of the ruling house divided the various regions of Oman among themselves. Thus, the unification of the coastal regions of Oman with the *dakhiliya*, a rare feat achieved by the Ya'ariba since the days of the first Imamate of the ninth century,[38] was lost to the Albusaidis.

The foundations of this division of Omani territories were laid in Ahmad b Said's own time. His two middle sons Sayf and Sultan, who were uterine brothers and related to the influential Ghafiri *tamima* of the Jubûr controlling the Sumayil area, Jâbir b Muḥammad, rebelled against him with the help of the latter in 1781.[39] At one point, the two brothers succeeded in taking possession of Muscat and imprisoned their brother Said,[40] their father's favourite, who already had invested in him authority over Rustaq, Nizwa, Izki and parts of the Sumayil area while Qays was in charge of Sohar.[41] The rebellion, however, failed, and the two brothers eventually withdrew into self-imposed exile in Makran[42] from where Sayf was subsequently to make his way to East Africa.

The most important point about this rebellion is that it was in no way influenced by the principles of the *nahda* (Ibadi revival) movement. It was purely and simply an attempt by Sayf and Sultan to redress what they must have perceived as an imbalance in the way their father wished to distribute power and revenue amongst his sons. The fact that the primary objective of the rebellion was directed solely towards the control of Muscat not only indicates the stature that Muscat had by then achieved in the Indian Ocean regional commerce but also highlights the commercial rivalries among the Albusaidis themselves. It is significant to note in this connection that, whilst their brother was in prison in Jalali and their father out of the way in Rustaq, Sayf and Sultan made the point of reassuring the mercantile communities of Muscat of their goodwill towards them and organised a special reception ceremony to exchange views with their leaders.[43] Thus, while keeping an eye on the traditional 'national-cum-Ibadi' core of the *dakhiliya*, the Albusaidis became preoccupied principally with the imperative of controlling Muscati commerce. The Omani international port, once again governed by the Omanis themselves, was recognised to have become through the energies of the Ya'ariba and their expansion overseas the political as well as the commercial centre of Oman.

European writers on Imam Said b Ahmad's reign all agree that although he had the apparent religious legitimacy to his rule, he was disliked by the majority of the Omani tribes. They do not, however, clarify why this was so.[44] Ibadi sources, on the other hand, dispute both the conduct and the validity of his election motivated as it was by his father's insistence that he should be recognised as successor.[45]

Table 2 The eighteenth-century Albusaidi rulers

Imam Aḥmad b Sa'îd	(1749–83)
Imam Sa'îd b Ahmad	(1783–89; remained nominally Imam until c.1821)
Hamad b Sa'îd	(1789–92)
Sulṭân b Aḥmad	(1792–1804)

Sources: Anon. Ms, 165–71; Kashf, 155; Juhaina, 136–8; Bathurst R.D., 1967, 323–5; Beckingham C.F., 1941, 257–60; IOR/P/381/33, Seton to Bombay, 9 July 1802.

During the early years of his father's reign, Said b Ahmad had been appointed as *wali* of Nizwa. His heavy-handedness in his dealings with the Ghafiris, and his open tendency to favour Hinawis when appointing tribal leaders to higher administrative posts, had sown the seeds of resentment against him.[46] To aggravate the situation further, once recognised as Imam, he involved himself in trading activities to such an extent that he gained a monopoly of the textile dyeing industry around Nizwa levying stringent taxes upon anyone else who had the temerity to compete.[47] These patently unpopular measures, considered by a number of *'ulama`* (religious leaders) as unworthy of an Imam, lost him considerable tribal support.[48]

The effective control of Muscat by his son Hamad, from 1789, has been characterised by a recent American study as the establishment of an 'independent' state in Muscat geared solely to commerce and dissociated totally from the tribal scene in the *dakhiliya*. After allegedly adopting the title of *sayyid*,[49] 'in 1785 Hamad bin Said made a clean break with Oman [*dakhiliya*]...and established an independent state at Muscat'.[50] There is no evidence, however, to support this contention. As discussed in the Introduction, the commercial fortunes of the coast and the *dakhiliya* have always been interdependent functioning symbiotically in times of accord and unification. Moreover, unlike the *dakhiliya*, the coast throughout Oman's history has never been able to sustain even a minimal degree of political independence. In those times when the two regions were not unified the coast was invariably under the control of a foreign power.

The evidence available for the 1780s shows clearly that Said b Ahmad remained, nominally at least, in his post as Imam in Rustaq until his death in c.1821[51] and he seems to have been well aware of the way events in Muscat were shaping up. As 'Abd-allah al-Salimi claims, Hamad may have been disgusted by his father's ostentatious ways unbefitting the conduct of an Imam,[52] but nevertheless Hamad's success in taking control of Muscat, according to both al-Mughairi and Badger, was achieved with his father's connivance.[53] The trickery and posturing that Hamad employed to gain control of Muscat alluded to in the accounts of Ibn Ruzaiq, were aimed more at undermining the influence of the *wali* of Muscat, Muḥammad b Khalfân Âlbûsa'îdî, and that of Ibn Ruzaiq's own family than that of the Imam.

Muhammad's father, Khalfân b Muḥammad, had been a merchant in Sohar when Ahmad b Said was appointed its *wali* by the Ya'ariba.[54] When Ahmad became ruler, he nominated Khalfan at first as his *wakîl* in Muscat but later, after marrying one of Khalfan's daughters, promoted his father-in-law to the position of *wali*.[55] Ahmad also allowed Ruzaiq b Bakhît, the chronicler's grandfather who had assisted the Albusaidi in his struggle against the Ya'ariba, to continue in his post as customs master of Muscat, a position he had held under Sayf b Sultan II al-Ya'rubi.[56] When Hamad took control of Muscat with the tacit approval of the *ulama*,[57] both of his grandfather's appointees to important commercially oriented positions lost their privileges. This may well be the reason for Ibn Ruzaiq's undisguised hostility towards Hamad.

Nevertheless, as a careful reading of the various narratives of Ibn Ruzaiq himself on this period show, with Qays established at Sohar, Hamad and his father Said appear to have had a thorough understanding of how the political situation was evolving. Moreover, they acted in concert in their effort to safeguard their own commercial interests at Muscat faced as they were with persistent intrigues from other members of the Albusaid.[58] Indeed, in addition to the commercial importance of Muscat, the notion of overseas expansion was also not lost to either of them. Both had ambitions to establish their authority further afield not only in East Africa but also in India.[59] Before they could do so, however, they had to consolidate their positions at home. Their greatest concern internally was the constant threat posed to them by Sultan b Ahmad. According to Ibn Ruzaiq, each time that they crossed paths with Sultan, they manifested a distinct uneasiness in his presence, afraid of what he next had in store for them.[60] During a meeting in which some `a'ayân (religious leaders and tribal notables) questioned Said about his unhappy relationship with his brother, the acknowledged Imam replied: 'For me the task of overcoming Sultan is far greater than that of establishing my authority at Mombasa or Bombay. Sultan is very brave and nobody can defeat him in a war'.[61] At the same moment and in a similar conference in Muscat, the Imam's son Hamad was echoing identical sentiments concerning his uncle.[62]

With the unexpected death of Hamad from smallpox early in 1792,[63] his father found himself in a very vulnerable situation. That father and son had been acting hand in glove is further evidenced by the grief that Said is reported to have manifested at Hamad's death. He composed elegiac poetry for the loss of his son and apparently thereafter evinced no further interest in the affairs of Muscat for which, as expected, he was immediately challenged by his brother Sultan.[64] After taking control of Muscat by a series of strategems and violent actions,[65] a year later, Sultan's position was recognised by all concerned. In a formal agreement, power in Oman was divided between the three principal sons of Ahmad b Said. Sultan remained in control of Muscat; Qays, while retaining Sohar, was awarded the forts and the revenue of Matrah; and Imam Said was to receive a pension with his authority circumscribed to Rustaq.[66] Other tribal leaders, such as Mâlik b Sayf al-Ya'rubî of Nakhl, continued to hold sway in their own recognised *dars*.[67]

This decentralisation of power in Oman and the implicit acceptance of the lapse of the Imamate into desuetude gave the leaders in East Africa a further opportunity to dissociate themselves from Albusaidi control. Furthermore, as it will be shown below, these factors were also to affect profoundly the subsequent course of history of both Oman and East Africa right until the middle of the twentieth century.

DEVELOPMENTS IN OMANI AND INDIAN OCEAN COMMERCE BY THE TURN OF THE NINETEENTH CENTURY

Given this division of Oman into petty chiefdoms in the last decade of the eighteenth century, coupled with the multifarious and continual internecine quarrels and shifting allegiances among the ruling house, it is a source of wonder that the Albusaidis managed to establish any sort of power base in East Africa by the following century. In spite of these conflicts in Oman, three factors combined at the turn of the nineteenth century to encourage the Albusaidi rulers to direct their attention towards East Africa: the commercial expansion of Muscat within the Indian Ocean regional system; the identification of the interests of Omani rulers with Banyan merchant groups and the increasing forays of Westerners into the Indian Ocean area.

During the eighteenth century, new opportunities for Muscati-based merchants arose independently of the internal political situation of Oman. Muscat's handling of the Yemeni-produced coffee trade, which had existed during the reign of Ahmad b Said,[68] virtually doubled in the 1790s.[69] By that time, the highly profitable sale of slaves to the French in East Africa received a boost while 50 per cent of the trade between India and the Gulf passed through the Omani port which also supplied the Gulf and the Levant areas with sugar procured from Batavia.[70] When Hamad b Said took control of Muscat he strengthened the traditional Omani commercial links with Sind and further encouraged Muscat's trade by abandoning the discriminatory customs tariff and introducing a flat rate of 6½ per cent for all foreign business. The old system, in existence since his grandfather's time, had favoured the Western Christian traders who paid only 5 per cent while Muslims paid 6 and Hindus and Jews 9.[71]

Under Sultan b Ahmad, Muscat once again experienced a dynamic upsurge in maritime activity side by side with commercial expansion.

Soon after his accession, Sultan sent a force to take Gwadar which he had acquired while in exile from the Khan of Kalat in 1784, although the oft-made claim that it had been given to him as a gift in perpetuity is a subject of some controversy.[72] He also annexed Chahbar further along the Makran coast, took control of the Gulf islands of Qishm, Hurmuz, Minab and Hanjam after allying himself with their rulers the Banû Ma'în and taking over from them the lease agreement with the Shah of Persia relating to Bander Abbas.[73] On the Arab coast of the Gulf, he neutralised the Qasimis (*Qawâsim*) by forging an alliance with their *Huwâla* rivals on the Persian side. The 'Utbis (*'Utûb*), the other principal Arab power in the Gulf, he chose to subdue by waging war against them on the pretext of forcing them to pay the *gumruk* (protective costs) of 2½ per cent which he had imposed on all local shipping entering the Gulf.[74]

In the commercial sphere, Sultan entered into trading agreements with ports in the Indian Ocean as far afield as Batavia, Sind, Shiraz and Abyssinia.[75] Like his Albusaidi predecessors and the Ya'ariba before them, he continued to encourage trading activities of the resident mercantile communities of Matrah and Muscat as witnessed by his reduction in 1802 of import duties to 2½ per cent for Muslims, 5 per cent for non-Muslims and the continued abolition of export duties.[76] As a result of this favourable treatment, Muslim, Hindu and Jewish merchants from India, Africa, Yemen, Egypt, Persia, Makran, Indonesia and Iraq were all involved in commercial activity at Muscat in the beginning of the nineteenth century.[77] A number of merchants and shipowners, predominantly from India and Persia, began at this time to settle in Muscat, encouraged by the protection given by the authorities against piracy and by the moderate duties already mentioned.[78]

Muscati traders, moreover, took advantage of the chaotic conditions prevailing in Persia during the civil war that followed the downfall of the Safavid Dynasty in 1722. The port of Muscat soon captured the trade of Goombroom (Bander Abbas), especially after the British factory there was abandoned in 1763 as political anarchy spread into Persia.[79] It is quite likely that Sultan b Ahmad was bent upon acquiring the lease of Bander Abbas because he did not wish the resurgence of competing commercial activity from another port in the vicinity, which would have detracted from the burgeoning role of Muscat:

> The people of Muscat accumulated unimaginable wealth at the end of the [eighteenth] century. In order to protect this wealth the Imam [*sic*] of Oman built a very strong naval force and became the strongest and most respected power in the area.[80]

This development in Omani commercial activity at Muscat and later at Zanzibar was due largely to Western influence which effectively propelled the Indian Ocean ports into the emergent international trade system. The origins of this process, as indicated above, go back to the time of the Portuguese seaborne empire in the Indian Ocean in the sixteenth century. The subsequent maritime expansion of the Dutch, French and British, and the integration of America into European commercial networks, generated a powerful force pulling together the various active ports of the Indian Ocean both in Asia and Africa. With the emergence of the English[81] and the Dutch East India Companies, later to be joined by the French Compagnie des Indes Orientales and other companies, increasing specialisation coupled with new long-distance trade and economic exchange practices gave rise to a system of trade more closely linked on a global scale. This system heralded further innovations. The organisation of the English and the Dutch East India Companies into joint-stock companies, exercising separation between the ownership of capital and management by a professional class of merchants and salaried administrators, was a new and unique phenomenon in commercial organisation.[82]

Trans-continental trade no longer was the exclusive preserve either of royal monopoly, as had been the case of the Portuguese–Spanish Crown, or of individual merchants or partnerships operating as separate entities and covering vast trading areas such as that between the Italian cities and the ports of India. Among the changes this situation wrought was a growth in the magnitude of trade between Europe and America on the one hand, and between these two continents and Asia and Africa on the other. Furthermore, the increase in the size of commercial purchases made by North Atlantic merchants in particular, together with the corporate structure of trade and the progressive concentration of financial resources, created a much closer link than before between the supplying and consuming markets. More significantly, these changes, as Professor Chadhuri has shown, introduced into the Indian Ocean trade system the principle of capitalism:

> The emerging pattern of long distance trade [following the establish-ments of the East India Companies] represented the beginning of a 'world economy'. It has certainly been interpreted as the first stage in the history of capitalism, leading eventually to the dominant role of industrial capital and the social transformations of the early nine-teenth century.... In functional terms, what happened in Western Europe during the sixteenth and seventeenth centuries may not have been quite unique after all. One can find strong parallel developments

in many areas of the Indian Ocean – areas long associated with emporia and trans-continental trade.[83]

As the North European 'bureaucratic chartered companies' developed, new methods of trade, bringing with them central distribution agencies which operated internationally on capitalistic lines, were grafted onto the pre-modern system of production. However, the pre-industrial capitalism of the Indian Ocean remained undefined in legal terms and its implications were not understood socially. Land and labour, factors of production other than capital, were regarded as socially divisible, since anyone with sufficient purchasing power could buy land and employ labour. But capital for trade and industry, as will be shown for the Omani case below, remained the sole prerogative of mercantile groups. It does not seem to have occurred to rulers in the Indian Ocean, accustomed as they were to age-old commercial methods, that the possession of title to commercial investments might have been better for generating permanent income than direct taxation of merchants. Had it done so, the need to define such titles and rights in law would have automatically followed.

With the enormous expansion in the trading activity of the Indian Ocean from the seventeenth century onwards, and the diversion of a large proportion of trans-continental trade of Eurasia from the Red Sea and the Persian Gulf to the Cape route, ports of trade in the Indian Ocean flourished and prospered. Merchant communities in these ports thus thrived not only by supplying the demands of Asian and African markets but also by supplying goods to the new emporia of the North Sea and the Atlantic: Amsterdam, London, Salem and New York.

Given this background, it is surprising that many historians persist in attributing the origins of the commercial rise of Muscat to the hostilities between France and Britain following the 1789 French Revolution and the subsequent Napoleonic Wars.[84] While it is true that Omani traders, both in Arabia and in Africa, did profit from these hostilities by capturing a large proportion of the carrying trade sailing as they did under neutral colours, it is evident that Muscat had already been enjoying a great degree of prosperity before the end of the eighteenth century despite political turmoil in the country. This prosperity has been graphically described by European visitors to Oman. Parsons, for example, who visited Muscat in 1775 has left us this account:

There are at present such immense quantities of goods in this town that, as there are not warehouses to contain half of them, they are piled up in the streets, and lie night and day exposed, without any watch or guard, yet there never happens an instance that such goods are robbed, or even pilfered of the least part.[85]

Ten years earlier, Niebuhr on his visit to Oman nearly two decades after the resolution of the Omani civil wars, had described it in the following way:

> The country afforded plenty of cheese, barley, lentils, with several different sort of grapes. Of dates, such abundance is here produced, as to yield an annual exportation of several ships lading; and there is a variety of other fruits and pulse.[86]

In fact, the most crucial impact that the Napoleonic Wars were to have on Oman was the initiation of what was to prove to be a long-lasting political association of the Albusaidi rulers with Britain. Conventionally, this association has been presented as having been motivated by strategic and defensive considerations having for their objective the exclusion of other European powers from activity in the Indian Ocean and later the protection of the lines of communication to British India.[87] The stimulus for the Omani–British relationship, however, in its initial stages arose purely for commercial reasons. Even when strategic and the so-called 'humanitarian' factors came into play later, as for example after the 1798 Napoleonic invasion of Egypt or during the British antislavery crusade, it was impossible to divorce them from the underlying commercial considerations that primarily motivated British policy towards Oman. It is to the emergence of this policy and the origins of British involvement with Oman that we turn our attention in the next chapter.

3 The emergence of British policy towards Oman: 1798–1804

THE ORIGINS OF BRITISH CONNECTIONS WITH OMAN

It was as early as 1624, at a time when the maritime outlets of the Indian Ocean were under Portuguese control, that Muscat came to the fore and started to feature in the commercial policies of the English East India Company.[1] Since merchants from the coastal settlements of Oman have traded with ports on the Indian continent from time immemorial it is hardly surprising that the English Company, based in Surat on the western coast of India, should have soon come into contact with these 'local' merchants. Nor is it unusual that this company, with time, attempted to forge alliances with these local merchants and their rulers in its struggle to compete for the available trade with other European powers, mainly the Portuguese and the Dutch.[2] Prominent among the local merchants, as already indicated, were Banyans from Gujarat who resided and traded at Muscat in the early seventeenth century. But there were also Omani merchants who lived in Surat and who were heavily involved in this early commercial activity.[3]

Following the expulsion of the Portuguese from Sohar in 1643,[4] the initiative was in fact taken by the Omanis when in 1645 Imam Nâṣir b Murshid al-Ya'rubî invited the English Company to trade formally at Sohar and Seeb at a time when Muscat was still under Portuguese control.[5] The Imam chose to have commercial alliances with Europeans, other than his Portuguese enemies, because he was aware that English merchants were already involved in the commercial activity of Muscat. During the first half of the seventeenth century, English merchants had been selling sugar, rice, cotton wool and tobacco at Muscat for a profit margin of 'no less than fifty per cent'.[6]

As a consequence of these early contacts, an agreement was signed in Sohar in January 1646 between the Imam Nasir b Murshid and Philip Wylde, representative of the company, granting the English trading privileges at Sohar.[7] It was this agreement followed by similar trading arrangements with other European powers that marked a new era in the history of Oman. Having entered into such agreements, Omani rulers were encouraged to obtain for themselves the commercial benefits hitherto accruing to the Portuguese, as a result of the latter's control of outlets on the Omani coast and in the Indian Ocean at large. There is no doubt that these commercially oriented agreements not only provided the Omani rulers with the impetus for working towards the final expulsion of the Portuguese from Muscat which, as already described, was achieved with the help of Banyan merchants; but they also fuelled the ambitions of Omani rulers to expand overseas in their quest for taking control of the other commercial outlets in the Indian Ocean still under Portuguese authority, especially in those areas such as East Africa, where resident Omani communities were resisting Portuguese domination.

The Ya'ariba continued to maintain friendly relations with the English following the signing of the 1646 Agreement at Sohar. After the Dutch–English wars of 1653–4, there was even renewed talk of establishing an English 'factory'[8] at Muscat, since such a facility had been offered by the Omanis in 1651: 'We were proferred with much importunity the best house in the town for a factory'.[9] During the wars Muscat came to be seen by the English as 'a port in these parts as that wee might call our owne...as wee are at present and are like to bee if these wars continue'.[10] However, although negotiations for a treaty to establish a factory were conducted by Colonel Rainsford, representative of the President of the Council of the English Company during his visit to Muscat in 1659, the Colonel died before negotiations were concluded.[11] And it was not until 1798, some 139 years later, under the Albusaid, that a full-fledged commercial treaty giving extensive facilities to the British, although not the privilege of establishing a factory, finally came to be signed between Oman and Britain. It is important to examine, in some detail, why this happened in 1798 and not before since this treaty and the circumstances associated with it were to affect the whole of the subsequent history of Oman.

THE 1798 TREATY BETWEEN OMAN AND BRITAIN: ORIGINS AND CONSEQUENCES

Throughout the long interval between the 1646 Agreement and the 1798 Treaty, numerous attempts had been made by Britain and by other European powers to obtain some sort of facility either in Muscat or in some other port of Oman for the purpose of either establishing a factory or having possession of a fort.[12] All such requests were, however, rejected although trade by the English was encouraged and did actually increase[13]: 'Surat says the King [who at that time must have been Imam Sultân b Sayf I al-Ya'rubî – r.1649–79] has gone back on his word. We can have a factory but not the fort [of Muscat]'.[14] By the 1660s, the English Company at Surat came to regard the possession of a fort in Oman as beneficial from a strategic as well as a commercial viewpoint: ''Twill be a very beneficial place and keepe both India and Persia in awe'.[15] Nevertheless, the Ya'ariba had by then grown more reluctant to hand over forts on the Omani coast to any European power.[16] The memory of their great struggle and the eventual expulsion of the Portuguese after more than a century of occupation of Muscat must have been too fresh in their minds.

The early Albusaidi rulers likewise 'continued to refuse applications which were repeatedly made to them for permission to establish a British factory at Muscat'.[17] With such precedents clearly aimed at safeguarding Muscat's position, it is important to analyse why Sultan b Ahmad in 1798 chose to agree to a treaty with the British which turned out to be the first step towards the political and economic stranglehold that Britain was to exercise over Oman throughout the nineteenth century and for the best part of the twentieth.[18] The signing and the ratification of this treaty by 1800 constituted, as it will be shown below, the first nail in the coffin of Omani independence of action in both the trade and the politics of the Indian Ocean.

Sultan b Ahmad: the apogee of Albusaidi power

It is unfeasible that in 1798 Sultan b Ahmad agreed to the treaty from a position of weakness. As seen earlier, by then he controlled both sides of the Straits of Hormuz. Thus commanding the entrance to the Gulf, he exploited this fact by imposing a Portuguese type of "Pass System" which required all shipping heading for the Gulf to stop at Muscat and pay protective costs for goods carried up the Gulf under an Omani escort.[19] Furthermore, Muscat in Sultan's time became a great entrepôt, described in a contemporary report as:

> being an exchange centre for articles from Surat, Bhavnagar, Bombay, the Malabar and Cormandel coasts, Makran, Sind, Punjab, Kutch, Bengal, Batavia and the Malay islands, East Africa and the Mascarene islands and of course the countries bordering the Persian Gulf.[20]

Under Sultan's rule Omani shipowners prospered and bought new vessels and there were at Muscat fifteen ships from 400 to 700 tons, three brigs, fifty dhows and fifty large dingies; at Sur and Jalan there were 250 dhows and baghlas...and Omanis were building ships at Bombay and repairing old ones to the amount of five lakhs [500,000] of rupees...[and they possessed] from 40,000 to 50,000 tons of shipping.[21]

As related in Chapter 2, trade had been the basic principle that had driven Sultan b Ahmad to take over the control of Muscat. Once in power, he remained obsessed with the perceived need to safeguard and nurture the commercial development of Muscat. From the beginning, he directed his energies to meet the challenges posed to Muscat from the newly emerging maritime principalities of the Gulf, notably those of the Utbis of Bahrain and the Qasimis of northern Oman.[22] For commercial purposes, he also maintained friendly relations with the French in East Africa and with commercially active rulers of India outside the British zone of control, notably Tipu Sultan of Mysore and Mîr Bejar of Sind, as well as with influential merchants in Bengal, Goa, Kutch, Bombay and as far north as Afghanistan.[23]

During his reign a personal dimension was added to Oman's traditional trade links with Sind as a result of an incident that had taken place in his father's lifetime.[24] The story goes that Mîr Bejar's uncle, like many Muslims from northern parts of India and Afghanistan, had travelled to Mecca via Muscat to perform the *hajj*. On his arrival at Muscat, the Sindi had been captured by *wakil* Khalfan b Muhammad's men and delivered over to some enemies of his family residing in Muscat while members of the Bejar household had at the same time been massacred in Sind. The enemies of this family in Muscat had apparently bribed the *wakil* to carry out the deed. Eventually, it had been none other than Sultan who had rescued Mîr Bejar's uncle from Khalfan's clutches taking the Sindi, who had bravely resisted capture, to his father Imam Ahmad in Rustaq. When Mîr Bejar and Sultan became rulers of their separate domains the Sindi ruler promised to send 30,000 maunds of saltpetre to Muscat every year as a token of gratitude following a visit by the Albusaidi to Sind.[25]

Muscat's relations with Tipu Sultan's Mysore were also strengthened during Sultan b Ahmad's time. Tipu's father, Haydar Ali (r.1761–81) who by the mid-1760s had taken control of the Malabar coast with its famous ports of Mangalore and Calicut, had cooperated with Sultan's father, Ahmad b Said, in overcoming a nest of pirates that had been hindering the flow of trade between Muscat and Mangalore.[26] Haydar had also established a factory at Muscat[27] while a *wakil* had been appointed at Mangalore to represent Muscat's interests.[28] Following the seizure of Mysore in 1784 by Tipu Sultan (r. 1782–99; also known as Tipu Sahib), the factory at Muscat was administered by a resident Mysori mission sent to Oman from April to June 1786.[29] During this period, commerce between the two areas was further encouraged as shipping facilities were provided at each others' ports and reciprocal trade agreements concluded. As a result of these, Muscat customs levied on traders from Mysore were reduced from 10 to 6 per cent while duties imposed on Omani traders at ports controlled by Tipu were halved.[30] Among the trade commodities imported by Muscat, apart from the all-important rice, were sandalwood, pepper, cloth, cardamoms and timber while Muscat supplied, directly or through its network of maritime connections, dates, saffron seeds, pistachio nuts, horses, mules, copper, chinawares, silkworms, sulphur, pearls, rock salt and raisins.[31]

Thus, by the time Sultan b Ahmad came to power in 1792 Oman already had formidable links with Mysore. During his reign a wide-ranging commercial network of connections was established, as related above, primarily between Muscat and other ports of the Indian Ocean. It was for no other reason than the safeguarding of these connections that in 1798 Sultan found himself obliged to sign the treaty with the British although Britain, as will be seen, was motivated also by considerations of a political and strategic nature.

Since its emergence from the sixteenth century onwards Muscat had established commercial contacts indirectly with Western Europe via India. During that long span of time between the sixteenth and the nineteenth centuries both the ports of India and the Omani international port itself had come to be increasingly connected with a worldwide economic system. Therefore, Muscat could never dissociate itself from the changing fortunes of the ports of the Indian coast with which its own economic well-being was intimately linked. Thus the origins of British political domination of Oman from 1798, and later of Zanzibar, can be seen as a consequence of the acquisition of extensive territorial holdings in India at the end of the eighteenth century by the East India Company. Thereafter, the British did all that was in their power to forestall any local, regional or Western power from challenging either their political or commercial hegemony in the area. This can be clearly seen, in the case of Oman, from the precautionary measures Britain took in the months leading up to the first Omani–British treaty.

In 1796, in an attempt to counter Muscat's commercial expansion, the East India Company threatened to terminate the free access that had until then been available to Omanis visiting British ports in India[32] while at the same time imposing a tax of 2 per cent on all non-British exports from Surat to the Gulf.[33] Britain's commercial concerns were, however, soon relegated to second place as the British authorities in Surat received the alarming news of Napoleon's triumphal entry into Cairo on 25 July 1798.[34] When the Surat authorities learned that Napoleon's main ambition was the eventual domination of India, they immediately engaged in a flurry of activity forging alliances with rulers of the Gulf in their effort to defend their Indian territories and to nip in the bud Bonaparte's challenge to their commercial and political position in the Indian Ocean. Hardly three months had gone by when a mission under Mehdi Ali Khan, a Persian recently appointed as the British Resident in Bushire, was sent to Muscat in October 1798 for the very purpose.[35]

Sultan b Ahmad, on the other hand, seeing his livelihood threatened by the increasing British domination of commercial outlets in India, agreed to sign the so-called *qawlnâma* (Per. = Treaty) that Mehdi was proposing. But it is significant to note that in doing so his main concern was to obtain some important commercial privileges for himself and for Omani merchants in British India at a time when Britain, preoccupied by its wider strategic interests, could not refuse him. Despite its earlier attempts to hinder Omani trade, Britain now in return for the treaty agreed to grant the following concessions to Omanis trading in British India: exemption from pilotage charges for all Omani ships; supply of free wood and water to one of Sultan b Ahmad's ships resorting annually to Bombay and to two of his ships sailing to Bengal every year; permission for each Omani ship to take 1,000 maunds of salt per year to Calcutta and for two of Sultan's own ships to take 5,000 maunds there annually.[36] Sultan, for his part, agreed to British demands 'to dismiss from his employ a certain person of the French nation',[37] and promised that in times of war between European nations the French and the Dutch would not be allowed 'a place to fix or seat themselves in, nor shall they ever get ground to stand upon, with this state'.[38]

Nonetheless, it must be stressed that Sultan was canny enough not to compromise his own relations with the French. He steadfastly refused to grant the British permission to establish a factory at Muscat on the grounds that it would lead to a confrontation with the French. Such a confrontation would have inevitably been detrimental to Oman's interests in East Africa and would have been prejudicial to Muscat's trade. Sultan agreed, however, to allow the British to re-establish their former factory at Bander Abbas whilst emphasising that such a privilege had recently been refused to the Dutch and the French.[39]

It seems that in 1798 the British authorities preferred to ignore the extent of Oman's associations with France which had originated on the East African coast since at least the 1740s.[40] There is no doubt that they were aware of these associations. But due to Oman's age-old commercial connections with India, the British perhaps conjectured that Muscati rulers would never put at risk their trading activities with British-controlled Indian ports by allying themselves with Britain's enemies, the French.[41] However, for Oman the East African link was as important as its link with India. Indeed, the fact that Britain now was out to gain control of more and more of Oman's traditional contacts in India had the result of propelling the Omani rulers and the Muscati merchants further towards East Africa.

The early Omani–French relations

The earliest recorded contacts between French and Omani merchants occurred as early as the 1670s.[42] At that time, it was not the British but the Dutch who, in 1671, had forcibly prevented French merchants from trading at Muscat.[43] Nevertheless, contacts between French and Omani merchants continued in East Africa and Omani rulers soon started a correspondence with Paris through the agency of the French resident at Basra.[44]

Ironically, the ever-increasing role played by French merchants, in the 1770s and 1780s on the East African coast, was to lead to the first direct external threat to the Albusaid's own authority at a time when leaders of Omani communities in Africa, like the Mazaria of Mombasa or the rulers of Kilwa, were striving to gain their independence from Oman. Furthermore some French traders, such as Morice, had conceived their own highly ambitious plans for France in East Africa. Morice in his 'Projet d'un Etablissement à la Côte Orientale d'Afrique' had not only put forward proposals for commercial treaties with the rulers of Oman but had also expounded ideas for the annexation of the whole East African coast by the French.[45] More significantly, he was actively supported in such schemes by de Cossigny, the governor of Ile de France[46] during the 1770s.[47] In the commercial sphere, there was fierce competition between the French and the Omani authorities in Zanzibar for the control of Kilwa's 'prosperous trade'.[48] However, the Albusaidi-installed authorities in Zanzibar managed to maintain their political hold on Kilwa and reinstated an Omani *wali* there in 1785 at the height of French activity. This was no mean feat if we bear in mind the fact that local rulers of Kilwa had wholeheartedly associated themselves with the French to shake off Albusaidi domination over them from Zanzibar.[49]

By the 1780s French merchants, operating from Ile de France and engaged in the slave trade centred on Kilwa and Zanzibar, made representations to Hamad b Said at Muscat to regularise the duties they were compelled to pay at Albusaidi-controlled ports in East Africa. This was followed by a mission under one Monsieur Rosilly who was sent to Muscat in 1785 by de Souillac, Governor of Ile de France, in order to negotiate a commercial agreement with Hamad. These French efforts were duly rewarded when on 10 March 1790, 'the Sultan presented to the French a consular house [at Muscat], something that he had consistently refused to Great Britain'.[50] Nonetheless, with the outbreak of the French Revolution in 1789, France became too pre-occupied with its own internal situation to pursue these inroads made with the Albusaidis.

During the Revolutionary Wars, the Albusaidi rulers of Muscat were unable to prevent themselves from being sucked into the web of the commercial and strategic interests of the European powers. Seeing the French active on the western side of their trading zone in the Indian Ocean and the British in the east, they were obliged at first to play a game of wait-and-see in the hope that the Europeans would dissipate their respective energies on the battlefield thus leaving the way clear for Muscat to step into the resulting power vacuum. Any ambitions that Muscat's rulers may have nursed of competing with the European powers and establishing their own authority soon evaporated, however, when Oman's own internal political imperatives dictated that they take sides with the eventual European victor, Britain.

THE WAHHABIS AND THE BEGINNINGS OF MUSCAT'S RELIANCE ON BRITAIN

As seen above, in signing the 1798 Treaty with Britain, Sultan b Ahmad had refused to endanger his relations with the French. After 1798, he in fact continued to freight shipments bound for Ile de France with large quantities of grain and brimstone.[51] He also maintained amicable relations throughout with Tipu Sultan of Mysore who in 1799, after forging an alliance with the governor of Ile de France, went to war with the British.[52] The Omanis at this time were purportedly giving considerable assistance to the French and it seems that this assistance was decisive in enabling Ile de France to hold out for so long against Britain during the Wars.[53] It is no wonder therefore that in 1799 Napoleon sent letters of support to both Sultan b Ahmad and Tipu Sultan of Mysore promising them aid in their struggle against the British.[54] Nevertheless, four years later in August 1803 the Muscati ruler refused even to receive de Cavignac, the newly appointed French consul, arriving at Muscat to take up his position. Having previously aroused the ire of the British by his actions and 'ignored the catalogue of misdemeanours [by the Muscati ruler] drawn up at Bombay',[55] Sultan b Ahmad now felt compelled to respond to British demands that he sever all ties with the French forthwith. For the evolution of subsequent Omani–British– French relations, it is important to analyse how such a turn of events came about.

As a result of an alliance concluded between Britain and the Ottoman Empire on 2 January 1799, the French advance into Syria in March of that year was halted at the fortress of Acre.[56] Two months later, Tipu Sultan of Mysore was killed during the famous battle with British troops at Seringapatam.[57] A year later, in June 1801, Cairo fell to a British–Ottoman force thus bringing to an end the French occupation of Egypt.[58] With Mysore defeated and any attempt by Napoleon to cross to India via the Gulf or the Red Sea rendered impossible,[59] the British had proved to all concerned who were to remain the undisputed masters of India.

In India, apart from Mysore, the whole coast of Malabar had also by then fallen into the hands of the British who held possession of every port at which a vessel could anchor all the way from Surat to Calcutta.[60] This scenario radically affected Muscat's commercial position. But these exogenous commercial factors, whatever their significance may have been for Muscat, were relegated to second place by the immense problems that the Omanis were at that time experiencing internally. For nearly four years now, since his agreement with the British, Sultan b Ahmad's landward frontiers had been under attack from the Wahhabis of Central Arabia whilst his adversaries at sea, the Qasimis and the Utbis, had been receiving moral and logistical support from these same Wahhabis to bring about the Albusaidi's downfall.

The rise of the Wahhabi movement or the so-called First Sa'udi State and its early relationship with Oman need not be repeated here in detail as it has been dealt with elsewhere.[61] What concerns us here is to examine the role played by this movement in relation to the internal political and economic situation of Oman and how it affected Oman's connections with Western powers. By definition the Wahhabi movement was expansionist. Its propagandist tract, entitled '*Kitâb Kashf al-Shubuhât*', attributed to Muḥammad b 'Abd-al-Wahhâb and containing an exposition of the doctrines of the *muwaḥḥidûn* (unitarians, as the Wahhabis called themselves), was sent to Muscat at the beginning of the nineteenth century along with an invitation to submit.[62] But the Omani religious-cum-tribal leaders dismissed this tract as 'untruthful

fabricated nonsense'.[63] Indeed, the Wahhabi doctrine was total ana-
thema to the Ibadi *ulama* as can be seen from the commentary of the
'âlim Abû Nabhân Jâ'id b Khamîs al-Kharûsî:

> The Wahhabi religion calls for Muslims to kill each other and
> declares other Muslims who do not adhere to its doctrines as
> polytheists allowing the plunder of their goods, the enslavement of
> their women and children, the taking of booty and the imposition of
> *jizya* [poll tax] and *kharâj* [land tax].... This religion has taken a bit
> from the \zâriqa and a bit from the Ḥanbalis.... In fact they have
> taken from every *madhhab* its worst aspects while claiming to
> have come across the true religion.... From the Azariqa, they have
> taken *tashrîk ahl al-qibla* [declaring non-adherent Muslims to be
> polytheists].[64]

Ibadism, on the other hand, has always insisted on recognising the
validity of the beliefs of other Muslims through the status of *ahl al-
qibla* (people who pray facing the Ka'ba in Mecca).[65] Therefore, the
doctrines preached by the Wahhabis, even in those aspects concerning
other Muslims, were in direct opposition to those of the Ibadis.

Although currently recognised by historians to have been one of the
numerous Islamic *salafîya* movements,[66] Wahhabism, characterised by
a bigotry inherent in such movements, stunned and confounded the
Muslim world directed as it was primarily against the Islamic `*umma*
(community) itself. Not only was it legitimate, in Wahhabis' eyes, to
desecrate the Shi'i holy shrines in Iraq, but Ibadis, Shi'is, Sufis,
Mu'tazila and even those Sunnis not adhering to the creed of Ibn Ḥanbal
were regarded as heretics fit only to be put to the sword if not converted
to the new creed. Furthermore, the movement emerged at a time when
leaders of Muslim societies were agonising over how to rationalise the
loss of their prestige of old and how to face the challenge posed by the
might of the newly industrialised Christian West with its advanced
techniques in warfare. Although Islamic leaders were enraged at the
Wahhabi conquest of the holy cities of Islam and the slaughter of the
Shi'is in Iraq in 1802,[67] there was little they could do engaged as they
were in their own struggle against the Europeans. The Ottoman Sultan
Selim III was far too preoccupied with the politics of Europe and
Constantinople. The Persian Fath Ali Shah was fighting the Russians on
his northern frontiers while Shah Alam II, the last of the Mughals in
Delhi, could only look on helplessly as the British extended their power
through Bengal to Oudh, central India and Rajputana.[68]

As far as Oman was concerned, the expulsion of the Omani garrison
from Bahrain by the Wahhabis in 1802 followed by the humiliating

experience of Sultan b Ahmad having to sue for peace with the Nubian slave, Sâlim b Hilâl al-Harîq,[69] the commander of the Wahhabi forces in Buraymi, shook the very foundations of Oman as a political entity. Sultan was obliged to submit in 1803 following al-Hariq's butchery and plunder of the Batina.[70] In return for a three-year truce, Sultan even agreed to pay an annual tribute of MT\$ 12,000 to Dir'îya (the Wahhabi headquarters), while Wahhabi preachers were permitted to propound their doctrines in the very streets of Muscat and Matrah.[71]

It was in these humbling circumstances that Sultan b Ahmad, forced to look on as the very foundations of his 'state' were crumbling, refused to receive the French consul at Muscat in the summer of 1803. He now realised that Britain was the only power capable of aiding him against his enemies. And he was no longer prepared to imperil his chances of British support by flirting with the French at such a critical time no matter what the consequences may have been for his interests in Africa, linked as they were with those of the French. Moreover, since most of Muscat's trade was with India, an alliance and a show of respect for British wishes were, in the long run, more beneficial to Muscat's commercial interests. At that time, in the words of the British chronicler Lorimer:

> It was directly intimated to Sultan more than once, that, were he to throw in his lot with the French, the British Government would have no alternative but to place his dominions under a commercial blockade from the side of India.[72]

Thus, to save his commercial links with India, the historical commercial partner of Oman, Sultan b Ahmad was forced to make concessions to the British. Henceforth the trading networks of the Indian Ocean or at least the western section of them, now increasingly dominated by the British, meant that the task hitherto undertaken by Oman now fell to Britain, namely the control of the high seas against depredations on cargo-laden shipping or 'piracy' as the British insisted upon calling them. Britain was now to join in the mêlée obliged as it was to compete not only with Muscat but also with other principalities of the Gulf, all out to seize control of commerce in the western Indian Ocean region. Throughout the eighteenth century and before, it had been Oman which had assumed the responsibility of that control often going to war with other forces in the region for that purpose. Now, Britain had to be reckoned with as well. And it was a matter of sheer coincidence that following the ratificaton of the 1798 Treaty on 18 June 1800[73] the first decade of the nineteenth century saw the interests of Oman and Britain converging as both sought to control attacks on shipping by the Qasimis who, in turn, were supported by the Wahhabis.

With regard to the internal situation of Oman, after the loss of Suwaiq on the Batina and the siege of Sohar by the Wahhabis in 1803, Sultan b Ahmad managed to summon the most prominent tribal leaders of Oman at Barka in a united front against the Wahhabi enemy. However, while preparations were being made to raise the siege of Sohar after recruiting some 12,000 tribal levies,[74] news was received in November 1803 of the assassination of the Wahhabi *amîr* 'Abd-al'Azîz b Muḥammad b Sa'ûd. The *amir* had been killed by an Iraqi Shi'i whose own chidren had been massacred at Kerbala.[75] At this al-Hariq, the Wahhabi commander, quietly withdrew from Sohar to his headquarters in Buraymi and the Omani forces were allowed to disperse without having entered the arena of battle.[76]

From a commercial viewpoint Muscat's position had by then markedly deteriorated. In addition to the above-mentioned loss of control of important trading outlets in India to the British, the Qasimis had managed to wrest the island of Qishm from the Omani garrison there,[77] thus obtaining a base at the entrance of the Gulf from which they could launch attacks upon Muscati and other shipping. Furthermore, Ali Pasha, the *wali* of Baghdad, on receiving the news of the Albusaidi's predicament decided to withdraw the subsidy that the Ottomans annually forwarded to Muscat. This subsidy was paid in return for Omani naval protection given for trading purposes to Southern Iraq in 1775 by Ahmad b Said, the founder of the Albusaidi Dynasty.[78] With these developments, after the truce with the Wahhabis following the assassination of their *amir*, Ahmad's son, Sultan, decided to take the initiative. While demanding the resumption of payment of the tribute due to Muscat he also entered into communication with the Ottoman authorities on the need for a joint effort to rid Arabia of the Wahhabis once and for all.[79]

Receiving an encouraging response from Ali Pasha, in 1804 Sultan sailed to Basra for the dual purpose of collecting the subsidy owed to him and of making the necessary military preparations for a combined Omani-Ottoman expedition against the Wahhabis. Nevertheless, on arrival he was disillusioned by the lack of preparations at Basra and receiving news subsequently of Ali Pasha's change of heart and refusal to join him in any military expeditions at that stage[80] Sultan, disappointed and angry, set sail for Muscat in November 1804. It was to be his last journey for on the way he was attacked by three Qasimi war vessels and was killed in what appears to have been yet another of those skirmishes so common among the warring maritime tribes of the Gulf.[81] Indeed, his assailants did not even know that they were dealing with the ruler of Muscat who, obstinate in his tribal pride, refused to reveal his identity when challenged to a military confrontation.[82] As the *alim* Sâlim b Muḥammad al-Darrmakkî lamented in his *marthîya* (elegy) for Sultan:

> Wonders never cease in these our times,
> The lion of lions has been assaulted by dogs.[83]

The extent of Sultan b Ahmad's reliance on Britain

It is significant to note that Sultan b Ahmad in his lifetime never once asked Britain for any military assistance. His readiness to undertake a major campaign against the Wahhabis in his last years shows that Muscat was still in a relatively strong position *vis-à-vis* the Wahhabis and the Western powers. Despite Bonaparte's débâcle in Egypt and British incursions nearer home, Sultan continued to keep a close watch on his commercial interests in East Africa which provided him, in the beginning of the nineteenth century, with a revenue of MT$. 40,000 annually from customs[84] compared to MT$ 112,500 from those of Muscat.[85] Motivated throughout his life, as already shown, by his ambition to enhance the commercial status of Muscat, Sultan had warned the British about his independence and his continuing commercial pursuits, even after the ratification of his treaty with them in 1800:

> I am the ruler of my own country and sovereign over it and the inhabitants thereof, and independent of everyone. The course that I am to observe with the French proceeds from the necessity I am under not to put an entire stop to the trade by sea of my subjects.[86]

Indeed, any troubles that Sultan experienced before his death from East Africa originated from the increasingly confident inroads that Britain had started to make in influencing the political situation there.

Following a British mission dispatched in 1799 from London to Zanzibar under John Blankett,[87] Omani leaders in East Africa began to seize the opportunity of the increasing show of British interest by offering to conclude alliances in order to get rid of Albusaidi suzerainty over them. For this reason Sultan b Ahmad, still experiencing dissent and opposition from the rulers of Kilwa and the Mazaria of Mombasa who also controlled Pemba,[88] had now to contend with another challenge to his authority from the rulers of Pate, the most powerful group in the Lamu Archipelago. In 1801 the ruler of Pate, one Muḥammad al-Nabhânî, sent two envoys to Bombay offering Britain the privilege of building a fort and defending the island against any aggressors in return for half of the island's produce.[89] Jonathan Duncan, the governor of

Bombay, at the time preoccupied with the French threat and anxious to get the Muscati ruler on his side, was all for applying pressure on the Albusaidi from East Africa and showed great interest in the Pate project. However, although he recommended British support for the idea it was rejected by his superiors.[90]

In any event, Sultan b Ahmad, then engrossed in the Wahhabi invasion of his territories in Oman, could only observe these events as he was unable to take any action. He may well have had plans for East Africa to be put into effect after his trip to Basra. But that was not to be. After him the political chaos that was to engulf Oman not only enabled Britain to bring Oman more and more within its fold; it also empowered the British to destroy the traditional competitive maritime trade system of the Gulf. How this came about will be the subject matter of the next chapter.

4 British policy towards Oman under the first Wahhabi threat: 1804–14

The political maelstrom into which Oman was plunged following Sultan b Ahmad's death in November 1804 accorded the tribal leaders in East Africa a further opportunity to dissociate themselves from the Albusaid. With Oman overrun by the Wahhabis and with no recognised Albusaidi successor the dominant Omani group in East Africa, the Mazaria of Mombasa, did in fact try to expand their realm in the Lamu Archipelago. But before turning to the situation in Africa we will first examine the events in Arabia.

THE WAHHABI–QASIMI THREAT TO OMAN AND BRITAIN

In Oman, Sultan's death gave the Wahhabis the opportunity of launching a final assault on Muscat and of bringing it within the Wahhabi domain. By now, with their movement well established in al-Zâhira, al-Shamâlîya and Bahrain,[1] they were able to use these places as bases from which they could launch further conquests of the region. At such a critical moment, however, they decided not to take any action against Muscat. It is interesting to analyse what may have been the reasons behind this decision.

While it is true that the new Wahhabi *amir*, Sa'ûd b 'Abd al-'Azîz, was preoccupied with asserting his authority in the Hijaz after his father's assassination, al-Rashid maintains that 'it is doubtful that the Hijaz campaigns could have completely diverted the Suudi efforts from the Southeastern frontiers'.[2] He goes on to suggest that perhaps it was the vastness of the territorial expanse of Oman, its 'ever quarrelling' tribes and 'its remoteness from the central government' that dissuaded the Dir'iya authorities from bringing Oman under outright Wahhabi rule.[3] However, this explanation is barely adequate since the considerations mentioned by al-Rashid had not changed appreciably from those of two years earlier when, on al-Rashid's own admission, 'the

Suudi Amir [had been determined] to exercise complete control over Masqat'.[4] Furthermore, in his conclusion al-Rashid states:

> Convinced of the universality of their reforms, the Suudi-Wahhabi leaders and followers recognized no geographical boundaries or political divisions within the peninsula. They resolved to enforce their views by totally subjugating certain districts, or else by winning local chiefs to their side and enforcing the reform practices through them.[5]

Nevertheless, although the Wahhabi authorities may have wished to subjugate Oman, they never planned an outright conquest of Omani territories. All they wanted was to subjugate tribal leaders forcing them to pay an annual tribute in return for peace. However, even when subjugated tribes did agree to pay this tribute it was never regarded as *zakât* in the sense of it being a tax due to a legitimate Islamic ruler as is claimed by al-Rashid. Rather, it was a *ṣulḥ* (peace) type of agreement which, as Wilkinson puts it, 'was an extortion to which the term "Danegeld" is more appropriate'.[6]

In the 1804 situation, it was also perhaps Oman's association with Britain that may have played its part in saving Muscat from the clutches of the Wahhabis. The Dir'iya authorities must have thought twice about the likely British reaction to any attempt of establishing their rule at Muscat. As it transpired it was not so much the Wahhabi designs on Muscat as the political and commercial ambitions of the Wahhabis and their allies, the Qasimis, and the challenge these presented to the commercial supremacy of Britain, and not that of Muscat as is propounded by most historians,[7] which finally provoked Britain into taking action.

By February 1805 the Qasimis had added to their control of Qishm that of Hormuz and Bander Abbas and had thus become masters of the Straits of Hormuz whence they could strike at any ship leaving or entering the Gulf. When two British ships belonging to Samuel Manesty, the British Resident at Basra, were attacked by the Qasimis late in 1804,[8] and when the Qasimis started to engage in battle gun cruisers belonging to the English East India Company in 1805,[9] Britain had no alternative but to respond. Here is how British officials saw the situation at the time. While Sultan b Ahmad had been alive, he had, according to these officials, managed to hold the Qasimis in check:

> Up to the close of 1804, they [the Qasimis] committed no acts of piracy; but with the exception of the attack on 'Bassein Snow' and 'Viper' [in 1778 and 1779] they manifested every respect for the British flag.[10]

Nevertheless,

the death of Syud Sultan, who had maintained some degree of control over the petty powers [of the Gulf], left these latter without check; the disturbances in consequence increased.[11]

Thus Britain, having assumed the role of protector of the Gulf trade formerly held by the rulers of Muscat, was now openly challenged by the Qasimis who continued to attack cargo-laden shipping, an activity which the mercantile communities of the Gulf, whether local or foreign, had been carrying out for centuries.[12] For this activity, although now dubbed by the British as 'piracy', was part and parcel of the commercial practice prevalent in the region. In the words of Landen, it was an 'occupation and a more or less accepted way of sustaining life or realising certain political and economic ambitions'.[13]

Like any important seaway the Gulf had experienced attacks on cargo vessels throughout its history. Indeed, there is evidence that British merchants themselves had carried out such attacks in their earlier efforts to acquire a share of the Gulf trade. In 1621 the British ships '*London*' and '*Roebuck*' attacked a Muscati ship 'about fourteen leagues from Diu [and took] 770 pieces of gold and 10,200 laris'.[14] In 1625, 'we capture a ship from Muscat with 37 Arab horses, besides dates, etc., with a total value of 41,470 Mahmudis'.[15] Towards the end of the century in 1698, evidence was adduced at the trial for piracy of one Henry Every, a British merchant, to show that he had captured a Muscati ship taking dates, rice and other goods after killing twelve of its crew.[16] In 1805 nevertheless, with Britain controlling some important maritime outlets of India, such depredations against British shipping and more importantly the readiness manifested by the Qasimis to openly engage British cruisers in battle came to be viewed in a very different perspective by the British authorities.[17] Britain insisted on calling Qasimi actions 'outright piracy' whereas similar plunder of its cargo vessels by the French, in the same period, was characterised as 'privateering'.[18] These labels could better have been attributed contrariwise since trade for the Qasimis, as for all the Gulf people, was crucial for their very livelihood and they consistently denied any illegality in their actions[19] which were no different in substance from those they and other merchants, including the British, had been carrying out for centuries before.

Britain and the post-1804 internal situation of Oman

After Bonaparte's defeat in Egypt, British attention towards Muscat had largely evaporated but there was now a quickening of interest when

Britain perceived that it shared a common purpose with the rulers of Muscat in thwarting the Qasimi forays against its shipping. Following the ratification of its treaty with Oman in 1800, Britain neither participated in nor indeed was it asked for its opinion regarding the various campaigns undertaken by Sultan b Ahmad in his final years. In fact, the British agency in Muscat was closed down at the end of 1803 after the neutralisation of the French threat to India.[20] However, with increasing Qasimi actions against British shipping, the former British Political Agent at Muscat (PAM), Captain David Seton, was ordered to go back to Muscat in March 1805.[21]

In the ongoing struggle for power at Muscat following Sultan's death, the thorny question now was with which contender was Seton to deal? For the first time in the history of Omani–British relations Britain was compelled to take the internal situation of Oman into consideration. But the British authorities could never grasp the complexity of the Omani political structure based as it was on tribalism and cloaked by a myriad of religious beliefs, often genuinely held but at times donned as a matter of political expediency. With modern European ideas of cohesive nation-states permeating their attitudes and guiding their footsteps, these authorities adopted a cautious approach by showing a willingness to support one of the sons of the former ruler although they advocated Seton to support the candidate 'whose pretensions shall appear to be founded on justice, provided that support can be afforded without the hazard of involving the British Government in hostilities with the state of Muscat'.[22] Furthermore, it was imperative that this was to be done without provoking disputes with the Wahhabis, the Ottoman Empire or Persia[23] at a time when the Wahhabis occupied parts of northern Oman and their allies, the Qasimis, controlled the access to Gulf waters.

The interlude of Badr b Sayf (r.1804–6)

As related above, Omani territories in 1793 had been divided between three sons of Ahmad b Said with Said the Imam taking possession of Rustaq, Qays of Sohar and Sultan of Muscat and of Oman's holdings overseas.[24] The situation had remained more or less static up to 1804 despite the plunder of the Batina and the unsuccessful siege of Sohar by the Wahhabis. The late Sultan b Ahmad, on his last departure to Basra, had appointed his relation and trusted friend Muḥammad b Nâṣir al-Jabrî, *tamima* of the powerful Ghafiri tribe of al-Jubûr controlling the Sumayil area, as Regent at Muscat and as guardian of his two minor sons Sâlim and Sa'îd, aged 15 and 13 respectively.[25] For Oman,

Sultan's death was 'a calamity which violently shook all corners of the country affecting every soul'.[26] It

> caused intense dismay throughout...threatened as the country was by external foes...the general consternation at the disappearance of the warrior, who had alone actively opposed the common foe and disturber of public peace, caused every chief to defend himself.[27]

In these circumstances, Qays at Sohar, now supported by his brother Said, the nominal Imam at Rustaq,[28] and by the Sharqiya Hinawis under Îsa b Sâlih I al-Hârthî,[29] grasped the nettle and endeavoured to seize control of Muscat.[30] Marching along the Batina Qays took Khabura, Seeb, Matrah and was threatening the very gates of Muscat.[31] Muhammad al-Jabri, the Regent, unable to defend the town, offered Isa al-Harthi, 'the most prominent of the leaders involved, large sums of money surreptitiously'.[32] al-Jabri also tried to buy off Qays by offering him a monthly pension of MT$ 2,000 if he returned to Sohar and adhered to the conditions agreed in 1793. But Qays, elated by his unexpected successes, rejected the offer and pushed on further towards his goal.[33] At this point it was the influence of Sayyida Môza bint Ahmad,[34] daughter of the founder of the Albusaidi Dynasty, which persuaded al-Jabri to call back to Muscat her other nephew, Badr b Sayf, who was at that time in exile in Qatar in a final desperate attempt to frustrate the designs of her brother Qays.[35]

Lorimer describes this Sayyida as 'a lady of unusual force of character',[36] and all al-Mughairî, Ibn Ruzaiq and Salma bint Sa'îd (later Emily Said-Ruete) agree that it was this lady who was in real control of Muscat affairs at the time.[37]

> My great-aunt [had] declared in the most decided manner that she would carry on the government herself until her nephew came of age...the ministers had to make their reports to her, and received her instructions and commands every day...she closely watched and knew everything...and put aside all rules of etiquette; regardless of what people might say she merely wore her *schele* in the presence of ministers...and dressed in men's clothes [on her inspection rounds at night].[38]
>
> At this critical stage Sayyida Moza sent one 'Alî b Fâdil al-Shî'î as an envoy to Badr summoning him to Muscat.[39] This Badr was the same man who only two years earlier had staged an abortive attempt to overthrow her brother Sultan seizing the opportunity of the ruler's absence at Mecca for *hajj* to take Muscat.[40] However, his plot to take possession of Fort Jalali had been discovered, interestingly enough,

by a Banyan merchant who had accordingly reported it to the Muscati authorities.[41] Having thus failed, Badr had fled to Dir'iya where he had allegedly embraced the new creed of the Wahhabis before proceeding to exile in Qatar.[42]

On his return to Muscat Badr was appointed by his aunt Moza as deputy ruler for two years until his cousin Said reached the age of 16.[43] Establishing himself at Barka, since Muscat was still under siege from Qays, Badr conceived plans of his own. He soon sent an appeal for aid to the Wahhabis who swiftly answered his call. A contingent of Wahhabi forces under Humayd b Nâsir al-Ghâfirî of al-'Aynayn (a fort in a strategic location in Wâdî al-Kabîr in central Oman) marched through Wâdî al-Jizzî towards Sohar, an action which forced Qays to fall back from Muscat to defend Sohar and to come to terms with Badr shortly afterwards.[44]

It was at this point in time, in May 1805, that the newly reappointed British PAM, Seton, arrived at Muscat. Having received instructions from his superiors to help the ruler of Muscat against the Qasimis, although he had been told not to interfere in any succession disputes,[45] Seton proceeded to assist Badr who was in the process of making preparations for the recovery of Qishm and Bander Abbas. In this way and solely for the purpose of its own commercial interests Britain became involved, albeit indirectly, with the enemies of Oman. Nonetheless, although Seton's efforts did result in an agreement with the Qasimis to observe a seventy-day truce and to respect British property and shipping,[46] in Oman itself hostilities did not come to an end.

During Badr's absence on his expedition against Qishm and Bander Abbas, Qays once again tried to seize Muscat. By the time Badr returned, Qays had already taken Matrah[47] obliging the former to appeal once more to the Wahhabis for assistance. A large land contingent together with a fifteen-vessel fleet manned by some 4,000 men were duly dispatched by the Wahhabis to Oman.[48] The arrival of the fleet from Bahrain caused great consternation among Muscat's cosmopolitan population especially the Shi'is amongst them who, as seen earlier, were on good terms with the Albusaidi rulers. The Wahhabi fleet arrived at Muscat flaunting trophies plundered during the sack of Kerbala and flew from the ships' masts strips of the sacred cloth torn from the tomb of the Shi'i Imam al-Husayn b 'Alî.[49]

In addition to the Wahhabi assistance to Badr, Qays also faced a formidable and swelling internal opposition to his plans to seize Muscat. By now, not only did al-Zahira tribes under Humayd al-Ghafiri stand against him but Imam Said at Rustaq and the Sharqiya Hinawis were also opposed to his takeover of Muscat.[50] It was this internal opposition that put Qays in a humiliating position obliging him eventually to surrender every place under his control except for Sohar while his brother and ally, Muhammad, was forced to hand the forts of Nizwa and Bahla over to Badr who was now effectively recognised as the ruler of Muscat.[51]

Nevertheless, it was Badr's misfortune that he had to rely so heavily on Wahhabi aid. He has been portrayed in many accounts as having become a strict adherent to Wahhabi doctrines allegedly expressing 'his loyalty to Amir Saud, promising to carry out his commands and to assist the state whenever aid was required'.[52] We will never know, however, how much his association with Wahhabism was borne of a genuine commitment to their ideals and how much it was motivated by his own political ambitions. His first brush with the Wahhabis had definitely originated from the latter following his failure to seize Muscat in 1803. And it was by sheer force of circumstances that he had been entreated by his aunt Moza to return to Muscat in 1805. His continued relationship with Oman's bitter enemies was nevertheless to prove a doomed partnership and it led inexorably to his eventual downfall. The available evidence quite clearly points to the fact that Badr realised that in achieving his end by such means he was unleashing forces he knew he would be powerless to control on his own.

He soon saw that the corollary of his heavy reliance on Wahhabi troops was the unchecked proselytising by Wahhabi preachers who roamed right in the streets of Muscat and Matrah terrorising their cosmopolitan and multi-religious populations and forcing the Muslims among them, under threat of punishment, to close down their shops regularly at times of prayer. As *amir* Sa'ûd b 'Abd-al-'Azîz himself put it: 'The Christians and the Jews...they have their books and must live by them; the Mohammedans alone are guilty and must choose between Wahhabism and death'.[53]

In a country proud of its Ibadi heritage and its tolerance towards other beliefs Wahhabi notions, such as the one expounded in the above quotation, could not go unchecked for very long especially if we consider how important trade was for Omani communities. This trade could never thrive without a tolerant, if not an encouraging, attitude towards Oman's mercantile groups whether they were Muslim, Hindu or of any other religious persuasion. 'The exodus of inhabitants from Muscat town'[54] at that time was certainly harmful to Muscat's fortunes. In fact, Badr himself was becoming alarmed at these developments but he refrained from taking any action until he received a letter from *amir* Saud, in the summer of 1805, in which he was instructed: 'Verily thou shalt speedily proceed to the Holy War in India by which thou wilt not be fighting for me but it is incumbent on thee to be obedient to God'.[55] Badr was so intimidated, as this clearly meant that he was to go to war against the British, that he wrote to Jonathan Duncan, the governor of Bombay, asking for British help to deal with the Wahhabis. In this he was supported by PAM Seton who, by including a translation of Saud's letter to Badr in his dispatch, warned Duncan of the potential disruption to British trade in the Indian Ocean should the Wahhabis gain the upper hand at Muscat.[56] While the British authorities were contemplating how best to deal with this situation, and interesting though it would have been to see *amir* Saud's reaction to Badr's refusal to his demands, both the British and the Wahhabis were spared the need to take any drastic measures. For it was the Albusaidis themselves who decided that Badr and his association with the Wahhabis should be dealt with once and for all.

THE RISE AND EARLY STRUGGLES OF SAID B SULTAN (r.1806–56)

There is no doubt that it was Sayyida Moza bint Said's influence, once again, that was crucial behind not only Badr's downfall but also the rise to power in his stead of her other nephew, Said b Sultan. A question often puzzling historians is why, of the three nephews (Salim being the third), should Moza's choice have fallen on Said. Salim was two years older than Said and, had Moza agreed, he could have ruled Muscat without having had to resort to calling Badr back from Qatar in the first place. In trying to give an explanation for why Salim was passed over some European accounts forward the reason that he was of a 'peculiar and unsuitable character' or that he suffered from paralysis, was unable to control his movements and was thus considered unfit to rule.[57] There is no mention of this, however, in Omani sources and Ibn Ruzaiq holds Salim in very high esteem.[58] Nonetheless, while leaving these unflattering portrayals of Salim out of the equation, there seem to have been three main reasons why Said was favoured by his aunt.

Firstly Said's mother, Sayyida Ghânî bint Sayf, was from an influential section of the Albusaidi House itself whereas Salim's mother was not even an Albusaidiya.[59] Secondly Said took as his first wife a daughter of Moza, 'Azza bint Sayf b 'Alî, a granddaughter of

Ahmad b Said, the founder of the Dynasty.[60] Thus, Said was not only a nephew but also a son-in-law of Moza and both he himself and his progeny must have been regarded as having a better pedigree than Salim or Salim's descendents. A third reason was that Salim was of a studious disposition and more interested in the perusal of religious scriptures than in the affairs of state.[61] Said, on the other hand, as subsequent events show, was much more versed in the affairs of the world and was from an early age considered fit to assume the mantle of leadership.

Having put Badr in power in the first instance Moza, two years later, realised that he would never relinquish it without a protracted struggle despite his earlier promises. By now the resentment borne towards Badr, and the deep humiliation felt at the Albusaidi House having to pay tribute to Dir'iya, made his continued rule at Muscat untenable. Therefore, Moza, according to al-Mughairi, 'incited Said b Sultan to assassinate Badr'.[62]

Badr himself, a year before, had used assassination as a method to divest himself of a powerful rival, Muhanna b Muḥammad al-Ya'rubî of Nakhl, *tamima* of the ousted Ya'ariba Dynasty. Muhanna had continued to remain loyal to Moza's camp and had shown not the slightest inclination to accept Badr as ruler of Muscat.[63] This deprivation of Moza and her supporters of their most loyal ally was the final straw which provoked the Sayyida into making Said execute their strategy conceived to break the stranglehold of Badr and his Wahhabi cronies. With the cooperation of al-Jabri, Said, then *wali* of Barka, lured Badr to that town on a pretext and in a treacherous plot murdered him on 9 July 1806.[64] Pleading his innocence to the Wahhabi commander at Barka and putting the blame for the crime on al-Jabri, Said made his way to Muscat where he was proclaimed ruler at the age of 16.[65] Fortunately for him, Said immediately received support from his uncle Qays at Sohar 'who had an utter detestation for Badr and his Wahhabi tendencies'.[66]

On 31 July 1806 Said wrote to Duncan at Bombay announcing his assumption of power and seeking British recognition.[67] The mere fact that he felt the need to write to the British authorities for recognition shows not so much his weakness but the immense influence Britain already exerted in the role it had taken upon itself as arbiter of the affairs of Oman and the Gulf. But the nefarious manner of his accession to power did not recommend him to the British authorities and recognition was withheld for a whole year. When finally granted it was not due to any British regard for the internal situation of Oman. It was simply because Britain, in its continuing rivalry with France in the Indian Ocean and its unremitting clashes with the Qasimis, had concluded that its interests would be best served by supporting Said despite having before envisaged that his rule 'begun amidst unfavourable omens, would be of short duration'.[68]

Said b Sultan's early relations with the British and the French

Said b Sultan, from a very early age, had been aware of British standing in regional affairs. As a boy of eight he had been present at Muscat, in 1800, at the reception ceremony held for John Malcolm, then Assistant Resident in Hyderabad and sent on a trade mission to Oman. Among the most prestigious gifts then received by Omanis from members of the mission had been double-barrelled guns, telescopes and pistols. Said and his brother Salim had been given, among other things, a model of a British ship with fifty mounted guns.[69] Having, from these early days, been impressed by British weaponry and having seen Britain triumph over France during the first few years of the nineteenth century, it was soon brought home to Said within a matter of months of his accession that any action he was to take in the Gulf as ruler of Muscat would have to be compatible with British wishes.

In the autumn of 1806 a French ship *'La Vigilante'* from Ile de France berthed at Muscat, as was quite common, for water and supplies. When, however, it was forced to leave Muscat harbour by the British cruiser *'Concorde'* at cannon-point and was later captured just outside Muscat cove, Said, fearing French reprisals, protested to Duncan that the action was an unjust violation of the neutrality of Muscat port.[70] To protect his interests in East Africa Said hastily despatched an envoy to General De Caen, Governor of Ile de France, to explain Oman's innocence in the affair. De Caen nonetheless, insisting on the return of the French ship and its crew, held by the British in Bombay, put the blame on both Oman and Britain.

While the British authorities were lengthily explaining to Said the meaning of Muscat's neutrality according to the terms of the treaty they had signed with his father, the French decided to make a show of their strength. Eight Muscati ships were soon afterwards captured on their way to Bengal by the French and their captains were told in no uncertain terms that the action was taken on the express orders of De Caen himself, in retaliation for the British capture of *La Vigilante*.[71] Said immediately sent envoys both to Ile de France and Bombay pointing out to De Caen that Muscat was not responsible for actions taken by the British. And as it was the British who had captured and now held *La Vigilante* Said pleaded for the return of the plundered Omani cargoes. From Duncan, Said requested the release of the French ship. Thus caught up in the wars between Europeans Said submitted various proposals to Duncan that his own ships be escorted to Calcutta by British vessels, that a British cruiser be permanently stationed at Muscat and that Britain give him substantial assistance in terms of troops, money and ships in return for Oman adopting an overtly hostile stance against the French.[72]

Said, as it can be deduced from his dispatch to Duncan, had already chosen sides. It had not taken him long to realise, as his father had done before him, that Muscat's interests dominated by its trade with India would be best served if he were to forge an alliance with Britain. For such an alliance it seems that he was prepared, at this stage, even to relinquish Oman's multifarious interests in East Africa or perhaps he hoped that Britain would assist him in Africa as well. There is no doubt that such a stand by Said, at that time, was prompted largely by his internal predicament in Oman where he had a negligible tribal power base and an increasing siege mentality induced by constant incursions of the Qasimis in the north and of the Wahhabis in the west.

Nevertheless, the British authorities rejected Said's offer of an alliance. It was precisely because of the precarious situation in which Said found himself internally that Britain decided to rebuff his overtures, unwilling to become entangled in the intricate web of Oman's politics. It is abundantly clear from the mass of despatches of its political agents that for all its involvements in regional affairs, Britain, throughout the nineteenth century, failed to acquire even an elementary grasp of Oman's internal dynamics and tribal-cum-religious political structures. In the 1806 situation, faced by recurrent protests by Said, Britain eventually even agreed to allow the French to trade openly with Muscat which was now to be regarded once again as 'neutral' in the British–French wars.[73] Thus, the British requirement of a total ban on French activities at Muscat, in the time of Said's father, could no longer be supported unless Britain was willing to give Muscat active backing. At a time when there was no direct threat from any Western power to the British position in the Indian Ocean Britain refused to become involved in Oman's internal situation even if it meant that Oman was to succumb more and more to Wahhabi demands. In this way, within a period of eight years, political realities had shifted to such an extent that the alliance that the British had been actively seeking with Muscat for over a century[74] was now rejected out of hand when offered to them on a plate.

Said b Sultan, thus rebuffed by the British, decided to try his luck with their rivals. He wrote to De Caen:

We attach ourselves very much to the need to cultivate the friendship of old that has always existed between our fathers and the French nation. We hope that Your Excellency would well consider our country as belonging to you, and being for ever ready to obey you, each time that you may wish to honour us with your commands.[75]

Following this, on 15 June 1807, De Caen signed 'a treaty of perpetual and inviolable peace between H.M. the Emperor of the French people and H.M. the Sultan of Muscat' giving both the Omanis and the French most favoured nation privileges in matters of commerce and navigation in each other's territories.[76] This treaty, however, was never ratified in Paris although the French authorities in the Indian Ocean were subsequently to act as if it had been.[77]

This brief interlude during which Muscat gained its 'neutrality' and was deemed unimportant by Britain soon came to a dramatic end.

In May 1807 Bonaparte signed a treaty with the Persians under the terms of which, in return for France recognising Georgia as part of Persia, the Persians agreed to cede some islands in the Gulf to the French.[78] This treaty was aimed principally against Russia but Britain became anxious that the islands might eventually be used in a French military expedition against India.[79] To aggravate British fears France also attempted to conclude an alliance with the Ottoman Empire in order to prohibit British troops from operating in Iraqi territories.[80] Furthermore, Bonaparte also at this time sent an envoy to the Wahhabi *amir* in Dir'iya in an attempt to obtain his cooperation for preventing British troops from crossing territories under his control.[81]

Britain became so alarmed at these developments that Seton was ordered back to Muscat[82] with instructions to persuade Said to sever all connections with the French and to cease supplies of grain to Ile de France.[83] Thus, the definition of Muscat's 'neutrality' was yet again changed, by Britain itself, as fear of a possible French invasion of India obliged it to associate more closely with the ruler of Muscat. Britain grudgingly restored to Said b Sultan the recognition of the strategic value of his international port for the defence of British India. Even when tensions subsequently relaxed following the Peace of Tilsit between Bonaparte and the Tsar Alexander I on 7 July 1807 and when Paris refused to ratify the French treaty with Persia,[84] Britain continued to move closer to Muscat. Britain felt obliged to do so at a time when its wars with France in the Indian Ocean remained inconclusive.

Interestingly, among Seton's instructions from Bombay at this time was a directive to find out about Said's standing in Oman and to report on 'what exactly was happening in the country'.[85] The PAM's verdict did not bode well for the Albusaidi:

> Syud Saeed, young and inexperienced, has lost the influence his father had acquired, and from the little consideration he manifested towards the Shaiks who visited Maskat, was left almost friendless. Of Oman he possesses only the sea coast, the upper country having become tributary to the Wahabees, and it was only by a degrading submission that the Imaum [*sic*] protected the low country from their inroads. Makran, with the exception of Guaden [Gwadar], has also become independent of the Imaum'.[86]

Internally, following the murder of Badr b Sayf in 1806, Said b Sultan, by disavowing any part in the assassination plot and declaring to Dir'iya his readiness to continue the payment of tribute, managed to obviate any punitive Wahhabi action against him.[87] A year later, however, with encouragement from his uncle Qays of Sohar, Said led an expedition against Khawr Fakkan which had been captured by the Qasimis in the confusion following Badr's death. The Qasimi leader, Sultân b Saqr, had built a fort and established a base to attack Gulf shipping from Khawr Fakkan. Although the Omani forces managed initially to capture the fort and put its garrison to the sword, al-Qasimi hastened to the relief of his troops with a superior force which decisively defeated the Omanis. Qays b Ahmad of Sohar, Said's uncle, was among those who were killed in this battle.[88]

Later in the autumn of the same year, 1807, Said fell out with his most powerful ally, Muhammad b Nasir al-Jabri. In this also the leading spirit was yet again Sayyida Moza bint Ahmad. In an attempt to bring under Albusaidi control the forts of Sumayil and Bidbid which were in al-Jabri's possession Said, instructed by his aunt Moza, summoned al-Jabri to Muscat under the pretext that he needed the counsel of his father's old confidant regarding some tribal affairs. Upon al-Jabri's arrival Said promptly imprisoned him while, in a similar scenario, Moza held al-Jabri's wife as prisoner in Sumayil itself.[89] Both aunt and nephew refused to release their prisoners until al-Jabri had agreed to deliver the coveted forts.

Disgusted by such behaviour especially after having previously risked his neck for this same Said and his aunt in complying with Badr's assassination plot, al–Jabri decided to proceed to Dir'iya to seek Wahhabi protection. On his way he paid a visit and declared his friendship to Humayd al-Ghafiri who continued to hold the fort of al-'Aynayn in Wadi al-Kabîr in central Oman.[90] The Wahhabi *amir*

Saud, thus receiving open support from powerful leaders in central Oman itself, not surprisingly, jumped at the opportunity of an alliance with al-Jabri and al-Ghafiri. He promptly sent a strong force to march on the Batina under Muṭlaq al-Muṭayrî, one of his ablest generals. With the assistance of Humayd al-Ghafiri and the support provided by tribes loyal to al-Jabri, notably the Banû Ruwâḥa, al-Mutayri soon expelled the Muscati garrisons from the forts of Sumayil and Bidbid and delivered them to al-Jabri. By the end of 1808, al-Mutayri had captured most of the ports on the Batina and had taken Shinas from 'Azzân b Qays I who had taken charge of the Sohar area following his father's death. Said's authority had by then been reduced to Muscat and its immediate environs.[91] In Ras al-Khayma al-Mutayri had also replaced Sulṭân b Saqr by his cousin Ḥusain b 'Alî of Rams to the leadership of the Qasimis since the former had entered into a secret alliance with Said b Sultan during the troubles.[92]

The newly Wahhabi-appointed Qasimi ruler was given specific instructions to seize, in the name of Wahhabism, 'all vessels in the Gulf and beyond, be they of heretics, renegades or unbelievers', and to remit to Dir'iya one-fifth of all the plunder taken.[93] Thus started a more vigorous Qasimi/Wahhabi campaign of assaults on all shipping in the Indian Ocean. In May 1808 yet another ship belonging to Samuel Manesty, the British Resident in Basra, was captured, this time by no less than fifty-five vessels belonging to the Qasimis who now cruised in squadrons of fifty to a hundred ships. Each squadron was commanded by a *nâ`ib* (deputy), who was responsible directly to the Qasimi leader, Husain b Ali.[94]

After capturing their prey the Qasimis/Wahhabis not only stripped the vessels of all their cargoes but they also, on occasions, according to one Western eyewitness account, ceremoniously killed everyone on board:

> They did so with circumstances of horrid solemnity which gave the deed the appearance of some hellish religious rite...the crew were led forward singly, their heads placed on the gunwale, and their throats cut with the exclamation used in battle of Allah akbar – God is Great.[95]

Possessing a naval strength estimated at sixty large vessels and some 800 smaller ones, manned by about 25,000 armed men,[96] the Qasimis/ Wahhabis started to expand their activities. By the end of the year, they were attacking ships even on the Gujarat coast of western India in the very heart of British Indian territory. In December 1808, after an incident in which twenty Gujarati ships had been plundered, prominent merchants all over the western coast of India petitioned Duncan, the British governor of Bombay, to take action if they were not to abandon for good their trading activities. Alarmed at these developments Duncan sent the ubiquitous Seton, then on a mission to Sind, back to Muscat to report on the situation there and to enquire how best could 'Britain's ally', Said b Sultan, deal with 'these pirates', as his father had so successfully dealt previously.[97]

On his way to Muscat, where he arrived in January 1809, Seton found that all the main shipping lanes were in Wahhabi/Qasimi control. During a meeting with Husain b Ali, the Wahhabi-appointed Qasimi leader had even had the temerity to suggest to Seton that Britain should pay him a salary in return for a guarantee that British ships wishing to proceed up the Gulf would be given protection by a Qasimi escort.[98] That was one method of dispute resolution to which the people of the Gulf were accustomed but Britain, convinced of the superiority of its own methods, would of course have none of it.

In Oman itself Seton for the first time took the trouble of finding out the extent of the Wahhabi hold on the country. He reported that Wahhabi preachers roamed even in the streets of Muscat where 'they had established a sort of inquisition in the town'[99] and where Said b Sultan had all but bowed to the powerful combination of Wahhabi and Omani forces marshalled against him. Said had even written to the Wahhabi leadership that he was willing to negotiate a more comprehensive settlement with them for the restoration of Shinas and some other Omani ports in the north. In reply *amir* Saud informed the beleaguered Muscati ruler that the ports would not be returned unless he agreed to participate in a joint Wahhabi/Qasimi/Omani expedition against Basra and, in addition, showed willingness to attack British ships in the Indian Ocean.[100] Moreover, if Said refused, the *amir* added, he would himself descend upon Muscat after performing the *hajj* in the spring of that year.[101]

Had Said agreed to the terms proposed by the Wahhabi *amir*, he would have put himself in direct conflict with the British. He had seen the magnitude of British power not only in India and in the Gulf in Badr's time but also against the French right under his nose in Muscat harbour. He had already offered, in the commercial interests of Muscat, to form an alliance with the British which had been summarily rejected as seen earlier. It was by sheer good fortune that, at this crucial moment when he was facing utter humiliation and defeat in his own backyard, British interests were to coincide with his own. Once they realised the extent of Wahhabi/Qasimi domination of the waters of the Gulf and the western Indian Ocean and once they were convinced that the ruler of

Muscat was powerless to intervene on their behalf, the British authorities decided it was time that they themselves took the matter in hand and thus organised an expedition against Ras-al-Khayma.

The 1809–10 Omani-British expedition against Ras-al-Khayma

It must be emphasised from the outset that the 1809–10 expedition against Ras-al-Khayma was not 'to preserve Oman's independence', as is often claimed by historians.[102] Western writers like Miles, Kelly, Landen, Nicholls and others, basing their accounts mainly on despatches forwarded by British political agents and officials in Oman and the Gulf, have reached this conclusion because they perceive Oman as a single political entity. In doing so, they have no doubt derived their ideas from the Western concept of a 'state' with recognised frontiers. No such thing, however, existed in Oman at this time and thus the concept of Oman's independence requires some readjustment. In any event, the geographical extent of this so-called entity has not been clearly defined in the accounts of these writers. Does the reference to Oman apply to the geographical area of the present Sultanate or to the traditional geographical region known as Oman which would today include most of the states comprising the United Arab Emirates and also some parts of Saudi Arabia? Furthermore, as it has been discussed above, even those areas under Albusaidi control in the core region of Oman were at that time divided amongst a number of the ruling tribe's influential members while other tribal and communal leaders controlled the affairs of their own *dars*.[103] Therefore, there was no such phenomenon as a single Omani political entity even in that geographical area of interior Oman here defined as the *dakhiliya*.

As the early despatches of British officials themselves quite clearly show the 1809–10 expedition against Ras-al-Khayma, from its inception, had nothing to do with the 'independence' of Oman:

> We consider it of some importance to manifest as much as possible, both by declaration and by action, that the expedition is directed not generally against the tribe [*sic*] of Wahabees but exclusively against the piratical branch of that tribe which has long infested the commerce of India and the Gulf.[104]

The expedition then was motivated solely by the adverse manner in which British commercial interests were being affected by the organised and ever-expanding Wahhabi/Qasimi depredations against British shipping. Ultimately, it was designed to put an end to the commercial competitiveness of the Gulf people following which, as we shall see,

Britain directed its energies to destroy the commercial challenge posed to it by Oman itself.

The afterthought by British authorities of inviting Said b Sultan to join in their expedition must have been viewed by the Albusaidi as a heaven-sent opportunity enabling him to disentangle himself from his desperate internal situation. When Seton asked him if he would participate he naturally agreed.[105] Having previously striven unsuccessfully to forge some sort of alliance with the British, a military association with them was beyond even Said's expectations as it greatly enhanced his standing among the local and regional tribes. News of a joint Omani-British expedition

> filled Muscat with joy.... Seyd Said, trusting in his powerful allies, immediately declared himself an enemy of the Vaabi, and ordered the envoy of Saout to leave his dominions. At the same time he levied an additional force, so as to increase his troops to 6000 men.[106]

Nevertheless, the joint venture proved to be a total failure and the main purpose for which Said had participated therein, namely the return of Shinas and Khawr Fakkan, did not materialise. This came about precisely because the British were not interested in Said's internal difficulties let alone the means of resolving them. They refused to go to battle with his enemies breaking off military action at crucial moments in both Ras-al-Khayma and Shinas upon hearing news of the arrival of Wahhabi reinforcements.[107] With the Wahhabis/Qasimis now launching a full-scale war against Oman, Said was bewildered by the inconsistency, to say the least, of British policy towards him. While British officials in Oman assured him that aid would be forthcoming and expressed support for his requests in their despatches to Bombay, British authorities in India responded with blunt replies of refusal.[108]

Very soon after, Said felt obliged to make further appeals to the British authorities informing them that his participation in the expedition had put him in the awkward position of being in a 'perpetual and implacable war with the Wahabees',[109] and requesting them to send 'under the auspecies of Heaven ships and victorious troops...having in view the annihilation of the deluded Wahabees who were the foes of us both'.[110] However, it was with these same foes that the British, behind Said's back and solely in their own interests, decided to enter into negotiations. In return for a guarantee from *amir* Saud that British shipping would no longer be molested in the Gulf, Britain promised the Wahhabi leader that, from then on, it would not interfere in 'his quarrels with other Muslims'.[111] Therefore, the reply they sent to Said's requests for reinforcements was that 'the British Government was no further interested in the contest between him and the Wahabees and it recommended the Imaum [Said] to grant the terms of a pacification solicited by the Wahabees'.[112] Despondent but not despairing, Said at first turned to the French for assistance. At that time Monsieur Dallons, an envoy from De Caen, Governor of Ile de France, happened to be in Muscat. When Said discussed with him the possibility of French aid Dallons, aware of the immense problems the French were themselves at that time experiencing in their war with Britain, advised Said that he should not only 'conclude a Peace with the Vaabi' but also 'embrace their religious opinions'.[113]

Said b Sultan's Mission to Shiraz

Rebuffed by both Britain and France and realising that his own resources were far too inadequate to overcome his adversaries in Oman, Said turned to Persia and sent his brother Salim to Shiraz on a mission to request Persian assistance. At the same time, in order to distract the attention of his enemies from further consolidating their positions and to gain some respite in Oman, Said attacked the Wahhabi garrisons at Zubara, Qatar and Bahrain in the summer of 1810. The Omani forces successfully raided Bahrain and managed to put the Wahhabi troops in Zubara to flight.[114]

Meanwhile Salim's mission was cautiously received at Shiraz. The Shi'i Persians initially had their doubts whether Omani Ibadis were any better qualified to merit their help against what was, admittedly, in their view, the more repellent Wahhabis. It was apparently the influence of a Muscati Shi'i companion of Salim, one Mûsa al-Mûsawî, who eventually overcame these doubts during discussions on Islamic ideology.[115] A Persian force, under Sa'dî Khân, consisting of 1,500 horsemen and four pieces of artillery, operated by about fifty Russian deserters, was duly dispatched to Oman.[116]

The first campaign undertaken by these forces in Oman was an attempt to wrest the control of Sumayil from Muhammad al-Jabri. Although in the beginning Sumayil fell to the Omani–Persian troops a subsequent attack by a force under the joint command of al-Jabri and al-Mutayri, the Wahhabi commander, inflicted a shattering defeat on the combined Omani–Persian forces.[117] When the remaining hundred or so Persian horsemen were sent back to Persia,[118] and when an envoy subsequently sent by *amir* Saud to Shiraz received assurances that no further help would be forthcoming for Oman,[119] Said b Sultan's downfall seemed imminent. Any prospect of aid from Britain or France, at this point, was further dashed when Britain captured Ile de France (renamed Mauritius) in December 1810. While France was itself in dire straits, having suffered a major setback to its imperial policies in the Indian Ocean, Britain no longer needed Muscat's cooperation to counter any designs that France or any other Western power may have had in India.

The fact that Said b Sultan and Oman were saved from being totally absorbed within the Wahhabi domain owed nothing to British, Persian or French intervention. It was due mainly to the arrogance of and the scurrilous methods used by the Wahhabi leaders themselves, then at the height of their triumph. After their troops had 'ravaged the outskirts of Masqat, plundered the town of Matrah and the village of Arbaq and [had] then swept through Eastern Hajar in a tornado of bloodshed and destruction',[120] Said in 1813 desperately attempted to buy off al-Mutayri by offering him large sums of money.[121] Although Said's offers were rejected, the Wahhabis themselves now started having problems.

Following the plunder of Medina in 1810 'when the Prophet's tomb was opened and its jewels and relics sold and distributed among the Wahhabi soldiery',[122] the Ottoman Sultan Mahmud II was at last moved to act against such outrage. But realising that he himself would be incapable of resisting the Wahhabis totally, engrossed as he was in confronting the European threat to his own dominions, he requested Muhammad Ali of Egypt instead to take the field against them.[123] While *amir* Saud and his forces were thus forced to turn their attention towards their possessions in western Arabia tribes in northern Oman started to revolt against the Wahhabis with more and more refusing to pay the tribute demanded.[124] This phenomenon of resistance against the Wahhabis from outside the Albusaidi domain was nothing new. Two years previously, in 1811, some members of the Utbis had joined in an Omani expedition under the command of Said b Sultan's cousin Hilâl b Muhammad, sent for a second assault upon Zubara and Bahrain. On this occasion, the Omanis had routed the Wahhabi troops in Bahrain and had captured their commander, 'Abd-allâh b 'Ufaysân.[125] Said b Sultan, having thus recaptured Bahrain, had allowed the Âl-Khalîfa Shaykhs, recently freed from imprisonment in Dir'iya, to rule Bahrain in return for recognition of Albusaidi suzerainty and payment of an annual tribute.[126]

In Oman, after al-Mutayri's death at the hands of Omani tribesmen in Sharqiya at the end of 1813,[127] Said prepared himself with his troops at Nizwa in order to meet the anticipated attack by the new Wahhabi commander, 'Abd-allâh b Mazrû', encamped at nearby Bahla. However, before the two sides could engage in battle, Said received the intelligence that his cousin Azzan b Qays I of Sohar had died on his way back from *hajj*. Said immediately proceeded to Sohar, where in appointing Sâlim b Sa'îd Âlbûsa'îdî as his own *wali*,[128] he made an enemy of Azzan's son, Ḥamûd. This enmity with the Awlad Qays branch of the Albusaidi House was to endure and create many problems for Said and his successors in the future. Following this incident, it must have been a relief to Said to learn that Ibn Mazru' and his forces had left Bahla and had returned to al-Zahira without taking any action. Shortly afterwards, *amir* Saud, whose efforts were now all directed against the Egyptian conquest of Hijaz, sent a delegation to Muscat to come to terms with the Albusaidi.[129]

With the Wahhabi threat thus lifted from Oman and with Bahrain once again under Albusaidi suzerainty, Said could now turn his attention to consolidating his position first in Oman and then in Oman's territories overseas. As for Muscat's trade, it continued unabated despite the departure of some merchants during times of trouble. Muscat's custom revenues however, as it was to be expected during such times, had suffered a slight decline. From an estimated value of between MT$125,000[130] and MT$180,000[131] in the era of Sultan b Ahmad, this revenue had declined to just under MT$95,000 at the time of Buckingham's visit to Oman in 1816.[132] But Muscat remained a bustling port as conveyed in Buckingham's own account as in those of other contemporary travellers visiting the town. According to Heude, Oman's 'bazaars supply everything in absolute profusion...the exports are coffee, brimstone, horses and camels'[133] while Buckingham adds dates, pearls and copper to the list of exports and includes muslin, spices, timber, rice, pepper, coffee, cotton, gold, ostrich feathers, ivory, tamarind, slaves and Chinese goods to that of imports.[134]

With regard to British policy towards Oman, following its capture of Ile de France (Mauritius), Britain decided to withdraw from Muscat its political agent who was not to return for another thirty years. When he did in 1840, the reason, as on previous occasions, had nothing to do with any British regard for Oman itself. It was motivated largely by another threat to British hegemony in the Indian Ocean. Although Britain by then had managed to pacify the Qasimis, Muhammad Ali's advance into Arabia coupled with the commercial challenge posed by Oman and the emergent United States of America, which in 1833 had signed a treaty with Said b Sultan, obliged Britain once more 'to cultivate with this prince [Said], who has ever evinced the most friendly disposition to the British, the most intimate relations'.[135]

Part II

The Albusaidi move to Zanzibar: exercise in empire building or survival?

5 Commercial, political and strategic attractions of East Africa

In the first half of the nineteenth century the continuing rise in demand for ivory in India, Europe and the United States of America; the expansion from the second decade onwards of the slave trade with slaves destined for both the local plantation economy and export; and the decline in the price of the leading imports, cotton goods, all contributed to make the terms of trade very lucrative on the East African coast.

At Zanzibar in the beginning of the nineteenth century the Banyans, despite their historical pre-eminence in the matters of commerce, were by no means the only group involved in the port's trade.[1] By 1811, 'a considerable number of Banyans...reside in the town [Zanzibar], many of whom appear to be wealthy and hold the best part of the [export] trade'. However, with regard to the local trade, it is recounted that 'the trade of this coast [is] chiefly in the hands of the Arabs...and a few adventurers from *Kutch and the coast of Scinde*'.[2] As for the nature and magnitude of the annual trade at this time, nearly 50 per cent of the imports at Zanzibar consisted of 'Surat clothes' valued at MT$545,000 in addition to approximately 50 tons of iron bar, sugar, rice, chinaware and other goods from Bombay, Surat and Muscat, the total value of the imports amounting to MT$1,100,000. Although corresponding figures for the export trade are not given in the sources, exports were also fairly significant providing the supplies and generating the capital to finance the import trade.[3] A close scrutiny of available evidence reveals that, contrary to what is often stated, ivory was definitely not 'the only significant branch of the export trade'[4] for in addition to ivory other export items at the time included slaves, coconuts, coir and copal, wax, cowries, turtle shells, and rhinoceros hides and horns.[5] It is important to note that, already by 1811, most goods for export were being brought to Zanzibar from other areas in East Africa for shipment.

SAID B SULTAN'S RELATIONSHIP WITH MERCHANTS FROM INDIA

A question that often creates difficulties for writers on East African history is the determination of nationalities of the various merchants involved in its trade. It may be appreciated from the foregoing discussion (Introduction and Chapter 1) that such an attempt is extremely problematic, if not impossible. Indeed, it is doubtful whether these merchants themselves at the time thought in terms of nationality in the modern sense although they no doubt recognised their ethnic, religious and, in the case of the Hindus, caste differentiations.

Historically members of merchant communities, having contacts at various points in the Indian Ocean trading region, had, for a variety of commercial, religious and political reasons, moved from environments where they had been relatively disadvantaged to ones where they were more favourably treated.[6] In nineteenth century East Africa many traders in Zanzibar were Omani Arabs, some of whom having chosen to migrate in order to join their 'co-nationals', already settled in Africa since at least the expansionist era of the Ya'ariba. Like their predecessors, these later arrivals were with time integrated, either wholly or partially, within the expanding 'Swahili' community. For example, Sa'îd b 'Alî al-Mughairî, the author of 'Juhaina', himself a 'Swahili' but who was during the 1960s and the 1970s described on his return to Oman as a 'Zanzibari', had ancestors who were originally from Oman but had migrated to East Africa during the Ya'rubi period.[7] As al-Mughairi himself explains, there was so much intermarriage between Omanis and Africans during the nineteenth century that 'nobody could tell the difference between an Arab and a Zinji [negro]'.[8] Other traders in East Africa originated from India, migrating to Zanzibar either directly or after long or short periods of residence in Muscat or in other Omani ports. These latter also, in time, became more or less 'swahilised'.[9] Perhaps the most striking point to note is that the Omani ruler, Said b Sultan, treated all traders migrating to Africa from Oman as 'natives of Oman'. All these 'natives', including the Indians but excluding any Western merchants residing in East African ports, were allowed to participate in the trade of the African mainland. According to Sheriff: 'This was the most guarded privilege granted to native traders and formed a corner stone on which Omani commercial empire was constructed'.[10] Had the 'Indians' from Oman been regarded by contemporary Omani rulers as 'foreigners', they too, like the Westerners, would have been excluded from the mainland.

From a linguistic point of view it is interesting to note that, by 1811,

Indians already had a good command of the Swahili language. Captain Smee, one of the earlier British visitors to Zanzibar, informs us that during his travels his companion was one Mallum Ali, 'the Hindoostani interpreter'.[11] On the other hand, the older settler 'Swahilis' could not even write a simple letter in Arabic[12] and even those who had acquired a little Arabic, primarily for religious purposes, could barely speak it.[13] Said b Sultan himself is said to have been able to speak Persian and Hindustani in addition to Swahili and Arabic.[14] But among the new arrivals from Oman, at the beginning of the nineteenth century, 'Arabic was spoken at Zanzibar only by Omanis and Indians'.[15] However, the label 'Indians' comprises a multitude of different communal and religious groups. To ascribe to the various Indian communities the blanket label 'Banyan', as was done by British officials and early historians, has caused not only a great deal of confusion among later writers but is also an expression that would be rejected as meaningless by those very communities. 'Banyan', in its strict sense, denotes those Indians who belong to the Vanya merchant caste and follow Hinduism as their religion.[16] In his oft-quoted source, Frere entitles his report as 'Banyans or Natives of India...' equating one with the other.[17] Kelly defines the Banyans as Gujarati traders without distinguishing among the various ethnic and religious elements that make up the Gujarati trading community.[18] To an Indian Muslim Ismaili or for that matter to the Banyans themselves, such an expression would not only be an inadequate description of their ethnic origins but would be objection-able on religious grounds alone.

As established above, the Banyan community was but one of the many Indian groups involved in East African trade at the beginning of the nineteenth century following their participation in the Indian Ocean commerce centred previously on Muscat. Among other groups thus involved were the Khojas[19] whose ancestors, just like those of the nineteenth century Banyans, are said to have had settlements on the East African coast from at least the fifteenth century prior to the arrival of Vasco de Gama who later described their presence there.[20] Moreover, in nineteenth century Zanzibar, it was not the Banyans but the Khojas who constituted the most numerous 'Indian' group.[21] Some of these Khojas had migrated to East Africa not only from India but also from Persia directly or after a period of residence in ports such as Bombay.[22]

Nonetheless, by the beginning of the nineteenth century, due to the commercial advantages accruing to them partly as a result of the anti-Muslim policies of the Portuguese,[23] it was the Banyans, despite their smaller numbers, who assumed the most prominent position in the Indian Ocean trade. But these policies were by no means the only reason why the Banyans came to dominate the commercial scene. Another important element contributing to their success was their Joint Family organisation which was adopted to varying degrees by other traders, such as the Khojas or some later Hindu converts to Islam, who frequently continued to adhere to their former Hindu practices even after conversion.[24]

The Joint Family organisation of the Banyans

The Joint Family organisation was a Hindu structure which was utilised by members of various mercantile communities but in which the Banyans, being Hindu, had an inherent pre-eminence. In sum, it was a legal concept which, before its modification by British law during the first half of the twentieth century, rested fundamentally upon the notion of the family in relation to the property it owned.[25] Any property holder within the family did not own that property personally but held it in trust for his ancestors on behalf of his descendants.[26] Banyans and certain Khojas in Muscat readily admit that their joint families were, and to some degree still are, a valuable feature of their commercial success.[27] In such families, since various members or groups in Zanzibar, Muscat or elsewhere behaved as satellites and continued, despite their dispersal far and wide, to defer to their own core kin groups in India, there was no possibility of any new core groups being formed outside India.[28] Thus members of a particular Joint Family could be scattered all over the region and be as mobile as commercial necessity dictated, ready to move from one area or from one port to the next at short notice.

This awareness of and adherence to the Joint Family entity also dictated settlement patterns in commercially active areas as businesses became established centred around the main ports such as Muscat and Zanzibar while family members were dispersed to other commercial outposts. Here is how Burton described the dispersion in East Africa of some members of one such family:

> Ladha Damha [correctly Dhamji] farms the customs at Zanzibar, at Pemba island his nephew Pisu has the same charge; Mombasa is in the hands of Lakhmidas, and some 40 of his co-religionists; Pangani is directed by Trikandas...; even the pauper Sa'adani has its Banyan; Ramji, an active and intelligent trader, presides at Bagamoyo, and the customs of Kilwa are collected by Kishindas. I need hardly say that almost all of them are connected by blood as well as trade.[29]

Furthermore, fortunes made abroad as a result of these commercial activities not only enhanced the prestige of the entire Joint Family but also provided the wherewithal to bring even more family members out to take up new positions in the expanding business arenas. A newly arrived member, although he could only expand his business with his own profits, had all the reserves of the family at his disposal relying on its members even for food and accommodation in the initial stages. If he failed in his enterprise he was not completely lost since his business, whatever the field, was conducted for the benefit of the family.[30] In this way, because of these commercial practices based on Joint Family legal principles and due to their traditional role in the trading sphere, greatly enhanced as it had been by the Portuguese, the Banyans attained an unassailable dominant position in the Indian Ocean commercial networks during the course of the nineteenth century.

For the nineteenth century rulers of Muscat (Said b Sultan from 1806 to 1856), it was absolutely vital that they should maintain any relations they still had with the Banyans now that Muscat had lost to the British any influence it may previously have exercised in parts of Western India. It is not surprising therefore in the context of this relationship that, according to Banyan traditions, it was a fleet belonging to a Bhattia[31] mercantile family of India that brought Said b Sultan from Muscat to Zanzibar and 'provided extra armed ships and man-power in his wars with Mombasa and feuds which arose in Zanzibar'.[32] This Bhattia Family was no other than that of Shivji Topan[33] which, together with the Gopal Bhimani Family at Muscat, were the two most prominent Indian families whose roles were vital for the nineteenth century commercial expansion of Oman at Muscat and Zanzibar. It must be stressed from the outset that these families originated from the Kutch region of north western India which, as was the case for Oman's other traditional commercial partner further north, Sind, were both outside the British zone of control. Therefore, it was as much in the interests of mercantile communities in these areas as it was in those of the ruler of Muscat not only to hold fast and to guard jealously their already established links but to cooperate and act in harness to resist the British challenge to their livelihoods.

Little information exists on the Gopal Bhimani Family. We know that the customs master at Muscat in 1801 was one Mowjee, described as a 'Banyan from Kutch'.[34] This Mowjee, although his full name is not given in the source cited, was undoubtedly a member of the Gopal Bhimani Family which according to its own traditions had established intimate relations with the Albusaid after settling to trade in Muscat in the middle of the eighteenth century.[35] His full name was in fact Gopal Mowjee Bhimani who is said to have been the first Banyan to hold the Muscat customs farm at the beginning of the nineteenth century. At that time he was also influential in commercial activities at Zanzibar where he also held the customs farm for a period of time and where he was known as Wat Bhima or Wad Bhimani which in colloquial Omani signifies 'the son of Bhima or Bhimani'.[36] This family maintained the control of the Muscat customs farm right into the 1840s and, as late as the 1870s, was involved in Muscati commerce.[37] In the first half of the nineteenth century it was instrumental in encouraging Said b Sultan to extend Albusaidi control over East Africa.[38]

Much more information is available with regard to the Shivji Topan family (See Figure 1). According to its family traditions it was Topan, Shivji's father, who was the founder of the family business. Functioning from the port of Mandvi in Kutch, he is said never to have ventured abroad himself but to have possessed, by the end of the eighteenth century, a number of ships involved in the coastal trade of western India. By the turn of the nineteenth century his two sons Shivji and Champsi working together with Topan Tajiani (known in Zanzibar as Topan b Tajir) had enlarged their small fleet to thirty ships, 'each armed with brass guns and manned by a crew of thirty', and had started to trade in earnest with Muscat.[39] This Topan Tajiani, originating from Lakhput in Kutch from a modest background of oil milling, was the father of the famous Sir Tharya Topan who was to have an influential role in Zanzibar as head of the Khoja community later on in the nineteenth century when Zanzibar came under British protection.[40]

With the increasing political subservience of India to British rule and the consequent difficulties created for Indian merchants outside the British sphere of influence, it was apparently Shivji's son, Ebji, regarded as 'the most famous personality of the family [who established] intimate relations' with Sultan b Ahmad. According to a contemporary report, Sultan, when he died in 1804, owed Ebji some MT\$12,000.[41] After his death the friendship continued between Ebji and Sultan's son, Said, and it was to reach such proportions that 'Ebji incurred, as a result, considerable enmity from the Sultan's enemies who attempted to murder him so frequently that tradition records that he never slept in the same place for two nights running'.[42]

In return for this loyalty, for his financial indebtedness and for the increasing influence that the Shivji Topan Family was acquiring in the expanding trade at Zanzibar, in 1818 Said b Sultan transferred the management of the Zanzibar customs from his *wali* to Ebji Shivji.[43] 'Given to their heirs in perpetuity', according to the traditions of the family, the Zanzibar customs lease was in fact to remain, despite some interruptions in the 1870s, within the Shivji Topan House until the heady days of the European 'scramble' for African territories in the late

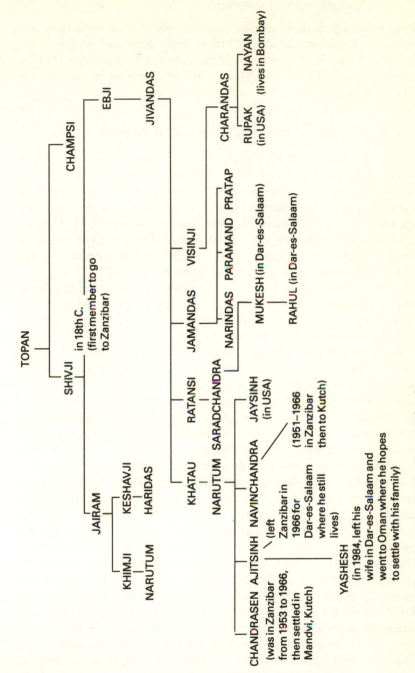

Figure 1 The Shivji Topan family (leading members).

1880s when the British company Mackinnon and Co. took over the control of Zanzibar customs.[44] Interestingly members of the same family were also in charge of the Muscat customs farm in the 1880s[45] long after Said b Sultan, Ebji Shivji and his influential brother Jairam had passed away.

Customs revenue and the commercial pull of Zanzibar

The customs revenue at Muscat in 1802 was estimated to be between MT$112,500[46] and MT$180,000.[47] Revenue from the East African coast at the same time was about MT$40,000. But it is significant to note that, even then, the sources specifically mention that the Zanzibar, Mombasa and Kilwa customs were all in the hands of Banyan merchants, although it is not possible to deduce whether the term 'Banyan' is used as a generic term applied indiscriminately to all Indians or describes Hindu Vanyas in its precise sense.[48]

By 1811, while Said b Sultan was engrossed in his efforts to extract himself unscathed from the Wahhabi onslaught against Muscat, his *wali* in Zanzibar, one Yâqût b 'Ambar al-Habashî, assumed the management of the customs.[49] It is noteworthy that Yaqut, a former slave loyal to Said's grandfather Ahmad b Said, had been appointed by Said's father Sultan as *wali* of Zanzibar around 1803 as a reward for his continued loyalty and for his neutrality in Oman's tribal intrigues. Yaqut also had substantial property holdings in Oman so that his appointment as *wali* far away in Zanzibar '[would] guarantee his fidelity to the prince [Sultan b Ahmad]'.[50] Sultan's son, Said, also pursued the same policy by appointing another former slave 'Ambar b Sultân al-Habashî as *wali* of Zanzibar sometime between 1812 and 1820.[51] At Muscat, Said's first *wali* had been a Baluchi by the name of Jum'a b Durra al-Bulûshî.[52] Thus it can be seen that the Albusaidis, from the beginning of the Dynasty, had relied heavily upon individuals from outside the core tribal complex of interior Oman, not only for the running of the customs but for important administrative posts as well.

In the commercial field, apart from a better guarantee of loyalty and a share in profits, the Albusaidi rulers' continued reliance on the 'Indians' also paid dividends in the matter of raising finance. As early as 1811, Said b Sultan sent a mission to Zanzibar for the purpose of raising MT$25,000 over and above the normal customs revenue to assist in the financing of his war against the Wahhabis/Qasimis. Although some Indian merchants protested at this extra demand on their resources, many Banyans and 'Muslim traders of Surat' are said to have willingly contributed.[53]

The emergence of Zanzibar

As a result of these widespread contacts between rulers and merchants, a system of trade in East Africa was already well established and thriving by the time Said b Sultan had the opportunity of consolidating Albusaidi authority there, that is after the first Wahhabi threat was lifted from Oman in 1813. This trade system did not suddenly spring into shape as a result of Said's so-called 'African Policy', inducing coastal Swahili traders to establish new links with the interior of Africa.[54] Nor was it founded 'exclusively through African initiative'.[55] It had in fact existed for the most part of the eighteenth century and incorporated African traders from the interior as well as a multitude of others on the coast.[56]

Nevertheless, contrary to conventional beliefs, ivory and slaves were not the sole items of trade for throughout this period the age-old exchange of dates, dried fish and Muscat cloth for African grain, mangrove poles (Om. = *kandal*), hides and wax continued uninterrupted.[57] That Zanzibar was to become the focus of this expanding commercial network was due as much to it being the political hub of the Albusaidi domain in East Africa as it was to geographical factors.[58] In addition to being a more accessible and safer port, Zanzibar was simply more favoured for trade by the *mawsimî* (seasonal or monsoonal) flow of winds. As the French trader Morice had commented in the 1770s, the central position of Zanzibar within the coastal wind patterns, which allowed local vessels to sail along the coast from Lamu to the Comoro Islands for most of the year, meant that Zanzibar was already by that time favoured as an entrepôt by local and regional traders:

> It is to them [Omanis] and to their centres in Zanzibar that the ships from India go in preference to unload their cargoes for distribution all along the coast. When the ships from India arrive in December, January or February, all the Moors [Swahilis] from Kilwa, Mafia, Mombasa, Pate, etc., go to Zanzibar to buy cargoes and distribute them subsequently in their districts in exchange for ivory tusks, provisions and slaves. In March and April all the Moors and Arabs come to the Kingdom of Kilwa to trade.[59]

Furthermore, the Portuguese stranglehold over trading activities in the southern Macuana region prompted African traders like the Yao, who had previously been involved in the southern trade but who were being gradually squeezed out, to move northwards where they found that they received not only higher prices for their goods but more advantageous terms of trade in general.[60]

With the growth of the maritime and coastal dhow trade and the multiplication of links between the internal and coastal African trade networks, members of various mercantile communities already established or newly arrived, whether Indian, Omani, Swahili, Hadrami, European or other, continued to participate in the expanding commercial activity. But among this motley collection of mercantile communities the Banyans, for reasons already enumerated, benefitted from a head-start in this trade. Thus the ruler of Muscat, Said b Sultan, had no alternative but to maintain his links with the Banyans. So intimate did these links in fact become that they prompted an early British visitor to Zanzibar to comment that 'Hindoos [were] amongst his most confidential servants'.[61] Said's continued appointment of Banyan merchants to the important post of customs master, both in Zanzibar and Muscat, pays eloquent testimony not only to his personal relationships with them but also to the economic clout that they wielded in both Muscat and Zanzibar from the beginning of the nineteenth century. For apart from the trade on the East African coast, it will be recalled that Muscati Banyan and other merchants had played an important part as carriers of the Indian Ocean trade throughout the region during the Napoleonic Wars.[62]

With the emergence of Zanzibar as an economic force, by the second decade of the nineteenth century the Treasury at Muscat began to receive increasing customs revenues from the East African coast at a time when Muscat's own customs revenues, subjected to the harmful effects of the post-1804 Wahhabi incursions on trade in general, were momentarily declining.[63] Nonetheless Muscat's annual customs revenues, despite extreme fluctuations in some years, remained more or less within the same bracket yielding between MT$100,000 and MT$180,000 throughout the nineteenth century. Those of Zanzibar on the other hand, as Table 3 and Figure 2 below show, increased by an average multiple of seven, rising from a mere MT$40,000 in 1802 to MT$800,000 in 1889.

THE COMMERCIAL POTENTIAL AND OPPOSITION TO SAID B SULTAN

The free flow of people, goods, information and ideas between the various regions of the Indian Ocean and the extent to which Omanis (including those already 'swahilised') viewed their settlements in East Africa and Oman as one integral whole are best exemplified by the relationships of the different tribal groups of Omani origin living in East Africa to the Albusaidi rulers in Muscat. One important such group, the Mazari'a, had opposed the rise of the Albusaid, as indicated above, even before the election to the Imamate of the founder of the

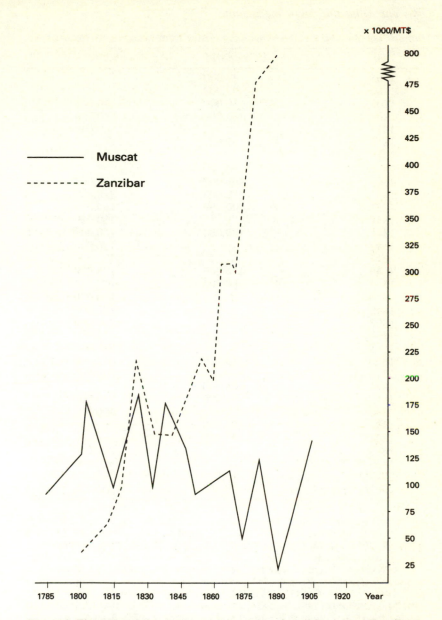

Figure 2 The Albusaidi rulers' customs revenue from Muscat and Zanzibar

Sources: Z = Zanzibar; M = Muscat.
1765, M: Niebuhr C., 1792, [tr.], II, 116; 1786, M: Waqayi', 28; 1802, M: IOR/P/381/33, Seton to Bombay, 9 July 1802, – Z: ibid.; 1804, M: Maurizi V., 1819, 29, – Z: Dallons P., 1804 in SD, 198; 1811, Z: IOR/L/MAR/C/586, Smee, 1811; 1816, M: Buckingham J.S., 1830, II, 392, figure given is 20,000 rupees, for exchange rate of 2.11 rupees = 1 MT\$ used

Table 3 The Albusaidi rulers' customs revenue from Muscat and Zanzibar

Year	Muscat/MT$	Zanzibar/MT$
1765	47,000	
1786	93,000	
1802	130,000	40,000
1804	180,000	40,000
1811		60,000
1816	95,000	
1819		80,000
1821	90,000	
1825	188,000	120,000
1827	188,000	220,000
1834	100,000	150,000
1837		150,000
1841	180,000	150,000
1842		150,000
1847		175,000
1848	136,000	175,000
1854	80,000	
1856		220,000
1860		196,000
1862		200,000
1864		195,000
1865		310,000
1868	115,000	310,000
1870		300,000
1871	105,000	
1875	51,400	350,000
1880		500,000
1883	125,000	
1884	131,000	
1888		800,000
1889		800,000
1892	17,000	
1907	140,000	

see Milburn W., 1813, I, 116, 173–4 and Landen R.G., 1967, 128–31; 1819, Z: Albrand F., 1838, 78; 1821, M: Fraser J.B., 1825, 16; 1825, M and Z: *Asiatic Journal*, 1825 cited in Bidwell R., 1978, 144; 1827, M: IOR/V/23/217, BS., 633, – Z: ibid.; 1834, M: Lorimer, IA, 469 – Z: ibid., IOR/P/387/58, Hart H., 1834, Report on Zanzibar; 1837, Z: US. Arch/ NEMA, Waters to Forsyth, 6 May 1837, 216; 1841, M: IOR/L/P&S/5/48, Hamerton to Bombay, 29 May 1842, – Z: ibid.; 1842, Z: PRO/FO/54/4, Hamerton to Aberdeen, 21 May 1842; 1847, Z: Loarer C. 1851, 296; 1848, M: Guillain-Documents, II, 250, – Z: ibid.; 1854, M: Landen R.G., 1967, 65; 1856, Z: Bennett N.R., 1978, 43; 1860, Z: ZA/AA12/2 and IOR/L/P&S/9/37, Rigby to Bombay, 1 May 1860; 1862, Z: PRO/FO/54/20, Playfair to Anderson, 15 June 1863; 1864, Z: USArch/NEMA, Hines to Seward, 25 Oct 1864, 532; 1865, Z: USArch/NEMA, Ropes to Seward, 5 Oct 1865, 540; 1868, M: Germain A., 1868a, 353, – Z: idem, 1868b, 534; 1870, Z: ZA/AA12/2, Rigby's Evidence to Royal Commission, 25 July 1871; 1871, M: IOR/l/P&S/5/266, Pelly to Bombay, 3 Feb 1871; 1875, Z: PRO/ FOCP/4673, 1880, 59; 1880, Z: PRO/ibid.; 1883, M: IOR/15/6/16, Miles to Ross, 5 Feb 1884; 1884, M: ibid.; 1888, Z: ZA/AA5/17, Memo on Duty collected, 19 Feb 1890; 1889, Z: ZA/ibid.; 1892, M: Curzon G.N., 1892, II, 433–46; 1907, M: Landen R.G., 1967, 391.

Dynasty.[64] But like all elements opposed to the Albusaidi rulers, be they the British, French, Persians, Wahhabis, other members of the ruling family or other tribal groupings, the Mazaria seized the opportunity they had been awaiting during the post-1804 political chaos in Oman and sought to assert their independence. For Said b Sultan, it was vital that he should crush the continuing Mazrui opposition if he and his allies were to reap the full benefits of the expanding commercial activity in East Africa at the turn of the nineteenth century.

Roots of the Albusaidi-Mazrui conflict

The Mazaria of Oman, not to be confused with a clan of the same name forming a section of the Banî Yâs in northern Oman, are a *fakhdh* (lit. thigh = clan) of the Ghâfirî Banî Jâbir. Although found in various parts of Oman, in Shinas and Lower Sumayil for example, in the past their main conglomeration was in their fortified section of Rustaq known as *Burj al-Mazâri'a*.[65] Together with the Mashâqisa (sing. Shaqsi), who were instrumental in the establishment of the Ya'ariba Dynasty, the Mazaria were among several other Omani tribes who readily acknowledged the election of the first Ya'rubi Imam, Nasir b Murshid, in 1624.[66] Subsequently it was under Mazrui and Baluchi commanders that the forces of the Ya'ariba eventually wrested Mombasa from the Portuguese.[67] Moreover, although the *nisba* of the first *wali*, Muhammad b Mubârak, appointed to Mombasa by Sultan b Sayf I al-Ya'rubi in 1665, is not given in the sources, it is more than feasible that he was a Mazrui.[68] However, the dynastic monopoly that the *awlâd* (lit. sons of = branch) 'Uthmân b 'Abd-allâh al-Mazrû'î were later to enjoy with regard to the governorship of Mombasa did not get under way until the appointment of Muhammad b'Uthmân 'in 1730 by Sayf b Sultân II al-Ya'rubi as other non-Mazrui *walis* had also occupied this position until then.

Following the recapture of Mombasa from the Portuguese in 1698 Nâsir b 'Abd-allâh al-Mazrû'î succeeded Muhammad b Mubarak as *wali* under Sayf b Sultân I al-Ya'rubî (Qayd al-ard).[69] Although Nasir met with stiff opposition locally and was ultimately dispatched unceremoniously to Oman in chains in 1727, he nominally remained in his position as *wali* until that date.[70] Between 1727 and 1730, in the chaos of the civil wars during which the ever opportunist Portuguese tried to benefit from the disruptions in Oman and made a final but unsuccessful attempt to retake Mombasa, two non-Mazrui *walis* were appointed to the town, Muhammad b Sa'îd al-Ma'marî and Sâlih b Muhammad al-Hadramî.[71] It is not clear, however, by which contending party in Oman these two were appointed although it may reasonably be assumed, as will become apparent below, that they were non-Ya'rubi pretenders. It is also important to note that during this period some Mazaria were even prepared to collaborate with the Portuguese in their bid to obtain the upper hand in Mombasa and to break the fetters of domination by Muscati rulers.[72] But this Mazrui bid for supremacy was opposed at that time by a number of Swahili/African tribes who were actively engaged in soliciting the support of Omani rulers in their joint struggle to overcome the Portuguese. One of the members of the 1729–30 East African delegation, which had proceeded to Muscat seeking Omani assistance against the Portuguese, had been a representative of the commercially active Swahili 'Mijikenda' tribe.[73]

When Sayf b Sultân II al-Ya'rubî, whose succession as a minor in 1719 had sparked off the civil wars in Oman, was deemed fit to be re-elected to the Imamate in 1728 having by then reached maturity, he felt it expedient to rekindle the embers of the old Ya'rubi-Mazrui alliance. He formally approached Nasir b Abdallah entreating him to return to his former position as the Mazrui *wali* of Mombasa.[74] But Nasir excused himself from reassuming the office on grounds of old age although his recommendation that his nephew, Muhammad b 'Uthmân, should be appointed in his place was accepted.[75]

Nevertheless, the re-established Ya'rubi–Mazrui connection did not last long as three years later Sayf II al-Ya'rubi was stripped of his Imamate after alienating the Omani *ulama*.[76] Sayf was eventually killed in battle but not before earning himself, as related previously, the *laqab* of *al-jâ`ir* (the tyrant) for having introduced Nadir Shah's Persian troops onto Omani soil.[77] However, if the Ya'ariba were soon to lose for ever their hold on the rulership of Oman, their reinforcement of the Mazaria hegemony over the governorship of Mombasa continued to hold fast for more than a century under the guardianship of the descendants of Nasir b Abdallah, as can be seen from Figure 3.

With the advent of the Albusaid to power in Oman, it is not surprising that Muhammad b Uthman, who like his predecessors was a Ya'rubi appointee, rejected the Hinawi-backed Albusaidi suzerainty over Mombasa.[78] Soon after, the Mazrui *wali* refused to send to Muscat the annual tribute he had promised to Sayf II al-Ya'rubi[79] and thus started the more-than-a-century-long struggle between the Albusaid and the Mazaria for the control not only of Mombasa but of the whole northern East African coast involved in the regional trade.

Although the first Albusaidi ruler, Ahmad b Said, in his day attempted to capture Mombasa and even sent assassination squads from Oman to murder certain Mazrui leaders,[80] the political fragmentation of Oman

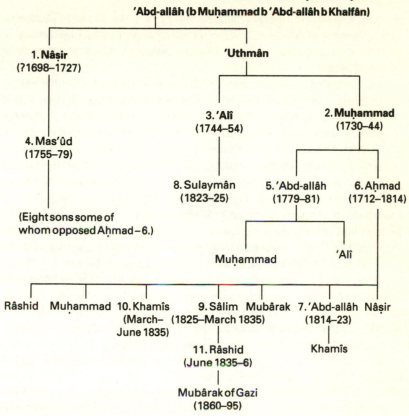

Figure 3 Awlâd 'Uthmân b 'Abd-allâh and Awlâd Nâṣir b 'Abd-allâh as Mazrû'î Wâlîs of Mombasa

Notes and Sources:
Numbers and dates show Walis in chronological order. Bold characters show those members who were born in Oman.
Juhaina, 118–39; Kitab al-Zunuj, 243; *Mombasa Chronicle*, 218; IOR/V/23/45, Miles, 1883–4; Cashmore I.H., 1968, 125; Nicholls C.S., 1971, 380; Berg F.J., 1971, chap. 3; Pouwels R.L., 1987, chap. 6.

after his death and the squabbles among the ruling family itself enabled the Mazaria to retain their position not only in Mombasa but also in Pemba where they were also influential.[81] With the political situation in Oman in a state of flux, the Mazaria were further encouraged to encroach upon other dominions held by the Albusaidis in East Africa. As early as 1727, they had attempted to seize Zanzibar itself and had even made an offer of a strategic alliance with the Portuguese.[82] Since these endeavours had met with a singular lack of success, as did a later military expedition to take Zanzibar in 1753,[83] the Mazaria started to seek alliances with other Omani and Swahili groups in East Africa in their attempt to extend the zone of their influence and to resist the rise of the Albusaid.

One such Omani group was the Banu Nabhan of Pate with whose cooperation the Mazaria tried to obtain a foothold in the Lamu Archipelago by offering to mediate in the local succession and other disputes.[84] But their best opportunity to spread their authority came in 1807. With Omani politics in disarray Pate's ruler, Fûm Ahmad (Fumo Madi), 'the last of the great Sultans of the Nabhans',[85] died during that year. In the ensuing succession dispute the Mazaria were asked to assume their customary mediatory role. Nonetheless, the *wali* of Mombasa at the time, Ahmad b Muhammad b 'Uthmân, although he himself had previously accepted to remain in that position as a vassal of the Albusaid,[86] now refused to recognise the deceased ruler's son, Fûm Lût (Fumo Luti) al-Nabhânî, as successor. Instead, he led a military expedition to Pate whereby Fum Lut was taken prisoner to Mombasa and a Mazrui garrison formerly expelled by Fûm Ahmad was re-established in Pate.[87] The newly appointed ruler of Pate, Ahmad b Shaykh, had Abdallah b Ahmad al-Mazrui, son of the *wali* of Mombasa, as a constant companion supervising and dictating his every move while Abdallah's very presence in Pate was meant to convey proof of ultimate Mazrui suzerainty over Pate.[88]

Fum Lut's supporters, however, refused to accept this state of affairs especially when the Mazaria started to impose taxes on the agricultural produce of the local people,[89] and they fled to Lamu which now became the theatre of conflict between the two parties. Between 1807 and 1811 the Mazaria led two expeditions against Lamu but in a later campaign, sometime in 1812 or 1813, the Mazrui troops were heavily defeated at the battle of Shela, a village south of Lamu town.[90] In the aftermath of this, fearing awesome reprisals by the Mazaria, two delegations, one from Lamu under Muhammad b al-Hâj al-Sa'sa'î and another from the ousted ruler of Pate, Fum Lut al-Nabhani, were sent to Muscat to solicit aid from Said b Sultan.[91]

It was fortunate for Said that he was in a position, by that time, to respond effectively to the entreaties of the envoys from East Africa. Gone were the gloomy days of 1810 and, as it has been shown, by 1813 the Wahhabi hold on Oman was weakening and Said, having taken the initiative, had expelled the Wahhabi garrison from Bahrain allowing the Al-Khalifa to rule there under Albusaidi suzerainty.[92] Moreover, Said, who had first visited Zanzibar as a boy of about 11 years of age in 1802,[93] must have realised the great potential of the ever growing

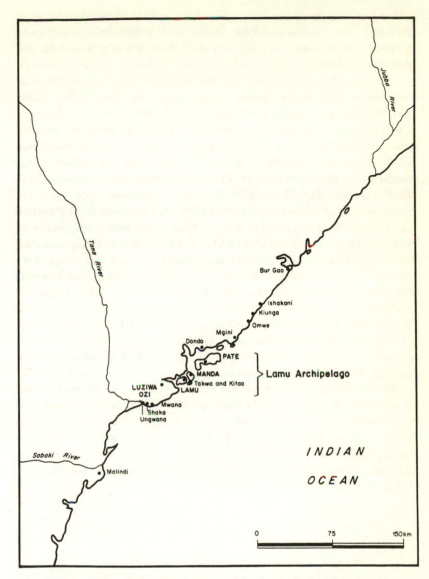

Map 7 East Africa: the northern coast and the Lamu Archipelago.

commercial network of East Africa converging increasingly upon Zanzibar. As already related, he was further encouraged to bring this network under Muscati control by his Banyan and other Indian allies who were even prepared to give him military assistance to achieve this objective.[94]

It is not surprising therefore that Said readily responded to these emissaries from Lamu and Pate. Initially he dispatched a garrison to occupy the port town of Lamu where soon after a fort was built and Muhammad b Nâṣir b Sayf al-Ma'walî was appointed as the Albusaidi *wali*.[95] The politics of Lamu, however, were so entwined with those of Pate that no *wali* could control Lamu without the cooperation of the ruler of Pate who remained a puppet of the Mazaria.

In 1814 Said's designs to strengthen further his position in East Africa suffered a serious setback when Abdallah b Ahmad succeeded his father to the governorship of Mombasa.[96] In the words of al-Mughairi: 'It was in the days of this wali that wars began between Said bin Sultan and the Mazaria'.[97] Abdallah, who had once been the commander of the Mazrui garrison before its expulsion from Pate and who had taken on the role of a supervisor there after 1807, had also been in the forefront of the army which had experienced the humiliating defeat at Shela.[98] Consequently he refused to have any truck with Muscat or with the Albusaidi-appointed *walis* in East Africa and was determined to increase his own influence in the Lamu Archipelago.[99]

Shortly after, when Said b Sultan sent Abdallah a letter with a special envoy from Oman who was also a Mazrui, Muḥammad b Sulaymân, warning him not to interfere in the affairs of Pate and ordering him to surrender Fort Jesus,[100] Abdallah reacted by sending his own emissary, Ḥasan b 'Alî al-Janâbî, to Muscat. Together with a letter, a cooking pot, a ladle, a coat of mail and a cup the Mazrui sent gunpowder and musket balls to the Albusaidi with the message that 'If you want to come, you will have to put on armour...[and by sending him these things he was telling him to] either come and fight or else stay in the kitchen like a woman and cook'.[101] With regard to the Fort, as the Swahili poet Mukâya b Ḥajjî al-Ghassânî (1776–1837) related of this incident, Abdallah's reply was:

'Hutaingia Ngomeni	You will not enter the Fort
na kuta zake hufiki	You will not even arrive near its walls,
pasi panga mikononi	Without swords in your hands
na midomo ya bunduki	Without the mouths of guns[102]

Mazrui resistance, however, was not the only problem that Said had to contend with at that time as there were more pressing affairs nearer home to which he had to attend. As it transpired, it was not until fourteen years later that he was able to grasp the nettle and respond to this insult. For the moment, he was obliged to tackle the internecine strife on his home ground before endeavouring to regain those commercial and political interests that his father had once controlled in the Gulf.

In 1814 the greatest thorn in Said b Sultan's side in the Gulf remained the Qasimis of Ras-al-Khayma following the failure of the joint Omani–British 1809 expedition due to the British refusal to fight Said's enemies at critical stages.[103] Qasimi depredations against shipping continued apace hampering the smooth flow of commercial exchange in the region.[104] After the fiasco of 1809, Said was even willing to assist his erstwhile enemy, Sultân b Saqr al-Qâsimî, in the latter's bid to control Ras-al-Khayma. Sultan, the former leader of the Qasimis ousted by the Wahhabis but having now escaped from imprisonment in Dir'iya,

> promised that if His Highness [Said b Sultan] would restore him to his hereditary possessions and consequence he would consider himself as a vassal of the Imaum [Said b Sultan] and his allies, and would never again, or his tribe, commit piracies.[105]

On the basis of al-Qasimi's promise, Said sent three expeditions against Ras-al-Khayma between 1812 and 1814. The first one in 1812 was a total failure. Being frustrated by Wahhabi interventions, Said attempted once again to solicit British involvement hoping that the new governor at Bombay, Evan Nepan, appointed at the end of 1811, would be more accommodating and more amenable than his predecessor, Jonathan Duncan.[106] The only reaction he managed to elicit, however, was that Captain William Bruce, the British Resident at Bushire, could accompany Oman's next expedition with a cruiser. From his safe vantage point Bruce early in 1813 was able to watch the second unsuccessful Omani attempt to take Ras-al-Khayma, which foundered due to the failure of aid, previously vouchsafed by Shaykh Shakhbût b Dhiyâb Âl-bû-Falâh of the Banî Yâs, to materialise. This time Said managed nonetheless to install Sultan b Saqr in the second principal Qasimi port of Sharja.

On his third attempt in 1814, the most Said was able to extract was a truce with Ras-al-Khayma accompanied by a promise that Muscati shipping would no longer be attacked.[107] A year later, however, instead of desisting from attacks on Omani vessels in the Gulf as agreed, the Qasimi fleet was threatening Said right in the heart of his domain with an attack on Matrah port itself. The Qasimi fleet was eventually driven away with great difficulty but not before inflicting a wound on the Albusaidi ruler himself by a bullet which, according to his daughter, 'settled in the hip, [and was to] cause him frequent pain and made him limp a little'.[108]

The Ya'rubi-Jabri challenge

Having thus resisted an external challenge, very soon after this incident in 1816 Said had to face what for a short while seemed an insuperable internal threat to his authority. He had to deal with the combined forces of his erstwhile friend and trustee, Muhammad b Nasir al-Jabri whom he had alienated,[109] and of the leaders of the old Ya'rubi regime.

Although the *tamima* of the Ya'ariba, Muhanna b Muhammad of Nakhl, in 1804 had wholeheartedly supported the ambitions of Sayyida Moza bint Ahmad for her nephews Said and Salim after their father's death, he had been murdered once Badr b Sayf had seized the reins of power.[110] The murderer, Mâlik b Sayf b Sulṭân al-Ya'rubî, had then been given charge of Nakhl by Badr to add to his existing dominion of al-Hazm.[111] Not surprisingly during the disruptions caused by the Wahhabi incursions in Oman, in the strategies adopted by Sayyida Moza to re-establish Albusaidi authority, Nakhl had been in the eye of the storm in the struggle between the Albusaid and al-Jabri especially after the latter had recovered Bidbid and Sumayil. Fortunately for the Albusaidis, at this stage they had the support of another Ya'rubi Shaykh, Ḥimyar b Muḥammad b Sulaymân, brother of the assassinated *tamima* of the Ya'ariba 'who hated Malik b Sayf for having killed his brother'.[112]

According to Ibn Ruzaiq, Said b Sultan eventually succeeded in taking Nakhl because its inhabitants detested Malik and were in favour of Himyar, obeying the latter's exhortations not to offer any resistance to the predominantly Baluchi and Ma'âwil forces sent by Said to capture Nakhl. However, although Himyar was at first allowed to remain in Nakhl by Said, albeit under the supervision of his *wali* Sa'îd b Sayf al-Ma'walî, he was later expelled by Said's uncle Tâlib b Aḥmad of Rustaq when the latter was given temporary charge of Nakhl.[113]

Under the tyrannical rule of the subsequently appointed Albusaidi *wali*, Khalfân b Sayf al-Ma'walî, the people of Nakhl pleaded with Himyar al-Ya'rubi, who was now settled in Ṭaww, to come to their rescue. 'When he procrastinated, they wrote to him that if you do not come soon, we will leave this area in a very short time. At this he got furious and sent them two hundred men from Taww'.[114] Thus started the war between the Albusaidi-supported Ma'awil and the Ya'ariba, now openly backed by al-Jabri who had marched into Nakhl with an army of a thousand men.

Incapable of taking on the combined Ya'rubi–Jabri might in the field, Said b Sultan resorted to the other method of disarming his enemies at which he was by now quite adept: that of bribery. He dispatched an emissary to al-Jabri with a promise that if the latter withdrew his support from Himyar, not only could he have as much money as he wished but he could take whatever forts he desired in addition to his own of Bidbid and Sumayil. The old confidant of Said's father had too many Albusaidi connections, including those of blood, to allow himself to preside over the demise of the Dynasty. By now, disillusioned by the havoc his former allies, the Wahhabis, had caused in Oman, he was very forgiving of Said's previous insults and soon decided to exit from Nakhl with his army.[115]

With the field now open to Said, he gathered a huge force composed of elements of the Ḥirth, Ḥājiryyîn, Banî (B) Kharûs, B Ḥasan, B Nizâr, B Hina, under the command of Nujaim b 'Abd-allâh al-Siyâbî, to retake Nakhl. He also sent envoys from the B Hasan to Himyar al-Ya'rubi offering him a pardon and safe passage out of Nakhl if he surrendered. When Himyar was, however, brought to him, he immediately threw the Ya'rubi in jail to the disgust of the B Hasan who insisted upon, and were eventually able to, obtain his release.

When Said chose to appoint Suwaylim b Salmîn as his next *wali* of Nakhl, Himyar decided to escape to his old refuge in Taww. But this was not the end of the affair. For very soon after, during a visit to Barka, Said wrote to Himyar demanding his presence. He also wrote to his *wali* Suwaylim with the orders 'to capture as many of the Ya'ariba leaders as he comes across in Nakhl and to send them to him in Barka'.[116] When they arrived, Said imprisoned them and they were all to languish and die in jail with the exception of Himyar's son, Sulaymân, who had refused to accompany his father to Barka, and Sayf b Mâlik b Sayf, a minor who was allowed by Said to return to Taww. Apart from the leader, Ḥimyar b Muḥammad b Sulaymân, other Ya'ariba Shaykhs thus eliminated were Mâjid b Sayf and Ḥimyar b Muḥammad b Ḥimyar.[117] Thus ended this tawdry episode of resistance undertaken by members of the old Dynasty against the new one. However, it was by no means the last stand as members of the Ya'ariba were later to make similar attempts to regain some of their old prestige among the tribes of Oman.[118]

Apart from the continuing political turmoil in Oman and the commercial and strategic attractions of the island of Zanzibar, developments in the Gulf also played their part in further driving Said b Sultan and his commercial associates to East Africa. In the next chapter these Gulf events will be examined before analysing the reasons behind the Omani ruler's move to Zanzibar.

6 The suppression of Omani interests in the Gulf and the Albusaidi move to Zanzibar

THE QASIMI AND UTBI THREAT TO OMANI COMMERCE

Following the elimination of a number of prominent Ya'ariba leaders in 1816 Said b Sultan succeeded in reasserting his authority in Oman. Although he had not yet won back the powerful al-Jabri over to his side, he turned his attention to avenging the humiliation he had suffered at the hands of the Qasimis a year before in 1815. His blockade of Ras-al-Khayma for a period of four months in 1816 did not, however, enable him even to retake Khawr Fakkan from them. No sooner had he returned to Muscat than he prepared for yet another expedition under the guidance of Shaykh Muḥammad b Khalaf al-Shî'î, this time against Bahrain where the Al-Khalîfa of the Utbis ('Utûb) had ceased paying the transit tax and the annual tribute due to Muscat.[1]

The Utbis had reneged upon their former promises to Said because they were benefiting from those very activities pursued by Said's enemies: the Qasimis were utilising Bahrain as a clearing house for the goods seized by them on the high seas. It is no wonder then that some Utbis, in addition to providing the Qasimis with basic commodities like food, were soon recruited to the Qasimi ranks gleefully participating in the plunder of Gulf shipping while others were profiting from the burgeoning trade between Ras-al-Khayma and Bahrain.[2] In response to this sustained direct threat to the commercial position of Muscat, Said b Sultan gathered a large force and sailed to Bahrain in June 1816. But his troops were routed by the combined Utbi/Qasimi forces. His brother Ḥamad, Shaykh Sa'îd b Mâjid al-Ḥârthî and, significantly, some of the 'principal sirdars' were among those who were killed on this occasion.[3] In the aftermath of this, Said retired to the Gulf island of Kung where he had been promised a supply of Persian reinforcements from Bushire on condition that, should Bahrain be taken, Said would agree to pay 10,000 tomans (= £7,500 = MT$35,600) as an annual tribute to the governor of

Shiraz for the possession of Bahrain.[4] However, having received news of his earlier defeat, the Persian authorities now had different ideas:

> Said fortunately discovered in time that he was being led into a snare by the Persians, who intended to carry him a prisoner to Shiraz, and abandoning his project against Bahrain, returned to Oman.[5]

In Oman, soon after his return, Said had to confront yet another challenge from among the last few remaining Ya'ariba. Sulaymân, the son of the murdered Ya'rubi Shaykh, Himyar b Muhammad b Sulaymân, having obtained assistance from another leading Ya'rubi Shaykh then in the service of the Albusaid, Muhammad b Sulaymân, the *wali* of Bahla, had attacked the Ma'awil and had gained the upper hand after ensconcing himself in Nakhl. Fortunately for Said, his call for tribal assistance against the Ya'ariba was this time answered by the Sharqiya Hinawis under Îsa b Sâlih I al-Hârthî,[6] by the Hajiriyyîn, the people of Suwaiq and al-Khadra under Sulaymân b Sa'îd al-Darmakkî and by the people of Rustaq led by Muhammad b Sulaymân al-'Adawî. On this occasion his forces prevailed. As for Sulayman b Himyar al-Ya'rubi, he was for a time given refuge by the Ya'rubi *wali* of Bahla following his defeat but his life was spared only after the intercession of the *alim* Abû Nabhân Jâ'id al-Kharûsî who escorted the Ya'rubi as a prisoner to Said in Muscat and pleaded for clemency on his behalf.[7]

The 1819 Omani-British expedition against Ras-al-Khayma

Externally, Said's struggle with the Qasimis and the Utbis remained unresolved. And it was not so much by dint of Said's own efforts as it was a result of the increasing Qasimi/Utbi display of contempt and total disregard for British warnings that once again compelled Britain to seek Muscat's cooperation. The intensification of Qasimi/Utbi activities against shipping was in fact nurtured not only by their victories against what were reputed to be formidable foes but also by the apathy of the British themselves, especially as they had done nothing to regain their prestige damaged by the 1809–10 débâcle. Moreover, when Said had asked for their cooperation in curtailing Qasimi activity on several occasions subsequently, they had flatly refused. Far from helping to avenge the heavy defeats suffered by their once 'most trusted ally', they had stood by and allowed the Qasimi fleet to grow from strength to strength. By 1817 this fleet could boast over a hundred large dhows with 400 cannon and 8,000 armed men[8] and had become bold enough once again to attack ships even in the ports of western India and to challenge vessels of the Royal Navy on the high seas.

The activities pursued by the Qasimis and their allies increased to such an extent that during the 1817–18 trading season the British authorities in Bombay were obliged to organise a convoy based at Muscat in order to protect their trade and to escort merchant shipping wishing to proceed up the Gulf.[9] Thus it was Britain once again that was forced to ally with the ruler of Muscat in order to safeguard its own commercial interests. Nevertheless, the final British triumph in the Gulf after 1819 was greatly facilitated by two other regional developments: the decisive defeat of the Wahhabis at the hands of the Egyptians in 1818 and the contemporaneous dismantling of the power structure of the Marathas in India.[10] The former enabled Britain at last to undertake military expeditions in eastern Arabia without running the risk of the long and protracted conflict with the Wahhabis that such an involvement during the last two decades would have undoubtedly entailed. The latter signified that Britain from now on had more resources at its disposal to use in its campaigns outside India. More importantly Britain no longer needed to solicit aid from the Egyptians against the Qasimis and their allies, an action to which the ruler of Muscat had shown himself to be totally opposed.[11] Thus in 1819, while Captain George Sadlier lingered on in Hijaz, waiting for a definite answer from Ibrahim Pasha with regard to such aid, at Bombay the decision had already been taken to take action against Ras-al-Khayma.

When the expedition sailed from Bombay on 4 November 1819 under Major General William Keir there was no question at that stage of it being a joint Omani–British venture.[12] A question often left unanswered by writers on this episode of Gulf history is why, given the background of frequent British refusals even to entertain the idea of cooperating with Muscat on this matter, should Keir have decided to touch at Muscat at all before proceeding to Ras-al-Khayma? The answer, apart from commercial reasons, is that Keir was aware of an offer of alliance that had recently been made by Hasan b Raḥma of Ras-al-Khayma to both Britain and Oman. Although he obviously knew that Britain had rejected the offer he was not sure what Muscat's response had been and accordingly went to see Said b Sultan to find out where Muscat's sympathies lay.[13]

Prior to Keir's arrival Said had in fact already rejected the overture made by the Qasimi chief knowing only too well that the Qasimis had approached him because they had of late become greatly alarmed at rumours, then spreading in the Gulf, of an impending Egyptian attack against Ras-al-Khayma. Despite his own apprehensions of Egyptian ambitions, Said had had too many abortive dealings with the Qasimis to consider an offer of an alliance with them even for a moment. On the contrary, when Keir arrived in Muscat, Said was contemplating yet another Omani attack against Ras-al-Khayma in harness with his allies, Sultân b Saqr of Sharja and Tahnûn b Shakhbût of Abu Dhabi.[14] Thus, for a second time, British interests coincided with those of Muscat with regard to Ras-al-Khayma.

After receiving assurances from Keir that there would be no Egyptian involvement, Said could not resist participating in what had become once again a joint Omani–British campaign against Ras-al-Khayma, a combined venture that Said had been striving to achieve since the 1809–10 failure. Therefore, he agreed to accompany in person an Omani land force of 4,000 men, joined by 800 troops on three ships of war.[15] Yet, when Ras-al-Khayma was finally taken Keir totally disregarded the interests of the ruler of Muscat. Contrary to Said's wishes, he refused to allow the ruler of Ras-al-Khayma to acknowledge Albusaidi suzerainty. In fact the newly re-installed Qasimi ruler, Sultan b Saqr, had in 1813, as seen earlier, pledged just such recognition in return for Albusaidi assistance to regain the control of Ras-al-Khayma.[16] Moreover, British authorities themselves, for a long time before the expedition, had reiterated their commitment to bring Ras-al-Khayma within the Albusaidi domain. Only now was it decided that due to Muscat's wide-ranging commercial relations, such a policy would be extremely detrimental to British commercial interests in the Gulf.[17] Nonetheless, whereas Said could accept an 'independent' ruler at Ras-al-Khayma, he could never come to terms with the release of the former Wahhabi-installed Qasimi leaders, the very ones who had relentlessly plagued him, undermined his rule, compelled him to divert so many of his resources from other fronts, been responsible for personal injuries from which he was still suffering and to whom, to his disbelief, Keir was now offering a treaty. Disgusted and powerless but categorically refusing to become involved in any such treaties, he returned to Muscat.[18]

The negation of Omani interests in the Gulf

Although the British authorities in India initially had their reservations about the General Treaty of Peace that Keir signed on the spot with the various Gulf Shaykhs in 1820, the treaty and later amendments thereto had come to stay with serious consequences for Oman.[19] As far as Muscat's interests were concerned, the treaty was a great blow to both the political and the economic fortunes of Oman. In one fell swoop, Keir had buried any ambitions that the Albusaidis may have had in the Gulf. For although rulers of Muscat before 1820 had now and again lost the allegiance of one tribe or another in northern Oman, that part of it now known as the Trucial Coast was irrevocably severed from the Albusaidi 'Omani' dominions. In any future conflict, Omani rulers had Britain to contend with and not the tribes themselves as had been the centuries-old state of play in the region.

Economically, Trucial Oman was henceforth to become nothing more than an extension of the British domain in India. And this was not all. Bahrain, that 'gem of pearl fisheries', which for quite a long period had been at the mercy of British policy makers being at times subjected to Oman and at others to Persia when it was expedient to pacify the Shah, was now also for ever lost to Muscat. It too became enveloped in Britain's cloak of domination when the Utbis were included in the General Treaty. But even if the Al-Khalifa after signing the treaty, fearful of the preparations then being made of a joint Omani–Persian expedition against Bahrain, agreed to recognise Muscati overlordship and promised to pay an annual tribute of MT\$30,000,[20] the Albusaid from now on could only deal through Britain in their relations with Bahrain.

Following the dismantling of Omani interests in India during his father's lifetime, by 1820 Said had thus also lost to the British just about all the possessions that his father had once controlled in the Gulf with the exception of Bander Abbas, which was on lease from Persia, and certain islands in the Gulf such as Qishm. In these circumstances he had no alternative but to salvage what interests remained to Muscat in other areas of the Indian Ocean and thus the clarion call for his move to Zanzibar was being sounded particularly as the French, since 1817, had shown a renewed interest in his dominions in East Africa and had even sent special emissaries to Muscat asking him for commercial privileges.

SAID B SULTAN'S MOVE TO ZANZIBAR: A NEW INTERPRETATION

It is generally assumed by most East Africanists and some other historians that Said b Sultan 'moved his court' to Zanzibar in 1840, allegedly from a position of strength in Oman to consolidate his 'empire' in East Africa.[21] The facts though would seem to give lie to such an assumption. As seen above, Said's position in Oman was far from strong and though following his 1840 trip he did remain for the longest period of time he was ever to stay in East Africa, this was in fact his seventh visit (see Table 4).

As early as 1829 Said had decided to move items of his household furniture and other personal effects to Zanzibar[22] having, a year before,

Table 4   Duration Of Said b Sultan's visits to East Africa

1802		brief visit at the age of about 11
January 1828	– April 1828:	first expedition against Mombasa
December 1829	– 9 May 1830:	second expedition against Mombasa
December 1831	– September 1832	
November 1833	– Spring 1835:	third expedition against Mombasa
Early 1837	– September 1839	
December 1840	– April 1851:	longest stay
December 1852	– April 1854	
19 October 1856:		died on his way to Zanzibar

Sources: al-Farsi, 1942, 77–80; al-Fath, 460; Juhaina 158; Guillain-Documents I, 589 and III, 454; French Archives quoted in Nicholls C.S., 1971, chap. 10; IOR/L/P&S/5/393, Said b Sultan to Bombay, 7 October 1839; IOR/P/386/61, Agent in Muscat to Bombay, 8 January 1830; US/Arch/NEMA, Jnl of R.P. Waters, 1836–1844, 189–215; IOR/P/387/58, Report by Capt. Hart, 10 February 1834; ZA/AA3/8, Hamerton to Bombay, 4 September 1852.

given orders for a palace to be built for him at Mtoni on the coast about 3 miles north of Zanzibar town.[23] The decades of the 1820s and the 1830s, generally treated at most in a perfunctory manner in most accounts, are crucial to the understanding of what motivated the ruler of Muscat apparently to abandon Oman after 1829 and to adopt Zanzibar as his base.

Despite the neutralisation of the Qasimis by the British in 1820, Said made a final attempt during the 1820s to regain some of his father's former stature in Gulf affairs. The impetus behind this attempt was engendered by a concatenation of several factors. Firstly, having by now more or less established himself in Muscat, he was able in 1820 to remove a major obstacle to his commercial endeavours by subjugating the Banî Bû 'Alî of Ja'lân in Sur. That he did so with British help was purely fortuitous.

The immediate cause for British participation was an on-the-spot decision taken by Captain Thompson to avenge the murder of a messenger despatched to the Bani Bu Ali port of Ashkhara to enquire into acts of plunder against shipping carried out by the tribe. The events of the so-called 'Bani Bu Ali expeditions'[24] may have taught the British government to think twice before launching any military campaigns by land in Arabia. But the expeditions were far from being used by Said b Sultan to test the resolve of his British 'allies to uphold the integrity of his territory' as has often been suggested.[25] No doubt the action taken by Captain Thompson, albeit for his own motives, did provide Said with a long-awaited opportunity to triumph over a tribe which had reputedly supported the Wahhabis and had adopted their tenets during the invasions of the first decade of the nineteenth century. More importantly Thompson's action was partly responsible for Said being able to take control of the important commercial outlet that Ja'lan was for the Sharqiya region of Oman, leading as it did to the coast at Sur and to the ports of East Africa beyond. Thus when Thompson approached him, Said readily agreed to join in the military expedition with a thousand men under the joint command of the now reconciled Muhammad b Nasir al-Jabri and the leader of the Sharqiya Hinawis, Isa b Salih I al-Harthi.[26]

With the town of Ashkhara eventually destroyed and opposing tribal leaders imprisoned, Said succeeded, albeit at the cost of personal injury, where he had failed at Ras-al-Khayma and was able to enhance Muscati commercial interests substantially by virtue of this victory. In taking Ja'lan, he could now control in this era of commercial expansion in East Africa the export of Omani products which, from the Sharqiya, constituted cloth, lucerne and dates grown in the extensive palm cultivations of the region.[27] Fortunately for him, Britain, at the time preoccupied to the point of obsession with the idea of 'the defence of India', did not even contemplate that Muscati possessions in South Arabia or in East Africa further afield would ultimately pose a challenge to its own commercial interests in the Indian Ocean.

Omani migrations to East Africa

As for connections between Sharqiya and East Africa, Sur, through which most of the commercial exchanges took place, had become a prosperous port boasting a fleet of about 250 sea-going vessels since the beginning of the nineteenth century.[28] It was also at this time that new waves of migrations from Oman to Africa took place. Apart from the movement of merchant communities from Muscat already discussed, extensive migrations notably of the Hirth (correctly al-Ḥirth; sing. al-Ḥarthî) Tôqî also took place from Sharqiya not only to East but to Central Africa as well. Among the various sections of the Harthi tribe, the most prominent ones thus migrating were the Ṭôqî,'Isrî, Sinâwî,'Urfî and Marhûbî from the villages of Ibra and the oases of Mudaybi and Sinaw.[29]

These were not of course the first Hirth migrations from Oman since others including the Khanâjira, the Ghuyûth, the Maḥârima and the Barâwina, 'the richest of the Omani tribes',[30] also from Ibra in Sharqiya, were firmly established in Zanzibar by the nineteenth century.[31] Some Hirth, together with the Banû Nabhân, are said to have been in East Africa before Portuguese times as early as the tenth century.[32] The Manâdhira, it is alleged, had lived in Mombasa as traders since at least the mid-sixteenth century.[33] As for other Omani tribes settled in East Africa by the turn of the nineteenth century or migrating there during the course of the century, mention in the sources is made of the following: 'Abriyîn, 'Awâmir, B Bahrî, Darâmika, Hawâsina, B Hina, B Ismâ'îl, Jahâdim, B Kharûs, Ma'âwil, Masâkira, Mazâri'a, Mughairiyîn, Mushâqisa, Awlâd Rabî'a, B Rasad, B Riyâm, B Ruwâha, B 'Umar, and the 'Utûb.[34] In addition to these, later sources also include the Bâsimî (or Ba'samî), Bâqashwayn, B Bû 'Ali, B Bû Hasan, Bulûshî, Hâtimî, Janâbî, Lâmî, Ma'marî, Muhâshimî, Ma'tâfi, Rajabî, Rumay'.î, Shukaylî, Timâmî and Zihâmî.[35]

The purpose of listing these tribal names is not to display prowess in recitation but to demonstrate the extent of the geographical dispersement of those tribes which enjoyed long-established links and had settlements in East Africa, encompassing as they do the majority of Omani tribes from Sur in the south to Buraymi in the north. And contrary to current popular beliefs in Oman, as this list shows, Omani links with East Africa were not only from the Sharqiya region. In addition to the Albusaid and their associates, the maintenance of commercial connections with East Africa in the nineteenth century was vital for the people of the whole of Oman including of course those residing in the Batina and Muscat whose activities have already been discussed.

The consolidation of Omani authority in East Africa: early nineteenth century attempts

A further indication of the scope of the expanding Indian Ocean trade network is found in the new recognition that, with Britain as master of India, Said b Sultan continued to accord to Africa throughout this period despite problems nearer home. It was not a sudden flight of fancy that motivated the Albusaidi to despatch his forces from Oman periodically to subdue the Mazaria during his so-called 'expeditions' against Mombasa.[36] Like his father, his dispute with the Mazaria and with other Omani groups was continuous and concurrent with his other struggles in Arabia, India and Africa. Rather, it was the Mazrui bid to extend their influence in the Lamu Archipelago that prompted the Albusaidi as early as 1813 to try and nip in the bud these pretensions that he instinctively realised would plague not only his own commercial ambitions in Zanzibar but also those of his Banyan protégés. Therefore whilst still facing the Utbi and the Qasimi resistance in the Gulf, compounded now by British intervention and troubled by the Ya'rubi and other opposition in Oman itself,[37] in 1817 Said decided to deal firmly with the ever present Mazrui threat. Another factor which no doubt galvanised him into action was the resurfacing of the ever simmering tradition of political rivalry between the Albusaid and the Mazaria.

For these reasons Said, in 1817, sent 4,000 men in thirty ships to attack Pate as a starting point in a general scheme to eradicate the Mazrui influence in the Lamu Archipelago and in Pemba as well as in Mombasa itself.[38] Pemba, '*al-jazîrat-al-Khaḍrâ*'' (the Green Island) and the 'granary of East Africa', was a coveted prize from both the political and the economic points of view.[39] As for Mombasa and the ports of the Lamu Archipelago, they, together with other outlets on the Somali coast, comprised the northern section of the expanding network of East African coastal agriculture and commerce that was beginning to converge on Zanzibar.[40] Thus, Mombasa and the northern ports were an indivisible part and parcel of this network, elements for the future expansion of which, as related above, were already present and operating in the late eighteenth century.[41] For Said b Sultan, it was imperative to control these outlets in order to profit from the massive potential for expansion. But to do so, he had to outmanoeuvre all his local rivals especially now that the most influential among them, the Mazaria, had started to employ deliberate measures to restrict the commercial activities of the Banyans and of the Muscati ruler's other agents and associates in the territories under Mazrui control.[42] The Mazaria had, moreover, started to trade directly with India from Mombasa thus threatening to establish an independent economic base outside Zanzibari control.[43]

However, the Mazaria were but one of the many Omani groups in East Africa which were opposed to the Albusaid. In 1819, while Said was preoccupied with his campaigns in Ras-al-Khayma, the ruler of Kilwa offered to cede Zanzibar to the French if they helped him regain the island from what he alleged were 'Albusaidi usurpers'. But the French at that time were negotiating a commercial treaty with those very would-be 'usurpers'[44] and were understandably apprehensive of British reactions should they have decided to take Kilwa under their wing.[45] The situation was further exacerbated in 1821 when the Barwani *wali* of Zanzibar, 'Abd-allâh b Jum'a b 'Âmir,[46] recently ousted on Said's instructions, sought French support and showed willingness 'to see Zanzibar under French rule'.[47] The Barwani clan of the Hirth was very influential around the area of Lindi. Abd-allah's brother, Muḥammad, who had taken Mafia in 1818 on Said's behalf and had subsequently been appointed as its Albusaidi *wali*, was now also stripped of his position by Said who had grown wary of the considerable wealth and influence that the Barwanis already mustered on the mainland and who was afraid that they might eventually create problems for him if he allowed them to continue to remain in important administrative posts.[48]

Having by now taken control of Ja'lan, it was vital for Said not to alienate the French or precipitate them into the embrace of any other of the Omani groups opposed to him. To pre-empt such a potentially dangerous eventuality, he sent his brother Aḥmad to Bourbon where a commercial agreement, sought by the French since 1817, was signed on 30 March 1822.[49] It was also in that year that Said sent another naval expedition from Muscat under Ḥammâd b Aḥmad Albûsa'îdî which succeeded in capturing Pate from its Mazrui *wali* Gharîb b Aḥmad Muḥammad.[50] With the cooperation of the Masâkira, Pemba was also taken and a Maskari, Nâṣir b Sulaymân, was duly appointed as its *wali*.[51] The capture of Pemba by the Albusaid must have been a great blow to the Mazaria, who, despite Mombasa's own agricultural base, relied heavily for their grain imports on Pemba.[52]

By 1824 Said b Sultan, with the help of tribes and communities already settled in East Africa, had managed to take control of the Lamu Archipelago in addition to Pemba,[53] thus strengthening his position in his struggle with the Mazaria. But before going any further, it must be emphasized that this so-called 'effective control'[54] did not mean that the Muscati ruler thereafter was out to establish an Omani 'empire' in the western Indian Ocean as is maintained by some commentators.[55] Said's quarrels with the Shaykh of Bushire and his blockade of Basra in 1826 have been interpreted as the pursuit of a general scheme of expansion.[56] Nevertheless, the former was merely a personal dispute with 'Abd-al-Rasûl Khân, the Shaykh of Bushire, who was opposed to the idea of Said marrying a Persian princess.[57] The blockade of Basra was undertaken for the same reason which had prompted his father to take identical action in 1804, namely to force the payment of the tribute promised by the Ottomans to Muscat in his grandfather's time.[58]

Furthermore, in East Africa, there was no question of any new institutions being introduced to consolidate these would-be 'imperial' designs. Apart from the appointment of a *wali*, a customs master and in some cases a *jamâdâr* (Baluchi word = chief of garrison), the 'effective control' that the Albusaidi exercised amounted to nothing more than an allegiance given to him by the majority of the communities, whether Swahili, Arab, Indian or African, in those localities which acknowledged him nominally at least as their ruler. Without such an acknowl-

edgement, which was the basis of the Omani tribal system of government, he could not have appointed any of his officials.

Whereas Said b Sultan had no 'imperial' plans in the strict sense, it is
true nonetheless that by the late 1820s he had grown much in stature
and confidence. Following his March 1824 visit to Mecca for the *hajj*,
where he received envoys from Muhammad Ali of Egypt and 'was
accompanied by a large escort and entertained with great sumptuous-
ness...[creating] everywhere an immense sensation',[59] coupled with the
fact that Britain at that time showed minimal interest in Omani affairs,
the Albusaidi decided once again to assert himself in the Gulf. Declaring
war on Bahrain in August 1828, assisted by Ṭahnûn b Shakhbûṭ of Abu
Dhabi and accompanied by Muhammad b Nasir al-Jabri,[60] the Omani
fleet blockaded Manama, the chief port, on 5 November. But during the
subsequent battle, the Omani forces were completely routed: 'His
Highness appears to have shown his usual personal courage, and was
carried off with great difficulty by his faithful Nubians, after being
slightly wounded'.[61] Despite this inauspicious start, Said kept up the
blockade and it was only after an outbreak of cholera and rumblings of
disloyalty that he felt obliged to abandon the siege and sail for Muscat
on 20 November. The consequences of Said's miscalculations were to
prove disastrous for Oman. Not only was the battle itself lost but in the
ensuing peace settlement, worked out of course under the aegis of the
British authorities in December 1829, the Albusaidi was obliged to
relinquish any claim to tribute from Bahrain.[62]

Having had his fingers thus burnt by yet another in a series of failed
exploits aimed at subduing the Gulf, Said experienced greater success
in Dhofar which he took under control in 1829 following the murder of
its enterprising leader, Muḥammad b 'Aqîl.[63] Although he did not seem
to be interested in Dhofar itself, whence he removed his garrison in
1832,[64] its seizure in 1829 further bolstered his position in the Arabian
Sea. He may have been motivated purely by commercial considerations
in the first place, seizing Dhofar as a precautionary measure to put a
stop to the possible re-emergence of a commercial rival in south Arabia
rather than by any grand political designs. Buoyed up by this triumph
but before finally making the move to Zanzibar, he engaged upon a
further pre-emptive strike in seizing and imprisoning another potential
rival, this time in Oman itself, his cousin Hilâl b Muḥammad b Aḥmad,
the *wali* of Suwaiq.[65] Leaving his nephew Muḥammad b Sâlim as his
deputy in Muscat[66] and appointing Sulaymân b Ṣâliḥ Âlbûsa'îdî as *wali*
of Sohar, he set sail for East Africa in December 1829.[67]

Said b Sultan's own purported reasons for his move to Zanzibar were
given in an 1833 despatch to his agent in Bombay:

My revenues in Oman are very small and my expenses very great...[and] it is now five years since all the chief men have died out of Oman and none but the low and mean remain, and I am ashamed to live near such despicable people.[68]

The 'low and mean' were presumably those who opposed him but these existed as much in East Africa as in Oman. Similarly, as far as revenues were concerned, although the Zanzibar customs revenues did indeed increase as already seen, they did not 'continue to surpass those from Oman' at this time.[69] In 1827 Said received MT$188,000 from Muscat customs compared to MT$220,000 from those of Zanzibar.[70] The corresponding figures for 1841 were MT$180,000 for Muscat and MT$150,000 for Zanzibar.[71] Therefore, since the explanation put forward does not withstand closer scrutiny the reasons why the Albusaidi preferred to remain in Zanzibar must be sought elsewhere than the financial revenue sphere.

An important factor governing Said's decision may have been the degree of security afforded by an island stronghold. More crucial perhaps was the fact that the Albusaidi financial and economic practices worked in such a way that they necessitated close proximity to those very customs masters and merchants who had originally encouraged and helped in the move to Africa. In their financial dealings the Albusaidi rulers and other members of the ruling family when requiring or owing money wrote *barwas* (chits) addressed not only to the customs masters but also to other prominent merchants ordering them to send or pay specified amounts to the bearers. Instead of currency, these merchants more often than not supplied merchandise up to the required value to those bearers. Similarly, the provisions for most of the households of the Albusaidi ruling family were supplied by merchants using the *barwa* method, especially the Banyans who monopolised the rice and grain markets.[72] It was then the duty of the customs masters and the other merchants to keep these *barwas* and make a record of them in their accounts opened specifically for members of the ruling family. This practice, which existed from at least the time of Sultan b Ahmad at the beginning of the nineteenth century, continues in Oman up to the present day.[73] Here is how Lt. Christopher described it in Said b Sultan's time during his visit to Zanzibar in 1843:

The Treasury and all money accounts of Government are answered by the following simple plan. When the Imaum wants money or goods he writes an order [*barwa*] on his Banyan [customs master] who instantly meets the demand and keeps the order as his authority, receipt & ca. A balancing of accounts takes place every three or four years, when the orders are produced in apposition to the yearly rent.[74]

As far as security is concerned, it is noteworthy that both in Zanzibar and Muscat the Albusaidi palaces were surrounded by quarters built especially for 'Indian' merchants, other communities including the interior tribes being kept well away from buildings belonging to members of the ruling family.[75] This foresight on the part of the rulers seems to have paid off handsomely in Zanzibar during the troubles of 1859 and in Muscat in 1895 when, at the time of rebellions by *dakhiliya* tribes, the life of Sultan Faysal b Turkî (r.1888–1913) was saved only by his escape from the palace to the nearby Banyan houses.[76]

Thus in addition to the economic growth of Zanzibar, the intimate personal and commercial relations between the Albusaid and their Banyan and other 'Indian' protégés would have been important factors behind the Albusaidi decision to move to Zanzibar. The relocation was undoubtedly also motivated by the need to survive, related as that was to the imperative of resisting the onslaught of that formidable commercial rival in India, Britain, which had been responsible initially for compelling both the Muscati ruler and his protégés to seek their fortunes in Africa. Said b Sultan and his associates had to ensure that they would be in a strong enough position to deal with the inevitable British reaction once Britain woke up to the considerable influence that Omani rulers and their associates would exert on the commerce of the Indian Ocean from their dual vantage points at Zanzibar and Muscat.

Part III

The development of Omani commerce and British reaction

7 The re-emergence of British policy towards Oman

Post-1833

BRITISH DISINTEREST IN OMANI AFFAIRS: 1811–33

By the turn of the nineteenth century various mercantile communities, including a number of African ones, continued in their age-old commercial activities which now came to be focused on Zanzibar for a variety of reasons. Until the 1830s, neither British merchants nor the British government took any special interest in these activities. In fact the latter, during the 1820s and since its triumph over France in 1810, took little notice of Oman itself let alone of its possessions overseas in spite of British merchants' and officials' initial thrust of enthusiasm in the affairs of Muscat which had been motivated mainly by the French threat to India.[1]

The only two events worth mentioning in Omani–British relations during the decade of the 1820s were both closely related to antislaving agreements: the Morseby Treaty of 22 September 1822 and the curious episode of Captain Owen's on-the-spot British protection given to the Mazaria of Mombasa in February 1824. Said b Sultan signed the former in Muscat to prohibit the sale of slaves to Christians in Zanzibar.[2] In the second incident, furious at the behaviour of Owen to whom he had personally given a guarantee of safe passage,[3] Said registered a vehement protest with the British goverment which hastily repudiated Owen's actions.[4] But despite this minor success and the growth in stature and confidence that he experienced during this period, the Albusaidi, far from having 'achieved by 1820 a secure position in Oman',[5] was increasingly beleaguered by a host of challenges to his authority both in Arabia and in Africa.

The 1820s and the 1830s: internal and external opposition to Said b Sultan

Notwithstanding Said b Sultan's gains in Sur, Dhofar and the Lamu Archipelago in the 1820s, in the perpetuation of the tribal system of government which necessitated his physical presence if only to assert his authority by attending the *barza* (court functions) and proclaiming his decisions publicly to the people, he found himself in an unenviable situation. Each time he left either East Africa or Oman, trouble inevitably ensued as tribal elements opposed to him seized the opportunity of his absence to further their own aspirations. When he was preoccupied with affairs in Arabia in 1826, following the disavowal of Owen's actions by the British government, the Mazaria approached the French authorities in Bourbon and were ready 'to cede their island to the French'. But France, having previously rejected similar offers from Omani groups in Kilwa and Zanzibar and having signed a commercial agreement with the ruler of Muscat in 1822, rejected the Mazrui proposal.[6]

Similarly, no sooner had Said left for East Africa in December 1829 than serious disorders broke out in Oman. With Sayyida Môza bint Ahmad Albusaidi, who had been so instrumental in the initial assumption of power by Said in 1806[7] and still deeply involved in Omani politics,[8] another Albusaidi lady emerged on the Omani political stage. This time a niece of Sayyida Moza, Sayidda Jôkha bint Muḥammad b Aḥmad, incensed at her brother Hilal's imprisonment, took up arms against Said's *nâ`ib* at Muscat, Muḥammad b Sâlim, and managed to capture the fort at Suwaiq with tribal support raised in the Batina.[9]

In the subsequent disturbances, Ḥamûd b 'Azzân seized the opportunity to re-install himself in Sohar, the hereditary fief allocated to his grandfather Qays b Ahmad in 1793 but taken by Said b Sultan on the death of Hamud's father in 1814. Hamud, however, was not content to confine his conquest to Sohar and soon took Khabura and Shinas, and commenced preparations for an attack on Muscat. Although the *nâ`ib*, and significantly some 'Indian' merchants, appealed to Bombay for help,[10] it was the tribal levies raised by al-Jabri from Sumayil for the defence of Muscat and the punitive raids (*ghârât*) on Sohar carried out by al-Jabri's supporters, the Banû Na'îm of northern Oman, that dissuaded Hamud from attacking Muscat.[11] Had Hamud carried out his threat it is doubtful, after the fiasco of the Bani Bu Ali expeditions, whether the British would have interfered to save Muscat. The official British policy at the time was 'to persevere in our system of neutrality'.[12]

The need for the ruler's presence to pacify opposing tribes and entice supporting ones into action can be nowhere better evidenced than by his experiences in Mombasa. Despite having persuaded the Mazaria, in 1828, to sign a convention recognising once again Albusaidi overlordship and accepting the stationing of a garrison in Mombasa, albeit after a show of strength comprising 1,200 men and over ten vessels,[13] the Mazaria lost no time in declaring their 'independence' once the Sultan had departed for Arabia. Furthermore, when his recently appointed *wali* to Mombasa, Nâṣir b Sulaymân al-Maskarî (the former *wali* of Pemba), was subsequently expelled following the recapture of Fort Jesus by the Mazaria, even those groups loyal to the Albusaidi in East Africa did not rally to his defence by taking the field against the Mazaria once he was not in their midst.[14] Similarly, when he was recalled to Muscat in 1830 to deal with Hamud b Azzan's challenge in the aftermath of another unsuccessful attack on Mombasa in 1829, the Mazaria managed to consolidate their position still further after ruthlessly strangling his *wali* Nasir al-Maskari in Fort Jesus.[15]

In Oman, Said was unable to dislodge Hamud from either Sohar or Khabura and had to content himself with the recovery of Shinas only. He even agreed to cede the former towns to Hamud at the end of 1830 in return for an annual tribute of MT$8,000.[16] However, as soon as it was politically expedient, he chose to renege upon this agreement by besieging Sohar in February 1831 where, for his pains, his troops suffered a heavy defeat in the ensuing battle.[17] With nothing remaining for him but to renegotiate his former terms with Hamud, Said set out once more for East Africa in December 1831. This time, he appointed his eldest son Hilâl as *wali* of Muscat but advised him 'not to proceed in anything without Muhammad b Salim's approval'.[18]

Soon after Said had left Muscat, however, his own *wali* at Barka Sa'ûd b 'Alî b Sayf, a nephew of Badr b Sayf (r.1804–6), took up arms in an effort to avenge his uncle's murder.[19] In April 1832, during a routine visit of Muhammad b Salim and Hilal b Said to Barka, the two were accompanied by Khalfân b Muḥaysin, a slave belonging to the Jubur. Saud accused Khalfan of being a partner with Said in the crime of his uncle's assassination and had him summarily beheaded after throwing Muhammad and Hilal into prison.[20] This incident heralded a period of further chaos in the Batina. With the Muscati leaders conveniently *in absentia*, Hamud b Azzan now accompanied by Hilal b Muhammad of Suwaiq besieged Rustaq while Sultan b Saqr al-Qasimi supported by Râshid b Ḥamad of Ajman at the same time seized Khawr Fakkan and Diba.[21]

To compound matters, war broke out in Nakhl between its *wali* Nâṣir b Khalaf al-Zâmilî and its people who had in the past supported the leaders of the old Ya'ariba Dynasty.[22] But as it had by now become the custom in Nakhl, it was the Ma'awil who came to the rescue of the Muscati-appointed *wali*. Meanwhile Saud b Ali, with Muhammad b Salim in chains by his side, made preparations to attack Masana.[23] In the resulting mayhem, it was Sayyida Moza bint Ahmad who decided yet again to take personal charge of Muscat affairs in the absence of her other but more favoured nephew and son-in-law, Said b Sultan.[24] Interestingly, it was Sayyida Moza's daughter, Said's first wife, who contemporaneously appears to have been the person in control of at least the household affairs in Zanzibar:

> [My father's] first wife, Azze bint Sef, a princess of Oman by birth, reigned as absolute mistress over the household. In spite of her very small size, and of her plain exterior, she possessed an immense power over my father, who willingly submitted to all her arrangements...happily for us she had no children of her own, who could not have failed to be as disagreeable in their way![25]

In Muscat Sayyida Moza, whilst appealing for help to the British authorities in Bombay,[26] also sent urgent messages to her old confidant Muhammad b Nasir al-Jabri urging him to send troops forthwith to defend Muscat. Al-Jabri, accompanied by his supporters, himself descended from Sumayil to defend Muscat[27] while 1,500 Ghafiri tribesmen loyal to him were able to recover Rustaq.[28] At Masana, two brothers of Muhammad b Salim, Hamad and Sarhân, took the field against Saud forcing him to retreat to his base in Barka.[29] But Saud held on to his prisoners until Sayyida Moza paid a ransom of MT$8,000 for their release.[30] Receiving this news in Mombasa where his attempts to retake Fort Jesus from the Mazaria had all proved ineffectual,[31] Said in September 1832 once again sailed for Muscat.[32] However, it was not by his efforts but once again through Muhammad al-Jabri's personal mediation that peace was brought to Nakhl and a reconciliation effected between the ruler and Saud. Since Talib b Ahmad of Rustaq had died shortly before Said's arrival, the latter agreed to appoint Saud as *wali* there on condition that he relinquished Barka.[33]

With the Batina for the moment subdued, the main preoccupation of the Muscati ruler at this time in Arabia was the recapture of his possessions in northern Oman recently taken by the Qasimis. Well aware though that his resources were already stretched in Mombasa, Said knew he could do nothing to regain these possessions without British help. However, having by now dealt with the British for over two decades, he harboured no illusions about their attitudes towards him and was well accustomed to the convolutions of British policy.

During the recent disturbances in Oman, he had even ordered the unceremonious return to India of a British cruiser which had been sent to Muscat by the Bombay authorities for reconnaissance purposes.[34] Nonetheless, he had at the same time written to Bombay: 'We have attached ourselves to you with a view of obtaining your assistance under pressure of weighty events and not for such trifling occurrences as these'.[35] But if the British authorities in Bombay had in principle shown their support for him by sending cruisers and issuing warnings to the 'rebels' during the recent troubles,[36] they flatly refused to give him any assistance in the 'weighty event' of recovering Khawr Fakkan or Diba. They advised him instead 'to remain at home in future and protect his Arabian dominions'.[37] But there were even 'weightier events' to follow. And it was not his African but these very same Arabian dominions that soon after came under a renewed external threat, that posed by his old foes, the Wahhabis, now experiencing a revival in their new capital at Riyad.[38]

The Wahhabi revival, at a time when Britain demonstrated a singular disinclination to become enmeshed in Omani affairs, was a great blow for Said b Sultan. Despite numerous rebuttals still painfully fresh in his mind, he made a last-ditch attempt to obtain British military assistance when 'Umar b 'Ufaysân, the Wahhabi governor of Hasa, marched into Buraymi in January 1833.[39] The unequivocal reply Said received from the British, however, confirmed his worst suspicions:

> Our concern is only with the maritime commerce of the Gulf and as long as that is not molested, it matters not to us whether one power or another holds dominion on its shores....We are not prepared to sanction the employment of British arms for maintaining the integrity of the continental possessions of the Imaum of Muscat.[40]

It was more than apparent that Britain was totally unconcerned whether the coast of Oman was ruled by their 'old ally' or by the Wahhabis so long as their own commercial position remained unchallenged. In this unwelcome but conclusive realisation, Said had enough political acumen to come to terms quietly with the Wahhabis ensuring that there was no British mediation which had already caused him so much distress in his dealings with other tribes of Arabia. Thus politically compromised and wrong-footed, he agreed not only to pay an annual tribute of MT$5,000 to Riyad but also to the stationing of a Wahhabi garrison in Buraymi.[41] With his standing in Arabia at a very low ebb he sailed once again to East Africa where he arrived in November 1833.[42]

THE 1833 OMANI–AMERICAN TREATY: CATALYST FOR CHANGE OF BRITISH POLICY

Following his humiliation at the hands of the Wahhabis in Arabia in 1833, Said b Sultan was no more successful in Africa in yet another of his confrontations with the Mazaria.[43] To aggravate the situation further, while holding siege to Fort Jesus he received the ominous tidings at Mombasa that his father's old trustee Muhammad b Nasir al-Jabri had passed away in the spring of 1834.[44]

British reaction to the political ambitions of Hamud b Azzan

At the time of his death, Muhammad al-Jabri, together with tribal support raised by Râshid b Humayd al-Ghâfiri of al-Aynayn, comprising elements of the 'Abriyyîn, Bulûsh, B Ka'b, B Kalbân, Mayâyiha, B Na'îm, Qatab, al-Shawâmis, B Shukayl and B Ya'qûb, was camped at Izki preparing for war against Hamud b Azzan who was backed by a combined force of the Hirth, the Hubûs, and the B Ruwâha. When Saud b Ali b Sayf, the former *wali* of Barka recently reappointed to that post at Rustaq was murdered by his nephew Sultân b Ahmad b Sa'îd, another of the latter's uncles had grasped the nettle and captured Rustaq. This uncle was none other than Hamud b Azzan who, in the process of capturing Rustaq, had also killed the then leader of the Ya'ariba, Sulaymân b Khalfân b Mâlik and had destroyed *burj al-Mazari'a*, the fort belonging to the Mazaria in Rustaq.[45] Hamud had steadfastly refused even to pardon Ghayth al-Ya'rubî who had come to submit to him but had put the new leader of the Ya'ariba to the sword.[46]

The increasing tribal back-up, now at the disposal of Hamud, had gathered momentum as a result of the alienation of the B Ruwaha in Sumayil by al-Jabri, the rivalry between the latter and another Jabri Shaykh Sarhân b Sulaymân and the personal ambitions of Isa b Salih I al-Harthi. These factors had combined to forge a regrouping of tribes opposed to the growing pretensions of Muhammad al-Jabri who, under the aegis of Sayyida Moza, had continued to champion the aspirations of her nephew and son-in-law, Said b Sultan.[47] Upon Muhammad al-Jabri's death therefore, the whole fragile edifice of Said's authority in Oman was threatened with collapse. With the Wahhabis in the north and Isa I al-Harthi and Sarhan al-Jabri out to bolster their own power bases among the tribes of Oman, Muscat was exposed to yet another attack from Hamud b Azzan. But if a Wahhabi onslaught on Oman was fortuitously pre-empted by the assassination of its leader Turki b Abdallah in 1834,[48] Hamud had to contend with the reaction of the British government in any plans he may have entertained to seize the 'treasure of Oman' (*kanz 'Umân*), the sobriquet now attributed to Muscat by Sayyida Moza.[49] To sound out British opinion Hamud decided to travel personally to Bombay.[50] But in the correspondence that followed his visit, he was categorically informed in the summer of 1834 that if he were to commit as much as a slight act of aggression against Muscat he would be considered as 'an enemy of the British government'.[51] It was apparently at this point, stripped of any vestige of hope (*ya`sa*) of receiving British support, that Hamud adopted a cloak of piety and joined the Ibadi *nahda* movement.[52]

It seems certain that had the British in fact been as indifferent as to who ruled Oman as they had been maintaining so vociferously in the recent past, with Omani politics in disarray after Muhammad al-Jabri's death and with Said and his forces bogged down at Mombasa, Hamud, now the recipient of increasing tribal support, would have found little resistance at Muscat. Only a year before in 1833, the British had declared that they did not give a hoot even if the Wahhabis controlled Muscat. Now, when one of Oman's own seemed poised to take over, what motivated them to come rushing to the rescue of their rediscovered 'old ally'?

As on previous occasions, it was Britain's own commercial and political interests that provided the impetus for this volte-face. It is true that in June 1833 Britain had professed its concern to be confined solely to the maritime commerce of the Gulf declaring that the British authorities were not interested in intertribal squabbles of Arabia. Towards that end Britain had entered into friendly relations with the Wahhabis[53] whilst keeping a watchful eye over developments in northern Oman. At this epoch, in the context of Britain's international rivalry with Russia, the former had also decided to adopt a high visibility policy of emphasising its supremacy in the Gulf while abandoning its former practice of supporting Persia against Russia.[54] But in the Gulf itself Britain had made certain that its options were kept open for any eventuality.

With the changed circumstances of 1834, it had been neither the Wahhabi leaders nor Hamud b Azzan nor any other chieftain of Arabia but the ruler of Muscat who had managed to sign a commercial treaty with a Western power. Said b Sultan, whose star had for some time seemed to be on the wane in Oman and whose aspirations in Zanzibar Britain had for so long chosen to ignore, had surprisingly been able to sign a full-fledged commercial treaty with the emergent United States of America in September 1833 without so much as resorting to any consultations with Bombay.[55]

The significance of the Omani–American Treaty

The importance for Said b Sultan of his treaty with the Americans was such that 'it was with unconcealed pride and gratification that he now for the first time found himself placed on a level with the rulers of the civilised states'.[56] It was this opening, amounting to an unequalled opportunity granted to a rival Western power to challenge British supremacy in the Indian Ocean, coming hot on the heels of the tumultuous chain of events set in train by the Egyptian Muhammad Ali and the repercussions of his entanglements with the French,[57] that obliged Britain to sit up and take more notice of the ruler of Muscat. Said b Sultan had after all shown himself not only to be more tenacious but also more able than other leaders of Arabia. His cooperation would be vital if the Egyptian challenge in Arabia, the reverberations of which were already being felt in Yemen by 1834,[58] was to be repulsed effectively.

Although American traders had been involved in East African trade since at least the last decade of the seventeenth century[59] and although merchants from the port of Salem in Massachusetts had been trading directly with Muscat from the early decades of the nineteenth century,[60] the impetus for the signing of the Omani–American Treaty had its roots for the Omani ruler in primarily military imperatives. When in 1828 the American trader, Edmund Roberts, complained to Said about the commercial impediments suffered by American traders in Zanzibar, the Albusaidi replied that in return for a treaty the United States should provide him 'with bombs and shells' to use against the long-standing enemies of Oman, the Portuguese. At a time when Britain shunned any active involvement in his affairs, it is significant to note the assurances that Said found necessary to seek from the Americans to the effect 'that it was essential that the English government should not know of his designs'.[61]

During this period, Said's main objective seems to have been to bring as much of East African trade as possible under his control and to ensure a smooth flow of this trade. Having subsequently signed an agreement with the Portuguese governor at Mozambique to facilitate trade,[62] the Albusaidi sent military expeditions to the Somali coast[63] and entered into alliances with communities as far afield as the Comoro Islands.[64] He even attempted to forge an association by marriage to Ranavalano, Queen of Madagascar, asking her at the time of proposal to send soldiers for his struggle against Mombasa. But in the replies he received from the Queen and her ministers:

> the Queen said she had been made happy by hearing from one who had long been in friendship with her father,...and wished he could pay [her] a visit...[or] send her a coral necklace of a thousand dollars...[but] because of their law it was contrary for her to marry but there was a young princess that he might have. As for the men, he might have as many as he pleased, and he had only to give them a musket.[65]

Disappointed by the Queen's rejection of his proposal, Said decided not to take up her offer of reinforcements. Instead, 'he offered to allow the Americans to erect factories where they pleased, at Zanzibar or on the East African coast, on condition of their rendering him armed assistance in the prosecution of his plans'.[66] Unfortunately, the American authorities did not take his demands for military aid seriously assuring him that, unlike Britain or France, they had no designs on his territories and that their sole concern was the pursuit of legitimate trade. When the treaty was signed in Muscat on 21 September 1833, one of its terms though was that the Americans were not to sell firearms or gunpowder to anyone at Zanzibar except the government.[67] In the field of commerce the treaty did not offer the Americans any more benefits over and above those that the British already enjoyed under the terms of their 1798 treaty with Oman: 5 per cent import duty and reciprocal 'most favoured nation' treatment for traders and vessels of each nation at the ports of the other.[68] But the news of Said's treaty with the American government 'was received in India with the reverse of pleasure...and Captain Hart was soon despatched [to Zanzibar where Said had proceeded] to observe the state of affairs'.[69]

Upon Hart's arrival in Zanzibar on 31 January 1834, according to the Captain himself:

> [Said] commenced by saying how pleased he was to see an English ship, and when he heard her firing a gun he was delighted, as he was sure she must be a man-of-war. He always considered the English as his best friends, and was happy to see them at all times....I told him the friendship was mutual; that the English had a great regard for him and his subjects, and we were glad to show our sincerity whenever we had an opportunity, and that in saying this I was only speaking the sentiments of my country towards him.[70]

Such assurances rang hollow in view of the opportunity that had arisen only a few months earlier for a show of that 'sincerity' and in the face of which British 'sentiments' had remained totally unmoved despite the strong possibility that the capital of their 'friend' had run the risk of being invaded by foreign troops!

Nevertheless, Said himself was of course delighted at receiving all this attention. From the beginning of his reign he had been impressed by the power the British wielded both in India and in the field against the French. He had, on many occasions, tried to secure an umbrella of British protection against his enemies. But it was the British who had refused to get embroiled in what they recognised would be complex and costly undertakings in matters tribal and religious of which their officials displayed total ignorance. Now, when their own interests were once again threatened, obliging them to cooperate with the ruler of Muscat, they found him ready and all too willing to please.

Apart from offering his ship *Liverpool*, which ironically from an Ibadi viewpoint was renamed *Imaum* once the British had acquired it,[71] as a present to the King of England, Said 'wished above all things to have an English person always with him to guide him'.[72] He even offered to revoke his treaty with the Americans if the British promised to support him:

> Mr. Edmund Roberts was an old, fat blustering man, and I was glad to sign the treaty to get rid of him, as I did not think it of any importance. I never saw Mr. Edmund Roberts sign it, nor anyone else nor had it any witnesses, they brought the paper to me and I signed it.... If the Americans came to attack me will the English give me support... [I] am willing to give the English everything even [my] country if they wished it. As for the Americans, they [are] nothing to [me], [my] attachment is to the English'.[73]

But the revocation of the treaty would have put the British in the very awkward position of having to defend the Omani ruler against any American protests that would have undoubtedly followed. In these circumstances, it was deemed sufficient that Hart should extract a promise from the Albusaidi never again to enter into treaty relationships with other powers without first consulting the British. Whilst eager to give that promise Said also, somewhat naively, admitted to Hart that he was at that very moment in the process of negotiating a commercial treaty with the French.[74]

As far as the official British reaction to the Omani–American Treaty was concerned, although '[the British] much regretted it...[they were] unable to discover any tenable ground upon which English interference to annul or modify its provisions could be upheld'.[75] Therefore the Omani–American Treaty came to stay as Britain found it could do nothing legitimately to have it annulled nor could it impose its will by force since it was not now dealing merely with tribal rulers of Arabia but the American government. Thereafter, Britain not only had to take cautious note of further developments at Muscat engendered by the internal dynamics of Oman and the situation in Arabia but it also had to guard carefully against being outmanoeuvred commercially in the Indian Ocean from Zanzibar. In both places, it had to reckon with its 'old ally, the Imaum of Muscat'.

THE BRITISH ROLE IN THE RESOLUTION OF THE ALBUSAIDI–MAZRUI CONFLICT

There is no doubt that the British declaration of support for Said b Sultan made openly through the agency of Captain Hart in 1834 was a great boost for the Albusaidi *vis-à-vis* his opponents both internally and externally. The belittling treatment received by his strongest opponent in Oman, Hamud b Azzan, at the hands of the British has already been discussed. But as usual these developments in Oman also found a strong echo reverberated in East Africa.

With the rise of the fortunes of the Albusaid and the corresponding loss suffered by the Mazaria of any foreign backing, coupled with the fact that commerce came to be concentrated increasingly in the hands of Albusaidi agents and associates, many Omani/Swahili leaders in Mombasa began to grow weary of intrigues and rivalries among the Mazaria themselves. The situation was exacerbated at the death of the Mazrui leader Sâlim b Aḥmad in March 1835.[76] In the ensuing and seemingly inevitable and prolonged succession dispute between the deceased's brothers Khamîs and Nâṣir and his son Râshid, the Shaykh of Kilindini, Mu'allim b Mwinyî al-Shâfi'î, and other local leaders decided that their energies and resources had been sufficiently dissipitated by these factional quarrels and journeyed to Muscat seeking Albusaidi assistance.[77]

On their arrival, they found Said in the process of preparing yet another 'expedition' against Mombasa. Encouraged by this breaking of the ranks at Mombasa, Said set sail from Muscat with the onset of the next monsoon in November 1836.[78] Al-Shafi'i, described by the missionary Krapf as 'a crafty personage who often tried to draw me into politics',[79] had an important role to play in the subsequent events. It was through him, albeit after a generous dispensation of gifts, that the Omani ruler garnered the backing of local tribes in Mombasa. Thus, with the way prepared by the Shaykh of Kilindini, the Albusaidi forces backed by Omani groups other than the Mazaria settled in Mombasa, notably the Matâfiyîn,[80] met with little resistance when they landed at Kilindini harbour.[81] By his lavish expenditure the Omani ruler even managed to win over to his side Khamis b Ahmad and Nasir b Ahmad, uncles of the now proclaimed ruler of Mombasa, Rashid b Salim.[82] Faced with the prospect of further defections from the ranks of his supporters, Rashid found he had no alternative but to negotiate with the Albusaidi. Accordingly in February 1837, a convention was concluded, similar in many respects to the pact of 1828, whereby Rashid in return for his recognition of Albusaidi sovereignty over Mombasa was allowed to remain as its *wali*.[83] Only this time the Mazaria were not allowed to reside in Fort Jesus which was now to have a garrison of 500 men under the command of one 'Alî b Mansûr.[84]

With Mombasa's political organisation virtually unaltered and the people of the hinterland little affected by the change of its masters, it mattered little to Said b Sultan if the Mazaria continued to assume the governorship of the town so long as they recognised and deferred to his overlordship and did not hinder the flow of trade. Unfortunately, however, the situation in Mombasa itself had now changed radically as those very groups which had participated in the overthrow of the Mazaria felt intimidated by elements still opposed to the Albusaid.

If Said himself was personally able to forgive and forget the humiliation he had in the past suffered at the hands of the Mazaria, he could not afford to alienate the Shaykh of Kilindini, the Matafiyin or other members of the new coalition in the town. Therefore, when his supporters insisted that Mombasa 'would never be tranquil so long as the family of the Msara remained at the helm',[85] the Albusaidi had no alternative but to take action to appease them. He at first requested Rashid al-Mazrui to resign from his post as *wali* of Mombasa offering him in return the choice of a pension and a villa on Zanzibar, the governorship of Mafia Island or that of Pemba. But Rashid refused all three, this time enticing back to his side his uncles Nasir and Khamis who, despite personal rivalries with their nephew, were agreed that the governorship of Mombasa should continue to remain a prerogative of the Mazaria as it had been since Ya'ariba days.[86] Fearful of yet another regrouping by the Mazaria against him now that they were reunited, Said decided that the time had come to eliminate this deeply implanted challenge to his authority and to remove once and for all the thorn for so long embedded in the flesh of his reign and that of his predecessors. With the participation of his powerful *wali* in Zanzibar, Sulaymân b Hamad b Sa'îd Âl-bûsa'îdî[87] and his son Khâlid, Said devised a plot whereby the Mazaria were seized and twenty-five of their leaders were reputedly sent in chains to prison in Bander Abbas where they all purportedly perished.[88]

Nonetheless, these extreme measures did not herald the end of the Mazrui opposition to the Albusaid for several of their leaders did manage to escape and sought sanctuary with their kinsmen already established at Takungu.[89] Others created new settlements for themselves in Gazi along the southern coast of Mombasa.[90] Unable to challenge the Albusaidi authority in Said's lifetime, they were later to re-emerge as an irritant to his descendants and were ultimately to play an indirect part in the final dismantling of the Omani power base in Africa by the Europeans. This part derived from the legacy of the inevitable resentment that they nursed against the Albusaid. Furthermore, the memory of the treacherous ruse employed by Said b Sultan to lure the Mazaria leaders to their deaths, when he had been manifestly incapable of defeating them in open battle, became engraved upon the collective Mazrui psyche. To this day, the mythology of the 'golden age of Mombasa under the Mazaria' that Said unwittingly helped to create has been perpetuated and lingers on to be periodically recreated in the popular folk-tales of Mombasa.

8 The 'Omani' and the 'Indian' roles in the nineteenth-century commercial expansion

One of the difficulties faced by researchers in the nineteenth century history of Zanzibar is the paucity of source material available before the arrival of the Europeans and the North Americans. Apart from oral traditions, Zanzibari written sources for that period are virtually non-existent. As late as 1859 the British consul Rigby, in his attempt to unravel the convoluted relationships of the Omani rulers with other members of the Albusaid, let alone those with their Arab, Swahili, Indian or African followers, was lamenting:

> Everything is arranged verbally in open Durbar; Arabs have a great aversion to writing; no records of any sort are kept at Zanzibar, the most important affairs are settled...without any written proceedings.[1]

Thus, since most accounts on Zanzibar are based mainly on consular reports and narratives of Western travellers and missionaries, the general impression received is that there was a spontaneous burst of commercial activity starting from the 1840s when Said b Sultan allegedly moved his capital to Zanzibar.

However, these consuls, travellers and missionaries had a negligible knowledge of Zanzibari affairs, the majority of them not arriving in Africa until late into the first half of the nineteenth century. Their much vaunted travels and their subsequent participation in African affairs were later to be incongruously described as the 'Great Discovery' of Africa as if this 'discovery' had somehow escaped the indigenous inhabitants or long-time residents from other areas. Perhaps the significance of this so-called 'discovery' lay in the way African history came to be recorded in the written traditions of the West since it was mainly to writers and readers of these traditions that Africa had remained the 'Dark Continent'. Since the demise of the Romans at Carthage followed by the Islamic conquests of North Africa from the eighth century onwards, it had been Europe which had been separated from Africa by a belt of Muslim territory stretching from Morocco on the Atlantic coast to Egypt on the Red Sea and the Indian Ocean beyond, despite the maintenance of a few commercial contacts. If the West throughout this period had turned inwards to absorb and assimilate its 'barbarian invaders', traders from Arabia, India and other parts of the Indian Ocean had continued to follow patterns evolved long before the seventh century rise of Islam. As noted earlier, these merchants had traded and intermingled with the indigenous populations of the eastern shore of Africa, giving rise to the now so important 'Swahili' culture and language.[2]

ROLE OF MUSCAT IN THE RISE OF ZANZIBAR

In the nineteenth century East African context, given such a background it is very difficult to determine, by superimposing later notions of statehood or nationality, what part was actually played by various mercantile communities involved in the commercial expansion of Oman and to give due recognition to the pivotal role of the two Omani international ports, Muscat and Zanzibar. Many writers, by their insistence on separating the 'Indian' or 'Swahili' from the 'Omani', even during the early period, give distorted views of the Omani role. They equate 'Omani' with what they term the 'Arab role' which they attribute to the activities of Said b Sultan and of later Omani migrants to East Africa. In this, many of them tend to overlook the fact that the Mazaria, Nabahina, Mashaqisa, Manadhira, Barawina and various other tribes of Omani origin were firmly established in East Africa long before the nineteenth century. Even if sections of these tribes had by the advent of the nineteenth century become 'swahilised' to varying degrees, they considered themselves just as 'Omani' or as 'Zanzibari' as the Albusaid. Indeed, most of the 'Indians' migrating from Muscat also regarded themselves as part of the Albusaidi 'Omani' or 'Zanzibari' entity.

In the commercial field, it is clear that traders from Muscat, Sur and other parts of Oman – whether Arab, Indian, African, Swahili, Baluchi or other – had been involved in East African trade long before the turn of the nineteenth century. However, the commercial impetus that Muscat gave to Zanzibar is in most accounts either simply ignored, awarded nothing more than a cursory glance or misinterpreted. Thus we find that recognised authorities in the East African field such as Cooper conclude somewhat naively, without any analysis of Muscat's role, that by the nineteenth century:

Zanzibar had become the center of the old Omani trading network as well as an agricultural center, while the commercial economy of Oman had not developed beyond its eighteenth century bounds. By mid-nineteenth century Oman was in decline, unable to maintain the eastern end of its trade roots.[3]

Similarly Nicholls, in her conclusion, states that 'in the first half of the nineteenth century the Swahili Coast was able to respond to opportunities for economic development in a manner that would have been impossible for a country like Oman'.[4] As recently as 1987, Sheriff, while recognising the Indian component in both the Muscati and the Zanzibari 'merchant classes', avoids any discussion of Omani rulers' special relationships with the most prominent members of these classes. And although he does not examine the nature of the role played by the Muscati merchant classes, he confidently asserts that 'settlement by Indian merchants in East Africa had preceded the shift of Said's capital to Zanzibar and was due to causes independent of the Sultan'.[5] As already shown, the role and the fate of the Muscati merchant classes were inextricably intertwined with those of the Albusaid and the special relationship between them had a crucial bearing on the shift from Muscat to Zanzibar which was motivated for their mutual benefit in the face of competition from their formidable rival in India, the British East India Company.

As for the role of Muscat, Sheriff declares that 'during the nineteenth century Oman...appears to have been economically stagnant or declining, particularly with the migration of many well-to-do merchants and landowners and the transfer of the capital to Zanzibar'.[6] However, it cannot simply be deduced that this transfer automatically signified a corresponding abandonment of all commercial interests by these merchants in Muscat. It is perhaps worth repeating the vital point that the Albusaidi relationships were mainly with merchants from Kutch and Sind provinces which were not incorporated into the British India political domain. Having by now lost their interests in areas like Mysore and the Gulf to the British, it was crucial for the Muscati merchant classes, which included the Albusaid, to safeguard or strengthen what commercial interests remained to them in the Indian Ocean region. At a time when Britain showed little interest or did not yet realise the commercial potentialities of the East African coast, the move by the Muscati merchants to the rising port of Zanzibar seems, in retrospect, to have been a most economically sound course of action.

Since the Ya'ariba days, merchants and rulers from Muscat, Sur and other parts of Oman as well as those from India and Africa itself, unhindered in their commercial pursuits by obstacles such as national frontiers, visas or passports, had been driven nonetheless by a number of political, economic, religious and geographical considerations to channel more and more trade towards Zanzibar. However, in the subsequent expansion of Indian Ocean trade and the rise of Zanzibar, there was in fact a parallel expansion in the Omani economy in Arabia which was far from having 'declined' as suggested by Sheriff or 'stagnated' as alleged by Cooper 'to its eighteenth century bounds'. The American trader, Edmund Roberts, who had been the driving force behind the 1833 Treaty with Oman and who had been motivated primarily by his ambition to obtain trading privileges for American merchants at Zanzibar, described Muscat's commercial activity during his 1833 visit there in the following way:

> The exports from Muscat are wheat, dates, horses, raisins, salt, dried fish and a great variety of drugs &c &c. Muscat being the key to the Persian Gulf is a place of great resort in the winter months for vessels from the Persian Gulf and the western parts of India.[7]

In fact as far as the export trade was concerned, Zanzibar and Muscat worked hand in hand as Banyan and other merchants attempted to derive the maximum benefits from the demand created by the Western newcomers. Here is how Guillain described this situation writing in 1841:

> In the Zanzibari market, what is not taken by the Americans or the English goes to Bombay and to Muscat; from Muscat [trade commodities] may still find their way to America, if not they are exported to Calcutta or Bombay.[8]

The Zanzibari entrepôt economy

In the external commercial field, long before the negotiations during the 1820s that were to lead to the Omani–American Treaty, the majority of imports at Zanzibar were from India and Oman and consisted of 'Muscat cloth', dates, dried fish, ghee and beads from Muscat; and 'Surat cloth', iron bar, sugar, rice and chinaware from Bombay and other Indian ports, the total value of all imports amounting to MT$1,100,000.[9] Export items at the beginning of the nineteenth century, in addition to ivory and slaves, consisted of mangrove poles, grain, hides and wax to Muscat and Sur[10]; and coconuts, coir, copal, wax, cowry shells, turtle shells and rhinoceros hides and horns to India either directly or via the Omani ports of Muscat and Sur.[11] In this external trade, largely carried by Muscati, Suri, Zanzibari and Indian dhows, Zanzibar already by 1811 had emerged as the commercial centre not only for the whole of the East African coastal strip but also for parts of the interior as most of the above items were by then brought to it from the mainland for export.[12]

The most important factor in the trend to centralise trade on Zanzibar was the estabishment of a link between the seaborne dhow trade and the trade routes in the interior of Africa. This coordination was to prove vital to later commercial development.[13] The need to maintain a steady supply of commodities to Zanzibar led to a further opening up of the interior region especially behind the littoral ports opposite Zanzibar long before the arrival of 'European discoverers'. This in turn was conducive not only to the development of these ports but also to the growth of settlements or commercial staging posts along the caravan routes of the interior.[14] Thus it is not surprising that in the few references we have in the sources on the early period, mention is made of coastal traders seeking the cooperation of interior Africans, Swahilis and Omanis in order to supply the expanding market at Zanzibar.

Among the early 'pioneers' on the African mainland, so called because they were fortunate enough to have their names recorded by the early Western visitors, mention in the sources is made of the Khojas Saiyân and Mûsa Mzûrî;[15] and of the Omanis/Swahilis Jum'a b Rajab al-Murjibî;[16] Sâlim b Sayf al-Ḥârthî nicknamed 'Msopora';[17] Snây b 'Âmir al-Ḥârthî;[18] Leif or Sayf b Sa'îd whose mother was a Nyamwezi;[19] 'Âmir b Sa'îd al-Shaqsî;[20] Muhammad b Sâliḥ and his father Sâliḥ al-Nabhânî;[21] Sâliḥ b Hiraimil al-'Abrî;[22] Sa'îd b Muhammad al-Akhbârî;[23] 'Abd-allâh b 'Abd-al-Karîm Jamâl, Ahmad b 'Abd-al-Karîm Jamâl, 'Abd-allâh b Sâlim al-Hârthî, Nâsir b Sâlim al-Hârthî, Sa'îd b Danîn, Muhammad b 'Abd-al-Qâdir , Sayf b Sa'îd al-Ma'marî, Sa'îd b Mâjid al-Ma'marî, 'Abd-al-'Âl and Ibn Ḥabîb described by Burton as 'Shiahs of Bahrayn', Ahmad b Ibrâhîm al-'Âmirî, 'Îsa b Ḥusayn, Khamîs b 'Uthmân, Ḥasan b Ibrâhîm and 'Abd-allâh b Jum'a al-Ḥârthî.[24] If nothing else, this list gives some indication of the extent of the participation by coastal traders in the trade of the African mainland in the first half of the nineteenth century.

Likewise, the interior African involvement in this trade was also well established by the turn of the nineteenth century. South of Kilwa, eighteenth century trade had been conducted through a network of relay systems which were later boosted by Zanzibari demands to develop into fully fledged trading expeditions along whole lengths of the existing or newly forged trade routes. Apart from the participation of the Yao in the Macuana hinterland, the French trader Morice described the slaves reaching Kilwa in the 1770s as 'com[ing] from quite a long way, of 200 leagues or thereabouts'.[25] The significant point in Morice's account is that African groups were by then so advanced and dominant in the commercial economy that they felt able to impose measures designed to preserve their monopoly on trading activities in areas under their control. The Frenchman states that he was informed by Swahili and Arab traders who frequented the interior that 'Africans do not allow those on this side of the river to go and trade on the far side'.[26] Another source cites the practice, already adopted by coastal traders, of borrowing goods from prominent merchants on the coast to exchange for commodities in the interior:

> The people borrow from the merchants and take many trade goods, and go to their former homes up-country: there they buy ivory and slaves. When they return from up-country, they give their goods to the merchants....The third trade is this: the people borrow goods and go inland to the Makonde and buy copal.[27]

Swahilis and Arabs of course had their own share in this eighteenth century trade:

> The Moors [Swahilis] can go everywhere. The Moors and the Arabs go to the mainland to trade with the Africans. The Arabs who go there dress like Moors, and...they go as far as the sweet water sea [Lake Nyasa].[28]

Significantly Morice also notes that 'the Africans recognise the need they have of the Moors. The well-to-do cannot do without all the materials that the Moors have been bringing them for 300 years'.[29] With regard to coastal merchants frequenting the mainland three centuries before the nineteenth, there is indeed corroborative evidence that Arab traders were involved in the commerce of Mutapa, East of Sofala, in the sixteenth and seventeenth centuries.[30]

A regional system of trade networks had also developed north of Kilwa by the turn of the nineteenth century involving Africans, Swahilis, Arabs and Indians.[31] By 1811, trade routes in these networks extended at least as far as Mount Kilimanjaro.[32] In this hinterland, Baxter tells us that Arabs around Pangani 'planted extensively the coconut, an import from India, and the betel-nut and sugar cane' for commercial purposes during the eighteenth century, an activity which, according to Baxter, they had been pursuing for centuries before.[33] Also, certain goods originating on the coast such as chinaware found their way as far as Buganda during the eighteenth century.[34] In the hinterland of Mombasa, due to demographic pressures and ecological factors, the Kamba also became involved in commercial activities, at first hunting for ivory and producing agricultural goods for the passing caravans. But as competition in trade intensified they, like the Gogo, started charging tolls on caravans traversing their territories whilst supplying them with the necessary provisions.[35] The link between the Kamba and coastal traders was apparently provided by the Mijikenda who, it will be recalled, had special relations with the Mazaria and other Omani/Swahili groups. As Sheriff puts it, 'the convergence of these two forces [the two extremes of the long-distance trade routes] was probably primarily responsible for the vaulting of the *nyika* wilderness that opened up a vast hinterland for Mombasa.[36]

From these beginnings, with the supply side of the internal trade geared for the most part to the provision of slaves for the French plantation colonies and of ivory for India, the whole of the interior caravan network received an enormous boost in the nineteenth century. Later when other merchants, particularly the Americans, decided to engage more heavily in the Indian Ocean commerce, new and more extensive markets were thereby created for local African and other Indian Ocean regional products. An important consequence of this was the growing commitment of the interior peoples of Africa (and of Arabia and parts of India as hereafter explained) not only to the Indian Ocean trade but now also to international commerce as a whole. African and Swahili peoples, notably the Makua in the south or those living near Lake Nyasa, the Yao, the Nyamwezi and others such as the Luguru, the Shomvi, the Zaramo, the Gogo, the Jiji and the Kamba, moved with the changing tide when they discerned that their goods were meeting with increasingly greater demand at outlets serving Zanzibar. In this way, three important trade networks took on a clearer shape and expanded to supply the demands of the international port that Zanzibar had in the nineteenth century become.

The development of African trade routes

Starting at the port of Kilwa Kisiwani, soon to be supplanted by neighbouring Kilwa Kivinje, the southern network led to Tungi Bay near Cape Delgado and inland to areas surrounding Lake Malawi and Central Africa beyond.[37] A central network of trade routes bordered to the east by the Mrima coast ports such as Bagamoyo and Sadani, extended through central Tanzania to regions along Lakes Tanganyika and Victoria and continued as far as Uganda in the north-east, eastern Zaire in the west and northern Zambia in the south-west. Of Zanzibar's total imports from the African mainland more than half came through

the trade routes of this central network.[38] The northern network had as
its ports places like Pangani and Mombasa and stretched inland as far as
Mount Kilimanjaro, across Kenya to Lake Victoria and through the
Somali ports up to the frontiers of Ethiopia in the north.[39]

With the mushrooming of the internal networks, the conventional
opinion is that 'settlements of Arabs and coastal Africans sprang up
along the routes, the resident traders flying the red flag of Uman and
Zanzibar and considering themselves part of the political–economic
system which centred on Said bin Sultan's African capital'.[40] Although
there was naturally an increase in the number of 'Arab' and 'Swahili'
traders penetrating into the interior, from the beginning they were
accompanied by Khojas and Banyan customs officers who must have
already been conversant with at least the coastal sections of the routes.
Curiously, some Khojas like Musa Mzuri are said to have become
'leading member[s] of the *Arab* community of Unanyembe' and surprisingly by a recognised Western authority on Zanzibar affairs such as
Bennett.[41] Nearly a century and a half earlier Albrand, in his attempt to
distinguish between the various peoples of Zanzibar, described them as
'these Moors [Swahilis], just like the Arabs are Shi'i Muslims, that is to
say, from the sect of [Imam] Ali'.[42]

Such statements coming from leading historians in the field, in their
own time, show not only the extent of the confusion resulting from the
mélange of the ethnic, national and religious make-up of the 'Swahili'
or for that matter the 'Omani'; they also indicate the futility of
attempting to identify the 'Omani', the 'Swahili' or the 'Indian' (let
alone the various sub-divisions of each grouping) within the generic
racial terms of 'Arab', 'African' or 'Indian' at this early stage when
European notions of political organisation and demarcation had not yet
been superimposed upon their existing structures. Furthermore, according to the available sources there was no sudden 'springing up' at this
time of 'Arab settlements' as the narrative of Ḥamad al-Murjibî (Tippu-
Tip) clearly shows. 'Arabs' had been in these localities before and, as
in former times, they lived and cooperated with other inhabitants, each
community functioning within the confines of its own sphere of
influence but all striving to gain from this expansion in commercial
activity despite intermittent quarrels among local rulers.[43]

It is important to bear in mind that these local rulers in interior Africa
included 'Swahilis' originating from Oman such as, for example, Jum'a
b Rajab al-Murjibî, Tippu-Tip's grandfather, who was an ally of
Mirambo's grandfather and, like the two grandsons later on in the
century, wielded enormous influence among local people.[44] The label

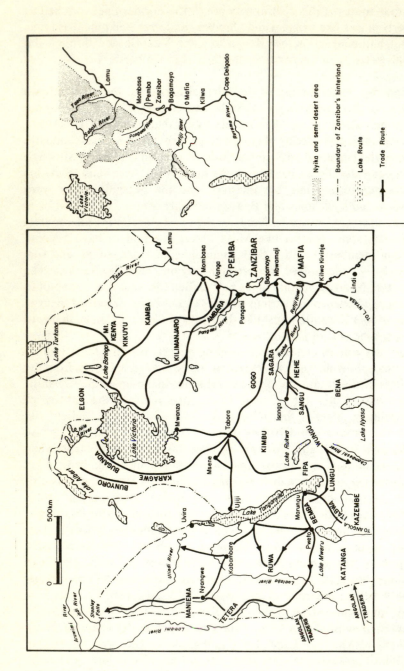

Map 8: East Africa: trade routes (c. 1873) and the Nyika.
Source: After Sheriff, A.M.H., 1987

of 'Arab settlements' as distinct from African or Swahili ones was a much later concept adopted to satisfy Western notions of categorisation. Such characterisations were introduced when the Westerners first began to intervene in Zanzibari affairs and were later reinforced by European colonialists.

Although the various mercantile communities and tribes in East Africa formed part of the integrated commercial system, this does not imply that all members had equal rights or shares within the system. The Omani tribal system of government, described by one nineteenth century British official as 'a crude system of patronage',[45] was stratified throughout with the ruler at the top of the social hierarchy even though he is said to have addressed his 'subjects' during his public audiences 'more as an equal than as a superior'.[46] Moreover, this system was never rigid and, as already shown, many other tribal leaders constantly challenged the power of the ruler. It was also quite possible for members from social backgrounds regarded as 'low' within the social hierarchy to move up to influential positions. The appointment of Baluchis as commanders, slaves as *walis* and Banyans as customs masters are cases in point. Within this flexible system, each community or tribe and even individuals recognised their 'status' and behaved accordingly. The important point is that they were all part of the system which had been functioning for centuries until it was dismantled, in the last decades of the nineteenth century, by European imperialism.

The Zanzibari agricultural economy

As a result of these early developments the Zanzibari entrepôt economy began to assume new dimensions. But the agricultural one, in existence also for centuries before, retained its importance. Zanzibaris were well accustomed to the cultivation of crops such as cassava, millet, rice and sugar. And despite the fact that in the early nineteenth century 'nothing can exceed the profusion of fruits abounding in every quarter, all of them excellent [but] left to rot on the ground that produced them',[47] (a fact also sadly noted in 1986 by this visitor), by 1811 only coconut products in the agricultural field contributed to the export trade.[48] With the arrival of new waves of migrations from Oman and India, those merchants involved in Muscat's commerce, being well acquainted with the export potential of Omani date cultivation and with the value of the traditional spice trade, could see for themselves the boost given by the French to their sugar and clove plantation economies in their island colonies.

As far as cloves were concerned, already by 1800 the French islands were producing them on a commercial scale with Ile de France (Mauritius) exporting some 20,000 lb annually.[49] But the export duties at that time paid for them by traders in Zanzibar were as high as 15 per cent.[50] During the same period the southern slave trade to the Mascarene Islands, based on Kilwa and dominated by Zanzibari merchants, collapsed as a result of the Napoleonic Wars. The resulting loss of a market of about 2,000 slaves per annum nearly halved the 1780s' level of slave prices which plunged to MT$20 per slave by 1822.[51] The situation was further exacerbated by the imposition of the antislavery policies pursued by the British early on in the century. This meant that there was a glut of slaves in the market place. Therefore, from the first decade of the nineteenth century three interrelated factors converged, encouraging Zanzibari traders to start experimenting with cloves and other export crops: their search for a greater share of the historically lucrative spice trade still monopolised by the Dutch from the Moluccas; the fact that they had by now seen at first hand the success of the French plantation economy in an African island environment similar to their own and the need to put slaves to a more profitable use.

Apart from cloves, cinnamon, coffee and nutmeg were introduced and sugar cane was 'extensively cultivated' before 1811.[52] There can be no doubt that this attempt to diversify the Zanzibari economy before the British antislaving measures had a stimulatory effect on this economy was a deliberate and conscious decision as evidenced by Said b Sultan's despatch to his agent in Bombay: 'In consequence of the abolition of the slave trade the collections [revenue] of Zanzibar have been diminished; it has therefore been deemed necessary to make plantations of sugar cane in the islands'.[53] Although the Omani ruler did not yet know it, it was the plantation of cloves during this period that was to prove vital to the expansion of the Zanzibari economy.

As it transpired, notwithstanding the failure in the production for export of some of the crops grown at the beginning of the nineteenth century such as sugar, in the case of cloves both Zanzibar and dependent Pemba proved that they had environments suitable enough to make them eventually the world's leading producers of the spice. As for the profitability of the trade in this spice, as late as 1834 by the time the Dutch monopoly over it had started to crumble, it was apparently yielding a profitability of over 1,000 per cent on its original cost of production.[54]

It is not clear though when exactly or under whose initiative the clove seed was first introduced into Zanzibar. East African traditions give the credit to the Omani Ṣâliḥ b Hiraimil al-'Abrî who, according to some, obtained the shoots from other would-be candidates, the Frenchmen Sausse or Desplant in La Reunion (Bourbon) in the late eighteenth or early nineteenth century. Alternatively it may have been, as al-Mughairi claims, one 'Abd-Allâh al-'Ajamî who was allegedly sent by Said b Sultan specifically for the purpose of bringing clove seedlings to Zanzibar from Ile de France.[55] Nonetheless, given the fact that most of the cloves were destined for India and merchants from India had for long been predominant in East African and Indian Ocean commerce, the initiator may well have been an 'Indian' or an 'Omani' from India. Be that as it may, the fact is that by 1822 clove-bearing trees were already as high as 15 feet in some areas of Zanzibar.[56] To reach that stage clove trees require at least seven to eight years and, according to Tidbury, do not give high yields until they are over 20 years old.[57] Therefore, they must have been planted in Zanzibar during, at the latest, the first decade of the nineteenth century.

Bombay trade figures show that small quantities of cloves were imported from East Africa right from the beginning of the nineteenth century.[58] It is reasonable to assume that, in this era, these found their way there via Zanzibar from the Mascarene Islands. There do not seem to be any production figures for the very early period for Zanzibar itself. However, the fact that this activity rocketed whilst experiments with other products, such as cinnamon or sugar, were pursued with less vigour proves that clove plantation must have been a lucrative business from its very inception. In this way the Omani ruler together with his associates, other traders and cultivators recognised and exploited a developing trend. It is only in this light that the Omani ruler Said b Sultan may be given the credit for being responsible, at least in part, for transforming clove cultivation into the overriding economic and social factor which, to this day, governs and shapes the lives of the inhabitants of Zanzibar and Pemba.

During the 1820s Bombay was importing increasing amounts of cloves and on a more regular basis from the African coast, significantly, via Muscat and Kutch,[59] that is to say nearly a decade before Said b Sultan decided to have a residence built for him in Zanzibar. Averaging about MT$4,600 in the 1820s, the value of Bombay's annual clove imports from East Africa alone rose to MT$25,000 by the 1840s.[60] Exports of the spice to the United States from Zanzibar also increased from a value of US$1,270 in 1830 to US$24,000 in 1839.[61]

By 1835 when Said b Sultan himself had reputedly acquired some forty-five plantations, the American visitor Ruschenberger remarked that cloves 'are found to thrive so well that almost everybody on the island is now clearing away the coconut to make way for them'.[62] As for Pemba, Guillain informs us that clove cultivation was first started there in 1839.[63] A decade later the island was producing some 35,000 lb of the spice.[64] However, due to the imposition of taxes on Pemba cloves and the decline in prices resulting from overproduction by the mid-century, Pemba did not become a major producer of the spice until after the devastating hurricane of 1872. The hurricane, which barely touched Pemba, destroyed more than two-thirds of the clove trees on Zanzibar.[65]

Slave labour and the Zanzibari economy

In the 'mania' of clove plantation during the 1830s,[66] the Zanzibari agricultural economy received a shot in the arm, ironically so, from the hullabaloo surrounding the British slave trade prohibition campaign. The vagaries and vicissitudes of this campaign are beyond the scope of this work and have in any case given rise to many a publication.[67] The 1822 ban on the export of slaves to British India and Christian nations had no effect on the numbers coming into Zanzibar. And though slave exports to Arabia, Persia and India continued even after the introduction of the 1845/7 measures which forbade slave exports to these places, the slave sector itself had by then undergone a profound transformation in Zanzibar and Pemba. Increasing numbers of slaves were now being used on the islands for the labour-intensive cultivation and harvesting of agricultural produce and in other commercial pursuits, as will be seen later on. In 1811, of an estimated number of 15,000 slaves arriving in Zanzibar, 7,000 were retained on the island and the rest exported. For 1844, the estimated figures were 20,000 arrivals with 5,000 retentions. The corresponding figures for 1860/1 were 19,000 arrivals and 10,000 exports.[68] Thus for the first six decades of the nineteenth century, an oscillating figure of between 25 and nearly 50 per cent of slaves reaching Zanzibar were retained there to provide cheap labour for the evolving economy.

As already discussed above, trade in slaves in the Indian Ocean area had been a pre-Islamic activity dating back into the realms of antiquity. Contrary to popular opinion perpetuated by the Atlantic slave trade from West Africa, the Indian Ocean slave trade did involve not only black African slaves but also the paler-skinned Indian, Circassian, Georgian and other slaves and concubines.[69] Nor was this trade one way from Africa only. In the nineteenth century continuing Franco–British rivalry for commercial hegemony, it is interesting to note the reaction of the French authorities to the basically British-imposed ban on the slave trade. Although we are not concerned here with the system of 'engages libres' that the French devised whereby Zanzibari slaves were made to 'volunteer' to go to French colonies before payments could be made to their owners, the fact that the French initially looked for ways of importing labour from Muscat is relevant. With the British at first preocccupied at the East African end and before they could take effective action in the aftermath of the 1839 Agreement with Said b Sultan to stop slave exports to Mauritius from Zanzibar, some 25,000 'Indian labourers' with a ratio of two women to five men were apparently imported by the French colonies from Muscat, India and Madagascar in the period between 1834 and 1839.[70] However, the 1839 British Act of Parliament forbidding the emigration of 'labourers' from India was revoked soon after by the 15 January 1842 Queen's Order in Council which permitted renewed emigration from India on an indenture basis. In the following year, 1843, 35,000 'Indian labourers' were thus taken from the above-mentioned places, including Muscat, to Bourbon and Mauritius.[71]

At the time, the French also had plans to import labour from China, 'the celestial empire, full to the brim with population' and further to 'encourage emigration to Mauritius of natives from India, Madagascar, Muscat and other countries with their families'.[72] Such measures on the part of the French prompted many Swahilis, Omanis and Indians, residing in or having connections with Muscat, to migrate to the Mascarene Islands not only from Zanzibar but also directly from Oman and India. Said b Sultan had to make special pleas to both the French and British authorities to ensure that the rights of 'Omanis' were upheld and properly looked after by the relevant authorities in the French islands.[73] As for 'slaves' from India, these were sold at Muscat, Zanzibar and other ports of the Gulf during the 1840s and the British consul Rigby mentions cases of Indian girls sold openly in the market at Zanzibar as late as 1860.[74]

MUSCAT AND ZANZIBAR: THE RESURGENCE OF THE OMANI ECONOMY

As far as the economy and social life in Zanzibar were concerned, the ban on the slave trade went far beyond affecting just the provision of cheap labour. It interfered with the day-to-day lives of the well-to-do as 'slaves' were used for a multitude of purposes from basic household servitude to military and protective duties. Thus, it is not surprising that influential individuals like Ahmad b Nu'mân b Muhsin al-Ka'bî, personal secretary to Said b Sultan, when hearing of this ban retorted disbelievingly: 'Arabs have carried on the [slave] trade since the days of Noah. Arabs must have slaves'.[75] At this juncture, it must be emphasised that Omani and Hadrami Arabs in Zanzibar never referred to labourers on their plantations as *'abîd* (slaves) but always as *khuddâm* (servants) although conversely domestic servants and concubines, according to some informants, were at times regarded as *abid*.[76]

The slave trade in Oman

Muscat, which together with Sur was the principal destination and port of transit for these slaves, was described by Sir John Malcolm during his 1800 visit as having 'vile narrow streets with strings of slaves for sale'.[77] Ten years later, Maurizi added that 'black slaves are constantly to be purchased in the bazaar...of Muscat', with the ruler allegedly drawing an annual revenue at that time of MT$75,000 from the slave trade alone.[78] By 1816 this trade had developed to such an extent that three slave markets per week were held in Muscat with prices ranging from MT$40 to MT$50 per slave.[79] And it had expanded even further by 1833 when 'daily slave sales...[were] made every evening towards sunset'.[80] In Matrah where the people in 1817 were adjudged by one traveller to be 'less Abyssinian looking than those of Muscat',[81] the area where the slave market was held in the south-east corner of what is now described as the old *suq* is to this day known as *Khawr Bembah* (the inlet of Pemba).[82] And just as there is a quarter outside Zanzibar town called *Mnazi Moja* (Ar. *nâzî môyâ* = lit. one palm tree) so there is a place also so called to this day in Matrah where slaves belonging to merchants in the town had their residential quarters.[83]

Of an estimated 1,365 slaves imported into Muscat annually during the 1830s, about half were re-exported while the remaining half were absorbed within the port and its environs.[84] However, despite Sheriff's assumptions and assertions to the contrary, it is impossible from the occasional figures quoted in the sources for Muscat to arrive at an estimate of 1,500 slaves as the total annual figure for the so-called 'northern' slave trade, as he attempts to do.[85] The very sources Sheriff quotes tell us that not only Muscat but Sur also

> are the principal primary ports to which slaves, from whencesoever shipped, whether Zanzibar or the Red Sea, are brought, and whence they are eventually carried into Turkey, Persia, Sind, the Arab States, and even our own territories on the Western coast of India.[86]

Indeed the 1841 table, from which Sheriff takes his figures, clearly indicates that the number of vessels employed for this trade at Sur was more than double that used at Muscat. In the three-month period from

August to October 1841, 36 Suri boats brought 355 slaves while 16 vessels took 166 slaves to Muscat. Furthermore the same source, which itself arrives at a grand total of 3,488 as the annual intake of the 'northern' slave trade, takes the trouble to put the reader upon his or her guard by saying:

> large as this number may appear, it is allowed with regret, that if any error has been made it has been on the side of detraction and not of exaggeration; and it must be further remembered, that it does not include the slaves brought into Muskat for sale on the spot, or for exportation, as before stated, to the ports of Sind, and even India.[87]

The above estimate also does not take into account any slaves that may have been re-exported directly from Sur to Sind or elsewhere. Nor does it make any allowances for a number of Indian slaves sold in the markets of Omani and other Gulf ports.[88] Thus, Sheriff's estimate of 1,500 slaves as the total annual figure for the whole of the 'northern' trade would seem to be an underestimate.

The ownership of plantations and slaves

By the 1840s most of the leading Omani families in Zanzibar, no doubt partly as a result of slave ownership, had become involved in the acquisition of plantations. This of course was nothing new. The Omani conquerer who wrested East Africa from Portuguese control, Sayf b Sultan I al-Ya'rubi (r.1692–1711) possessed such vast estates that he reputedly owned a third of the land and water rights in Oman, qualifying him to earn his *laqab* (sobriquet) of *Qayd al-arḍ* (Master of the Land).[89] He allegedly owned 1,700 slaves who were employed not only to plant some 30,000 date and 6,000 coconut palms but also to construct seventeen new *aflaj* (irrigational channels) and to renovate a number of others.[90] Similarly in nineteenth century Zanzibar, just like their merchant–ruler predecessors, it was in the interests of the Albusaid merchant princes to perpetuate this tradition.

Sulayman b Hamad Albusaidi,[91] Said b Sultan's 'prime minister...and a man of great wealth and personal character [having] more influence here [in East Africa] with the Swahilis and Africans than any other Arab'[92] is said to have owned a staggeringly unbelievable number of 30,000 slaves and 12,000 clove trees[93] which were yielding an annual crop of 210,000 lb of the spice by the end of the 1840s.[94] Said's own plantations yielded nearly 1,050,000 lb at that time and increased to 3,150,000 lb by the mid-century when they provided nearly a third of the total production of the islands.[95] By then members of the Hirth had also become 'proprietors of large landed estates' with their leaders reputedly owning up to 1,500 slaves.[96] 'Almost every one of the Sultan's subjects own[s] slaves, the poorer about five, and the wealthier from 400 to 1,500' wrote British Consul Hamerton in 1841.[97]

Nor was this slave ownership confined to 'Arabs' only. Africans, such as the Nyamwezi, developing into what Unomah describes as 'a new agrico-commercial bourgeiosie', also imported slaves from the Maniema country in eastern Zaire for agricultural purposes. Indeed these slaves were used primarily for the production of foodstuffs for sale to the passing caravans.[98] Many Banyans and other Indians also owned slaves.[99] Jairam Shivji, having by 1843 replaced his brother Ebji as customs master, owned from 200 to 400 slaves while the Omani ruler at the same time is said to have possessed some 12,000.[100] However, Jairam did not use his slaves for cultivation purposes but for military protection and domestic duties. Therefore, in the case of the Banyans, the figures of slave ownership quoted cannot be taken as an indication of the real worth of the slave masters. Furthermore, Banyans were discouraged from personal ownership of slaves by the insistence of British officials that they were British subjects, and as such 'were forbidden to participate in the slave trade' pursuant to the legislation in force governing the participation of British subjects in the slave traffic.[101]

The reason conventionally advanced to explain why few prominent Banyans owned plantations, despite their enormous wealth, is that Banyans did not acquire land because they never settled in regions outside India where they purportedly left their families to whom they always returned. It is proven nonetheless that Banyans did indeed settle, together with their families, in Oman from at least the days of Narutem in the 1640s through to the eighteenth century, when Niebuhr estimated them in 1765 to number 'no fewer than twelve hundred...liv[ing] agreably to their own laws,...bring[ing] their wives hither,...set[ting] up idols in their chambers and burn[ing] their dead',[102] and up to the present day. The fact that they did not acquire plantations in Oman or in Zanzibar until the late nineteenth century, was due in part to the absence of agricultural tradition within their family structure as compared to other 'Omanis' who were accustomed to date cultivation. It was also partly due to the way the whole system of business methods functioned in Oman and East Africa which will be discussed in the next chapter.

Muscat's manufacturing and entrepôt economy

Although Banyans, from the beginning of the nineteenth century, provided credit in the form of advance finance in Oman, and in parts of western India as well as in East Africa, and were thus responsible for injecting an important element of capitalism into the Indian Ocean trade system, they remained throughout more concerned with their primary role as traders rather than as financiers. In Oman, Banyan and other merchants based at Muscat, the port of shipment, employed either their own agents or independent brokers (*dallâl*) working on a commission basis to advance money not only to farmers specialising in date cultivation but also to various manufacturing centres of handicraft industries.

By accepting a part payment of the final price the producers bound themselves, by custom and convention rather than as a matter of strict contractual law, to deliver the required goods at a specified time. This injection of capital funds into industry, operating with largely imported raw materials, had made Matrah the principal cloth-weaving centre of Oman by the 1830s. The main articles, manufactured for both local consumption and export, included *musar* (pl. *misâr* = square woollen or cotton piece of cloth used by Omanis as turbans); *wizâr* (pl. *wizara* = rectangular cotton piece of cloth worn to cover the lower part of the body = the Indian *lungî*); *'abâ`ah* (pl. *'abâ`ât* = black cotton or woollen cloak-like wrap used by women = the Persian *châdôr*); and *bisht* (pl. *bushût* = woollen outer cloak worn by men).[103] There is evidence that these types of cloth had been exported from Muscat to East Africa from the eighteenth century and conceivably prior to that era.[104] In the nineteenth century, Fraser, on his visit to Muscat in July 1821, left us this description of Omani textiles:

> Omaun is by no means celebrated for its manufactures. Turbans and waistbands, or girdles of cotton and silk, striped or checked with blue, and having the ends ornamented with red, green or yellow borders; cloaks called abbas, of sheep's wool or camel's hair, of various degrees of fineness; cotton canvas...these comprise their fabrics.[105]

Fifteen years later Wellsted described Matrah as 'a considerable town [where the] principal employment is weaving cloth, or fabricating the woollen cloaks so generally worn in Arabia...[and where there was] scarcely a hut but contained its spinning wheel, with a female busily employed before it'.[106] These females included even the ruler's mother, Ghani bint Sayf, for when Pauline Helfer visited the Albusaidi household in 1836, 'the Imaum's mother was simply dressed and busy at sewing...which she said she had learnt from European ladies'.[107] Apart from Matrah, the Bilad-Bani-Bu-Hasan region of Sharqiya also had a major silk-weaving industry.[108]

Closely related to these textile industries was the manufacture of embroidered caps (Ar. = *qohfîya* = Om. *kumma* = Sw. *kofiyya* or *kumma* = In. *tôpî*), widely worn by Omanis and Zanzibaris and now forming a part of both the Omani and the Zanzibari national dress. Although these caps have recently been replaced by the cheaper machine-made versions imported from China and retailing at a price of between RO (Rial Omani) 2 and RO10 (£4 and £20), it is the hand-woven cotton ones that have been traditionally, and are still, particularly sought after by the affluent classes. Because of the element of time and skill involved in making the latter ones, their price nowadays ranges from RO30 to RO100 (£60 and £200) per cap.[109]

During the nineteenth century these embroidered caps were made not only in Matrah, Suhar and Sur in Oman but in Zanzibar, Mombasa and other parts of East Africa as well (this tradition in East Africa, as personally witnessed in 1986, is still being carried out in Zanzibar, Pemba and Mombasa). In his portraits of Omanis and Swahilis drawn between 1846 and 1848, Guillain clearly shows that both caps and turbans (*musar*) were widely worn as head dress in Zanzibar before 1850.[110] Burton, a bit later, remarked that 'respectable Waswahili dress like Arabs in Koffiya'.[111] Moreover, he has left us the following description of the trade in this head-gear in East Africa:

> The skull-caps are of two kinds. One is a little fez, locally called kumma and costing between MT$5 to MT$9 per dozen. The other, the cheaper kind is preferred in Unyamwezi; it is carried up from the coast by Arab slaves [?] and Waswahili merchants and is a favourite wear with the [local] sultan and the mtongi. At Unyanyembe the price of the fez rises to one dollar. The 'Alfiyya' is the common Surat cap, worked with silk upon a cotton ground; it is affected by the Diwans and the Shomwis of the coast.[112]

Interestingly some Omani merchants, following in their forefathers' footsteps and specialising to this day in this embroidered cap trade, insist that the best ones traditionally came from Zanzibar. 'Zanjbari Topi was the best' is the view repeatedly expressed by Khoja merchants of Matrah in many a recent interview.[113] In Zanzibar, on the other hand, where people because of their relative poverty have been more receptive in recent times to cheaper Chinese imports, it is still believed that the best-quality caps have always come from Oman.[114]

Another activity connected with the textile industries was that of the dyers (Om. *ṣabbâgh* = In. *khattrî*) who were primarily involved in dyeing cloth with the ubiquitous and ever popular blue indigo dye (Om. *nîl*). With the probable exception of Dhofar, this activity was spread throughout Oman. Apart from Matrah, the main centres were Ibri, Bahla, Firq and Sur, and to a lesser extent Nizwa, Hamra, Ibra and Rustaq. Many of these places made use of the Omani- manufactured dye extracted from plants cultivated specifically for the purpose or which grew wild locally.[115] So widespread and popular was this activity in the eighteenth century that the last 'elected' Albusaidi Imam, Said b Ahmad (r.1783–9), alienated many Omani tribes and mercantile communities when he monopolised the dyeing industry at Nizwa and imposed taxes on others wishing to pursue it.[116] Notwithstanding that this was a contributory factor to the Imam's downfall and to the assumption of power at Muscat by his son Hamad,[117] the indigo dyeing industry continued to flourish throughout the nineteenth and twentieth centuries and is still today practised in Matrah, Bahla and Ibri. Some Khoja and other merchants in Matrah are to this day referred to by the now Omanised Indian *nisba* of Khattrî.[118]

Other handicraft industries, some of which are still currently known by their Indian equivalent in Oman, included the blacksmiths (Om. *ḥaddâd* = In. *lôwârâ*) who were found in many of the larger towns of Batina and the interior and made hardware items such as copper pots or arms like spear heads, daggers, swords, matchlocks and cannon for the ruler's navy. Jewellers (Om. *ṣâyigh* = In. *sônâra*), allegedly brought from India to Muscat by the Albusaidi rulers in the eighteenth century to manufacture gold and other ornaments for the ruling family, later opened their shops to the general public.[119] Among others, carpenters (Om. *najjâr* = In. *wâdâ*), sandal makers (Om. *raqqâ'* = In. *môchî*), rope makers (Om. *ḥabbâl* = In. *rassaiwâlâ*), porters (Om. *ḥammâl* = In. *hammâlî*), mat makers (Om. *nâsij al-ḥuṣur* = In. *hasirwâla*), water bearers (Om. *mishkî* = In. *pânîwâlâ*) and even barbers (Om. *ḥallâq* = In. *hajjâm*) were involved in this commercial expansion in Oman.[120] In 1835, Edmund Roberts tells us that in Muscat 'Hindoo barbers carry on their trade generally in the streets'.[121] Bread making of the thin flat type, an important part of the Omani diet, was carried out mainly by the 'Ajam (Persian) bakers (Om. *khabbâz* = In. *mânîwâlâ*) who used open clay furnaces (*tannûr*) and who were found in most of the Batina towns.[122] These 'Ajam dominated the bread-baking trade from those times right up to the 1970s when they were recruited to work in the new government departments, having had their trade monopoly broken by the post-1970 trend of bringing into Oman Indian, Pakistani and Bangladeshi bread makers by the new breed of Omani entrepreneurs.

Omani agricultural economy

In the agricultural field, apart from grapes, wine making in the Jabal Akhdar, export of lemons and limes from Sohar and the cultivation of wheat for local consumption,[123] fruit 'is so plentiful that only a tenth of the crop is picked...[and] in few parts of the world can the necessaries, nay even the luxuries of life, be obtained in greater profusion [than in Muscat]'.[124] Refining of sugar was also carried out in Muscat and Nizwa where Omani *halwa* (a confection made of honey, ghee, almonds and sugar) was made and exported to India and Iran.[125]

With regard to dates, some Muscati merchants went in person or sent their agents, at six monthly intervals, to inspect the date-bearing branches of the palm trees in Nakhl, Sumayil and in parts of the Batina and Sharqiya. The *gidd* (time when branches are cut from Ar. *yajiddu* but pronounced in Oman with a hard g) of the *busûr* (yellow dates = In. *khârik*) was in the month of June and that of *tamr* (wet dates also known in Oman as *suh* = In. *khajûr*) took place two months later in August. On both occasions, Muscati merchants or their agents would pay deposits for their orders after negotiating terms with local farmers as to price, quality and quantity of the dates they required. When the dates were ready [in the case of the *busur* they had to be boiled and left to dry on *pallow* (Omanised In. = mat sheeting)], they were transported by camel to Matrah where *zakât* (tax), normally 5 per cent of the total value, was collected for the government.[126] Only after collections of specific advance orders had been completed were the rest of the dates sold off to other brokers for general sale. If any merchants at this stage required more quantities of either type of date, they had now to deal through the appointed brokers.

Most of the *busur*, packed in *gûnîya* (Omanised from In. *gûnî* = jute bag), were shipped to India. But before the *tamr* could be exported, the dates had to be put on a *jirâb* or a *khisfa* (Om. = tightly woven mat with no holes). The small ones of these were then made into a *mîchân* (Om. = date basket), the bigger ones into sacks where the *tamr* were tightly packed by the action of stamping upon them with bare feet. This activity and the subsequent transport by the porters of the sacks of both the *busur* and the *tamr* were carried out mainly by Baluchis and African/ Swahilis who took them in their *hawârî* (sing. *hôrî* = native wooden vessel) and loaded them onto ships for export.[127]

Apart from India, the places where the *tamr* were destined for included Java, Mocha, East Africa, the Mascarene Islands and the USA.[128] Although unfortunately no figures exist for this early date trade, its importance is reflected and reiterated in the accounts of most

Western visitors to Oman at the beginning of the nineteenth century.[129] There is also evidence that already by 1843, companies in the USA, which was to become by the latter half of the nineteenth century an important importer of Omani dates, were sending ships from Salem and New Bedford to load dates at Muscat.[130] In India, the town of Mandvi in the province of Kutch, from which the Shivji Topan Family originated and where Sindi merchants whose ruler had been a special ally of Said b Sultan's father were predominant in the commercial sphere, it was described as early as 1818 as 'the principal sea-port and the most populous town in Cutch'.[131] In its 'brisk trade with Arabia, Bombay and the Malabar coast in which upwards of 800 boats of from 40 to 50 candies tonnage are employed', we are told that large quantities of 'kharik and khajoor were imported from Maskat'.[132]

9   Beginnings of the integration of Muscat and Zanzibar into the world economy

In the early decades of the nineteenth century, a system of credit similar in its essentials to the one described in the preceding chapter for Oman also existed in Kutch and East Africa. This system was controlled at the three outlets of Mandvi, Muscat and Zanzibar and was linked to Bombay by merchant groups or their agents who dominated the triangular East Africa–Gulf–western India maritime trade network. Interestingly this triangular network, using Omani ports as entrepôt stages for the re-export of East African goods to India and further afield towards the east, was described by al-Mas'ûdî as early as the tenth century:

> The land of Zanj produces wild leopard skins. The people wear them as clothes, or export them to Muslim countries. They are the largest leopard skins and the most beautiful for making saddles.... It is from this country that come [ivory] tusks weighing fifty pounds or more. They usually go to Oman, and from there are sent to China and India. This is the chief trade route.[1]

INTRODUCTION OF CAPITALISM IN THE INDIAN OCEAN COMMERCIAL SYSTEM

In nineteenth century Zanzibar, as early as 1843, Arab plantation owners were reported by British Consul Hamerton to have been heavily indebted to 'Indian' money lenders whom they repaid with the produce of their plantations.[2] In Mandvi merchants advanced money to cotton growers further inland to provide the wherewithal to finance the highly lucrative textile industry.[3] Thus in all three ports of shipment of the triangular maritime network, merchants gave financial inducements in return for the provision of not only agricultural produce but also other goods which were in great demand for local consumption or export.

In this general expansion of Indian Ocean trade, the traditionally favoured Banyans came to assume an even more enviable degree of control over the production system of the artisans and agriculturalists. However, their central concern remained the procurement of the final product by the provision of finance and not the day-to-day running or management of the production system itself. Thus they were responsible for the introduction of important elements of capitalism as a system and a force within the trade networks and were instrumental in causing local exchanges to become increasingly monetised. Nonetheless, in their dealings with the Omani rulers at Zanzibar and Muscat, in lending to members of the ruling family and in collecting taxes, they had no formalised system whereby they could institutionalise their public credits into marketable assets and were thus unable to capitalise fully upon their initiative. Accordingly they could not develop into a fully fledged capitalist class, in the Western sense, as they remained dependent on the goodwill of the ruling family for their very *raison d'être*.

Furthermore, having always confined themselves to their own quarters throughout the course of their settlement in Omani territories, they continued to observe the ancient and honoured laws of reciprocity among which adherence to non-ownership of land seems to have been the most compelling. Against such a background a question arises as to why the Banyans, who had been living in Muscat since at least the seventeenth century, started to acquire the legal right to ownership of property only from the nineteenth. The reason may be due partly to surviving concepts at the beginning of the nineteenth century of the early traditions of Omani Ibadi/tribal laws whereby, unlike other Muslims (the *ahl al-qibla*; those who pray towards Mecca), the *mushrikun* (polytheist) Banyans were not allowed to have rights of exclusive ownership. The Banyans were tolerated for trading purposes only in the international ports of Oman where reciprocal taxation arrangements applied to them under *aman* agreements in the same way as they did to Omanis residing abroad.[4] That the Banyans started acquiring property in the late nineteenth century, in Muscat as well as in Zanzibar, was due mainly to the grafting of British legal notions onto the commercial fabric of the Indian Ocean.

As a direct result of the increasingly interventionist policies of the British, Omani Arabs and Swahilis came to be progressively alienated and estranged from the Banyans and were consequently forced to cede their lands, mortgaged initially to these Banyans in return for commercial benefits. Lawatiyas and Khojas, being Muslims, experienced no such problems regarding the ownership of land. '*Sûr Lawâtiya*' (the enclosed residential quarters in Matrah) was acquired by its inhabitants from at least the 1760s,[5] but the Lawatiya exercised no financial clout nor enjoyed commercial privileges as did the Banyan. It was only later during the nineteenth century, with new migrations of commercially affluent Ismaili/Khoja communities to Oman and their intermingling with the Lawatiya of Matrah following the conversion of the former to Ithna'ashari Shi'ism, that the Lawatiyas/Khojas (now recognised as one group) came to gain ascendancy in the Omani commerce.[6] It is not surprising therefore that in Zanzibar where there were no Lawatiya settlements and where Banyans were predominant, early visitors described the 'Arabs' as 'generally the lords of the soil',[7] whereas the Banyans were invariably portrayed as being obsessed with financial investment:

> They can cash drafts upon Zanzibar, Mandavi and Bombay; provide outfits, supply guards and procure the Pagazi or porters who are mostly their employees.... They will also buy up the entire cargoes of American and Hamburg ships. The ivory of the interior is consigned to them, and they purchase the copal from the native diggers.[8]

On the other hand, the 'Arabs', including the Hadramis, some of whom allegedly had the largest slave holdings,[9] were preoccupied markedly with their social status within the stratified Omani society[10] as demonstrated by the number of plantations and slaves they had in their possession. The greater the number of these the more power and prestige the 'Arab' thought he had.[11] Even in later years of successive crises, the 'Arabs' would rather incur more debts by borrowing at very high interest rates from 'Indians' (this time specifically mentioned as Indian Muslims), than relinquish their plantations.[12]

EXPANSION OF THE OMANI ENTREPÔT AND AGRICULTURAL ECONOMY

One of the important consequences of the early experimentation with cash crops in Zanzibar and the subsequent success of clove cultivation was the linking up of the trade routes in the interior of Africa to the maritime trade of the Indian Ocean which was dominated by dhows. To a considerable extent, these dhows operated from or were owned by merchants based in the Omani ports of Sur, Muscat and Zanzibar or the ports of Mandvi and Bombay in western India. With the increasing number of slave arrivals in Muscat and Zanzibar, despite the prohibition measures enforced by Britain, the commercial economies of both places now supplemented to varying degrees by agricultural ones profited from the ready pool of slave labour. At the same time the economies of both ports, that is the economy of Oman as a whole, received a further stimulus from new waves of migration in the first half of the nineteenth century from Gujarat, Kutch and Sind, places which had always had important historical commercial relations with Oman as well as with East Africa.[13]

As far as slave labour was concerned, it meant that rival areas of production, such as the Mascarene Islands which competed with Zanzibar for most regional and local markets, found themselves at a grave disadvantage since those very slave trade prohibition policies, adapted by their home governments in Europe, hindered them by depriving them of the cheap labour necessary to compete successfully with Oman. And though Basra, the rival of Muscat in date cultivation, flooded the Omani market with its produce during the nineteenth century, its dates, regarded as inferior in quality to Oman's own produce, were used mainly in the Batina for cattle-feed while it remained throughout dependent for its slave supplies on the Omani ports of Muscat and Sur.[14]

Expansion of the Zanzibari economy

As described in the previous chapter, slave labour was employed for far more than cultivation purposes. In Oman, this labour (employed more in domestic and professional services just as Indians, Pakistanis, Koreans, Bangladeshis and others have been employed more recently in the 1970s and 1980s) was exploited for a variety of functions including fishing, pearl diving, date cultivating, transport, gathering of natural products and in employments such as water bearing, porterage, and the performance of household and military duties. Similarly in East Africa, as Zanzibar evolved into an international trans-shipment port, slave labour, apart from being employed in agriculture, was used also to perform a multitude of other functions especially in those areas stimulated by the growing demand for both import and export commodities. As the nineteenth century wore on, in addition to being employed in greater numbers as cultivators on the islands, slaves also came to be used increasingly on the mainland as porters, together with the free *pagazi* recruits, and as gatherers of natural products. That so many goods were transported on human shoulders rather than on beasts of burden was due to all sorts of factors ranging from the absence of roads, the lack of use of the wheel in the African interior, the undomestication of the African elephant and the ravages of the tsetse fly which periodically decimated entire herds throughout enormous swathes of the continent.[15]

Of the export commodities other than slaves, the most important one was of course ivory which was brought to the coast by these porters. From an estimate of 6,000 tusks carried annually to the coast in the first half of the nineteenth century, this number nearly quadrupled to 22,000 by the 1870s.[16] The boost the ivory trade received was not only due to the expansion of the existing demand in the markets of India; but it also received a tremendous stimulus from the insatiable demands of the new American and English markets, the latter receiving its supplies via Bombay (Table 5).

Table 5 Average annual ivory exports from Zanzibar to Bombay and the USA

	Value in MT$ (Bombay)	Value in MT$ (USA)
Before the 1850s	213,145	72,350
During the 1850s	547,089	250,000

Sources: PRO/FO/54/17 and IOR/L/P&S/9/37, Rigby to Wood, 1 May 1860; Sheriff A.M.H., 1971, Appendices A and C; Loarer quoted in Nicholls C.S., 1971, 324–75.

The value of annual ivory exports to Bombay in the first half of the century was in the region of Rs454,000 (= MT$213,145). This figure for the decade of the 1850s had risen to Rs1,165,300 (= MT$547,089) per year.[17] American ivory imports from Zanzibar, Muscat and other ports were valued at MT$23,700 in 1825/6.[18] To satisfy the demands of Salem merchants who in the 1840s complained that they were not receiving anywhere near sufficient quantities of the product to meet all the orders of their customers,[19] Zanzibar alone in 1848 and 1856 provided the American market with ivory valued at MT$121,000 and MT$175,000 respectively.[20] By 1859 when more than three-quarters of all the ivory available to Westerners in Zanzibar was channelled to the American markets,[21] this value had escalated to MT$325,000.[22] And even if ivory prices in Zanzibar naturally rose steeply as a corollary of the fact that demand constantly outstripped supply, there was a comparable price increase in the American home market which assured the continued, albeit at times reduced, profitability of the trade in the USA.[23]

Whilst disregarding (because of the lack of available figures), the ivory which did not touch at Zanzibar but was exported directly from ports like Mombasa and Lamu,[24] if the value of ivory exports to Bombay had more than doubled by the 1860s, that to the United States, as the above figures show, increased by a staggering multiple of no less than thirteen within a span of thirty-five years. Nonetheless, despite these trends towards market diversification, in terms of quantity and value the ports of western India retained their ranking as the principal direct importers of East African ivory, although an increasing proportion of the quantity imported by Bombay was in fact re-exported to London.

In addition to ivory, two other natural products carried by porters from the mainland to Zanzibar were copal and cowries. The former, used mainly for the manufacture of lacquer and varnishes and 'as an incense in incantations and medicinings' by the Nyamwezi and other African/Swahili communities,[25] together with ivory, were regarded by the Americans as the two most valuable import commodities for their home market.[26] Of its two varieties, only raw copal (*chakazi*) was found on Zanzibar Island itself.[27] The pure or ripe copal (In. *sandrus* = Sw. *sandarusi*) was the produce of the mainland coast between Mombasa and Cape Delgado up to thirty miles inland, the best-quality varieties being found between Kilwa and Pangani.[28]

Traditionally exported in considerable quantities to Arabia and India, the copal trade, like its ivory counterpart, also received a fresh impetus at first from the American demand and later from that of the German newcomers on the Zanzibari commercial scene. But as in the case of ivory, the American appetite for copal also seems to have been insatiable. In 1844 the American trader, Captain Gallop, found that he could only manage to procure 9,000 lb in the Zanzibar market before his departure having beforehand received instructions from his firm to bring 40,000 lb in his return cargo.[29] A year later an American merchant with $2,000 cash set aside specifically for copal, could not obtain any supplies whatsoever during his stay in Zanzibar.[30]

Prior to the participation of the Germans in the copal trade, the Americans appear to have dominated the market (Table 6). Their share of it in 1845 was 630,000 lb valued at $108,000 of the total exports of 1,487,500 lb worth $284,250 or 42.5 per cent of the total market.[31] After 1849, the situation changed with the participation of the Germans.[32] Their forceful unequivocal entry into the market was described by one American merchant in the following way:

> About copal I hardly know what to say. But this new German house [William O'Swald and Co. of Hamburg] will give much attention to this article; and 3 or 4 German vessels may be expected in the next 6 months; and then the American transient vessels will take more or less [of what remained].[33]

With the demand curve for copal rising steeply and the price, despite occasional and extreme fluctuations in certain years increasing steadily, the supply side went through a tremendous phase of expansion; from

Table 6 Copal exports from Zanzibar before and after the entry of the Germans in the market

Year	USA			India			Germany		
	Quantity (lb)	Value ($)	Price ($/lb)	Q	V	P	Q	V	P
1845	630,000	108,000	0.17	420,000	18,000	0.18	–	–	–
1859	595,000	93,500	0.16	86,000	13,500	0.16	210,000	54,000	0.26

Sources: PRO/FO/54/17 and IOR/L/P&S/9/37, Rigby to Wood, 1 May 1860; Nicholls C.S., 1968, chap. 8; Cochet quoted in Nicholls C.S., 1971, 343.

1,085,000 lb exported in 1841,[34] the figure leapt to some 19 million lb leaving Zanzibar annually by the mid-century making copal the port's chief export at that time.[35] Within a span of ten years from 1849 to 1859, although the value of copal exports to India fell by more than a quarter, the value of imports by Germany almost doubled while that to the United States remained more or less at comparable levels to those of previous years.[36] But as the figures in Table 6 show, in 1859 the price of $0.26 per pound paid by the Germans far exceeded that of $0.16 paid by the Indians and the Americans. This further illustrates the fierce competitiveness of the Germans who seemed to be willing to pay considerably higher prices to guarantee their share of the market. It is more than feasible that the Banyan and other Indian merchants preferred to sell to the Germans at these prices on the spot market rather than forward their supplies for future trading to their agents in India or elsewhere. This would account for the reduction in the level of exports to India.

Indeed the Germans were not only in competition with other Westerners for the commodity markets at Zanzibar. From the start of their operations they endeavoured, albeit unsuccessfully, to substitute some of the traditional Omani and Indian supplies to the African market by their own products:

An enterprising Hanseatic merchant hit upon the idea of imitating the famous Muscat turban. He found that he could import from Hambro [Hamburg] an equally good looking (in my view better) article at a reduced price: but the Arabs and Sowahaille men about town decided the colours were a little too bright: the article was forthwith gossamer to a beaver. Another gentleman sampled a large pink bead. The only objection to it was, that it did not sell in Uniamesi, among the Mountains of the Moon. Similar accidents happened in piece goods; a stripe too broad or a line too little was sufficient to make the conservative ladies of the Negro races doubt quality, and stick to the original Surat, Broach, or Bengal.[37]

The cowry trade, one of the principal items of exchange during the seventeenth and eighteenth century between Pate and the Comoro Islands but traditionally channelled mainly to the West African coast where cowries were used as currency, was also re-invigorated with the advent of the Germans.[38] By 1859 cowries constituted the major commodity exported by the Germans from Zanzibar. Within ten years of establishing its agency in Zanzibar, by 1859 the German firm of W. O'Swald & Co. was purchasing some 7,800,000 lb worth $230,000 of the total 8,016,000 lb valued at $245,000, or 97.3 per cent of the total quantity exported annually.[39]

The strengthening of connections between mercantile groups in the maritime triangular network of the Indian Ocean, coupled with the extension of these connections into interior Africa, forged a close link between the maritime long-distance trade and older land-based patterns of commerce. The maritime and the internal networks complemented each other and expanded in parallel encouraged as they constantly were by Zanzibar's intensified commercial control over its hinterland.

However nominal and tenuous, in the European political sense, this Zanzibari control may have been, it was perfectly consistent with the tribal and communal concepts of organisation with which Omani leaders and their followers were familiar. In any event, before the colonial onslaught of the Europeans, this control had proved to be more than adequate for the purposes of commercial expansion. By putting their Banyan allies in the important position of the customs master, by establishing a monopoly over the trade of the Mrima mainland and reserving it for 'native' traders, and by imposing a differential system of taxation for goods coming from the mainland,[40] Zanzibari control, albeit indirect, was assured over production in a vast and expanding hinterland.

However, the commercial exploitation of this hinterland, which went side by side with the development of the caravan trade system, would not have been viable without long-term credits. And it was the Banyan allies of the Omani rulers, having historical links within the maritime network, who were ideally placed to provide such credits. Although these credits were to be supplemented at a later date by injections of capital by the Americans, these latter would never have been able to participate in the existing financial system without the cooperation of the Banyans.

As the internal network grew, despite the increasing protection costs compounded by greater risks involved in transporting goods over longer distances and through often hostile terrain, so high was the demand at Zanzibar for commodities coming from the interior that the profitability of the trade was guaranteed.[41] Conversely the price of the import commodities, such as cotton goods and other manufactured merchandise sought after in the interior, declined due to the healthy competition between the old established coastal merchants and the relatively newly arrived Westerners.[42]

The monetisation of the East African economy

With the expansion of the caravan economy not only export products like ivory, copal or cowries but also internal trade commodities such as dried fish, salt, palm oil, copper and iron came to be exchanged over great distances. More importantly, interior people like the Jiji and the Nyamwezi, in a similar fashion to their Omani/Swahili coastal counterparts in places like Bagamoyo, being dependent on both kinds of trade, were able to respond vigorously to the increasing international demand at Zanzibar. If the residents of Bagamoyo adjusted their traditional fishing and boat-building enterprises in coastal trade to include caraveneering and large-scale ferry services, the Jiji and the Nyamwezi likewise expanded their customary commercial pursuits to include new goods, new markets and new practices such as, for example, the use of bead money in exchange for ivory.[43]

As the dynamics of long-distance and traditional local commerce developed, centres along the former trade routes like Bagamoyo, Tabora and Ujiji became points of collection and exchange for both kinds of commercial activity. Before the familiarisation of the interior peoples with the idea and practice of monetary exchange in return for goods, multiple staged trade practices of exchange by commodities evolved in the interior in the initial phase of expansion whereby, depending on the area, cloth was exchanged for Katanga copper, copper for ivory, beads for salt and palm oil, and salt, beads, brass wire, firearms and cloth for ivory, slaves and other interior products such as copal, hides, teeth and horns.[44]

At the same time, the needs of the growing populations in and around these commercial nodes and of porters and slaves who marched in huge numbers through these places to the coast prompted greater production of local goods. Thus Bagamoyo's local fish and produce markets burgeoned[45] while cultivation of new crops for local consumption was greatly enhanced. Tabora, another such commercial node, was transformed into a major food producer where 'Arabs looked more like great farmers, with huge stalls of cattle attached to their houses'.[46] To provide for local needs, rice cultivation became so extensive in the region surrounding Nyangwe and Kasongo in the Upper Congo that it came to be known as 'New Bengal'.[47]

It must be borne in mind that these places in the African interior did not spontaneously spring up in response to frenetic commercial activity but must have gone through many years of evolution to have attained such levels and degree of sophistication as described by Western missionaries and travellers who set foot in these regions after the mid-century. With the extension of the internal trade routes, the enlargement of market places and the increasing monetisation of commercial exchanges, even more goods, services and labour became obtainable through market transactions. With time, this transformed the caravan economy into a market-dominated one integrating it through its connections with Zanzibar to the emergent capitalist system of the Indian Ocean which itself was now linked to the world economy.

Muscat and Zanzibar: an integrated economy

With these developments in Africa, in the same way as some goods arriving in Zanzibar were directed primarily to the Muscati entrepôt market – notable examples being slaves, timber and coconut palm products – so home production in Oman also became geared to the dictates of the Zanzibari market. This received a further shot in the arm as Zanzibar started to import increasing quantities of Muscat textiles, dried fish, dates and salt, and other products such as grain which, although originating in India, found their way to Zanzibar via Muscat.[48] Similarly the traditional dhow trade, whether plied along the East African coast or involved in long-distance commerce, gained an extra impetus. Dhows now not only transported grain all along the coast but they also, among other goods, carried timber (Ar. *haṭab* = Om. *kandal*), much sought after in Oman, from Lamu to Zanzibar and to ports as far afield as Muscat and Bombay.[49]

Of the great variety of goods imported into Zanzibar the traditionally important cotton goods remained a significant commodity throughout this period. These cotton goods constituted the principal export item for the Americans though their better quality but relatively cheap 'merekeni'[50] unbleached cloth soon competed with Muscati and Indian clothes also exported to East Africa. However, as the Americans soon found when entering the Zanzibar market, the bleached varieties of their cottons were unpopular in the regional trade. To remedy this, some of the American unbleached variety found its way to Muscat where it was dyed with *nil* (indigo) before being re-exported to Zanzibar. It was apparently in this form that the 'merekeni' gained acceptance in the local Omani and African markets.[51]

Nonetheless, despite the more than quadrupling of the American export value in the Zanzibari textile market rising from some $84,000 in 1841 to $381,000 by 1859, the value of Indian textile exports remained greater and was worth $443,000 by 1859.[52] In that year Indian textiles constituted nearly 40 per cent of the total Zanzibari imports but unfortunately we do not have any figures for Omani textile exports to enable us to establish a more comprehensive comparison. After cottons, the second most valuable import item to Zanzibar from India was of course rice while that from the United States was, not surprisingly, firearms and gunpowder, commodities which had proved to be such vital factors in the initial stages of the American negotiations and which had induced Said b Sultan to conclude the 1833 Treaty.[53]

In 1859, the value of India's rice exports to Zanzibar was $104,000 while that of American firearms and gunpowder was $68,150.[54] Since the United States was the most prominent of the Western nations involved in the Zanzibari trade of this period,[55] the figures cited above for both imports and exports show that India, despite the vigorous entry of the Western nations in Indian Ocean commerce, retained its traditional place at the top of the league table of principal trading partners of Oman at Zanzibar as it had been at Muscat for centuries before.

In all this tremendous commercial explosion in the Indian Ocean region as a whole, the resurgence of the Albusaidi in Muscat and Zanzibar was bound to be construed as a challenge to the position of the British. But as previously noted, since the signing of the 1833 Omani–American Treaty, the British had in any event been forced to acknowledge at least the commercial importance of Oman and its dependencies. However, if British merchants found that they faced fierce competition from established traders in the Albusaidi dominions in East Africa, their government looked for other ways of eroding the Omani role in its search to safeguard its own dominant position in the backyard of its Indian possessions. In addition to the exploitation of its antislavery crusade, among other weapons employed for this end was Britain's insistence that Banyan and other Indian traders, including those coming to Zanzibar from Muscat, were all British subjects and thus under British jurisdiction. The way Britain achieved its goal will be the subject of the next and final part of this study.

Part IV

Internal and external factors in the subjugation of Oman

10 Commercial and political rivalry and British encroachments in East Africa

In the remarkable trade expansion of the Indian Ocean region, stimulated by the increasing absorption of the triangular Zanzibar–Muscat–western India commercial network into the international capitalist system, the resurgence of the Albusaidi-controlled ports of Muscat and Zanzibar was to lead inevitably to a confrontation with the British authorities. But Britain, which had shown a preference for non-intervention in Omani affairs after 1810, was now prompted firstly by the Omani–American Treaty of 1833 and secondly by regional and global developments to sit up and include the Omani ruler in its regional equation. With Muscat figuring prominently in the political strategy of British India, the economic threat posed by the Omanis and their associates at various points of the triangular commercial network was no less significant than strategic considerations. To maintain its hegemony in the Indian Ocean, Britain was compelled to deal decisively with both the political and the economic facets of the Omani challenge.

Said b Sultan's submission to the British

The fact that Britain was able to achieve its aim ultimately at little cost was due mainly to the receptive attitude of Said b Sultan himself. The Albusaidi, who had been spectacularly unsuccessful during the early struggles of his career in engaging the British in any affair which concerned solely his fortunes, predictably rejoiced now that Britain was becoming steadily enmeshed in the affairs of Zanzibar and Muscat. Steeped as he was in age-old tribal institutions and accustomed to ancient unwritten methods in commercial dealings and in political associations, the Omani ruler did not seem to realise that the corollary of his reliance on Britain, with its new ideas and technology, was the loss of his own independence. Said b Sultan may have been a warrior of some renown but his military prowess, dictated by the need to preserve the integrity of his territories on both land and sea, appears to have extended only to the Qasimis, the Utbis, the Wahhabis, the Persians, the Mazaria and his other local rivals. When it came to the British, he seemed to have something of a blind spot and consistently failed to assert himself or to claim his own rights against them even when his internal fortunes momentarily took a turn for the better in the 1830s.

It is true that the Omani ruler also showed interest in the military strength of other Western powers.[1] During a visit to Muscat in 1831, the traveller Stocqueler described Said as 'a warrior and trader, just governor and chivalric lover [who] asked penetrating questions about the recent French Revolution'.[2] However, Said had himself witnessed at first hand the British triumph over the French not only in India and the Indian Ocean but in Egypt as well. With regard to the Americans, Said had been motivated by the hope of receiving military aid from them, to enter into treaty relations. But the American government had rejected his proposals of military assistance assuring him that, unlike Britain and France, America was not interested in his territories and that Americans were in the Indian Ocean solely for trading purposes.[3] Little wonder then that when the British showed their displeasure, barely five months had elapsed following the signing of his treaty with the Americans than the Albusaidi was declaring himself to be 'willing to give the English everything even [his] country if they wished it'.[4]

In these circumstances, Britain had little difficulty in disposing of the Omani commercial challenge since the Muscati ruler himself had all but laid down a red carpet heralding their arrival. Nonetheless, to appease other powers involved in Indian Ocean affairs, Britain made more use of its diplomacy than its muscle to convince them of its hegemony, at times even giving a considerable share of its power to other European nations when political imperatives in Europe so decreed.[5] In its humanitarian guise, Britain found that its antislavery campaign, often fuelled by the centuries-old Christian crusade against Islam, provided it with a most expedient pretext for establishing its influence regionally. Its insistence upon commandeering and adopting the 'Muscati' Banyans and other traders hailing from India as British subjects was another stratagem which enabled Britain to make inroads into Omani strongholds.[6]

THE CONSOLIDATION OF BRITISH AUTHORITY IN THE GULF

Most historians believe that Oman reverted to being a 'forgotten backwater' following the 1861 British-sponsored dismemberment of the Omani 'State' into the two Zanzibar and Muscat Sultanates. The subordination of Oman (including its overseas dominions) to British influence and the subsequent loss of independence of Zanzibar, and of Muscat in all but name, can, however, be traced back to as early as the heady days of the 1830s.

Following the British upbraiding of the Muscati ruler for signing his treaty with the Americans without consulting them, the ever-obliging ruler of Muscat, Said b Sultan, informed Britain that France also at that time was seeking a similar treaty with him.[7] If Britain was powerless to have the American treaty revoked, it could at least for the time being afford to ignore the Americans who seemed to have no ambitions beyond commercial profit in the East African domain of the Muscati Sultan. Britain could not, however, turn a blind eye to the political motives of other powers.

In the wake of the French involvement with Muhammad Ali and the Egyptian advance through Arabia, Britain once again became anxious to bring Muscat to its side. The British were further obliged, by the deterioration of their own relations with Persia over Afghanistan especially as Persia was becoming increasingly entangled with Russia in the late 1830s,[8] to eliminate any rival influence at Oman's international ports in Arabia. Thus, in addition to the economic challenge from Zanzibar, affairs nearer India forced the British authorities to draw in tightly the net over Oman so conveniently provided for them by the Omani ruler himself. To give Said b Sultan due credit, he did not at that time have any alternative. For apart from the persistence of the Wahhabi threat, only a few months after showing their displeasure at his treaty with the Americans, it had been the British who had been responsible, albeit indirectly, for rescuing Muscat from the clutches of Hamud b Azzan after Muhammad al-Jabri's death.[9]

With the changed circumstances of the late 1830s, British fears were further aroused when Muhammad Ali of Egypt succeeded in obtaining the allegiance of Shaykh Ahmad b 'Abd-allâh Âl-Khalîfa of Bahrain on 7 May 1839.[10] Britain was aware that as early as 1831 Muhammad Ali had put forward a proposal to Said b Sultan as to the possibility of collaborating in a project aimed at bringing both Hasa and Bahrain under joint Omani–Egyptian control.[11] Now with the Wahhabis entrenched in northern Oman and the Muscati ruler preoccupied at

Mombasa, was Muscat to be the next target of the ambitious Egyptian?

In 1838 British apprehensions in this regard had been allayed when Muhammad Ali, in response to their enquiries, had assured them that he had no designs over Muscat:

> As for the Persian Gulf, there, there is only one country which is Muscat, the chief of which country he [Mohammed Ali] loved and esteemed, because he had declared himself the partizan of civilized reforms, and the conquest of that country (Muscat), even if possible, could not be of any advantage to him, since it was so well governed.[12]

Even if the Egyptian Pasha may have experienced a change of heart with regard to his benevolent stance *vis-à-vis* Muscat following his declaration of independence from the Ottomans on 25 May 1838, his requests for Omani cooperation in a joint Omani–Egyptian campaign in June 1839 came too late as Britain only a month before had signed a commercial treaty with the 'Imaum of Muscat' at Zanzibar. It did not help matters any when the Egyptian emissaries to Muscat told Thuwayni b Said and Mohammad b Salim, who were entrusted with the affairs of state, that the Egyptians were taking control of Buraymi and demanded the resumption of the payment of MT\$5,000 to them as annual tribute which had previously been paid to the Wahhabis.[13]

By 1839 British attitudes with respect to the Omani ruler had undergone a rapid transformation. Instead of the indifference shown towards him in the pre-1833 era, he was once again described as: 'The Imaum of Muscat is one of the oldest and has ever been one of the most faithful of our Eastern allies'.[14] The British Resident in the Gulf even suggested that in return for Muscati cooperation in repelling the Egyptians, British troops would provide logistical support to help Said not only in overcoming Hamud b Azzan, who had by then taken Suwaiq and Rustaq, but also in recapturing Bahrain.[15]

Said b Sultan, who had given up hope of ever retaking Bahrain after the débâcle of 1828 and the subsequent meddling of the British,[16] was obviously pleased at this volte-face in British policy. Having by now overcome the Mazaria in Mombasa,[17] on his return to Muscat in September 1839 he agreed to the British proposals on condition that he received British military support in a joint expedition not only against Bahrain but also for the recapture of Buraymi.[18] But though he was assured of active British military involvement, he was told to wait until the arrival of naval forces from England since the British troops in India were then heavily engaged in Afghanistan.[19] Despite these fulsome promises the British were in fact playing their customary waiting game:

The present would be a very inopportune occasion of undertaking military or naval operations for the purpose of putting His Highness in possession of Bahrain. Any such expedition would be premature before we are acquainted with the results of the war in Syria, and with the manner in which the Egyptian question is likely to be settled.[20]

As it turned out, the Albusaidi never received any British help but he stubbornly nurtured the forlorn hope that it would be forthcoming eventually. In nursing these futile aspirations, he was even prepared to alienate the French further rather than undertake an attempt to recruit them as a possibly more constant ally.

Whilst France in the mid-1830s had been using one Sa'îd b Khalfân as its native agent in Muscat,[21] the Omani ruler had agreed with the French Captain Guillain, during his 1838 visit to East Africa, that he would welcome a French consul in his territories.[22] Nevertheless, in the interim, the renewal of closer British relations with Muscat, coupled with the increasing French activities on the East African coast which were perceived by the Albusaidi as prejudicial to Omani interests, had further driven him into the British camp.

In 1838 a deputation from the Sakalava people of Madagascar had been sent to Said b Sultan in Zanzibar to enlist his aid against their enemies, the Hova. Said had not only sent forces but also given instructions for the construction of forts in Sakalava territory after signing an agreement to take the Sakalava people under his protection.[23] But when the Sakalava had subsequently been forced to flee to neighbouring Nossi-Bé, an island now coveted by France,[24] the Omani ruler had thus found himself in direct conflict with the French. In addition, the French had been making enquiries openly both at Zanzibar and Muscat as to the possibility of establishing French 'factories' on the Somali coast.[25] Against this backdrop of rising tension, when the recently appointed French consul M. Noel accompanied by Captain Guillain arrived in Zanzibar in June 1840, Hilal b Said, in his father's absence, refused to receive the consul on the pretext that he could not do so without his father's permission.[26] Guillain and the consul thereupon proceeded to Muscat but not before visiting Nossi-Bé where their offer of protection was apparently rejected.[27]

In Muscat where he was anticipating the arrival of British reinforcements, Said b Sultan also refused to receive the French consul despite Guillain's reminders of the ruler's earlier promises. It will be recalled that this was not the first time in the history of Omani–French relations that a French consul had been thus humiliated at Muscat. In similar circumstances in 1803, Said's father, when northern Oman was overrun by his foes and Britain had shown willingness to cooperate, had also refused to have any truck with Consul de Cavignac.[28] Now, whilst stalling M. Noel on the pretext that he could not receive a consul in his territories without the prior conclusion of a treaty, Said told the two British agents then present in Muscat, Hennell, the Resident in the Gulf, and Hamerton, who had been sent on a reconnaissance mission to Buraymi, that he would hold the French at bay until he received advice from the British authorities regarding the French and the assistance promised to him.[29] Despite displaying an overwhelming and at times inexplicable preference for cooperating with the British, the Omani ruler was now endeavouring to play, somewhat naively, his French card for all it was worth.

At this time the Albusaidi's apprehension for what he perceived to be his possessions in East Africa is clear from his despatches to both the British and the French authorities. To Palmerston he wrote: 'The French nation have their eyes on our possessions in and about Zanzibar. Is it possible that you could restrain them and keep them from us and our posterity or do you advise us to agree to their demands?'[30] At the same time, in his letter of protest to the French governor at Bourbon, Said, in making his claims, requested:

> Your Excellency is aware that the inhabitants of the island in question [Nossi-Bé] belong to me and are my subjects. What I therefore hope from Your Excellency, considering the friendship susbsisting between us, is that you will forbid your people from seizing my territories and possessions.[31]

In January 1839 the British, intent upon maintaining their pre-eminent position, had seized Aden in response to French exploratory expeditions around Abyssinia with the aim of preventing their arch-rivals from obtaining a coaling station for steam navigation 'in the backyard of India'.[32] It is not surprising therefore that when Palmerston received the Omani ruler's request for advice, he wrote back that Said was to 'refuse to comply with any demands which the French nation may make upon you...[and] to rely upon the support of England'.[33] But the vouched 'support of England' for the Albusaidi's inquietudes nearer home was never to materialise. When the Egyptian army was defeated in Syria in November 1840, Said finally came to the realisation that all his machinations were to no avail and that there no longer remained any hope of active British military participation on his behalf. Without the British dimension, he knew he would not have an iota of a chance of retaking Buraymi let alone Bahrain. Resignedly, he made preparations forthwith to set sail for East Africa[34] to ensure that he was not to lose to the Europeans bedding down there what he had irretrievably lost to the British who now not only controlled India but also held unassailable sway in the Gulf and the Red Sea.

BRITISH ENCROACHMENTS IN EAST AFRICA

Although the 1839 Omani–British Treaty incorporated clauses concerning the slave trade, bankruptcies, disputes, shipwrecks and sundry provisions,[35] it did not offer the British any more concessions in the commercial sphere than their 1798 Treaty with Oman had done.[36] Indeed, the provisions of the 1833 Omani–American Treaty[37] had been based on this 1798 Treaty concluded by the British authorities with Said's father, Sultan b Ahmad.

The existence of this first Omani–British Treaty would seem to have escaped the attention of most East African specialists. Curiously, we find that Bennett accuses Said b Sultan of double-dealing during his negotiations with the Americans claiming that Said, in asserting that Oman had treaty relations with Britain, 'was merely bluffing; there was no English Treaty!'.[38] More recently, Sheriff follows the same line of argument.[39] Nicholls, although cognisant of the existence of the first treaty, like the above-quoted and many other writers, suggests that 'he [Said b Sultan] was drawn into the British net when the British feared they were being commercially outmanoeuvred by the Americans [in East Africa]'.[40] But even if this proposition held true for the situation in Zanzibar, there was much more involved, as already shown, elsewhere in East Africa and in Arabia for Britain to take into account when signing the 1839 Treaty. Furthermore it is important to bear in mind that, contrary to the line adopted by most East Africanists, all treaties so far signed with Oman had been with Muscat and not Zanzibar. The question remains nevertheless that if the British already enjoyed the same commercial privileges as the Americans why did they feel the need to sign a new treaty in 1839 with the Muscati ruler?

Apart from the situation in Arabia and the British determination to keep the French at bay, this was the first British treaty not solely connected with the slave trade, to be entered into with Said b Sultan. Moreover, Said, though still not firmly established at home after thirty-three years of struggle, was nonetheless recognised by now as ruler of Muscat and Zanzibar by all Western nations involved in Indian Ocean commerce. Of equal importance is the fact that the 1839 Treaty was signed with the 'Imaum of Muscat' at Zanzibar.

British apprehensions at the growing American influence at Zanzibar

If Britian could afford to ignore the basically commercially oriented activities in the Zanzibar of the early 1830s of a tightly knit community of Americans hailing mostly from Salem, it could not stand aside and watch its commercial position in the Indian Ocean be shaken by the increasing dynamism of the Omani ruler and his associates. In the wake of the 1833 Omani–American Treaty, the situation took a serious turn, as far as the British were concerned, when the first American consul R.P. Waters, appointed as 'United States Consul for the island of Zanzibar, Muscat', arrived in Zanzibar on 17 March 1837.[41] Throughout the nineteenth century American consuls were non-careerists who received nominal salaries for their diplomatic functions. They made their fortunes though in their capacity as merchants or agents of mercantile concerns at home and abroad.

Although in his early days Waters tried to operate independently in the commercial sphere, at times competing with already established firms in Zanzibar such as the Shivji Topan House and demanding those concessions provided for in the 1833 Treaty,[42] he soon realised that if he were to achieve any significant measure of success he would have to adapt to and exploit the commercial system as it existed rather than to try and introduce innovations. After a dispute with 'Âmir b Sa'îd al-Shaqsî when the consul was set upon and beaten by slaves belonging to the Omani merchant, the American was unable to find any Zanzibari who would translate his letters of protest to the ruler.[43] Aware at the same time of the fact that the State Department did not want any friction in lands as far away as Zanzibar where the United States, in any case, 'had no warships in the area to defend its rights as the Europeans did',[44] the American consul decided that life would be a lot more amenable if he were to stop resisting the established order and co-operated instead with existing commercial concerns.

Waters correctly divined that Shivji Topan's son Jairam, now in charge of the Zanzibar customs, was the most powerful local commercial figure. This enviable status did not of course only stem from the fact that Jairam held the customs lease but was attributable to the very nature of the intricate financial structure of the 'Omani State' built as it was upon the intimate interdependence of the Albusaid and the Kutchi House, as previously detailed in Chapter 5. It was to Jairam, in Consul Waters's time, that all foreign merchants and agents:

> must first apply [and who would then] call the native merchants together, make known their offer, then take it upon himself to say

through what House the business must be transacted, and there [was] no alternative. Refuse to comply with his terms and [one] would be driven from the market with doing little or nothing.[45]

Even when the American consul managed, on occasions, to present his grievances to the ruler, the latter would invariably support Jairam,[46] a stance not altogether surprising in view of the way his fortunes were inextricably bound up with those of the customs master.

The crucial nature of this symbiotic relationship between the Albusaid and the Shivji Topan House was graphically illustrated to Waters in 1841 when, upon the expiry of the customs lease, Said b Sultan refused to grant the renewed term to a rival claimant even though that rival was offering $15,000 more per year than was Jairam.[47] Already indebted to the Kutchi House in more than mere financial terms, the Albusaidi preferred to forego the increase offered rather than jeopardise his relationship and ultimately his own financial and commercial security. In this context, the American consul was quick to realise that his interests would be best served if he entered into a 'partnership' with the customs master. When he did that, already by 1840 he was conducting nine-tenths of his business through the Shivji Topan House which reciprocated by giving priority to the American consul's requirements.[48] But this commercial cooperation between Jairam and Waters was of short duration since, by 1842, Waters succeeded in diversifying his local clientele and competed on a local level like any other merchant.[49] However, during the period when this cooperation was blossoming from the late 1830s and up to 1842, it gave rise to grave disquiet amongst not only British traders in Zanzibar but also the British authorities since by that time the commercial system in India itself had undergone a radical transformation which did not augur well for British commercial prospects in those territories that were outside its political control.

Kutchi Banyans and the post-1833 reorganisation of British commerce

One of the consequences of the reorganisation of the East India Company in 1833 had been the termination of its foreign trade monopoly with the result that native Indian business concerns received a tremendous encouragement to expand in overseas commerce.[50] Those Indian companies having an impressive established network of associates abroad found themselves in a vantage position and inevitably exerted themselves to exploit this network thereby reaping untold commercial benefits. One of the results of these developments was the emergence of what came to be known as the Managing Agency System (MAS) which was soon to experience a surge in popularity being utilised to satisfy the demands of the new economic environment.[51] For foreign firms seeking trade opportunities in places like Zanzibar and Muscat the use of the MAS, after 1833, proved to be the most convenient method of participating in faraway markets. While the affairs of foreign firms would be managed by merchants not directly employed by the parent concern, those merchants or their agents resident abroad could nonetheless provide expert knowledge and immediate access to the local economic system.

The only drawback of the MAS was the ever-present risk of fraud or mismanagement by the appointed local agents.[52] In effect, however, since the Muscati and Zanzibari Banyans operated for the most part within their Joint Family structure,[53] it was highly unlikely that their agents in Muscat or Zanzibar would jeopardise their own long-term prospects by undermining the parent family concern in Mandvi or Bombay. Therefore, the traditionally favoured Banyans in the commercial field, especially those who had now come to be closely associated with the Albusaid, received yet another stimulus in the 1830s. It was inevitable, bearing in mind the pre-eminent role of the Kutchi Banyans in Muscat and Zanzibar, that Indian trade with East Africa in the first few decades of the nineteenth century was presided over by Kutch. And just as the Shivji Topan family came to be known by the *nisba* of 'Swally'[54] (Ar. *Sawâhil* = coast; same Arabic root as for Swahili), so did this trade beween East Africa and Kutch come to be termed as the 'Swally Trade'.[55] During the first three decades of the nineteenth century, compared with the British-controlled ports of Bombay and Surat, Kutch imported twice as much ivory from East Africa and supplied three times the quantity of cotton goods.[56] Mandvi, 'the principal sea port and the most populous town in Cutch',[57] had at the same time 'a brisk trade with Arabia, Bombay and the Malabar coast'.[58] Interestingly, of the East African products received by Bombay at this time, we are told that between 26 and 29 per cent came from Muscat and other Gulf ports.[59]

In contrast to this vision of enterprise and prosperity was the spectre of a series of recurrent disasters which devastated Kutch and neighbouring Gujarat in the early decades of the nineteenth century. The famine of 1813 allegedly decimated nearly half the population of Kutch obliging many survivors to resort to migration. Famines are also reported to have struck in 1803, 1812, 1823–4 and 1833–4.[60] Therefore only those merchants already established in the commercially active ports of the western Indian Ocean could have benefited from the above-mentioned expansion in the export trade of India. Among these the Kutchi Banyans in Muscat and Zanzibar seemed destined to play a prominent role but they did not remain unscathed by the British.

In India, once Bombay assumed the mantle of intermediary in the ivory trade between East Africa and London, the British authorities immediately introduced heavy duties on all goods arriving at Bombay from other non-British Indian ports.[61] When Jairam Shivji, in 1837, proposed to expand Zanzibar's trade further by chartering American shipping for the carriage of goods to Kutch, the British authorities at Bombay rejected the proposal and immediately curtailed any further attempts at such a venture.[62] To have acceded to such a proposition would have entailed the prospect not only of increased commercial competition but also of unwelcome inroads being made by the nationals, if not the government itself, of another Western power into Britain's own domain.

Early British commercial activities in East Africa

In East Africa, bona fide non-'Indian' British merchants were also involved in Oman's trade expansion at Zanzibar. Prominent among these was the London firm of Newman, Hunt and Christopher. In its drive for a massive assault upon the commercial sphere, this firm appointed Robert Norsworthy as its resident agent in Zanzibar during the 1830s.[63] At the beginning of its operations, the firm seemed poised to reap its due share from the commercial windfalls at Zanzibar. It engaged a local Omani partner, 'Âmir b Sa'îd al-Shaqsî, and an interpreter Khamîs b 'Uthmân who could reportedly speak fourteen languages and who was sent by the firm on a mission to London in July 1834.[64]

However, the firm's fate served to highlight the merits of the Managing Agency System and the importance of having loyal and trustworthy local partners. It not only suffered from embezzlement and mismanagement by its agent Norsworthy but, to compound this indignity, it was also allegedly defrauded by its local partner al-Shaqsi. When it advanced MT$30,000 worth of goods to its Omani partner, Amir apparently ignored the requirements of the firm and used the money instead to set himself up in business on a grandiose scale.[65] Nonetheless the English firm's ultimate failure lay in its refusal to participate in the Zanzibari commercial system as it functioned. Instead, its owners attempted to establish a direct link between East Africa and England by short-circuiting the ivory trade to London via Bombay, thereby infringing upon the vested interests of not only the Zanzibari merchants but also other British traders in Bombay. Moreover, by refusing to cooperate with the Shivji Topan House, a condition precedent for commercial success as the first American consul had discovered to his cost, the firm further alienated Jairam, the customs master and the prominent commercial associate of the ruler, and was thus doomed. By the end of the 1830s the firm had incurred losses of about MT$115,000 and by the 1840s had substantially rationalised its operations although it did not relinquish its East African connections altogether.[66]

Nevertheless the commercial failure of Newman, Hunt and Christopher gave rise to vehement representations by its agent, Norsworthy, and by other British traders in Zanzibar who exhorted the British authorities to intervene on their behalf in such circumstances. Apart from the desirability of curbing the unchecked behaviour of local partners, these traders claimed that there existed a 'monopolist ring' in Zanzibar involving Jairam Shivji, the American consul and the ruler, which effectively excluded them and which they had no hope of breaking without British official sanction.[67] At the same time, other British merchants, notably Robert Cogan (who had been involved in Zanzibari affairs since the early 1830s and had been asked by Said b Sultan to take his ship *Liverpool* to London as a gift to the King of England in 1834[68]), repeatedly wrote to the Foreign Office regarding 'the necessity of arranging a treaty with Zanzibar to offset American influence there'.[69]

These factors undoubtedly played their part in further convincing Palmerston at the Foreign Office of the wisdom of signing the 1839 Treaty with Said b Sultan. But even if these factors in East Africa are left out of the equation, there were compelling political and economic reasons emanating from the international and regional realities in Arabia and India for signing such a treaty with 'the Imaum of Muscat' as Said was invariably referred to in British official correspondence of the time. It was Muscat which was once again accorded its due recognition by the British. And this is further proven by the fact that when Atkins Hamerton was appointed to the dual role of British Consul and Political Agent of the Bombay government in 1840, he was instructed to proceed to Muscat and not Zanzibar.[70] It was only after the sudden departure of the Omani ruler to East Africa in December 1840, in the wake of the Egyptian army's débâcle in Syria, that the newly appointed consul was obliged to follow the Omani ruler.

As already noted, Said's precipitous return to East Africa on this occasion, now that the Mazaria threat no longer existed, was prompted by French intrigues on the Somali coast, around Madagascar and in the Comoros. On his arrival, the Albusaidi received a letter from Queen Seneko of the Sakalava informing him that a French general with 600 men had taken Nossi-Bé and that she had been forced to capitulate as no reinforcements had been forthcoming from Zanzibar.[71] When the Albusaidi, who had only recently accepted British advice in Muscat not to have any truck with the French and 'to rely upon the support of England',[72] wrote to Palmerston to take him up on his word,[73] Said's request was dismissed in Zanzibar in the same manner as it had been before in Muscat. Palmerston now wrote to him that 'there is a material difference between territories which have for a length of time belonged to a sovereign and districts which have only recently tendered their submission to such a sovereign'.[74] With Muhammad Ali's advance in Arabia halted and his intrigues with the French checked, there was once again no question of Britain becoming embroiled militarily in East Africa, Arabia or anywhere else for the sake of defending the interests solely of the Omani ruler.

11 The subordination of Muscat's rulers and their associates from India

As early as 1834 Said b Sultan had indicated to the British that 'he wished above all things to have an English person always with him to guide him'.[1] However, when Hamerton arrived in Zanzibar on 4 May 1841,[2] far from being the long-awaited guide, he proved himself to be a downright nuisance to the ruler. Described by the British merchant Cogan, who had himself wished the presence of a British consul in Zanzibar, as 'quick-tempered and overbearing in his conduct towards the Prince and the people of Zanzibar',[3] Hamerton, from the beginning, felt the overt hostility of the local people engendered by British policies towards the slave trade. These policies had affected the very livelihood of the Zanzibaris necessitating no less than a revolution in their traditional lifestyles. Hamerton, on the other hand, coming from a milieu of British dominance in India and Arabia where he had seen the British whip and diplomacy at work and where the British way of thinking had been imposed without too much difficulty, immediately felt isolated in Zanzibar. Soon after his arrival he was lamenting: 'Our influence at Zanzibar is at the lowest possible ebb while that of the French and the Americans is very considerable, particularly the latter'.[4]

He misunderstood the fact that American influence, as exemplified by the activities and the cooperation of the American consul with the Shivji Topan House at that time, had no political undertones. The Americans had learnt to play the commercial game and had succeeded while Norsworthy and other British merchants, in trying to bypass the Kutchi House and prohibited by British Law from using slave labour, had been unable to compete and had thus come to grief.

BRITISH CONSUL'S EXPLOITATION OF THE NATIONALITY QUESTION AND THE ANTISLAVERY CRUSADE

In the wider commercial sense Hamerton could now see for himself that the Kutchis and other traders, having links with Muscat and India and through their special relationships with the Albusaid, diverted a considerable slice of the commercial cake from British India. He soon realised that the whole economy of both Zanzibar and Muscat was underpinned by these traders who were treated and enjoyed the same privileges as the 'natives' and were allowed to trade on the mainland. As an agent of the Bombay government, Hamerton understandably looked for ways to change this state of affairs but he could do nothing without first establishing himself locally.

In his search to obtain more leverage in local affairs where all business disputes and bankruptcy cases were handled by the *wali* Sulayman b Hamad Albusaidi, Hamerton resorted in his capacity as consul to the other method available to him, namely to exploiting 'the rabidly antislavery sentiments of the Foreign Office'. Falling back on the idea then in vogue in British official circles that all 'Indians' abroad were to be regarded as British subjects, Hamerton reported to his superiors that the 'Indians' in Zanzibar were all slave dealers.[5] By doing so, Hamerton paradoxically destroyed any chances that bona fide British merchants may have entertained of benefiting from local commerce now that they had a consul in their midst. Cogan, who had been the driving force behind the 1839 Omani–British Treaty, had decided, despite the prior commercial demise of British firms such as Newman, Hunt and Christopher, to try his fortunes further in Zanzibar's commercial field. In the 1840s he agreed to act as an agent for the Bombay-based British firm of Henderson and Co. He also entered into commercial partnership with Said b Sultan himself for the production of sugar and for the exploitation of guano deposits on Latham Island to the South of Zanzibar.[6] Although the guano project failed due to the bird droppings being washed away by an unusually high tide,[7] Cogan found that his other commercial projects could not begin to compete in the local market without employing slave labour. As a direct result of the treaty with the Omani ruler that he had previously so vigorously advocated, he could no longer use slaves now there was a British official on the spot to supervise him.[8]

While reviling the 'Indians' for their slave dealings, Hamerton from the moment he arrived in Zanzibar sent reports on the need to be firm with the ruler: 'No negotiation nor remonstrance of any kind, nor on the part of anyone, will succeed with His Highness for the suppression of the Slave Trade in his dominions unless backed by force.[9] Reluctant as always to incur the expense involved in using force and with too much at stake elsewhere in the Indian Ocean region, the British authorities advised their consul instead to approach Said b Sultan and persuade him to issue a proclamation forbidding his subjects from buying or selling slaves to British Indians.[10] A whole new dimension, 'a hornets' nest', was thus introduced into the picture. The question arose as to who exactly were British Indians and which groupings of the Indians in East Africa and in Oman could be classified as Omani subjects. Some of the Indians in Zanzibar prior to their arrival had been settled in Muscat. Others had been born either in East Africa or in Oman. Unhappy with Hamerton's demands and with the resentment he and the British agent at Muscat were causing among members of various mercantile communities, Said felt obliged to appeal to their superiors. To Aberdeen he wrote that he was:

> constantly perplexed by the petty annoyances from your consul Captain Hamerton at this place and from the jew agent Reuben at Muscat, they are the only servants of the British Government we have ever had occasion to complain of, but it is the constant vexations caused by them that compels us to speak out.[11]

On the nationality question, Said also asked Aberdeen whether those 'Indians' born in Omani dominions or resident there for a long time with local wives and children were to be regarded as Omani or British subjects.[12]

In his reply Aberdeen reassured the Albusaidi that only those Indians residing in territories directly under the British Crown 'were entitled to British consular protection'.[13] Furthermore, even Hamerton recognised the fact that not all Indians in Zanzibar and Muscat could possibly have been British subjects.[14] He knew that the 1819 Treaty of Alliance between the East India Company and the Rao of Kutch had not placed Kutch under the British Crown while the rights of its ruler 'to be free from all British authority in [his] domestic affairs [had been] recognised'.[15] Ironically Hamerton's actions once again prejudiced the interests of those very people he had set out to protect, the bona fide British merchants. If Sindis could no longer, after the 1840 British takeover of Sind,[16] be regarded as 'Omani' thereafter falling within the territories of the British Crown, Kutchis were still excluded from the consul's designs and could continue exploiting slave labour. Recognising this fact, Hamerton regretfully reported to Bombay that increasingly British Indians were being excluded from Zanzibar's trade to the benefit of the Kutchis.[17] This was hardly surprising. The simultaneous British-imposed antislavery measures placed many British Indians at the mercy of the 'Arab' and Swahili landowners whose plantations were mortgaged to the former. These British Indian mortgagees were no longer allowed to employ slave labour even for the purpose of recovering the value of their mortgages.

As far as Said b Sultan was concerned, being more accustomed to his tribal world than to the new notions the Westerners persisted in imposing upon him, he once told the American consul Ward during a debate on the nationality question, that: '[since] the English had earlier helped him in Arabia...it was immaterial to him whether the Banyans were subjects of England or Zanzibar. He added that he considered the English and the Arab [Omani?] people as one!'[18] As for the antislavery measures that Hamerton was now proposing to the Omani ruler, that was a different story. Said repeatedly told the British consul that he considered such measures 'the same as the orders of Azrael [Izrâ'îl], the Angel of death'.[19] But though he resisted and even sent 'Alî b Nâṣir al-Ḥârthî on a mission to London 'to plead his case with the Queen and the Foreign Office', when he finally bowed to British demands he did not even receive the compensation initially promised to him for signing the antislavery treaty, let alone British support against the French or in the capture of Bahrain as he had hoped.[20]

Before he eventually agreed to sign the treaty, due to the hostile reactions he had received from the people of the region as a result of his earlier concessions to the British, the Albusaidi looked for facesaving ways to solve the conundrum he was then facing. He issued orders that slave dealing should be relocated from its traditional areas to places outside Zanzibar town.[21] Similarly instructions were sent to Muscat that slaves were only to be sold inside the residences of recognised brokers.[22] However, the British authorities were not fooled nor were they impressed by these compromises and half measures. Their patronising self-righteous attitude towards the Omani ruler at this time – an attitude considered to be a divinely ordained sanction towards all Arabs in general – would perhaps be best summarised by quoting a despatch of the Foreign Office in response to Said's objections and which was later to be reiterated word for word to his son Mâjid in 1861:

Captain Hamerton should take every opportunity of impressing upon these Arabs that the nations of Europe are destined to put an end to the African Slave Trade, and that Great Britain is the main instrument in the Hands of Providence for the accomplishment of this purpose. That it is in vain for these Arabs to endeavour to resist the consummation of that which is written in the Book of Fate, and that they ought to bow to superior power, to leave off a pursuit which is doomed to annihilation, and a perseverance in which will only involve them in losses and other evils.[23]

To make matters worse for the Albusaidi, the early 1840s were a period of British–French *rapprochement* under the direction of the French Premier, Guizot, and the British Secretary of State for Foreign Affairs, Aberdeen. Having previously been instructed to have no dealings whatsoever with the French, Said was now informed by Aberdeen that the British would have no objection to the re-establishment of his relations with France. The British did not even raise an eyebrow when Said signed his treaty with the French in 1844.[24]

By then in Africa, the French had occupied Mayotte and had established themselves in the Grande Comore and in the Mozambique Channel where some local rulers unfamiliar with and resistent to European ways continued to consider themselves under Albusaidi suzerainty. Notable among these were Queen Seneko of the Sakalava and King 'Abd al-Raḥmân of Mohilla.[25] To counter these French moves, in 1844 the British decided to take Anjouan (Johanna) under their wing.[26] The manoeuvrings of the European powers, which were a prelude to the colonial onslaught of Africa and Arabia coupled with the declining influence of Oman, the only remaining local power able to withstand the Western challenge, had already gathered momentum.

Nevertheless when Said b Sultan did eventually sign the antislavery treaty of 1845 with the British, it was not so much these European incursions in the Indian Ocean as his own desperate military situation that constrained him to agree to British terms despite his earlier declarations that such a course of action would be tantamount to economic and political suicide. By 1845 the Albusaidi's campaigns against Siyu, the northern coastal town of what is now Kenya, had met with nothing but disaster.[27] In the latest expedition consisting of a force of 2,000 men despatched in March 1844 from Zanzibar, Said had lost not only the majority of his forces and most of his artillery and stores but also the commander of his troops, Ḥammâd b Aḥmad al-Sammâr Âlbusa'îdî, and a number of prominent personalities including Jum'a b 'Alî al-Mughairî, 'Abd-allâh b Sulayîm al-Ẓâhirî and 'Alî b Nâṣir al-Ḥârthî, his late envoy to London.[28]

From Muscat Said had also received the ominous news that the Wahhabis, having now recaptured Buraymi, were by 1845 demanding tribute and had started a series of raids on the Batina. His son Thuwayni's appeals to Bombay for help had brought forth the advice 'to maintain a friendly understanding with the Wahabees and to accept any terms compatible with his father's dignity'.[29] Having recently seen his military might annihilated in East Africa, the Albusaidi wrote to his son 'enjoining him to strengthen Burka, Semayle and Nukkul, and in the event of a rupture with the Wahabees, to confine himself to the defence of the forts, and on no account to leave Muskat'.[30] Although Hennell, the British Resident in the Gulf, sent two cruisers to patrol the Batina and wrote letters of protest to the Wahhabi authorities, it was once again:

> the fact that the Omani tribes were gathering in formidable numbers to oppose him [that] induced Sa'eed-bin-Mutlak [Sa'îd b Mutlaq, the Wahhabi commander in Buraymi], to accept terms, and he eventually withdrew his forces for an annual tribute of MT$5,000, the authorisation for which Thoweynee had received from Zanzibar.[31]

Yet again there was no question of active British military participation. Indeed, the official British policy regarding Muscat and the Wahhabis remained as it had been since the early 1830s:

> even if the worst contingency that can be supposed likely to take place were actually to happen, and the Wahhabis were not only to acquire possession of the port of Muscat, but also to commit acts of piracy on the Gulf Trade, it is conceived that it would be much cheaper and easier to chastise them under these circumstances than to take up the question in its present state and constitute ourselves the guardians of the possessions of the Imaum of Muscat against all his enemies.[32]

Despite this unbending attitude prevalent amongst his superiors, Hamerton in Zanzibar persisted in his demands for the antislavery agreement with promises of support and compensation as bait. With his military fortunes waning and having, in response to his protests, been advised by the Foreign Office 'to bow to superior power [and] to leave off a pursuit which [was] doomed to annihilation',[33] Said's agreement to the 1845 Treaty may indeed have been a face-saving device to avoid a confrontation with the British which he knew would be doomed to failure in these times of trial. However, even after this treaty, which prohibited slave exports to Arabia, came into force as agreed on 15 Muharram 1263 (1 January 1847), Hamerton continued to complain that 'it is notorious that the Imam's officers pay little attention to any orders he ever issues, which they consider at variance with their own interests and inclinations'.[34] Thus the use of slave labour, on which the greater part of the Omani and the East African economies were based, continued even if the ever unobtrusive British Indians were now, theoretically at least, forbidden from its practice.

As for Hamerton's own position in Zanzibar, gone was the period of isolation he had encountered in his early days. By 1851, the American consul Ward summed up the situation in the following way: 'From conversations I have had with the English consul, it is the Policy of the British Government to take possession of the East African coast at no distant day'.[35] But Britain as yet was in no hurry for that day. It knew only too well that it already had the Albusaidi Sultan bridled and could tighten or loosen the rein as and when it suited British interests.

With regard to the Omani ruler's relations with the British, even Said b Sultan in the latter years of his life had become so disillusioned with Britain that in 1856 he refused British mediation in his dispute over Bander Abbas with Persia.[36] Having in 1854 ceded the Kuria Muria islands 'to Queen Victoria...of the powerful nation (England) of my own free will and pleasure, without force, intimidation, or pecuniary interest whatsoever',[37] a year later the officials of that same Queen proscribed him from enlisting support from amongst tribes in northern Oman to resist Persia. Disheartened, tired and in a precarious state of health, he accepted Persia's terms even though Britain itself was at that time at war with his enemy. By accepting Persia's terms in a hurry to get back to deal with yet more troubles in Zanzibar, Muscat not only had to pay an increased rent for the lease of Bander Abbas which was raised from 6,000 to 16,000 tomans (MT\$13,800 to MT\$37,500) but the Omanis also lost the islands of Qishm and Hormuz conquered by Said's father in 1798.[38] In any event the Albusaidi no longer had the time to wait for the denouement of the Persian–British conflict as a major revolt had broken out in East Africa following the death of his son Khalid, his *nâ'ib* in Zanzibar, in November 1854.[39] Said also apparently had a premonition of his own impending end[40] and despite his haste he was never again to set eyes on the coconut-fringed shores of Oman's island in East Africa for he died at sea during his return voyage on 19 October 1856.[41]

Beginnings of the extension of British authority to East Africa

Following the lines already established, Hamerton's successors in Zanzibar intensified the high-handed methods adopted by him in the exploitation of the nationality question and the antislavery crusade. However, if Hamerton had shown willingness to follow international regulations to the letter and had at least recognised the distinction between the Kutchis and the British Indians, his successor Christopher

Rigby displayed no inclination to be bothered with such subtleties. In lumping together all Indians regardless of their exact legal status or loyalties, he not only demanded the wholesale and immediate emancipation of all their slaves but also initiated a system of levying a fine of MT$10 for each slave freed, ordering, at the same time, that plots of land should be provided for the freed slaves' sustenance.[42] Under his direction, the practices of public flogging, imprisonment and deportation of those Indians he considered guilty of cruelty towards their slaves were also introduced.[43] His zealousness was taken to such extremes that he started to punish the slave owners among the Baluchis and the Zadgalis from Makran maintaining that if they were not 'Arab' then they must be 'Indian' and therefore British subjects.[44]

Although the Zanzibari ruler, Sultan[45] Mâjid b Sa'îd Âlbûsa'îdî (r.1856–70) at times protested, he was effectively powerless to check the excesses of the British consul. Majid himself was far too dependent upon Rigby's goodwill to ensure his own position and to enlist support in his struggles with his brothers Thuwayni at Muscat and Barghash in Zanzibar. The British consul's attitude, on the other hand, towards the Sultan and other prominent personalities in Zanzibar was characterised by utter mistrust verging on undisguised contempt. While Majid, like other *a'ayân* (notables) in Zanzibar, held the *wali* Sulayman b Hamad in high esteem describing him respectfully in his correspondence to the consul as *al-wâlid* (our father),[46] Rigby in turn had no such feelings for the venerated old confidant of Said b Sultan. He depicted Sulayman instead as 'an old scoundrel and a notorious old slave dealer'.[47] As for Omanis in general Rigby described them as 'all wasting their substance in drunkenness and debauchery, the degraded victims of the system of slavery, by which they regard any kind of honest industry as beneath an Arab, and only befitting negro slaves'.[48]

Nor was Majid himself spared the sharp edge of the British consul's tongue. When the Sultan, in desperation, wrote to the consul:

> If I put a stop to the traffic in slaves it will ruin these countries, and it will ruin my subjects; and I am sure that the British Government would never agree to this; my friend, it is in my wish to comply with all the desires of the British Government but these countries cannot do without slaves. For the British Government is far off, and does not know the circumstances of these countries.[49]

Rigby, whilst enclosing Majid's letter in his despatch to his superiors, added this comment:

> By his extraordinary want of firmness, his apathy and inattention to

affairs, His Highness is fast alienating all the Arabs from him. Debauchery...ha[s] brought him to a dreadful state of pain and disease, and he will not take any medical advice.[50]

On leaving Zanzibar, ironically for health reasons after three years' tenure of office, Rigby furthermore proclaimed after bidding farewell to the Sultan that he wished 'never to see the false, vile scoundrel in this world again'.[51] But if the consul, by 1861, could gleefully boast that he had 'had the satisfaction of giving liberty to upwards of 8,000 slaves [including those] belonging to natives of India whether British subjects or nationals of the protected states',[52] his departure was regarded by those same Indians as nothing less than 'the termination of a great catastrophe'.[53]

THE SUBJUGATION OF THE 'INDIANS'

Rigby's successors in Zanzibar did indeed recognise the fact that British consuls had no legal right to put the Kutchis under British jurisdiction and therefore no sanction to deprive them of their slaves.[54] However, in 1865 Majid was prevailed upon to issue a decree that any local woman marrying a British Indian would automatically be regarded as British.[55] At the same time, seeing their livelihoods threatened, Zanzibari and Muscati Kutchis and some other communities long resident in Oman continued to register their protests now supported by two Sultans at either end. In Muscat as early as 1858, Sultan Thuwayni managed to obtain a guarantee from the British that those Lawatiyas and Khojas settled in Oman before the British conquest of Sind in 1840 were not to be regarded as British subjects.[56] Nevertheless any further complaints by the Sultans or the Kutchis themselves regarding their status, and consequently their commercial practices in Muscat and Zanzibar, were finally muzzled in April 1869 when the British decided to resolve this state of affairs once and for all. They persuaded the Rao of Kutch to issue a proclamation whereby from then on:

> the claims and disputes of [people from Kutch] who permanently reside in, or frequent for the purpose of trade, the port of Muscat and all other places in Africa, Arabia and the Persian Gulf should be settled by the British government in the same way as if they were its own subjects.[57]

By then, the practice of the British government settling the disputes of the Omani rulers themselves had become commonplace. With Imam 'Azzân b Qays Âlbûsa'îdî at that time struggling for his survival at

Muscat mainly against elements supported by the British, Majid's objections to the Rao's authority over Kutchis in East Africa were easily silenced. John Kirk, then only a subordinate official in Consul Churchill's absence, threatened 'to bring matters to a crisis' if Majid continued 'to stand in open antagonism to the will of H.E. the Governor of Bombay'.[58] To drive the point home, the Rao was later further induced to issue another proclamation directed at the Kutchis in general and which threateningly declared:

> If you continue to carry it [the slave trade] on, or be in any way concerned in it, the British Government will deal with you as with its own subjects and punish you severely, and your property in Kutch will be confiscated by this Government.[59]

By such methods, successive British consuls managed to bring the Kutchis and other Indian associates of the Albusaid under their control. In so doing these consuls not only succeeded in exercising a powerful influence on the financial administration of the now disunited 'Omani State'; they also averted the threat that the continuation of the centuries-old commercially successful Muscati–Banyan cooperation and a united Oman would have undoubtedly posed to the British position in the Indian Ocean. Their forceful actions were also responsible for alienating the Indians by creating ill-feeling between the different classes of Omani society, which included many who were of Indian origin, and by causing resentment between the indebted landowners and the money lenders amongst them. With more and more enforced emancipation of Indian-owned slaves, some Indian merchants from as early as 1850 became reluctant to advance money on the security of landed properties with the result that plantation prices plummeted.[60] By 1862 the value of many plantations had fallen by nearly 75 per cent from what they had been worth before the mid-century.[61] To exacerbate this state of affairs, 'Indians' also suffered from the fact that they could no longer resort to employing slave labour even for the purpose of recovering the value of those plantations mortgaged to them.

As far as trade was concerned, Rigby in 1861 could not understand how Oman could have risen to such commercial eminence as he was then witnessing at first hand in Zanzibar: 'The trade is certainly surprising, when it is considered that it has been developed under the primitive rule of an Arab chief'.[62] But he was happy to note at the same time that 'four-fifths of the entire commerce of Zanzibar pass[ed] through the hands of [what he considered were] British subjects'[63] who, by then according to Rigby, either owned or were the mortgagees of three-quarters of the total immovable property on Zanzibar.[64]

However, in spite of the British-enforced slave trade prohibitions, even Bartle Frere during his 1873 antislavery mission to Muscat and Zanzibar admitted that it was 'nearly impossible to feel sure that no part of commercial transactions [was] connected directly or indirectly to the slave trade'.[65] After all, if some 'Indians' continued to play the vital role of financing the slave-labour dominated agricultural and caravan economy of the interior, so did the Western traders or their agents at the international ports of Muscat and Zanzibar rely ultimately on that economy for the sale of their imports and the purchase of their exports.

Thus, by the time the opening of the Suez Canal in 1869 added a further strategic dimension to the situation concerning both Zanzibar and Muscat, Britain had succeeded through the Kutchi and other Banyans to tighten the knot around the economic jugular of Oman. It is perhaps no coincidence that the Rao's proclamation was issued in the same year as the Suez Canal was opened.

The humanitarian, religious and commercial aspects of the anti-slavery crusade

The humanitarian guise of the antislavery crusade under cover of which the British rent asunder the Albusaidi–Indian alliance, which had been so vital in the initial and the subsequent commercial rise of Oman, had an overt religious dimension. After the mid-century arrival of Christian missionaries in Africa, intent on pursuing their 'civilising mission' in 'heathen Africa', this dimension acquired such a high profile that in the latter part of the century the British Press was full of reports similar to the following:

> Are we to stand by and see Mohammedanism carried by fire and sword through Central Africa...and stifle those more peaceful influences by which Europe has hoped to develop African resources and to ameliorate the condition of the natives of Africa? If England, over-weighed with responsibilities elsewhere...should refrain from using her influence to check these Arabs then will not Germany look to it? Any action by her part in this direction will be welcomed by all natives, all classes, and all sections of the Christian creed who have at heart the real welfare of the Africans.[66]

In so far as such statements were prompted by humanitarian considerations which, according to the vociferous proclamations of the British during the nineteenth century and the statements of some writers even of our day, were the main targets behind the British 'crusade' against the slave trade, it is ironic to note that when 'Rule

Britannia' did eventually become established, the lot of the 'slave' population did not take a turn for the better as the earlier actions and lofty pronouncements would have justified. Unwilling to encounter either economic ruin or social disorder in its Protectorate of Zanzibar, proclaimed in 1890, the official British policy regarding the slave trade henceforth became subtly distorted 'to resort only to such measures for its abolition as being gradual in its operation [which] may effect the change without unnecessary disturbance',[67] nor 'be injurious to the industry of the islands [or] result in an early and permanent deficit in your [the Protectorate's] budget'.[68]

The cynicism and alacrity with which the humanitarian factors were discarded in the interests of economic and political expediency, once Britain assumed responsibility of Zanzibar's administration, were startling and revealing of true British designs. If 'Britons never never shall be slaves', it was deemed perfectly reasonable that others should remain so in spite of the high-flown statements previously made to the contrary and the destruction of a 'flourishing state' in the process. The needs and the comforts of the new masters, now openly proclaiming their intellectual and racial superiority, were the imperatives of the moment even if this meant the perpetuation of the old order which they had been 'divinely appointed' to crush when it had been in the hands of others. The British were of course not the only Europeans who adopted such attitudes. German officials in 1890 were openly buying slaves in Bagamoyo to the utter disbelief and disgust of local 'Arab and Swahili' residents.[69]

Notwithstanding the change of masters, it must be mentioned that the old Kutchi associates of the Albusaid continued to maintain their loyalties to the Omani rulers. Although Jairam Shivji himself left Zanzibar in 1853 and died in Bombay in 1866,[70] the firm established by his father, the Shivji Topan House, kept control of the Zanzibar customs well into the 1880s, bar a five-year interruption between 1876 and 1880.[71] In the early 1880s, the same house is said to have also controlled the customs at Muscat.[72] In any event during the interruption at Zanzibar, it had been a son of another old associate of the Albusaid, Tharya Topan, who had held the customs lease. His father, Topan Tajiani (or Topan bin Tajir as he was known in Zanzibar), it will be recalled, had been encouraged by Shivji Topan himself to enter into commercial associations with Sultan b Ahmad at the turn of the nineteenth century.[73] Before his death in 1851, Topan Tajiani obtained the greater part of his business in Zanzibar through Jairam and his brother Ebji.[74]

Commercial activities thus continued unabated based primarily on the Zanzibar–Muscat–western India triangular network and, locally, on the agricultural and caravan economy which still relied on slave labour despite fluctuations during times of recurrent crises such as the 1872 hurricane in Zanzibar. In Majid's time, Zanzibar's total import and export trade almost doubled between 1861 and 1865[75] at a time when the American trade was temporarily on the decline, due to the American Civil War, with India, as always, remaining the principal trading partner.[76] The increasing premiums paid for the customs' lease both in Zanzibar and in Muscat also bear testimony to the continuing commercial growth at both ports.[77] Under Barghash b Sa'îd (r.1870–88), annual state revenue in Zanzibar rose to $1,000,000 by the early 1880s compared to $300,000 in 1870.[78] Similarly in Muscat, custom revenues rose steadily from MT$51,000 in 1875 to MT$131,000 by 1884 increasing, despite some bad years in the 1890s, to MT$140,000 in 1907.[79]

Post-1856 indebtedness of the Albusaidi rulers to the Banyans

Nevertheless, through the legacy that the new Albusaidi rulers inherited from their recent forebearers, they predictably found themselves indebted to the 'Indian' Commercial Houses, especially those controlling the customs. Although there were, as previously examined, more than mere financial considerations involved in the Albusaidi–'Indian' relationships, British consuls insisted on limiting them to just these considerations, delighted as they were at the thought that the Sultans were so much in debt, in financial terms, to the 'Indian British subjects'. So much so that Rigby relished in reporting to Bombay that:

> the agent of the Custom Master acts as Treasurer and Banker and scarcely a dollar reaches His Highness or any of his family except through him. Being indebted to him in so large a sum, His Highness is entirely dependent on his goodwill for any money he requires.[80]

To quantify just how much this debt was, successive British consuls started demanding tabulated statistics. To pacify them, the customs masters duly produced the figures required while obstinately holding fast to their long-established financial and commercial links with the ruling family.

Basing his figures on the information provided by Ladha Damji, the customs master and agent of the Shivji Topan House, Rigby estimated that Majid, on assuming power, owed the Kutchi House some $250,000.[81] Since no distinction had been made between the personal fortune of the late Said b Sultan and the State Treasury, massive amounts had to be added to this figure. For Majid soon discovered that he not only had to borrow enormous sums of money from Ladha Damji in order to buy back from members of the ruling family the apparatus of state; but he was also, theoretically at least, obliged to transfer his father's inheritance to those members of the ruling family resident in Zanzibar.[82] The total inheritance estimated to be worth MT$1.5 million, according to the British consul's estimates, could be divided between Said's remaining thirty-four children with $57,917 going to each son and $28,958 to each daughter.[83] By the end of the decade Consul Kirk, not surprisingly, estimated that Majid's debt to the Shivji Topan House had risen to $540,000.[84]

This indebtedness of the Omani rulers to the Banyans had not spontaneously arisen in the era after Said b Sultan. It dated back at least to the time when Sultan b Ahmad had used warships provided by Kutchi Commercial Houses in his military campaigns at the turn of the nineteenth century. The difference was that no monetary value had been attached to this indebtedness during that epoch since the Banyan Commercial Houses in return enjoyed reciprocal commercial and protection rights in the Omani ruler's territories. These rights, though not committed to writing, had been tacitly understood and the same system had been perpetuated by Said b Sultan. In Majid's time, however, now that the British had claimed the Kutchis and other Indians as their own subjects, British consuls felt the need to put a figure, however arbitrary, upon this indebtedness in order to establish just how much the Omani rulers were indebted to those who were now the consuls' recognised co-nationals.

In spite of these radical changes, the special Albusaidi–Indian relationship continued both in Zanzibar and Muscat well into the twentieth century.[85] From a commercial standpoint, the net losers in all these developments were the Albusaidi rulers themselves. Unable to react with any effect to the arrogance of British officials, they were forced by internal developments in both Oman and East Africa to squander their resources further in the defence of their thrones in the dawning realisation that even then they could only keep hold of the reins of power with British approval and support. Indeed there were cases of Albusaidi rulers repudiating their thrones only to be forced by Britain, for its own and at times impenetrable motives, to reoccupy them. And even if the Sultans continued to receive financial support from a number of Banyan, Khoja and Lawatiya associates, the commercial upper hand came to be increasingly held by those Indians who were now closely associated with British and not Omani interests. Whereas the Muscati Banyans of the early 1840s had responded with an outright rejection of British claims to jurisdiction over their commercial affairs,[86] by 1895 the new generation of Banyans in Muscat was writing letters of gratitude to the British Resident 'for assurances given as regards safety of our life, property and trade in this *foreign* territory'.[87]

12 Post-1856 succession dispute and British intervention

None of the four principal sons of Said b Sultan – Thuwayni and Turki in Oman, Majid and Barghash in East Africa – were uterine brothers. The jealousy, treachery and hatred, the seeds of which had been sown by the machinations and intrigues conducted in the corridors of power of the *harim* (wives and concubines) by their respective mothers on their behalf for Said b Sultan's favours, added a further dimension to the tradition of internecine feuding so engrained in the psyche of the Omani tribal people. When Hilal, the eldest son [born c.1817], fell into disfavour in 1844,[1] his aunt Khurshîd, the Malabari woman, succeeded in her designs to have her son Khalid [born c.1819][2] appointed 'to be ruler over all our possessions on the continent of Africa'.[3]

Khalid, however, did not live long enough to reap the fruits of his mother's labours as he died in 1854 while his father was away on his campaigns against the Persians in Bander Abbas. In the aftermath of Khalid's death, it was Majid [born c.1833][4] who assumed responsibility for the running of Zanzibari affairs with the backing of the influential *wali* Sulayman b Hamad.[5] While Thuwayni [born c.1820][6] was *nâ`ib* at Muscat and Turki [born c.1832][7] was *wali* of Sohar, this left the youngest of them, Barghash [born c.1837],[8] a constant companion of their father in the 1850s,[9] without any established authority. The absence of any demarcated sphere of influence for Barghash to accede to after their father's death proved to be a decisive factor in determining Barghash's subsequent career.

THE SUCCESSION DISPUTE AND THE DIVISION OF SAID B SULTAN'S REALM

The question of whether or not Said b Sultan intended to divide his realm amongst his sons after his death has long exercised the minds of many a writer.[10] This discussion is based primarily on Said's above-quoted 1844 letter to Lord Aberdeen as the will left by the Omani ruler dealt exclusively with the disposal of his personal property and made no provisions whatsoever with regard to succession (see Appendices 2 and 3). But in his letter to Aberdeen, whilst appointing Khalid as ruler of his African dominions, Said had also declared that 'in like manner, we appoint our son Said Thoweenee to be ruler over all our possessions in Oman in Arabia, in the Persian Gulf, and on the coast of Persia'.

Although this declaration of *de facto* partition may be adduced as a convincing proof of Said's intent to divide his realm, in the historical context it can equally convincingly be construed as purely a strategy adopted by the ruler to ensure that his wishes for the disinheritance of his other son, Hilal, would be guaranteed after his death. Said knew only too well that Khalid, without British support, would have no chance of holding out after his death against a challenge from the popular Hilal. By 1856, all three of them, Said, Hilal and Khalid were dead. Perhaps the most important aspect of this episode lies in the fact that, despite Said's marked reluctance to involve the British in the domestic affairs of his own family, Hilal's actions of personally visiting London and begging for British intervention[11] had constrained him to do precisely what he had feared most. His letter to Aberdeen amounted to nothing less than an open invitation to the British to mediate in his family disputes.

Another factor with a crucial bearing upon Said b Sultan's intent to effect a partition or otherwise is the contemporary perception in defining the Omani dominions. It is inconceivable that the Omani ruler could ever have thought of his far-flung dominions as a homogeneous entity constituting an 'empire' or even a 'state' in the modern European sense. From his own political experience of Omani tribalism he knew that tribal allegiances and loyalties were built on shifting sands. As long as he enjoyed at least a nominal recognition from the major tribes in a particular area, whether in Africa or in Arabia, then that area was considered to fall within his domain. As Coghlan himself, appointed by the British authorities as the head of the 1861 Muscat–Zanzibar Commission to investigate and report on the succcession dispute, commented when he at first rejected the idea of Said b Sultan ever having wished to partition his possessions: 'His late Highness in his arrangements actually made or prospectively designed, had nothing more in view than to allot subordinate governorships to one or more of his sons under the paramount Sovereign of Oman'. Among Said's surviving sons, the one best qualified to assume the role of that Sovereign, according to Coghlan, was Thuwayni.[12]

As for the Omani method of resolving succession disputes, during a visit to Zanzibar in 1859 Hilal b Muhammad Albusaidi, the *wali* of Suwaiq, explained this method to Consul Rigby in the following way:

> Generally on the death of a chief his sons disputed the succession and the one who had most influence with the tribe or who gave the greatest hopes of being an efficient leader was elected...; no law of progeniture is recognised...[but] might coupled with the election by the tribes is the only right.[13]

The Albusaidi brothers were of course familiar with the tribal method described by Hilal. Nevertheless, before the intervention of the British, it was the association of Thuwayni and Barghash with the Barawina of East Africa that introduced a new aspect to the Omani method of resolving succession disputes.

From the early days of Said b Sultan's reign, the powerful Barawina of Zanzibar and Lindi, as noted earlier, had nurtured their own political ambitions not only of independence but also of territorial expansion.[14] Despite the fact that, as in the case of the Mazaria, the Nabahina and certain other Omani groups, the Barawina opposition had been offset by the growing commercial prosperity initially beneficial to all Omanis, the personal ambitions of the leaders of these groups had nonetheless not evaporated but remained latent ready to re-emerge at the first available opportunity. Indeed, to pre-empt any outbreak of political activity by the Barawina, Said b Sultan had always taken one of the most troublesome Barawina leaders, 'Abd-allâh b Sâlim, with him as a hostage every time he had left Zanzibar.[15] When Khalid died of pneumonia on 7 November 1854,[16] the Barawina, now having grown intensely resentful of the harmful economic side-effects generated by the ruler's submission to the British on the slaving issue, seized the opportunity and rose in rebellion in Said's absence.[17] But at that very moment, Abdallah b Salim at Muscat was pledging his support on behalf of all his Barawina followers to the Albusaidi ruler in the presence of both Thuwayni and Barghash.[18]

There seems little doubt that Khalid's death and the Barawina uprising were the main catalysts behind Said's hastily conducted negotiations with the Persians over Bander Abbas and his wish to return promptly to East Africa to stop the insurgency from gaining further momentum. Although Said b Sultan himself was never to complete his return journey to Zanzibar, it is important to bear in mind for the evolution of subsequent events that two personalities on board with his corpse were Barghash and Abdallah b Salim al-Barwani.[19]

Barghash b Said's early unsuccessful attempts to seize power at Zanzibar

In these circumstances, the ambitious 19 year old Barghash saw an unparalleled opportunity to seize power for himself. Although four years younger than Majid, he knew that his brother suffered badly from epilepsy and could not be considered fit to rule: 'He [Majid] frequently suffered from severe spasms, and for this reason he was hardly ever left without an attendant to render immediate assistance'.[20] Also, another factor of paramount importance to note in this context is the fact that although Majid had assumed the *de facto* reins of power at Zanzibar after Khalid's death, he had never been nominated as successor nor even appointed as *wali* or *nâ`ib* by his father. Accordingly, during the night following his arrival at Zanzibar on 25 October 1856, Barghash

> sent no information to Sayyid Majid nor to anyone else.... He ordered soldiers to surround the houses of Sayyid Majid and of his brothers so that no one should go in or out. He went with a few of his people and secretly buried his father in their graveyard Makusurani.[21]

However, Barghash's plan miscarried as the Baluchi *jamadar* of the Zanzibar garrison refused to allow him to take Majid prisoner. At the moment of Barghash's arrival at the Palace, his brother was suffering from a fit of epilepsy.[22] The following morning, it was Abdallah b Salim rather than Barghash who proceeded to the British consulate to ask 'what they should do, as the island was without a ruler'.[23] Turning him out of the building, Hamerton informed the Barwani leader that 'if he attempted to disturb the peace, his head would fall within twenty-four hours'.[24] Thus Majid's position was preserved and Barghash's initiative, such as it was, failed for three reasons: the Baluchi *jamadar's* action; the prompt response that Hamerton took on Majid's behalf; and more importantly, the overt support he received from the Zanzibar *a'yan* led by the influential Sulayman b Hamad who had openly backed Majid to take control of Zanzibar's affairs following Khalid's death.[25]

With Majid proclaimed as the new ruler of Zanzibar on 2 November 1856,[26] Hamerton could report a week later that the disturbances had been quelled and peace reigned once again over Zanzibar.[27] Although this may have held true at that time the resentment between the two brothers had by now reached such an advanced stage that it could not be quenched. Barghash's hasty excuses for his behaviour in the aftermath of his abortive attempt to seize power were unconvincing and fell on stony ground: 'I came ashore in secret and buried him [Said b Sultan] like this because he was in a horrible condition after being seven days unburied and I did not want him to be seen by the people in this condition'.[28] This explanation could not satisfactorily account for the surrounding of Majid's Palace by Barghash's men.

It is not evident, at this stage, whether Thuwayni at Muscat was aware of the actions of either Barghash or the Barwani leader. But such an eventuality and the possibility of Thuwayni being behind the movement against Majid seems unlikely at this juncture. For soon after Barghash's débâcle, Thuwayni despatched Hamad b Sâlim Âlbûsa'îdî as an emissary to Majid ostensibly for an amicable settlement of the succession dispute. To appease Thuwayni, Majid agreed that he would send MT$40,000 as an annual free gift to Oman and promised that he was willing to send extra funds on condition that Thuwayni recognised him as the sovereign of Zanzibar.[29] At the same time, Majid also pacified Abdallah b Salim by offering to pay him a yearly stipend of MT$12,000.[30] But with his financial resources already far too stretched on other fronts and his Treasury under assault from all sides,[31] Majid had no way of fulfilling these undertakings. He was constrained to seek the necessary funds elsewhere and, in 1857, sent a *barwa* to the branch of the Shivji Topan House in Bombay requesting that it pay the amount he had promised to Thuwayni on his behalf.[32] Other measures taken by Majid in order to meet these multifarious financial strains upon his purse during the first two years of his reign, included his heavy reliance on the property belonging to those minors of his immediate family who had inherited a share of his father's legacy as well as on the MT$180,000 bequeathed by Said b Sultan to the latter's first wife, 'Azza bint Sayf. Although Azza now resided in Oman, her share of the inheritance had been handed over by Said's Executors to Ladha Damji, the customs master in Zanzibar, for safe-keeping.[33]

Majid's inability to discharge his financial obligations in the second year sparked off a collaboration between his old rivals, Barghash and Abdallah b Salim, and Thuwayni at Muscat. After Hamerton's death on 5 July 1857,[34] Barghash started to borrow considerable sums of money from the Barwani leader to buy arms and provisions for the imminent plot to dethrone his brother. To procure these sums, Barghash entered into written agreements pursuant to which Thuwayni was declared as guarantor for the loans contracted by Barghash.[35]

The summer of 1857 was also the period of the Indian Mutiny.[36] With the prolonged absence of a British agent at both Muscat and Zanzibar, there was much agitation regarding the security of the British position in the wider context of India. Undoubtedly other powers, most notably France, lost no time in gaining advantage by adding to the prevailing ferment in Oman and East Africa and generally inflaming the already aroused passions for their own motives. As Consul Rigby was later to comment:

> There had been no British agent or consul here [in Zanzibar] for 13 months; this was the period of the Indian mutinies and the French had persuaded the Sultan and the Arabs that the British had lost India, and that no British consul would ever reside here again.[37]

Thuwayni was not slow to take the initiative as in the summer of 1858 he took the decision to proceed to Zanzibar in person, accompanied by a naval force, with the intention of settling the affair with Majid once and for all.[38] The execution of his plan had to be postponed, however, until the advent of the north-east monsoon which did not start before November. In the interim, on 27 July 1858, Rigby arrived to take up his position as the new British consul to Zanzibar. It is no surprise that Majid was so delighted at Rigby's arrival that he 'repeatedly expressed the gratification it afforded him to again welcome a British Resident in Zanzibar'.[39] Undeterred by the presence of a British consul in Zanzibar or perhaps unaware of the fact, and with his expedition already fitted out, Thuwayni together with 2,500 armed men sailed from Muscat at the start of the monsoon. Before the bulk of his fleet could reach the East African coast, in February 1859 the British authorities despatched a warship under the command of Griffith Jenkins to intercept Thuwayni's expeditionary force.[40]

Meanwhile, in Zanzibar, Majid and Sulayman b Hamad were making their preparations for the defence of the island in constant consultation and liaison with Rigby:

> Such was the commotion at Zanzibar that trade had come to a standstill and buying and selling had completely stopped. Many people from the interior of the island and from the mainland had gathered, each one ready to defend against the awaited enemy. Anyone running in the streets could hear nothing but the random sound of gunfire, with people at a high pitch of excitement and armed to the teeth.[41]

Indeed, such was the local resistance against Thuwayni that a number of *baghlas* (dhows) from his fleet that had managed to evade capture by the British warship were forcibly prevented from landing at various points along the East African coast. Their half-starved and disheartened crews had no strength to put up any resistance to their capture when they subsequently arrived in Zanzibar.[42] Furthermore many local leaders, still regarding themselves under the suzerainty of the Zanzibari Sultan, rallied around in support of Majid. Said b Muhammad, the ruler of Mohilla for example, came armed with 150 men and took charge of one of Majid's ships for the defence of his sovereign.[43]

Majid then was not so defenceless nor so 'helpless', resignedly awaiting the arrival of the so-called 'invasionary forces', as is suggested by Rigby's reports to his superiors.[44] During Thuwayni's preparations for his expedition in the summer of 1858, Majid had sent not only money but also guns and ammunition to his other brother Turki at Sohar inciting him to attack Muscat.[45] These 'defensive' actions no doubt took a heavy toll on Majid's already strained finances. More importantly they enabled Rigby, through the ruler's increased reliance on 'British Indians', to tighten the knot of the noose that Majid himself had tied around his own neck unwittingly putting the ends of the rope in the hands of the British consul.

Ultimately, with the threat he had posed now neutralised by the superior military force of the British, Thuwayni was forced to comply with British demands that he 'should address the British Government in the first instance if he has any claims to proffer against his brother Syed Majid'.[46] Thuwayni reluctantly agreed to submit his case with regard to his sovereignty over Zanzibar to British arbitration.[47] It was in this way that the British finally responded to the invitation extended to them fifteen years earlier by Said b Sultan to intervene in Omani succession disputes. Oman's own methods of resolving such disputes were now a thing of the past. From now on it was to be the paramount power, Britain, who assumed the role of kingmaker in Zanzibar as well as in Muscat.

THE BRITISH ROLE IN THE DISMEMBERMENT OF OMAN

At the beginning of 1859, the British authorities were generally in favour of maintaining the status quo, that is the formal unity of the Omani 'State'. But the concatenation of Rigby's high-handed intervention at Zanzibar the reliance of British authorities on his often biased portrayals of events and the tide of local opinion in both Oman and East Africa persuaded even a person like Coghlan, who at first had been totally against the idea of partition, to change his mind.[48]

Having taken a leading role in the organisation of Zanzibari resistance against the Muscati fleet, Rigby in the first flush of success could not now be stopped from intervening directly in the succession dispute at a local level. Although the Muscati fleet had been intercepted in February 1859, news that the expedition had been abandoned did not reach Zanzibar until 21 March 'caus[ing] the greatest consternation among the conspirators...[with] Said Barghash confin[ing] himself to the upper part of his house and admitt[ing] no one'.[49]

A few days later came the first unsuccessful attempt to assassinate Majid when Barghash fired 'a volley of musketry' at the ship of the newly proclaimed ruler as it was passing in front of his house on the seafront of Zanzibar town.[50] Enraged, Majid ordered Said b Muhammad of Mohilla to anchor his ship with its guns trained upon Barghash's house and to be always on the alert and ready to fire. Majid also declared that he would no longer pay the monthly allowance of MT$700 that he hitherto had been paying to his brother.[51] With Barghash in self-imposed confinement, there was a move at this juncture by Abdallah b Salim al-Barwani for reconciliation with Majid but the latter refused even to receive him or any of his followers in his *barza*.[52]

Two weeks after the first assassination attempt, on 18 April Thuwayni's envoy, Hamad b Salim, arrived once again in Zanzibar on the pretext that he had come to collect the money Majid had promised earlier. The ruler, however, immediately referred him to the British consulate insisting that all negotiations were henceforth to be conducted through Rigby:

> Had he not made war on me, I should not have withheld the money from him; nor was it ever my intention to deprive the subjects of Oman of the benefits which they receive from Zanzibar...but one who acts in this manner is not to be trusted.[53]

On presenting himself to Rigby, the Muscati envoy was informed in no uncertain terms that Majid 'would never pay a farthing' to Muscat and his interview with the consul was abruptly terminated.[54]

The 1859 Rebellion

The uncompromising and arrogant posturing of the British consul into whose hands Majid had delivered not only his fate but also that of Zanzibar, coupled with the recent arrival from Oman of new recruits to the resistance movement, were the catalysts for the hatching of a new conspiracy against Majid. Having anticipated the possibility that his envoy may meet with an unfavourable reception, Thuwayni had drawn up contingency plans, the main element of which was that Hamad should attempt to enlist the support of the influential *wali* Sulayman b Hamad whose backing the Muscatis knew would be absolutely crucial for any plot to succeed. But it was not to be as the Muscatis had hoped. Thuwayni's letters to the *wali* were accompanied by threats that 'if he [did] not comply with Syed Thuwenee's wishes, then he must take the consequences'.[55] Instead of forwarding a reply, Sulayman, the old trustee of Said b Sultan, passed these letters over to Rigby.[56]

While Nâsir b 'Alî b Tâlib and Sâlih b 'Alî al-Hârthî, the leader of the Sharqiya Hinawis, were busy at Zanzibar inciting the populace to revolt against Majid,[57] Barghash was using the greater part of the money he had received from Muscat to buy off other local leaders.[58] However, even within the Barawina, two camps emerged, one supporting Barghash and the other his brother. While Abdallah b Salim supported Barghash, 'Alî b Mas'ûd al-Barwânî and Husain b Muhammad b Salâm al-Barwânî, two other leaders of different factions of the Zanzibar Barawina, were firmly behind Majid.[59] So were the Ghâfirî Masâkira, the Mughairiyûn and the Banû Riyâm.[60] Furthermore, the leading *'alim* of Zanzibar of the time, Sulaymân b 'Alî al-Mandharî, also backed Majid[61] whilst even members of the House of the Albusaid were divided amongst themselves and their quarters became the scene of many a plot and counter-plot.[62]

Although by April the conspiracy had erupted into open rebellion, to Rigby's relief

> the unusual sight of three of Her Majesty's ships of war being in this port at the same time has greatly raised the prestige of British power and its watchfulness to prevent hostilities and to protect the interests of British subjects resident here.[63]

At Rigby's instigation, on 7 July Majid personally forced his way into Abdallah b Salim's house where he found a cache of 400 muskets stacked up in one of its rooms.[64] But before the ruler could arrest Abdallah and his people, Muhammad b Nâsir b Îsa al-Barwânî took out his gun in an attempt to shoot Majid on the spot. 'It was a matter of fate that his gun became jammed',[65] and thus Majid's life was saved in what was effectively a second assassination attempt though it was not the last one. With Barghash's house now surrounded by Majid's troops, it was Thuwayni's envoy, Hamad b Salim, who bribed a Baluchi soldier in Barghash's service with MT$3,000 to kill the ruler. The plot, however, was discovered and the Baluchi duly thrown in jail in the early days of September by which time Hamad himself had taken the sensible precaution of fleeing from Zanzibar.[66]

Under house arrest, Barghash on receiving this news momentarily faltered and sent Ladha Damji, the customs master, as his messenger to Rigby stating that he agreed to the consul's terms whereby his life would be spared if he left Zanzibar.[67] In his house, however, under the influence of his determined sister Khawla, 'Barghash would not listen to anything like submission'.[68] Collecting into one room of his house all his younger brothers and sisters and their mothers, he placed several barrels of gunpowder in the lower storey and threatened that he would blow them all up if Majid's people as much as set foot in the house.[69] Soon after, by bribing some of Majid's Baluchi soldiers, he sent messages to his remaining supporters to gather all their arms and ammunition at the fortified *shâmba* (Sw. = plantation) known as 'Marseilles' outside Zanzibar town.[70]

The most serious problem which still remained to be resolved, however, was the way in which Barghash was to escape from his house and join his supporters when it was surrounded on land by Majid's troops and had a ship's guns trained and ready to fire upon it from the sea. This problem also, in the end, was resolved by the ingenuity of his sisters:

> Armed to the teeth, Barghash at last consented to be wrapped in a sehele [Ar. = *'abâ`a*], which only left his eyes free and Abd il Aziz...scarcely twelve years old at the time...was disguised in the same way. We chose the tallest woman of our retinue to walk by the side of Barghash, to render his height less conspicuous; and before starting we each said a little prayer, which for all we knew, might be our last.[71]

The following morning on 9 October, news reached Rigby that Barghash had escaped and was in the process of strengthening the defences of 'Marseilles' while 'openly express[ing] his intention to seize the government of the island'.[72]

Exasperated by 'the habits of procrastination peculiar to the Arabs' and by Majid's inability after the passage of a whole week 'to induce his troups to storm the position of the rebels', Rigby called upon Commander Adams and Lieutenant Berkeley of the visiting British warships to attack Barghash's stronghold. One hundred British marines equipped with a twelve-pounder howitzer and followed by 5,000 of Majid's men succeeded after a heavy bombardment of 'Marseilles' in crushing the revolt on 16 October.[73] Barghash, however, had once again given his pursuers the slip having escaped during the night before the final assault. But contrary to his original plan, the idea of plundering and setting fire to Zanzibar town had been rejected by his own Harthi companions who, at the last minute, had been unwilling to put their own families residing in the town at risk.[74] The following morning Rigby himself arrested Barghash who was forced to sign whilst swearing an oath upon the Quran 'that he was never to associate with either the French or the Hirth...[and] to solemnly promise to quit Zanzibar for ever'. On 21 October, Barghash was finally sent into exile on a boat bound for Bombay.[75]

The dismemberment of Oman

In the sequence of events of the 1859 Rebellion worthy of a modern-day Hollywood thriller, the main actor had of course been Rigby. From the moment he arrived to assume his post as consul, he had been greeted by a troubled Majid who, from the first, had been forced to rely heavily on the former's goodwill. More importantly, Rigby had been welcomed by a willing and cooperative Sulayman b Hamad who had been prepared to lay the considerable assets he possessed at the consul's disposal for the sake of defending Majid's position. But in his preoccupation to save Majid's neck at all costs Sulayman, no doubt unwittingly, had also provided Rigby with a powerful leverage *vis-à-vis* the commercial activity at Zanzibar. Surprised at first by the rising profitability curves of Zanzibar's trade, the Consul had single-mindedly set himself upon a course designed to ensure that the beneficiary of this trade would be British India and not Oman (see Chapter 11).

Rigby's intervention in Oman's succession dispute was also the first time that Britain had taken military action to support the claims of an Omani ruler. That this should have happened in Africa was ironic given the fact that Said had spent most of his life endeavouring to get precisely such British involvement in Omani possessions in Arabia. The irony is further compounded by the fact that when Britain finally chose to intervene militarily it was not, by their own admission, on behalf of the legitimate successor to Said b Sultan. That prerogative, as expressly declared by Coghlan at the time and despite Said's 1844 letter to Aberdeen, belonged to Thuwayni who paradoxically had been prohibited by Britain's military intercession to lay a claim on part of his realm in Africa.

In London, Rigby, like Hamerton before him, managed to get his iron-fisted methods rubber stamped by provoking the 'rabidly anti-slavery sentiments of the Foreign Office'. To rationalise his actions further, Rigby also invoked the notion of 'the protection of our British Indian subjects' and in addition openly exploited the almost pathological fear of the old French bogey by alleging that both Thuwayni and Barghash were in league with the French.[76] The truth was that although Thuwayni and Barghash may have turned to the French for succour, especially as the French were once again challenging the British position overseas at this time and had lost no opportunity in taking advantage granted to them by the absence of a British consul in Omani territories in the aftermath of the Indian Mutiny, there was no question of military cooperation as Rigby's reports would imply. As Barghash himself made clear during the 1859 Rebellion:

> My brother Majid's wish is to give the country to the English....We, however, will not give our country either to the English or to the French or to the Americans, or to anyone else; but if we sell it, we shall do so only at the cost of our blood and war until we all die.[77]

Having put Majid on Zanzibar's throne, Rigby naturally took on the role of main prop and advisor to the ruler though there was never the slightest doubt as to who was the dominant party. When he was pressed in 1861 to release a number of Harthi leaders captured in 1859, the consul had the temerity to suggest that in exchange for their release, the Harthi tribe should be forced to assume the responsibility for the payment of the annual MT$40,000 due to Muscat.[78] Normally in Oman's traditions, it was the rulers who distributed bounty to gain the support of tribal leaders. But Rigby, like so many other British officials before and after him, convinced of the infallibility and superiority of Western methods, evinced not even a modicum of interest as to how the Omanis ran their own affairs.

By the time Rigby left Zanzibar in September 1861 for health reasons, he was greatly despised even by those who had at first welcomed and cooperated with him. But if his departure was regarded as the 'termination of a great catastrophe',[79] his partisan accounts and the very support he had originally received from the local *a'ayan* had done enough damage to have persuaded Coghlan that 'such being the altered condition and circumstances of the African dependencies, it seems consonant with reason and justice...that the people of those countries should have a voice in the election of their sovereign'.[80] This, combined with the facts that 'the separation of Zanzibar from Muscat would deal a great blow to the slave trade' and that it would be nigh impossible for one ruler to govern both areas, effectively led Coghlan to remark further as he now recommended partition: 'Fortunately, the *expediency* on which they [Coghlan's conclusions] are based, and which would hardly suffice to justify the severance of that state from the parent state of Muscat, is adequately supported and confirmed by the arguments founded on *right*'.[81]

Although Coghlan's views on the *expediency* part could be explained by the content of the two previous quotations, it is not evident nor did Coghlan anywhere clarify whether the *right* he referred to related to that of the Omanis or the British. If Majid did indeed have any rights, Coghlan did not indicate on what criteria any such rights may have been based especially as he himself previously, in the same report, had declared: 'I am led to conclude that Syud Majid's claims to the independent sovereignty of Zanzibar...must be pronounced untenable'.[82] As for Thuwayni, even before the deportation of Barghash from Zanzibar, and with continuing strife in Oman, he had given up any hope (`âyasa min 'azmihi`) of ever acquiring Zanzibar.[83] Following his agreement to British arbitration, and long before even the British authorities had appointed Coghlan to his mission, Thuwayni already seemed resigned to the fact that Zanzibar was forever lost to Muscat.[84]

On 2 April 1861, working on Coghlan's recommendations, Lord Canning duly effected the formal partition of the Omani 'State' into two Sultanates with Zanzibar obliged to pay to Muscat an annual subsidy of MT\$40,000.[85] The Canning Award, as it came to be known, constituted nothing less than the imposition of the European notion of statehood on the African and Arabian sections of the Omani 'State'. Oman's own structures and institutions were far too inadequate to deal with the realities of the latter half of the nineteenth century particularly when compared to those introduced by Britain. Nor were they sufficient even to administer Oman's expanding trade connections, viewed in European terms as a far-flung 'empire'. And even if the rulers of the two newly formed Sultanates, henceforth officially addressed like the Ottomans by the grand title of 'Sultan', continued for many years thereafter to function in their old ways within their separate spheres of influence, the most radical change was not their mutual independence but the greater ease with which Britain could now control the two separate entities. As the reactions of the two Sultans to the Canning Award clearly indicate, they could not have grasped the full significance of the division of their father's realm, steeped as they were in Oman's tribal traditions. Nor could they have appreciated the implications of the Award with regard to their own independence. Here is how they responded to Lord Canning's decision:

> We heartily accept...and thank God for your efforts on our behalf, praying also that your goodwill may be rewarded and that you may never cease to be our support [Thuwayni];

> I feel very much obliged to the British Government for all its kindness and favour, and for having averted from my dominions disorders and hostilities. During my lifetime, I shall never forget the kindness which it has shown to me [Majid].[86]

These reactions clearly show that whereas Britain had established an economic stranglehold over Oman by exercising control over the 'Indian' merchant population, it was now able, by its manipulation of

the Sultans through the Canning Award, to confirm its political para-
mountcy over both Zanzibar and Muscat.

International recognition of the division of Oman

The French intrigues in Zanzibar which had so exercised Rigby's
imagination, although dismissed as exaggerated and without basis in
some accounts,[87] appear to have been genuine when viewed against the
backdrop of the resurgence of French colonial expansion in Africa at
that time.[88] As early as 4 June 1859, before Barghash's exile, Napoleon
III had written to Majid effectively recognising him as the new ruler of
Zanzibar:

> We have with great interest learnt about your accession to supreme
> power, after the death of your beloved father, Sultan Sayd, of
> venerable memory, who had always shown himself to be a sincere
> and devout friend of France....It gives us pleasure to repeat to you our
> congratulations...and we would always attach ourselves dearly to
> favour the joyous development of reciprocal relations, and we
> present to you the sentiments of our high estimation and goodwill.[89]

In the aftermath of this when Majid agreed in 1860 to provide facilities
to the French Catholic Mission,[90] these paved the way, somewhat
fortuitously, for an international recognition of the division of Oman.
By agreeing to provide a building in Zanzibar to the Bishop of Réunion,
Majid may have been hoping that the industrial and agricultural
projects that the French Mission promised to execute in Zanzibar would
provide benefits similar to those provided by clove cultivation in his
father's time.[91] But these facilities were described by an alarmed Rigby
as the establishment of a 'large barrack' by the French on the island.[92]
Rigby's reports together with the mutual distrust which characterised
the relationship between the consuls of France and Britain in Zanzibar,
further compounded by their misunderstanding of each other's actions
(the French thinking that Britain had initially supported Thuwayni in
his take-over bid for Zanzibar and the British being apprehensive of the
resurgence of French colonial expansion on the northern coast of East
Africa), eventually led to the 10 March 1862 British–French Declaration.[93] Outwardly this declaration guaranteed the 'independence' of the
two newly formed Sultanates but effectively it suppressed any ambitions that France may have had at Zanzibar encouraging the French
instead to confine their ambitions and reinforce what interests they
already had in Madagascar and the Comoro Islands. For Oman this
'guarantee of independence' had precisely the opposite meaning since

all powers, other than Britain, were now barred from intervening in the affairs of the Sultanates. The stage was thus left clear for Britain to 'rule the waves' in both Oman and Zanzibar at least until other European powers, notably Germany, Belgium and Italy, with their own colonial ambitions, started to encroach on the British-controlled zones in the late nineteenth century.

Conclusion

Since the time of the Ya'ariba Dynasty, despite the vicissitudes of Muscat's political and economic fortunes, commercial development in Oman had been a continuous evolving process. With the expulsion of the Portuguese from Omani-controlled trading outlets in the Gulf and on the East African coast, mercantile communities based in, or associated with, the commercially active port of Muscat increasingly reaped the benefits of the burgeoning trade in the western Indian Ocean region.

From these early days, commercial profits had been generated to a large extent by the alliance of Muscati rulers with merchants from India, some of whom had been long-standing residents in the Omani international port and, like other mercantile communities in Omani territories, continued to benefit from the centuries-old established connections at either end in India and in East Africa. The need for an alliance between Muscati rulers and the Hindu Banyans in particular had been dictated primarily by the vigorous 'Christian Crusade' type of policies pursued by the Portuguese against Muslims, which had favoured the Banyans who emerged as the dominant trading class of the Indian Ocean commercial networks. The rise of the Banyans had also owed a great deal to their own commercial practices governed by the principles of their Joint Family structure and these practices continued to play their part in the development of trade at Muscat and Zanzibar during the eighteenth and the nineteenth centuries.

By the time the Albusaidi Dynasty came to power in Oman, the role of Muscat in the regional trade had become so pivotal that it was the catalyst behind a series of intrigues and quarrels among Albusaidi leaders as they vied with each other to gain control of the trade. In the early nineteenth century, those leaders amongst them who did succeed in establishing their authority over Muscat soon realised that, with the loss of their traditional outlets in India to the British, their continued alliance with the Banyans and other Indians from areas outside the British-controlled zone provided them with the best opportunity to compete with the relatively newly arrived Western merchants and to hold on to what remained to them of their commercial standing regionally. Notable among these areas were the provinces of Sind and Kutch, Oman's traditional commercial partners.

Whilst Britain had few commercial and strategic interests in East Africa, this alliance and the resultant military cooperation between Omani rulers and the militarised Indian mercantile fleets paid handsome dividends, not only in boosting commercial activity in East Africa but also in subduing Omani and Swahili groups opposed to Albusaidi rule. In the commercial field, the remarkable development of Omani-inspired trade in Zanzibar, which increased by a multiple of almost five during the first half of the nineteenth century, shifted the focus of Omani trade from Muscat to Zanzibar where commercial prosperity was to reach its zenith during the late 1870s and early 1880s.

Nonetheless, contrary to what has hitherto been alleged, Muscat remained a vibrant commercial force in the triangular trading network connecting the ports of East Africa, Oman and western India. Indeed, the phenomenal rise in the commercial activity of East Africa would not have been possible without the participation of Muscati merchants in the evolving commercial activity centred on Oman's international port in Africa, Zanzibar. The foundations of this commercial expansion had been in existence during the eighteenth century when the prevailing trade system had been developed by the commercial practices of Omanis, Swahilis, Africans, Indians and a number of Europeans, particularly the Portuguese and the French, all residing on the African continent.

However, the nineteenth century commercial development of Oman owed its genesis, in the final analysis, to the Industrial Revolution of the West. While the Omani economy (together with its East African component) was being increasingly integrated into the international economy, the suppression of the European slave trade gave it an added stimulus as the ensuing surplus slave labour was exploited locally for agricultural and commercial purposes. The demand for commodities such as ivory and cloves from Africa or dates and textiles from Arabia, produced using traditional tribal and communal labour, rose as production was boosted by the increased availability of slave labour. This trend, coupled with a corresponding decline in the prices of imported manufactured goods, provided the dynamics of an enormous commercial expansion in both Omani-controlled localities.

In East Africa, as in Oman, an important consequence of the

expansion in trade was the participation of greater numbers of mainland Africans and interior Omani tribes in the internationally oriented commerce which was financed mainly by those Indians having close relations with the Albusaid. As trading activities in Oman and on the African mainland proliferated, the economy of the African interior, like that of the *dakhiliya* of Oman, became progressively monetised. The subsequent process, whereby interior manufactured and cultivated commodities were geared to the international market, resulted in the integration of both the Zanzibari and the Muscati component of the Omani economy within the nascent global capitalist system. With the mushrooming of trade networks on the African mainland, the frontiers of Zanzibari control in those areas which recognised at least a nominal Albusaidi suzerainty extended to the heart of Africa as far as present-day Zaire in the west, to parts of the Comoro Islands in the south and to the marchlands of Somalia in the north.

However, at the same time as these events were unfolding in the Omani domain, Britain was also going through an historic revolution that was to transform it into the foremost capitalist power in the world. Said b Sultan unwittingly began to challenge the British position by exceeding the bounds of Omani rulers' traditional alliances with the Indians. When he then entered into treaty relations with the Americans, the British were finally forced to respond decisively to quell what they perceived as the Omani-inspired threat to their supremacy in the Indian Ocean. With the systematic suppression of Omani interests, first in India and then in the Gulf, successive British consuls looked for ways to divert the benefits of Omani-generated commerce in the western Indian Ocean away from Oman and towards British India. At first, they managed to achieve their goal by forcing British nationality on those very 'Indians' who had long-term associations with Omani rulers including those from Sind and Kutch who had resided at Muscat prior to their move to Zanzibar. Later on, when the fortunes of these 'Indians' declined partly due to the legislative prohibitions upon their use of slave labour, Britain displayed no hesitation in replacing them in Omani ports with its own Indian agents thereby becoming the major beneficiary of Oman's remaining trade, notwithstanding the continued reliance of that trade on slave labour.

In addition to the 'nationality question' and the consequent increased British interference in Omani affairs under the pretext of 'the protection of our British subjects', two other factors contributed to facilitate British subjugation of Oman. Although the British antislavery campaigns were presented for public consumption as 'humanitarian' missions and may at times have been genuine, effectively they were skilfully exploited to appease other Western powers and Christian public opinion when Britain deemed it expedient to rationalise and disguise the often ruthless and far from 'humanitarian' measures it itself employed against the Omanis.

Ultimately Britain managed to achieve its goals at little cost to itself because the Albusaidi rulers of the second half of the nineteenth century found themselves totally powerless to assert their own legitimate rights. The roots of this impotence can be traced back to the time of Sultan b Ahmad who, as a result of the Wahhabi threat to his dominions and the Qasimi/Utbi challenge to Muscat's commerce, felt compelled to sign the 1798 Treaty with Britain, overawed as he was at the time by the unrelenting march of the British military machine as it rolled through India acquiring more and more territories and triumphing over all those who resisted its advance, notable among whom were the French and the ruler of Mysore, both former commercial allies of Oman.

After Sultan, the British acquired even more leverage in Oman's affairs during his son Said's long reign from 1806 to 1856. Far from marshalling his military resources to challenge Britain's iron-fisted policy towards Oman and beset with problems internally from the outset, Said b Sultan was obliged to make concessions to the British authorities. Using most of his military might to maintain his position within the tribal configuration of Oman, confronted as it continued to be by external challenges posed by a combination of forces such as the Qasimis, Utbis and the Wahhabis, Said was forced not only to ask the British for military succour but also to mediate in his own affairs when threatened by influential members of his family.

Said's various attempts to extricate himself from this state of dependency came to naught. After his overtures for military assistance to the determinedly neutral Americans had been unequivocally rebuffed, and witnessing in his own time the succession of British victories over France, the other major contender in the power-broking stakes, Said became even prepared to cede territories under his control to the British at a moment's notice so long as the latter provided him with an umbrella of protection against his internal and external enemies. It was Britain though which showed itself to be averse to becoming enmeshed in the internal web of the tribal-cum-religious affairs of Oman except in those cases when the need to protect its own interests dictated such an involvement. Whilst a certain degree of political symbiosis existed between the British authorities and Said b Sultan, with Oman evolving by the mid-century from a position of an 'independent state' to one having a 'client status' relationship with the British, the '*modus vivendi*' thus established lasted throughout Said's lifetime.

After Said, the increasing show of interest by other Western powers in Oman and its overseas territories compelled Britain to take more notice of Oman in its regional, political and commercial equation in an attempt to nip in the bud any threat that might be posed to British supremacy in the backyard of India. The prerogative already handed to the British authorities by Said to intervene in the succession dispute after his death, together with the 'nationality question' and the 'antislavery crusade', were the means by which Britain succeeded in imposing its authority over Oman. By dividing Said's realm in 1861, Britain could control the two Sultanates with greater ease. In the era leading up to the 'scramble', due to its established relations with Oman, there was a certain inevitability that it would be Britain rather than any other Western power which eventually assumed control of Zanzibar while Oman, failing to attract the same degree of attention from other Western powers, remained only nominally independent.

Even those rulers among Said's successors, such as his son Barghash, who were aware of the imperative to face up to the British, found that their predecessors had left them with neither the institutions nor the resources to match those of the already established and recognised British Empire. Omani rulers became fully aware, as successive British consuls unfailingly pointed out to them, that without the approval of the paramount power they would never have been able to assume power, such as it was, in the first place. In addition, Said's successors became preoccupied with the need to conserve their own social and religious traditions which came to be progressively challenged by imported notions that the Westerners had brought along with them. They soon discovered the futility of mounting any sort of resistance and one by one they were convinced by events that they had no alternative but to respond to the local and regional policies forged by the dominant power in the region.

Already by Barghash's time, the 'Omani State' had been divided up and the ground was being prepared for the future absorption of Omani dominions in Africa within the European colonial systems and the subjugation of those territories once controlled by Oman in the Gulf to the British. Thus the roots of Muscat's dependence, laid down in the ill-fated 1798 Treaty with Britain which was purportedly motivated by such lofty aims and aspirations as 'the friendship of the two States may remain unshook till the end of time, and till the sun and moon have finished their revolving career', had branched out by the end of the nineteenth century into a complete British stranglehold over the political and economic interests that Oman formerly enjoyed in the western Indian Ocean region.

Appendices

APPENDIX 1: 1750 LETTER FROM THE RULER OF ANJOUAN TO AHMAD B SAID ALBUSAIDI

In the Name of God.

From Sultan Sayyid Ahmad ibn Salih and all the People of Anjouan

To the Imam of all Moslems, Ahmad ibn Said Albusaidi

After compliments and kindest inquiry of the 'august' health:

We have received your honoured letter by our brother Sulayman: it gave us much satisfaction to get it: we read it and understood its contents. With regard to your demand for men and money, we beg to state that we are quite willing to offer you whatever you demand but we have got one request to lay before you: it is this, our country is a very small one, it only extends to about half a day's march both in length and breadth, our people are very few and in order to increase our number we are obliged to keep our youths and get them married and have them live with their wives. If we allow them to leave the country, our country will be depopulated. We are very few in number and most of us are poor and needy. We therefore beg of your clemency to spare our men. Your predecessors made a similar demand of us but when we explained the matter to them they spared us. We shall feel greatly obliged if you will spare us the demand for our youths. If you still insist on enforcing your demand then we will submit to it without demur. We also request you to spare us from the payment you require but if you insist on having both, then we will be prepared to submit without demur. In any case we beg to repeat our entreaties to you to spare us from sending men because our country is a small island. Please, Sir, send us your reply whether favourable or unfavourable. Be assured, Sir, that we are loyal, obedient and consider ourselves as your subjects and we will never gainsay you in anything. Wassalam.

Dated Wednesday, 12th Jamad al-Awwal, 1163 [= 19 April 1750].

Source: ZA/PMMR/ARC/55

APPENDIX 2: SAID B SULTAN'S 1844 LETTER TO ABERDEEN

From His Highness the Imaum of Muscat to the Right Honourable the Earl of Aberdeen

Dated Zanzibar, 6 Rajab 1260; 23 July 1844

Be it known to your Lordship that we are always grateful for, and sensible of the kindness of the British Government. We are, as it were, overwhelmed with a sense of received favours.

In the Treaty between us and Her Majesty Queen Victoria of England, concluded and signed at Muscat on the 22nd July 1840, it is mentioned that the obligations are binding on us and our posterity: and for which we all feel happy; please God, during our lifetime, all will be duly fulfilled on our parts – we will abide by it.

And after us (on our death) we constitute and appoint our son Syud Khaled to be the Ruler of all our African possessions; that is to say all places on the continent of Africa between Magadosha, situated in about 2°10" north latitude, and Cape Delgado, situated in about 10°42" south latitude, together with the adjacent islands now subject to our rule and under our dominion. And in like manner, our son Syud Thoeenee to be Ruler over all our possessions in Oman in Arabia, in the Persian Gulf, and on the coast of Persia. And please God the two before-mentioned, our sons Syud Khaled and Syud Thooenee, will strictly conform to the stipulations of the Treaty; and furthermore, do all things in conformity with the wishes of the British Government; and our hope and desire is, that the British Government may be favourably disposed towards these our sons Syud Khaled and Syud Thooenee; and we feel certain that the Government will not withhold its friendship from them.

Whatever you require of us, it is for you to signify.

From the expectant of God's mercy,

(signed) Syud bin Sultan. (True translation) (signed) Atkins Hamerton.

Sources: ZA/CA4/1/3; PRO/FO/54/6 and IOR/L/P&S/5/501

APPENDIX 3: SAID B SULTAN'S WILL, 1850

In the Name of the Most Merciful God

Syud Saeed bin Sultan bin el Imaum Ahmed been Saeed Al boo Saeedy wills, with regard to what is incumbent upon him from his property after his decease in respect of all the funeral rites after his death until his burial, 500 dollars of his property, after his death, to whosoever washes his body with the washing of the departed, and to whoever digs the grave in which he is interred after his death. Also 500 dollars of his property, after his death, to his relatives who do not inherit anything from him. Also 1,000 expiatory prayers, each expiatory prayer (to be of the value of) what will feed sixty poor people. Also remuneration to whoever shall fast for him for the space of fifty months, in lieu of what was incumbent on himself for the transgression of the fast of the months of Ramadhan, and the remuneration is to be defrayed from his property, after his death, at the discretion of his executors. Also remuneration to whoever shall perform in his stead the pilgrimage of the Mussulmans to the Holy House of God, which is in the renowned (city of) Mecca, and shall visit in his stead the tomb of our Prophet Mahomed (upon whom be peace), which is at the Medinah of Yathrib, and shall, in his stead, offer up the salutations of peace to him and to his two companions the faithful Aboobekr and Omar-ibn-el-Khattab (God be gracious to them!) and shall perform in his stead, in such pilgrimage and visitation, the proper duties and ceremonies, and whatever God has ordained as well-pleasing (to Him); the remuneration for this is to be defrayed from his property, after his death, at the discretion of his executors. And whatever arms or weapons of war he possesses, he bequeaths to his male children. And his two ships, the 'Feid Alim' and 'Caroline', he gives, after his death, as a legacy to the Treasury of the Mussulmans. And whatever other ships he possesses besides those two ships are to be sold after his death, and their value to be divided among all his heirs according to what God has ordained in His law – to each one his share of the inheritance. And the said Syud Saeed declares to be free all the male and female slaves which shall remain in his possession after his death, excepting those who are at his plantation; for the sake of the Almighty God, and in the hope of His mercy. And he bequeaths to each one of them whatever each may possess – it is to be theirs. And he bequeaths to every Abyssinian male or female slave fifty dollars out of his property after his death. And to each of his concubines one hundred dollars out of his property after his death; and whatever she may possess, it is to be hers. And the said Syud Saeed has constituted all his houses at Bunder Muscat, and all which are at Bunder Zanzibar and at

Watiyyah, an endowment for ever to his heirs collectively as a bequest from him. The said Syud Saeed bequeaths whatever shall remain of his apparel, after his death, to his male children. And he has forbidden the sale of whatever furniture or utensils his houses may contain; but they are to be divided among his heirs according to what God has ordained in His law – to each one his share of the inheritance. And the said Syud Saeed has appointed his wife, the daughter of Seif bin Alli, and his nephew Mahomed bin Salem bin Sultan, and his son Khaled bin Saeed, his executors in regard to whatever he may possess or owe, he appoints them, his executors therein, to execute this Will which he has willed. And he confirms all that he has directed to be placed to his account, and directs that it be done and carried out into effect out of his property after his death. Whether the same be obligatory upon him or not, he has made it obligatory upon himself, hoping that his executors will duly execute the same, and that his heirs will be satisfied therewith. God is the witness over all.

Done on Monday, the 26th day of Ramadhan, of the months of the year of the Hegira of the Prophet, 1266 [= 6 August 1850], and written for him, at his direction, by the hand of his servant (the poor towards God) – Saeed bin Nasir bin Khalaf-el-Maooly [al-Ma'wali].

(The following, in the original, is in the handwriting of the late Syud Saeed, the testator.)

What is written in this Will is true, and it was (written) of my own free-will, and in my sight. This is written by the hand of the vile Saeed.

(Codicil) And I bequeath to the liberated slaves, Georgians and Abyssinians, who have no children, or whose children are not grown up, as also the Abyssinian eunuchs, the produce of the plantation of Showeni: all its proceeds are for their subsistence, except the female slaves who may marry – such are to have nothing; and if any shall separate from their husbands, those are not to have anything. Salaam.

Written by the vile Saeed with his own hand.

(Codicil) The male slaves at the plantation of Showeni are also to share in the plantation for their subsistence.

(True translation) (signed) George Percy Badger

Sources: ZA/CA4/1/3 and IOR/L/P&S/5/507

Glossary

âl	family; clan; people
'âlim	sing. of 'ulama (q.v.)
'aṣabîya	tribal or group cohesion
`awlâd	lit. = sons of, genealogical branch
`a'yân	notables, political or religious leaders
barza	public audience given by the ruler
dâkhilîya	[Om.] interior
dallâl	broker
dâr	(pl. diyâr) house, tribal territory
fakhdh	lit. thigh = clan
falaj	(pl. aflâj) irrigational channel
ḥajj	pilgrimage to Mecca
ḥarîm	women or women's quarters, for wives and concubines
hijrî	Islamic date commencing from Prophet Muhammad's emigration from Mecca to Madina in 622 AD
Imâm	prayer leader; [Om.] elected leader with political and religious authority
laqab	nickname; sobriquet
madhhab	Islamic School of Law
nahḍa	Ibadi reform or revival movement
nâ`ib	deputy
nisba	clan or affiliative name
qâḍî	(pl. quḍât) religious judge
salafîya	Islamic reform or revival movement
sayyid	descendants of the Prophet Muhammad; in Oman title for members of the ruling family
shâmba	[Sw.] plantation or plot of land
shaykh	(Sw. = shehe or mzee) leader of a tribe or clan
sulṭân	title for a secular ruler; not to be confused with the

	personal name Sultân
tamîma	paramount leader of a tribal confederation
taqîya	precautionary dissimulation of one's faith
ṭarîqa	religious order; sufi brotherhood
'ulamâ`	(sing. 'âlim) learned men, religious scholars or leaders
wâdî	valley
wakîl	(Per. = vakîl) representative; commercial agent
wâlî	(Per. = vâlî) governor

Notes

INTRODUCTION

1 al-Marhûbî, 'Âmir b 'Umayr, 1986, 'al-Ḥaḍârat al-'Umâniyat al-Qadîma'; Tosi M., 1983, 'Early Maritime Cultures of the Arabian Gulf and the Indian Ocean', preliminary paper delivered in Bahrain Through the Ages Conference, quoted in Wilkinson J.C., 1987, 'The Imamate Tradition of Oman', 33.

2 Braudel F., 1973, 'The Mediterranean and the Mediterranean World in the Age of Philip II', tr. Reynolds S, II.

3 For this idea see notably Coupland R., 1939, 'The Exploitation of East Africa, 1856–1890', 4–5; Ingham K., 1962, 'A History of East Africa', 19 et passim.

4 Allen C.H., 1978, 'Sayyids, Shets and Sultans: Politics and Trade in Masqat Under the Al Bu Said, 1785–1914', Ph.D. Dissn., Uni. of Washington, 68–93 et passim.

5 Hamilton A., 1727, 'A New Account of the East Indies', I, 44–5.

6 Chaudhuri K.N., 1985, 'Trade and Civilisation in the Indian Ocean, An Economic History from the Rise of Islam to 1750', 163.

7 Bathurst R.D., 1972, 'Maritime Trade and Imamate Government: Two Principal Themes in the History of Oman to 1728', in Hopwood D. [ed.], 'The Arabian Peninsula: Society and Politics', 99.

8 Steensgaard N., 1972, 'Carracks, Caravans and Companies: The Structural Crisis in the European–Asian Trade in the Early Seventeenth Century'.

9 Juhaina, 105; Bennett N.R., 1978, 'A History of the Arab State of Zanzibar', 11.

10 Juhaina, ii and 15; Cooper F., 1977, 'Plantation Slavery on the East Coast of Africa', 30.

11 Wilkinson J.C., 1969, 'Arab Settlement in Oman: The Origins and Development of the Tribal pattern and its Relationship to the Imamate', D.Phil. th., Uni. of Oxford, ii; Wilkinson J.C., 1987, Part III; see also Ennami A.K., 1971, 'Studies in Ibadism', Ph.D. th., Uni. of Cambridge.

12 For a detailed discussion see Wilkinson J.C., 1987, chaps 5 and 8.

13 Wilkinson J.C., 1987, chap. 3.

14 Khazanov A.M., 1983, 'Nomads and the Outside World', 3 and 296, passim.

15 Eickelman D.F., 1985, 'From Theocracy to Monarchy: Authority and

Legitimacy in Inner Oman, 1935–1957', in IJMES, 17, 4; idem, 1987, 'Ibadism and the Sectarian Perspective', in Pridham B.R., [ed.], 'Oman: Economic, Social and Strategic Developments', 32.
16 Spear T., 1981, 'Oral Traditions: Whose History?', in *History in Africa*, 8, 165–81.
17 Barth F., 1987, 'Complications of Geography, Ethnology and Tribalism', in Pridham B.R., [ed.], op. cit., 17–31; idem, 1983, 'Sohar: Culture and Society in an Omani Town', 191 et passim.

1 OMAN'S LINKS WITH INDIA AND EAST AFRICA: HISTORICAL PROBLEMS AND PERSPECTIVES

1 Nicholls C.S., 1971, 'The Swahili Coast–Politics, Diplomacy and Trade on the East African Littoral, 1798–1856', 217.
2 ZA/AA12/2, Ahmad b Nu'mân al-Ka'bî quoted in Rigby to Wilson, 5 September 1861; Brunschvig R., ''Abd' in EI2; Lewis B., 1976, 'The African Diaspora and the Civilization of Islam', in Kilson M.L. and Rotberg R., [eds], 'The African Diaspora: Interpretative Essays', 37–57; for slavery in pre-Islamic times see Irwing G.W., 1977, 'Africans Abroad, A Documentary History'; for a speculative study discussing earlier works on slavery and Islam in the East African context see Cooper F., 1981, 'Islam and Cultural Hegemony: The Ideology of Slaveowners on the East African Coast', in Lovejoy P.E., [ed.], 'The Ideology of Slavery in Africa', 271–309.
3 For the early links between Oman and East Africa see Hourani G., 1951, 'Arab Seafaring in the Indian Ocean in Ancient and Medieval Times', 80; extracts from al-Mas'udi and al-Idrisi in SD, 14–21; Froelich J.-C., 1968, 'Les Arabes en Afrique de l'Est', in *Revue Française d'Etudes Politiques Africaines*, 26–40; Trimingham J.S., 1975 a, 'The Arab Geographers and the East African Coast', and idem, 'Notes on Arabic Sources of Information on East Africa', both in Chittick H.N. and Rotberg R.I., [eds], 'East Africa and the Orient, Cultural Synthesis in Pre-Colonial Times', 115–47 and 248–72; see also Juhaina, passim.
4 Bathurst R.D., 1967, 'The Yarubi Dynasty of Oman', D.Phil. Dissn., Uni. of Oxford, passim.
5 For these notions, see Ingrams W.H., 1931, 'Zanzibar, Its History and Peoples'; Reusch R., 1954, 'History of East Africa'.
6 Alpers E.A., 1975, 'Ivory and Slaves in East Central Africa', 127.
7 Alpers E.A., 1969, 'The Coast and the Development of the Caravan Trade', in Kimambo I.N. and Temu A.J., [eds], 'A History of Tanzania', 45–7; for similar views see Nicholls C.S., 1971, 101–2; Gray J.M.,1962a, 'History of Zanzibar from the Middle Ages to 1856', 111; Coupland R., 1938, 'East Africa and its Invaders', 151–3; Cooper F., 1977, 30; Berg F.J., 1971, 'Mombasa under the Busaidi Sultanate: the city and its hinterland in the nineteenth century', Ph.D. Dissn., Uni. of Wisconsin, 76; Pouwels R.L., 1987, 'Horn and Crescent, Cultural Change and Traditional Islam on the East African Coast, 800–1900', 99.
8 For views of a northern coastal birthplace see Chittick H.N., 1974, 'Kilwa, an Islamic Trading City on the East African Coast', vols 1 and 2; Pouwels

R.L., 1978, 'The Medieval Foundations of East African Islam', Parts 1 and 2 in IJAHS, vol. 11; for views of a southern coastal settlement see Allen J. de V., 1982, 'The "Shirazi" Problem in East African Coastal History' in *Paideuma*, vol. 28, 9–29; but cf. idem, 1981, 'Swahili Culture and the Nature of East Coast Settlement' in IJAHS, vol. 14, where Allen seems to be more in favour of a northern coastal birthplace; see also Shepherd G., 1982, 'The Making of the Swahili: A view from the Southern End of the East African Coast', in *Paideuma*, vol. 28, 129–49.

9 Gray J.M., 1954, 'The Wadebuli and the Wadiba' in TNR, 36; Chittick H.N., 1965; Freeman-Grenville G.S.P., 1962, 163, 289–90; Gray J.M., 1962a, 23–30.

10 Ali T., 1927, quoted in Gregory R.G., 1971, 'India and East Africa', 5.

11 For a standard account see Trimingham J.S., 1964, 'Islam in East Africa'; see also Pouwels R.L., 1987.

12 Juhaina, ii and 15; al-Qahtaniya, 395; Wilkinson J.C., 1975, 'The Julanda of Oman', in JOS, 1, 97–109; Kirkman J., 1983, 'The Early History of Oman in East Africa' in JOS, 6, 41–59.

13 Kirkman J., ibid., 43.

14 Juhaina, p. ii of Introduction.

15 Pouwels R.L., 1974, 'Tenth Century Settlement of the East African Coast: the case for Qarmatian/Ismaili connection', in *Azania*, 9; see also Trimingham J.S., 1965, 'Islam in Ethiopia', 62–8; for views on the origins of the word 'Swahili' see Tolmacheva M., 1976, 'The Origin of the Name Swahili', in TNR nos 77–8; Eastman C., 1971, 'Who are the Waswahili?' in *Africa*, 41, 228–35; Prins A.H., 1961, 'The Swahili-speaking Peoples of Zanzibar and the East African Coast'.

16 Ricks T.M., 1970, 'Persian Gulf Seafaring and East Africa: Ninth to Twelfth Centuries', in AHS, 3, 339–57; Martin B.G., 1974, 'Arab Migrations to East Africa in Medieval Times', in IJAHS, 7, 367–90; Gregory R.G., 1971, 5, passim; Pouwels R.L., 1987, 137–8, passim; Juhaina, passim.

17 For the Shirazi Dynasty of Kilwa see Chittick H.N., 1965; idem, 1974; idem, 1975; for a publication of the Kilwa sira, BL Ms. Or. 2666, see 'Kitâb al-Salwa fî Akhbâr Kilwa', MNHC, Muscat, 1985.

18 Freeman-Grenville G.S.P., 1978, 'Shi'i Rulers at Kilwa' in *Numismatic Chronicle*, 8, 187–90.

19 Wilkinson J.C., 1981, 'Oman and East Africa: New Light on Early Kilwan History from the Omani Sources', in IJAHS, 14, 272–305.

20 Chittick H.N., 1980, 'East Africa and the Orient: Ports and Trade before the arrival of the Portuguese', in UNESCO, 'Historical Relations across the Indian Ocean', 16.

21 Stern S.M., 1960, 'The Early Ismaili Missionaries in North-West Persia and in Khurasan and Transoxania', in BSOAS, 23, 56–90; idem, 1949, 'Ismaili Propaganda and Fatimid Rule in Sind', in *Islamic Culture*, 23, 298–307; al-Hamdani A., 1956, 'Beginnings of the Ismaili Da'awa in Northern India'.

22 Faḍl al-lâh, 'Jâm'i al-Târîkh', 1960 edn, 9; Nanji A., 1978, 'The Nizari–Ismaili Tradition in the Indo-Pakistan Subcontinent', 35; for the spread of the *da'wa* in Gujarat see al-Nu'mân, al-Qâḍî Abû Ḥanîfa, 'Risâlat Iftitâḥ al-Da'wa', 1970 edn; for detailed studies of early Arab relations with India see al-Nadwi S.S., 1930, 'Arab-o-Hind ke Ta'alluqât'; al-Ṭîrâzî, 'Abd-allah,

1403/1983, 'Mawsû'at al-Ta`rîkh al-Islâmî wa al-Hadârat al-Islâmîya li bilâd al-Sind wa al-Panjâb fî 'ahd al-'Arab', vols 1 and 2; Jehangir B.H., 1973, 'The Arabs in Sind', Ph.D. Dissn., Uni of Utah.

23 Wilkinson J.C., 1972, 'The origins of the Omani State', in Hopwood D., [ed.], op. cit., 76; see also idem, 1975, 102; idem, 1974, 'Bayasirah and Bayadir', in *Arabian Studies*, 1, 84, n. 10.

24 For mercantile financial aid to Ismailism see Salibi K., 1980, 'A History of Arabia', 101–15; for Ibadism see Wilkinson J.C., 1972, 75.

25 al-Mas'ûdî, 'Murûj al-dhahab wa Madâ`in al-Jawhar', 1965 edn, I, 198; al-Istakhrî, 'Kitâb al-Masâlik wa al-Mamâlik', 1927 edn, 175; see also Esmail A. and Nanji A., 1977, 'The Ismailis in History', in Nasr S.H., [ed.], 'Ismaili Contributions to Islamic Culture', 233.

26 Nadvi S.S., 1930, op. cit.; Hamdani A., 1956, op. cit.

27 Tuhfa I, 263–4.

28 Lewis B., 1949/50, 'The Fatimids and the Route to India', in *Révue de la Faculté des Sciences de l' Université d' Istanbul*, vols 1–4, 50–4; Hamdani A., 1967, 'The Fatimid–Abbasid Conflict in India', in *Islamic Culture*, 41, 185–91.

29 Tuhfa I, 123; see article on Daybul in EI2.

30 Whitehouse D. and Williamson A., 1973, 'Sasanian Maritime Trade', in *Iran*, 11, 29–49; Wilkinson J.C., 1979, 'Suhar (Sohar) in the Early Islamic Period: The Written Evidence', in *Proceedings of the fourth International Conference of South Asian Archeology*; idem, 1972, 'Arab–Persian Land Relationships in the Late Sasanid Period', in *Proceedings of the sixth Seminar for Arabian Studies*.

31 Williamson A., 1973a, 'Sohar and Omani Seafaring in the Indian Ocean'; Wilkinson J.C., 1979, op. cit.

32 Chaudhuri K.N., 1985, 121; Nadvi S.S., 1966, 'Arab Navigation', 39; for Meccan merchants' fear of the sea under Caliphs 'Umar and the Umayyad Mu'âwiya see al-Tabarî, 'Târîkh al-Tabarî', 1879 edn, vol. I.

33 Tuhfa I, 154–5.

34 Pocock D.F., 1955, 'Indians in East Africa, with special reference to their Social and Economic Situation and Relationship', D.Phil. th., Uni. of Oxford, 16.

35 Irwing G., 1977, 139–67; Battacharya D.K., 1973, 'Indians of African Origin', in *Cahiers d' Etudes Africaines*, 40, 579–82.

36 Allen J. de V., 1985, 'Habash, Habshi, Sidi, Sayyid', in Stone J.C., [ed.], 1985, 'Africa and the Sea', 131–52.

37 Pires T., 'Trade Relations of the East Coast with Europe, Arabia and the Far East', in SD, 126; for pre-Portuguese direct links between East Africa and India see Yule H., [ed.], 1871, 'The Book of Marco Polo', 346 et passim; see also Gregory R.G., 1971; Boxer C.R., 1969, 'The Portuguese Seaborne Empire'; and Alpers E.A., 1976, 'Gujarat and the Trade of East Africa', in IJAHS, 9, 22–44.

38 Strandes J., 1899, 'The Portuguese Period in East Africa', Kirkman J.S., [ed.], and Wallwork J.F., [tr.], 1961, 93.

39 Chaudhuri K.N., 1985, 208.

40 Das Gupta A., 1970, 'Trade and Politics in 18th Century India', in Richards D.S., [ed.], 'Islam and the Trade of Asia', 181–215.

41 ibid.

42 Pocock D.F., 1955, p. vi of the Introduction; see also Das Gupta A., 1979, 'Indian Merchants and the Decline of Surat'.

43 Thoothi N.A., 1935, 'The Vaishnavas of Gujerat', 20; Das Gupta A., 1970, op. cit.

44 al-Tirazi A., 1983, 107.

45 al-Idrîsî, 'Nuzhat al-Mushtâq', in Elliot H.M. and Dowson J., [eds], 1867–77, 'The History of India as told by its own Historians', I, 77; for Arab cultural influences see Lombard M., 1971, 'L'Islam dans sa Première Grandeur'.

46 Mangat J.S., 1969, 'A History of the Asians in East Africa', p. ix of the Preface.

47 The identity of these various communities and their commercial role will become clear when we discuss trading activities in Part III.

48 Two notable exceptions of researchers who have managed to obtain some information on Banyan Family histories are Pocock D.F., 1955 and Allen C.H. 1978; through interviews and correspondence between 1981 and 1988, I have also managed to gather some information about Banyan and other Indian families involved in Muscat's trade, as will be shown in the course of this book.

49 See Chaudhuri K.N., 1985, chap. 5.

50 'Banyan' here is not used as a general term to describe 'natives of India' as was done by British agents and consular officials throughout the nineteenth century, causing great confusion as to which ethnic or religious groups different members of the Indian community actually belonged. Here 'Banyan' refers to the Hindu Vanya merchants. For the way the Banyans fit into the Hindu caste system see Enthoven R.E., 1920, 'The Tribes and Castes of Bombay'; Pocock D.F., 1955, chap. 5; Chopra P.N., 1982, 'Religions and Communities in India', 86–90.

51 See, for example, Cooper F., 1977, 42, n. 70; for other similar views see the works cited in note 7 of this chapter.

52 For the Joint Family organisation of the Banyans and its beneficial impact upon trade see Chapter 5.

53 Serjeant R.B., 1963, 'The Portuguese off the South Arabian Coast', 43; Chaudhuri K.N., 1985, chap. 3; see also Pearson M.N., 1976, 'Merchants and Rulers in Gujerat: The Response to the Portuguese in the Sixteenth Century'.

54 Chaudhuri K.N., 1985, 66; see also Chaudhuri K.N., 1965, 'The English East India Company: The Study of an Early Joint-Stock Company'; and Mollat M., 1970, [ed.], 'Sociétés et Compagnies de Commerce en Orient et dans l'Océan Indien'.

55 Chaudhuri K.N., 1985, 66, passim.

56 Floor W., 1985, 'A Description of Masqat and Oman Anno 1673 A.D./1084 Q.', in *Moyen Orient et Océan Indien*, vol. 2, 1–69.

57 For a contemporary report mentioning this incident see Wilmson G., 1673, 'A Description of the Government and Trade of Oman', reproduced as part of Floor W., 1985 in the preceding note; incident also mentioned in al-Fath, 286–91, tr. 81–7; cf. al-Qahtaniya, 429 and Tuhfa II, 64 where the daughter in question is that of another Banyan named Sakabila who, like Narutem, was allegedly an agent for the Portuguese.

58 al-Qahtaniya, 456; al-Fath, 291.

59 Alpers E.A., 1975, 70–98.
60 ibid., 90; Sheriff A.M.H., 1971, 'The Rise of a Commercial Empire: An Aspect of the Economic History of Zanzibar, 1770–1873', Ph.D. th., Uni. of London, chaps 2 and 3.
61 Morice-Projet, 106, 109, 137, passim; see also Alpers E.A., 1975, chap. 5.
62 IOR/P/381/29, P A M Seton's Jnl, 5 November 1801; his full name was Sa'îd b Aḥmad b Muḥammad b Khalaf; see also al-Fath, 350.
63 Portuguese Archives quoted in Alpers E.A., 1975, 90, 101, n. 60; for lack of ships in Ahmad b Said's own fleet see Floor W., 1979, 'A Description of the Persian Gulf and its Inhabitants in 1756', in *Persica*, 8, 163–86.
64 Anon. Ms, 161; Bathurst R.D., 1967, 319, n. 1; for Ahmad b Said's treatment of the Persians see al-Fath, 342–7, tr. 152–55; or for a less colourful version Anon., 160ff.
65 Padbrugge R., 1673, 'A Description of Masqat', in Floor W., 1985, op. cit.
66 ibid., 25.
67 For these relations with Sind and Mysore see Chapter 3
68 IOR/P/381/3, Hajji Khalil to Duncan, n.d. but sometime in January 1801; Hajji Khalil was Sultan b Ahmad's customs master at Bander Abbas.
69 Pocock D.F., 1955, 16; Bathurst R.D., 1967, 176.
70 On the horse Trade see Elliot H.M. and Dowson J., [eds], 1867–77, 8, 28–35; Mookerji R., 1912, 'Indian Shipping, A History of the Seaborne Trade and Maritime Activity of the Indians from the Earliest Times', 195; Digby S., 1971, 'War Horse and Elephant in the Delhi Sultanate: A Study of Military Supplies', part 2.
71 Floor W., 1982, 'First Contacts between the Netherlands and Masqat or A Report on the Discovery of the Coast of Oman in 1666...' in *Zeitschrift der Deutschen Morgenlandischen Gesellschaft*, 132, 289–307.

2 THE IMPORTANCE OF COMMERCE TO THE EARLY ALBUSAIDI RULERS

1 Tuhfa II, 98; Kashf, 113; Bathurst R.D., 1967, 260.
2 Qisas, 123–131; al-Shua'a, 271, passim.
3 Anon. Ms, 163–4; Bathurst R.D., 1967, 322; Tuhfa II, 169, quoted by Wilkinson J.C., 1987, 226, gives the election date as 1167 AH = 1753/4 AD; for a resolution of 1749 as being the correct date, see Beckingham C.F., 1941, 'The Reign of Ahmad ibn Said, Imam of Oman', in JRAS, 28, 257–60.
4 Darwîsh, Madîha Ahmad, 1982, 'Salṭanat 'Umân fî al-qarnayn al-thâmin 'ashar wa al-tâs'î 'ashar', 80.
5 Miles S.B., 1919, 'The Countries and Tribes of the Persian Gulf', 258; for the unimportance of the Albusaid at that time in Oman's tribal structure see al-Siyâbî, Sâlim b Ḥamûd, 1965, 'Is'âf al-a'ayân fî ansâb ahl 'Umân', 97–8.
6 Tuhfa II, 162.
7 For Nadir Shah's campaigns in Oman see Lockhart L., 1935–7, 'Nadir Shah's Campaign in Uman, 1737–1744', in BSOAS, 8, 157–71; see also Bathurst R.D., 1967, 278–313 ; Tuhfa II, 137–67; and al-Shua'a, 328–49.
8 Tuhfa II, 161; al-Ma'walî, Abû Sulaymân Muhammad b 'Âmir, 'Fî dhikr nihâyat al-Ya'âriba', printed as Section 7 of MNHC edition of Kashf, 156.

9 Tuhfa II, 138; Bathurst R.D., 1967, 259 and 279.
10 al-Qahtaniya, 453.
11 Niebuhr C., 1780, 'Voyage de M. Niebuhr en Arabie...', 1792, [tr.], II, 122; Risso P., 1986, 'Oman and Muscat, An Early Modern History', 43 and Appendix 4; Risso, quoting the same source, maintains that Ahmad actually married a daughter of Sayf b Sultan al-Ya'rubi but the English translation used here says only that he married a lady from the ruling family.
12 al-Qahtaniya, 453ff.
13 ibid.
14 Juhaina, 118; Tuhfa II, 142–3.
15 Lockhart L., 1935–7, op. cit.
16 al-Qahtaniya, 450.
17 For Ahmad b Said's efforts to control the East African coast, see Guillain-Documents I, 547.
18 Lorimer J.G., 1908–15, 'Gazetteer of the Persian Gulf, Oman and Central Arabia', IA, 416.
19 Tuhfa, 121–9; Kashf, 125–38; Risso P., 1986, 42–4, passim; Peterson J.E., 1978, 'Oman in the twentieth century: Political Foundations of an Emerging State', 112; Kelly J.B., 1968, 'Britain and the Persian Gulf, 1795–1880', 4–5.
20 For an attempt to categorise the various tribes, including the coastal mercantile communities according to their territories in Oman, see Wizârat al-Dâkhilîya (Ministry of Interior), 1982, 'al-Murshid al-'âm li al-Wilâyât wa al-Qabâ`il fî saltanat 'Umân'.
21 See note 3 above of this chapter.
22 al-Adnaniya, 134; Anon. Ms, 165–6; Tuhfa II, 172; Kashf, 155, Bathurst R.D., 1967, 323–5; prominent among these 'Attabi Shaykhs was Nâsir b Muhammad al-Ghâfirî.
23 Anon. Ms, 165.
24 Milburn W., 1813, 'Oriental Commerce', I, 115; Bathurst R.D., 1972, 100; for a description of the Omani fleet and its strength in 1695 see Chaudhuri K.N., 1985, 156.
25 Floor W., 1979, 163–86.
26 Parsons A., 1808, 'Travels in Asia and Africa', 206.
27 ibid.; for a description of the various boats see Risso P., 1986, Appendix 1.
28 These plots against Ahmad b Said will be discussed below, in this chapter.
29 Niebuhr M., 1792, [tr.], II, 113.
30 Guillain-Documents I, 543; Mombasa Chronicle in SD, 217.
31 Guillain-Documents, ibid.
32 ibid.
33 Bathurst R.D., 1967, 317.
34 Pate Chronicle printed in Stigand C.H., 1913, 'The Land of Zinj', 57.
35 See below in this chapter for events after the succession.
36 Guillain-Documents I, 556; Nicholls C., 1971, 32.
37 Anon. Ms, 171; al-Fath gives the wrong date of 1188 = 1774/5, see note 3 above of this chapter.
38 For the First Imamate see Wilkinson J.C., 1969, 109–16.
39 al-Qahtaniya, 459; Anon. Ms, 170.
40 al-Qahtaniya, ibid.; Anon. Ms, 170–1.
41 Juhaina, 137–8; al-Qahtaniya, 463; al-Fath, 387; Anon. Ms, 169; Hilal was

Ahmad b Said's eldest son – he was partially blind and died in Sind while seeking a cure.

42 IOR/P/381/33, Seton to Bombay, 9 July 1802; Anon. Ms, 170–1.
43 al-Qahtaniya, 459; until the 1970s the two forts of Mirani and Jalali in Muscat were used as prisons.
44 See notably Kirkman J., 1983, 'The Early History of Oman in East Africa', in JOS, 6, 53; Kelly J.B., 1968, 10.
45 al-Qahtaniya, 463; for the views of Abû Nabhân Jâ'id b Khamîs al-Kharûsî, a prominent *'âlim* of the eighteenth century, see Tuhfa II, 183-6 – Abu Nabhan is used extensively as a source by Abdallah al-Salimi in Tuhfa.
46 Tuhfa II, 181; al-Fath, 386–8.
47 al-Fath, 388; al-Qahtaniya, 463.
48 Tuhfa II, 183–6.
49 The titles 'Sayyid' for men and 'Sayyida' for women were never Albusaidi inventions, as is frequently claimed by a number of European writers; they were used in Ya'ariba times and are still used today in Oman before the first names of members of the ruling family; they are used to show respect and do not have the religious significance that the same titles have for the Shi'is who address only the descendants of the Prophet Muḥammad through his daughter Fâtima as Sayyids or Sayyidas.
50 Allen C.H., 1978, 28; see also idem, 1982, 'The State of Masqat in the Gulf and East Africa, 1785–1829', in IJMES, 14, 117–27.
51 For a discussion of these various dates see Wilkinson J.C., 1987, 352–3, n. 5; see also Kelly J.B., 1972, 109.
52 Tuhfa II, 168–9.
53 Juhaina, 138; IOR/L/P&S/5/507, Report by Percy Badger in Coghlan to Andreson, 4 July 1860.
54 al-Qahtaniya, 454; al-Fath, 364; IOR/P/381/33, Seton to Bombay, 9 July 1802.
55 IOR/ ibid.; al-Qahtaniya, ibid.
56 al-Fath, 365; the Customs House at Muscat, according to Padrugge R., 1673, op. cit., was built in 1624 by the Portuguese; see also IOR/15/6/4, De Rozario A.G., 1862, 'An Account of Muscat', in Green to Bombay, 25 October 1862; Miles S.B., 1919, 463.
57 Tuhfa II, 168; al-Qahtaniya, 463–7.
58 al-Qahtaniya, 463–7; al-Fath, 404–15; Juhaina 138; IOR/L/P&S/5/507, Report by P. Badger in Coghlan to Anderson, 4 July 1860.
59 al-Qahtaniya, 466; al-Fath, 409–10.
60 al-Qahtaniya, 467.
61 ibid.
62 ibid.
63 ibid.; al-Fath, 414.
64 IOR/L/P&S/5/507, Report by P. Badger in Coghlan to Anderson, 4 July 1860; for Said b Ahmad's poetry see Tuhfa II, 169; al-Qahtaniya, 467; al-Fath, 415.
65 For Sultan b Ahmad's plots see Anon. Ms, 170–1; al-Qahtaniya, 467–71; al-Fath, 416–38.
66 Miles S.B., 1919, 286; Lorimer J.G., 1908–15, IA, 421.
67 IOR/P/381/33, Seton to Bombay, 9 July 1802.
68 Risso P., 1986, 60.

69 IOR/G/29/25, Manesty S. and Jones H., 1790, 'Report on the Commerce of Arabia and Persia', printed in Abu Hakima M., 1970, 'Ta`rîkh al-Kuwayt', I, 21–82 and 59–60.
70 Amin A.A., 1967, 'British Interests in the Persian Gulf', 131–40.
71 IOR/G/29/25, Manesty S. and Jones H., 1790, op. cit., 28; Niebuhr C., 1792, [tr.], II, 116.
72 IOR/V/23/53, Miles S.B., 1887–8, 'Sketch of the Career of Seyyid Sultan bin Ahmed of Muscat' in 'Muscat Political Agency Report for 1887–8'; Ross E.C., 1866, 'Memorandum of notes on Mekran...' in TBGS, 18, 31–77; al-Fath, 429; Lorimer J.G., 1908–15, IA, 602.
73 IOR/V/23/53, Miles S.B., 1887–8, op. cit.; Landen R.G., 1967, 'Oman since 1856, Disruptive Modernization in a Traditional Arab Society', 218; Lorimer J.G., 1908–15, IA, 603.
74 IOR/ ibid.; IOR/P/381/19, Seton to Bombay, 29 December 1800.
75 IOR/P/381/31, Seton to Bombay, 19 May 1802.
76 IOR/P/381/33, Seton to Bombay, 9 July 1802.
77 Buckingham J.S., 1829, 'Travels in Assyria, Media and Persia', II, 395; for similar communities earlier in the eighteenth century see Niebuhr C., 1792, [tr.], II, 115.
78 IOR/P/343/14, Seton to Bombay, 21 August 1804.
79 Amin A.A., 1967, 139; Chaudhuri K.N., 1985, 195.
80 Amin A.A., 1967, 140.
81 The term 'English' rather than 'British' is used here because it was not until 1706 under Queen Anne (1702–14) that England and Scotland united into one British kingdom.
82 For the role of joint-stock companies see Chaudhuri K.N., 1965, 411–53.
83 Chaudhuri K.N., 1985, 209.
84 Nicholls C.S., 1971, 97; Bennett N.R., 1978, 'A History of the Arab State of Zanzibar', 16; Sheriff A.M.H., 1987, 'Slaves, Spices & Ivory in Zanzibar', chap. 1, passim.
85 Parsons A., 1808, 287.
86 Niebuhr C., 1792, [tr.], II, 114; for an earlier description of Muscat see Hamilton A., 1727, 'A New Account of the East Indies', I, 44–5.
87 Peterson J.E., 1978, 137; Nicholls C.S., 1971, 106; Sheriff A.M.H., 1987, 23–4.

3 THE EMERGENCE OF BRITISH POLICY TOWARDS OMAN: 1798–1804

1 Bathurst R.D., 1967, 67.
2 ibid.; for early Dutch contacts with Oman see Floor W., 1982, op. cit.
3 Issawi C., 1970, 'The Decline of Middle Eastern Trade, 1100–1850', in Richards D.S. [ed.], 1970, 'Islam and the Trade of Asia', 265; Das Gupta A., 1970, op. cit.; see also idem, 1967, 'The Crisis in Surat, 1730–32', in *Bengal Past and Present*, 148–62.
4 Bathurst R.D., 1967, 100.
5 Foster-Factories, VIII, 28; the Portuguese were expelled from Muscat itself in 1650.
6 Foster-Factories, V, 120.

7 IOR/H/628, Wylde and Wilton to Surat, 19 February 1646; the text of the agreement from this source is printed as Appendix C in Bathurst R.D., 1967.
8 Factory in this context means a trading post.
9 Foster-Factories, IX, 73.
10 Quoted in Bathurst R.D., 1967, 164; see also Floor W., 1985, op. cit.
11 Bathurst R.D., 1967, 165.
12 Floor W., 1985, op. cit.; idem, 1982, op. cit.
13 For this trade see Bathurst R.D., 1967, 149–79.
14 Foster-Factories, XI, 250.
15 ibid., XI, 306.
16 For the Ya'ariba apprehensions see Floor W., 1985 and 1982, op. cit.
17 Lorimer J.G., 1908–15, I, 420.
18 Text of 1798 Treaty is in IOR/V/23/217, BS, 248–50; Aitchison C.U., 1892, 'A Collection of Treaties, Engagements and Sanads Relating to India and Neighbouring Countries', 287–8; Risso P., 1986, Appendix 2.
19 IOR/P/343/14, Seton to Bombay, 21 August 1804. This type of pass system did not originate with the Portuguese as is commonly believed. For its earlier uses in the Gulf before the Portuguese, in medieval Islamic times and under the twelfth century rulers of Qays, see Wilkinson J.C., 1977, 'Water and Tribal Settlement in South-East Arabia, A Study of the Aflaj of Oman', 9; for enforced toll payments by the merchants of Malabar in the fourteenth century see Mookerji R.K., 1912, 195; for the way the Portuguese-imposed system functioned, see Das Gupta A., 1967a, 'Malabar in Asian Trade', 9–12.
20 IOR/P/381/33, Seton to Bombay, 9 July 1802.
21 IOR/ ibid.; IOR/P/343/14, Seton to Bombay, 21 August 1804.
22 See Chapter 2.
23 IOR/P/381/20, Seton to Bombay, 12 March 1801; IOR/P/381/33, Seton to Bombay, 9 July 1802.
24 Details of the incident are in IOR/P/381/33, Seton to Bombay, 9 July 1802.
25 IOR/ibid.
26 al-Fath, 371–2; on Haydar Ali, see Fernandes P., 1969, 'Storm over Seringapatam, The Incredible Story of Hyder Ali and Tippu Sultan', chap 3–9.
27 Waqayi', 14; IOR/P/380/69, Josey to Bombay, 27 December 1797.
28 Tipu Sultan's *wakil* in Muscat was one Mir Qasim while Sultan b Ahmad's in Mangalore was Ghaws Muhammad Khan; Tipu Sultan's *dallal* in Muscat was Seth Maoji [?Mowji], see Kirkpatrick W., 1811, 'Select Letters of Tippo Sultan', 239–40 and Appendix E on Commercial Regulations; Gopal M.H., 1971, 'Tipu Sultan's Mysore: an Economic Study', 22; Hasan M., 1971, 'History of Tipu Sultan', 128–30.
29 Tipu Sultan's emissaries (*sardârs*) to Oman were Nûr-allâh Khân, Ghulâm 'Alî Khân, Lutf 'Alî Khân, Ja'far Khân, accompanied by two secretaries, Sayyid Ja'far and Khwâja 'Abd-al-Qâdir, the author of the Waqayi', see Waqayi', 1–2; Kirkpatrick W., 1811, Appendix E.
30 Kirkpatrick W., 1811, 240–1.
31 Waqayi', 14; Kirkpatrick W., 1811, 231–41 and Appendix E.
32 Nicholls C.S., 1971, 105.
33 IOR/P/343/14, Seton to Bombay, 21 August 1804.

34 Holt P.M., 1966, 'Egypt and the Fertile Crescent, 1516–1922', 156.
35 Tuson P., 1979, 'The Records of the British Residency and Agencies in the Persian Gulf', 184; Lorimer J.G., 1908–15, IA, 425–8.
36 IOR/P/381/3, Bombay to Sultan b Ahmad, 30 May 1799.
37 This French person was the physician Morier (at times spelt Maurelle, Mord or Maureer) who, being in the employ of Sultan b Ahmad, used an Omani pass and traded under the Omani flag. The British duly replaced him by the British surgeon Archibald Bogle who in 1800 became the first British political agent to reside at Muscat; see IOR/P/381/12, Bombay to Bogle, 16 April 1800; Aitchison C.U., 1892, XI, 287–8; Lorimer J.G., 1908–15, IA, 432.
38 IOR/V/23/217, BS, 248; Article 3 of the Treaty in Aitchison C.U., 1892, loc. cit.
39 IOR/P/380/71, Bombay to Mehdi Ali Khan, 4 September 1798.
40 For Oman's early relations with France see al-Sudairan Nasser, 1973, 'La France et Mascate', Thèse de 3ème cycle, Université de Bordeaux III.
41 IOR/P/E/10, Duncan to Sultan b Ahmad, 1 July 1796.
42 Bathurst R.D., 1967, 171.
43 ibid.
44 Nicholls C.S., 1971, 103.
45 For Morice's plans see Morice-Projet.
46 This island, occupied by the Dutch, in 1598, was called Ile Maurice after the name of its governor. The French, taking it in the eighteenth century, renamed it Ile de France. The British, when they seized it in 1810, changed its name once again to Mauritius.
47 Morice-Projet, 89.
48 Sheriff A.M.H., 1971, 45–65; Nicholls C.S., 1968, 'European and Arab Activities on the East African Coast, 1798–1856, and the local reaction to them', D.Phil. th., Uni. of Oxford, chap. 2.
49 Nicholls C.S., 1968, chap. 5; idem, 1971, chap. 6.
50 Kajare F., 1914, 'Le Sultanat de l'Oman, la Question de Mascate', 75; for the term 'Sultan' see 'Conventions' above.
51 Nicholls C.S., 1971, 106.
52 IOR/P/381/7, Bombay to Rainier, 8 May 1799.
53 IOR/ibid.
54 Text of Bonaparte's letter is in Coupland R., 1938, 'East Africa and its Invaders', 89.
55 IOR/P/381/7, Bombay to Malcolm, 3 December 1799.
56 Holt P.M., 1966, 158.
57 IOR/P/381/3, Duncan to Sultan b Ahmad, 30 May 1799; Forrest D., 1970, 'Tiger of Mysore, The Life and Death of Tipu Sultan', 292–3.
58 Vatikiotis P.J., 1969, 'The History of Egypt', 45; Holt P.M., 1966, 159.
59 On the control of the Red Sea by Britain see Kelly J.B., 1968, 68.
60 IOR/P/381/10, Malcolm to Bombay, 4 February 1800.
61 On the rise of the Wahhabis or the First Saudi State see Ibn Bishr, 'Uthmân b 'Abd-allâh, n.d., ''Unwân al-Majd fî Târîkh Najd', I and II; al-'Ajlânî, Munîr, n.d., 'Târîkh al-Bilâd al-'Arabîya al-Sa'ûdîya: al-Dawla al-Sa'ûdîya al-`Ûla', I–IV; see also IOR/L/P&S/C 240, Saldanha J.A., 1904, 'Précis of Najd Affairs, 1804–1904'; al-Rashid Z.M., 1981, 'Su'udi Relations with Eastern Arabia and Uman, 1800–1870', 25–30; for Ibadi views on Wahhabism see al-Fath, 446–7; Tuhfa II, 187 and 254.

62 al-Fath, 431.
63 ibid.
64 Tuhfa II, 187 and 254; see also al-Fath, 445–7.
65 For a detailed discussion of these see Wilkinson J.C., 1987, chap. 8.
66 For *salafiya* movements see Hodgson M.G.S., 1974, 'The Venture of Islam', vol. 3; Levtzion N., 1986, 'Eighteenth century renewal and reform movements in Islam', in *Proceedings of the British Society for Middle East Studies*, 1986; Voll J.O., 1982, 'Islam: Continuity and Change in the Muslim World'; Naff T. and Owen R., 1977, 'Studies in Eighteenth-century Islamic History'.
67 IOR/V/23/217, BS, 430, IOR/15/1/5, Seton to Mehdi Ali Khan, 25 April 1802; IOR/P/381/32, Seton to Bombay, 8 and 10 May 1802.
68 Spear P., 1965, 'A History of India', II, chaps 6–11; Wolpert S., 1977, 'A New History of India', chaps 13–14; Yapp M.E., 1987, 'The Making of the Modern Near East, 1792–1923', chap. 2.
69 al-Fath, 432ff; cf. al-Rashid Z.M., 1981, 47, where he gives the name as Sâlim b Bilâl al-Harq.
70 IOR/V/23/53, Miles S.B., 1887–8, op. cit.; Lorimer J.G., 1908–15, IA, 424.
71 IOR/ibid.; Lorimer, ibid.; for the tribute not being regarded as *zakat* see below, Chapter 4.
72 Lorimer J.G., 1908–15, IA, 430–1.
73 Aitchison C.U., 1892, XI, 288.
74 Miles S.B., 1919, 298.
75 IOR/V/23/217, BS, 431.
76 IOR/ibid.
77 Allen C., 1978, 46.
78 al-Fath, 438.
79 IOR/V/23/53, Miles S.B., 1887–8, op. cit.
80 Corancez L., 1810, 'Histoire des Wahhabis', 67.
81 al-Fath, 439–40; al-Qahtaniya, 474–5.
82 Juhaina, 139; Ibn Bishr, I, 127; al-Fath, 438–40; al-Qahtaniya, 19–20; the Hijri date, given in Juhaina for Sultan b Ahmad's death, is 13 Shaban 1219 = 17 November 1804.
83 Quoted in al-Qahtaniya, 475 and al-Fath, 441.
84 IOR/P/381/33, Seton to Bombay, 9 July 1802; Dallons P., 'Zanzibar in 1804' in SD, 198.
85 IOR/ibid.
86 IOR/P/381/16, Sultan b Ahmad to Bombay, n.d., but received on 12 May 1800.
87 IOR/P/381/4, Bombay to Sultan b Ahmad, 20 June 1799.
88 Bennett N.R., 1978, 13.
89 IOR/H/478, Sultan of Pate to Bombay, petition presented by Bwana Kanga and Ali b Ahmad, 3 October 1801.
90 IOR/H/478, Duncan to Wellesley, 11 November 1801.

4 BRITISH POLICY TOWARDS OMAN UNDER THE FIRST WAHHABI THREAT: 1804–14

1 Ibn Bishr, 149; see Map 6.
2 al-Rashid Z.M., 1981, 59.
3 ibid., 59–60.
4 ibid., 58.
5 ibid., 130.
6 Wilkinson J.C., 1987, 84.
7 Notable among these and used extensively by later writers is Kelly J.B., 1968, 105–16 et passim.
8 IOR/V/23/217, BS, 303; Tuson P., 1979, 184.
9 IOR/ibid., 135.
10 IOR/ibid., 303; cf. Dubuisson P., 1978, 'Qasimi Piracy and the General Treaty of Peace (1820)', in *Arabian Studies*, vol. 4, 49, where she says that the first Qasimi attack on British shipping occurred in 1797.
11 IOR/V/23/217, BS, 175.
12 For a modern Qasimi viewpoint see al-Qasimi, Sultan Muhammad, 1986, 'The Myth of Arab Piracy in the Gulf'.
13 Landen R.G., 1967, 8.
14 Foster-Factories, I, 227; a lari was a Persian silver coin worth about a shilling in sterling.
15 Foster-Factories, III, 61; contemporary exchange rates were 100 mahmudis = 80 laris = 50 Abbasis = 1 toman, according to Floor W., 1985, op. cit., 63, n. 127.
16 Jameson J.F., 1923, 'Privateering and Piracy', 175.
17 Dubuisson P., 1978, op. cit.
18 al-'Aqqâd, Salâh, 1974, 'al-Tayyârât al-Siyâsîya fî al-Khalîj al-'Arabî', 91; Landen R.G., 1967, 8, 10 and 26; Jameson J.F., 1923, 175 et passim.
19 Dubuisson P., 1978, 50; Pelly L., 1863–4, 'Remarks on the tribes and resources around the shore line of the Persian Gulf' in TBGS, XVII.
20 IOR/F/4/192/4155, Duncan to Seton, 14 August 1805.
21 IOR/ibid., Duncan to Seton, 20 February 1805.
22 IOR/ibid., Duncan to Seton, 3 March 1805.
23 See the beginning of this chapter.
24 Juhaina, 139; Said-Ruete R., 1929, 'Said Bin Sultan (1791–1856), Ruler of Oman and Zanzibar', 10.
25 al-Fath, 440.
26 IOR/V/23/53, Miles S.B., 1887–8, op. cit., Miles S.B., 1919, 303.
27 Badger G.P., 1871, 'History of the Imams and Sayyids of Oman', lxvi; Lorimer J.G., 1908–15, IA, 437.
28 Tuhfa II, 185.
29 IOR/V/23/217, BS, 176.
30 Tuhfa II, 185; Badger G.P., 1871, lxvi.
31 Tuhfa ibid.
32 Said-Ruete R., 1929, 10; al-Fath, 466.
33 Tuhfa, ibid.; al-Fath, ibid.
34 In al-Fath and al-Qahtaniya, no first names of the Albusaidi women are given 'out of respect'. Other names, given for this same *sayyida*, are Fâkhira in Juhaina, 140; Â'isha in Said-Ruete E., [formerly Salma bint Said b

Sultan], 1886, [Eng. tr.], 1907, 'Memoirs of an Arabian Princess', 159, [the pages quoted here are from the English translation]; Moza is given in Said-Ruete R., 1929, 10 and Lorimer. J.G., 1908–15, IA, 437; that it was undoubtedly Moza is shown by the Sayyida's own correspondence to the British authorities as in, for example, IOR/F/4/1453/56726, Moza bint Ahmad to Bombay, 8 April 1832.

35 al-Fath, 464.
36 Lorimer J.G., 1908–15, IA, 437.
37 Juhaina, 140; Said-Ruete E., 1886, 159–62; al-Fath, 464–6.
38 Said-Ruete E., 1886, 160–1.
39 al-Fath, 466.
40 Juhaina, 140; IOR/V/23/217, BS, 176.
41 IOR/V/23/45, Miles S.B., 1883–4, 'Biographical Sketch of the Late Seyyid Sa'eed-Bin-Sultan Imam of Muscat', in 'Muscat Administration Report for 1883–1884', 21; Miles S.B., 1919, 297.
42 IOR/ibid.; Juhaina, 140.
43 See the second section in this chapter for the reasons why Salim was passed over.
44 IOR/V/23/53, Miles S.B., 1887–8, op. cit.
45 IOR/P/382/3, Duncan to Seton, 2 February 1805.
46 IOR/F/4/256/5646, Seton to Bombay, 14 March 1806.
47 IOR/15/6/483, Ross E.C., 1883–4, 'Muscat Administration Report for 1883–4'.
48 IOR/V/23/217, BS, 176; cf. Kelly J.B., 1968, 107, where he gives the figure of 1,500 men.
49 IOR/ibid.
50 IOR/ibid.
51 al-Fath, 488; Lorimer J.G., 1908–15, IA, 440.
52 al-Rashid Z.M., 1981, 62.
53 Amir Saud b Abd-al-Aziz quoted in Said-Ruete R., 1929, 14; see also Tuhfa II, 187.
54 Lorimer J.G., 1908–15, IA, 440.
55 IOR/V/23/217, BS, 431; IOR/F/4/192/4155, Seton to Duncan enclosing Badr b Sayf to Duncan, 22 Sha'ban 1220 = 21 October 1805.
56 IOR/ibid., Seton to Duncan, 16 November 1805.
57 Notable among these and used extensively by later writers is Lorimer J.G., 1908–15, IA, 440–1.
58 See Ibn Ruzaiq's numerous eulogies to Salim in Sabayik, 8, 12, 13, passim.
59 Juhaina, 139.
60 Guillain-Documents, II, 224; Said-Ruete E., 1886, 8.
61 Sabayik, 48; al-Qahtaniya, 475.
62 Juhaina, 140; see also al-Fath, 480–91.
63 al-Fath, 470; for Muhanna al-Ya'rubi's good relations with Sultan b Ahmad, see al-Qahtaniya, 473–4.
64 For a contemporary description of the murder see Maurizi V. (Shaikh Mansur), 1819, 'History of Seyd Said, Sultan of Muscat...', 10–11.
65 al-Fath, 461, gives the date of birth as 1206 which is equivalent to 1791/2 but R. Said-Ruete confirms, as the date in the title of his book indicates, that it was 1791.
66 al-Fath, 491.

67 IOR/F/4/257/5650, Said b Sultan to Duncan, 31 July 1806.
68 Lorimer J.G., 1908–15, IA, 440.
69 Kaye J.Y., 1856, 'Life ... of Sir John Malcolm', I, 105–10.
70 IOR/P/382/26, Said b Sultan to Duncan, 22 December 1806.
71 IOR/P/382/23, Said b Sultan to Duncan, 15 January 1807.
72 IOR/ibid.
73 IOR/P/382/29, Calcutta to Bombay, 23 April 1807.
74 See above, Chapter 3.
75 French translation of Said b Sultan's letter is in Sudairan N., 1973, 53.
76 Clerc De, 1864, 'Réceuil des Traités de la France', I, 201–3.
77 al-Aqqad S., 1974, 81–4.
78 ibid., 85–7; De Clerc, 1864, I, 205.
79 ibid.
80 al-Aqqad, 1974, 86.
81 Gardane A., 1865, 'La Mission du Général Gardane en Perse sous la
    Première Empire', 81.
82 The Political Agency had been left vacant since March 1806 when Seton
    had gone on sick leave, see Tuson P., 1979, 185; Low C.R., 1877,
    'History of the Indian Navy', I, 320.
83 IOR/L/P&S/20/C 284C, Saldanha J.A., 1906, 'Precis of the Corres-
    pondence regarding the Affairs of the Persian Gulf', 81.
84 al-Aqqad S., 1974, 84–91.
85 IOR/V/23/217, BS, 178.
86 IOR/ibid.
87 al-Ajlani M., n.d., IV, 75.
88 IOR/ibid.; al-Fath, 493; Miles S.B., 1919, 310; cf. Kelly J.B., 1968, 110.
    Kelly says that after Qays's death, Said b Sultan excluded Azzan, his son,
    from the succession and appointed his own *wali* at Sohar; but according to
    the evidence available, Said and Azzan were on friendly terms, and it was
    not until later in 1813, at Azzan's own death, that Said took control of Sohar
    thus alienating Hamud b Azzan.
89 al-Adnaniya, 134–5; al-Fath, 495.
90 al-Adnaniya, ibid.; al-Fath, 494–6.
91 al-Fath, 517; IOR/V/23/217, BS, 130–1.
92 For details of al-Mutayri's campaigns, see al-Rashid Z.M., 1981, 63–71;
    Kelly J.B., 1968, 110–28; and IOR/ibid.
93 IOR/P/383/2, Seton to Malcolm, 22 February 1809.
94 IOR/P/383/7, Seton to Bombay, 8 July 1809.
95 Wellsted J.R., 1840, 'Travels to the City of the Caliphs, along the Shores of
    the Persian Gulf and the Mediterranean', I, 101.
96 IOR/P/383/8, Manesty to Duncan, 8 July 1809.
97 IOR/P/382/55, 9 December 1808; Seton had been called back from Muscat
    only a few weeks after his arrival there in January 1808 for a mission to
    Sind.
98 Lorimer J.G., 1908–15, IA, 183.
99 ibid., IA, 442.
100 IOR/V/23/217, BS, 432.
101 IOR/ibid.
102 See, for example, the often quoted works of Kelly J.B., 1968, 115 who
    himself relies heavily on Miles S.B., 1919, 316.

103 See above, Introduction.
104 IOR/P/383/3, Calcutta to Bombay, 3 April 1809.
105 IOR/ibid.; al-Fath, 518.
106 For an eye-witness account of these events see Maurizi V., 1819, 53ff; see also IOR/V/23/217, BS, 432–60.
107 IOR/V/23/217, BS, 180.
108 IOR/ibid.; IOR/P/383/16, Smith to Warden, 14 April 1810.
109 Quoted in Coupland R., 1938, 145.
110 IOR/P/119/8, Saud b Abd-al-Aziz to Smith, n.d., received on 15 April 1810.
111 IOR/P/383/16, Smith to Warden, 14 April 1810; see also IOR/L/P&S/20/C 240, Saldanha J.A., 1904, op. cit.
112 IOR/P/383/16, ibid.
113 Maurizi V., 1819, 75.
114 IOR/ibid.
115 al-Fath, 504–12.
116 Maurizi V., 1819, 80–1; Said-Ruete R., 1919, 30.
117 Ibn Bishr, n.d., I, 189; al-Fath, 510–15.
118 al-Rashid Z.M., 1981, 68.
119 IOR/V/23/217, BS, 435.
120 Lorimer J.G., 1908–15, IA, 444; Arbaq, until the late 1960s, was a small fishing village near Matrah; it now forms part of the huge port of Mina Qabus.
121 ibid., IA, 445.
122 Kelly J.B., 1968, 128.
123 Kelly J.B., 1965, 'Mehmet Ali's Expedition to the Persian Gulf, 1837–1840', I, 350–81; II, 31–65.
124 IOR/V/23/217, BS, 182–3.
125 IOR/ibid; IOR/V/23/45, Miles S.B., 1883–4, op. cit.
126 IOR/V/23/217, BS, 183; Kelly J.B., 1968, 126.
127 Ibn Bishr, n.d., I, 159; al-Fath, 523; Maurizi V., 1819, 87; Guillain-Documents, II, 172.
128 al-Fath, 524; according to Ibn Ruzaiq, Azzan himself had appointed Salim as *wali* during his absence and had told him to be obedient to Said b Sultan.
129 IOR/V/23/217, BS, 435.
130 IOR/P/381/33, Seton to Bombay, 9 July 1802.
131 Maurizi V., 1819, 29.
132 Buckingham J.S., 1830, II, 392; the figure given is 20 lakh = 200, 000 rupees, the conversion rate used is 2.11 rupees = 1 MT$; for exchange rates at the time see Milburn W., 1813, I, 116, 173–4; Landen R.G., 1967, 128–31.
133 Heude W., 1819, 'A Voyage up the Persian Gulf', 20–34.
134 Buckingham J.S., 1830, II, 394.
135 IOR/L/P&S/5/381, Calcutta to Bombay, 31 January 1840.

5 COMMERCIAL, POLITICAL AND STRATEGIC ATTRACTIONS Of EAST AFRICA

1 See, for example, Sheriff A.M.H., 1971, 101–28; Sheriff finds difficulty in distinguishing Indians from Omanis and says that 'the Indians tacitly

accepted their status as local citizens' on p. 115 but see below, this chapter.

2 IOR/L/MAR/C/586, Smee T., 1811, 'Description of Zanzibar Island'; idem, 6 April 1811, 'Observations during a Voyage of Research on the East Coast of Africa...' in TBGS, VI, 1844, reprinted in Burton R.F., 1872, 'Zanzibar: City, Island and Coast', II, Appendix 3; the emphasis on Sind and Kutch is mine to highlight the importance of these two places for Omani commerce, as will become clear below.

3 IOR/ibid.; IOR/P/381/33, Seton to Bombay, 9 July 1802; Bird J., 1839–40, 'Commercial and Geographical View of East Africa', in TBGS, vol. 3, 112–22.

4 Sheriff A.M.H., 1971, 116.

5 IOR/L/MAR/C/586, Hardy Lt., 1811, 'Account of the different rivers on the coast from Qualiffe towards Mozambique'.

6 For a discussion of such migrations see Chaudhuri K.N., 1985, 164–6 et passim; see also Ricks T.M., 1970, op. cit.; Martin B.G., 1974, op. cit.; Juhaina, passim; Gregory R.G., 1971, 5 et passim.

7 See the Introduction in Juhaina.

8 Juhaina, 189. For a discussion of the term 'Zinji' as used by Arab geographers to describe Africans see Tolmacheva M., 1986, 'Towards a Definition of the term Zanj' in *Azania*, vol. 21, 105–13.

9 PRO/Adm/52/3940, Emery J.B., 1824–6, 'Jnl. of Lt. J.B. Emery'; see also, for examples of 'Indians' becoming 'Swahilis', Berg F.J., 1971, 'Mombasa under the Busaidi Sultanate: the city and its hinterland in the nineteenth century', Ph.D. Dissn., Uni. of Wisconsin, 59.

10 Sheriff A.M.H., 1971, 114; idem, 1987, 87.

11 IOR/L/MAR/C/586, Smee T., 6 April 1811, 33.

12 Burton R.F., 1872, I, 421–3.

13 Burton R.F., 1856, 'First Footsteps in East Africa or an Exploration of Harar', I, 71; Martin B.G., 1974, 383.

14 Keppel G., 1837, 'Narrative of a Journey from India to England', 9–33.

15 Nicholls C.S., 1971, 71; Albrand F., 1938, 'Extrait d'une memoire sur Zanzibar et sur Quiloa', in *Bulletin de la Société de Géographie*, vol. 10, 65–84.

16 Chopra P.N., 1982, 88–90; Pocock D.F., 1955, chap. 5; Pearson M.N., 1976, 26–7; Das Gupta A., 1979, 69–70; for the caste system and the Banyans see Enthoven R.E., 1920.

17 PRO/FO/84/1391, 'Memorandum regarding Banians or natives of India in East Africa', in Frere to Granville, 7 May 1873.

18 Kelly J.B., 1968, 13; for various components of Gujarati traders see Pearson M.N., 1976, 25–9.

19 Khojas, strictly speaking, are Sevener Shi'is who later became Ismaili Nizari Agha Khanis and should not include the Ithna'asharis (Twelvers). Personal information from Professor C. Beckingham, London, 4 April 1985.

20 Ravenstein E.G., 1898, 'A Journal of the First Voyage of Vasco de Gama, 1497–1499', 39; Esmail A.A., 1972, 'Satpanth Ismailis and Modern Changes within it with special reference to East Africa', Ph.D. th., Uni. of Edinburgh, 112; Berg F.J., 1971, 56.

21 IOR/V/23/230, Rigby C., 1 July 1860, 'Report on the Zanzibar Dominions';

Coupland R., 1939, 44; for the Banyans being pre-eminent in India see Pearson M.N., 1976, 26.

22 IOR/L/P&S/5/50, Council to Secret Committee, 22 October 1844.

23 On Portuguese policies see above, Chapter 1.

24 Int. Noor al-Din'Ali Bhay Mulla 'Abd-al-'Ali Noorani, Zanzibar, 24 July 1986; see Bhacker M.R., 1988, 'Roots of Domination and Dependency: British Reaction to the Development of Omani Commerce at Muscat and Zanzibar in the Nineteenth Century' D.Phil. th., Uni. of Oxford, 305–6; for Hindu influences on Muslim legal practices see Fyzee A.A., 1966, 'Cases in the Muhammadan Law of India and Pakistan', intro.; Misra S.C., 1964, 'Muslim Communities in Gujarat...'.

25 Information on Joint Families was obtained from various merchants and other individuals in Muscat, Zanzibar and India between 1981 and 1988; see also Pocock D.F., 1955, chap. 3.

26 Pocock D.F., 1955, 103–5; Esmail A.A., 1972, 87.

27 Pocock, ibid.

28 Int. Kamâl 'Abd-al-Ridâ Sultân, Muscat, 4 January 1984. A good example of Joint Family principles still functioning in Matrah in Oman is found in the Lawatiya company of 'W.J.Towell & Co.' which has the afore-mentioned Kamal as one of its directors.

29 Burton R.F., 1872, I, 328–9.

30 Loarer M., 1851, 'Ile de Zanzibar', in *Revue de l'Orient, d'Algérie et des Colonies*, vol. 9, 290–9; Int. Dr Garang Mehta and Mr Shirali Muhammad Ali Champsi, Zanzibar, 8 July 1986; for the personal histories of these two individuals see Bhacker M.R., 1988, 306.

31 The Banyan Bhattia caste was originally a warrior caste, which later became a fishing and sailing caste and later still a trading caste; see Chopra P.N., 1982, 80–2; for its relations to other castes see Pocock D.F., 1955, 21–ff; for a history of some of its members in Oman see Allen C.H., 1978.

32 Quoted in Pocock D.F., 1955, 21; same information supplied in int. Dr Mehta and Mr Champsi, Zanzibar, 9 July 1986, see note 30 above; for the wars in Mombasa see below, this chapter and Chapter 7.

33 The Shivji Topan Family is more popularly known as the Jairam Sewji Family due to the later role of Jairam in the commercial activities of East Africa made more widely known by American visitors and merchants in Zanzibar. The family name, according to the informants in the preceding note and note 30 above, is Shivji Topan. To obtain its correct pronunciation it would be transliterated as Shîvjî Tôpan. Sewji gives a completely different and incorrect pronunciation.

34 IOR/P/381/19, Seton to Bombay, 9 January 1801.

35 See the Bhimani Family traditions quoted in Allen C.H., 1978, 111.

36 ibid.; on Wad Bhima see IOR/L/P&S/9/49, Kirk to Bombay, 9 December 1871.

37 IOR/ibid.; IOR/F/4/2174, Agent at Muscat to PRPG, 17 October 1845.

38 Allen C.H., 1978, 110.

39 Quoted in Pocock D.F., 1955, 20; for the relations between the two families later at Zanzibar see US/Arch/NEMA, Emerton's Jnl, 1848, 410, McMullan to Shepard, 28 January 1851, 474–6, and Jelly to Jackson, 27 April 1851, 482.

40 Int. Dr Mehta, 8–9 July 1986; Topan M.T., 1962–3, 'Biography of Sir

Tharia Topan Kt.', I, 2, 17–19; III, 95; according to Dr Mehta, it was Ebji Shivji, a good friend of Topan Tajiani, who encouraged the latter to migrate to Zanzibar.

41 PRO/Adm/52/3940, Emery J.B., 1824–6, op. cit.
42 Quoted in Pocock D.F., 1955, 21; for Ebji's involvement in Zanzibar's commerce see US/Arch/NEMA, Waters to Abji Bin Siwji, 20 September 1839, 222 and Fabens to Shepard, 4 January 1845, 340.
43 IOR/L/P&S/5/408, Hamerton to Bombay, 9 February 1842.
44 Int. Chizuko Tominaga, Zanzibar, 8 August 1986; Bhacker M.R., 1988, 307; ZA/AA12/1, Webb and Bates to Hamerton, 23 July 1844; PRO/FOCP/ 4637, 1880, 59; ZA/AA1/61, Khalifa b Said to Mackinnon & Co., 1 dhu al-hijja, 1305 = 10 August 1888.
45 IOR/15/6/16, Miles to Ross, 5 February 1884.
46 IOR/P/381/33, Seton to Bombay, 9 July 1802.
47 Maurizi V., 1819, 29.
48 For a definition of 'Banyan' see above, Chapter 5; IOR/P/381/33, ibid.; Dallons P., 1804, 198; PRO/Adm/52/3940, Emery J.B., 1824–6, op. cit.
49 IOR/L/MAR/C/586, Capt. Smee's Log, 24 February 1811.
50 Dallons P., 1804, 198; see also Juhaina, 119; Smee T., 6 April 1811, op. cit.
51 Gray J.M., 1962a, 126.
52 al-Fath, 462.
53 IOR/L/MAR/C/586, Smee T., 1811, op. cit.
54 For Said b Sultan's alleged 'African Policy' see Coupland R., 1938, 299; Allen C.H., 1978, 68–93; Wilkinson J.C., 1987, 56.
55 Alpers E.A., 1967, 'The East African Slave Trade', 13; but cf. idem, 1975, where Alpers seems to have changed his mind.
56 On these political relationships between the coast and the interior see notably the following works: Mckay W.F., 1975, 'A Precolonial History of the Southern Kenya Coast', Ph.D. Dissn., Boston Uni.; Berg F.J., 1971; Ylvisaker M., 1975, 'The Political and Economic Relationship of the Lamu Archipelago to the Adjacent Kenya Coast in the Nineteenth Century', Ph.D. Dissn., Boston Uni.; Spear T., 1974, 'The Kaya Complex: A History of the Mijikenda Peoples of the Kenya Coast to 1900'; Ph.D. Dissn., Uni. of Wisconsin and Alpers E.A., 1975.
57 IOR/P/381/33, Seton to Bombay, 9 July 1802; Sheriff A.M.H., 1971, 39; Grant D.K., 1938, 'Mangrove Woods of Tanganyika Territory, their silviculture and dependent industries' in TNR, vol. 4.
58 Hoyle B.S., 1967, 'The Seaports of East Africa', 14–17; Datoo B.A., 1975, 'Port Development in East Africa: Spatial patterns from the ninth to the sixteenth centuries', 43–7; Datoo B.A., 1974, 'Influence of the monsoons on the movement of dhows along the East African coast' in *East African Geographical Review*, vol. 12, 23–33.
59 Morice-Projet, 82; see also PRO/Adm/52/3940, Emery J.B., 1824–6; Prins A.H., 1965, 'Sailing from Lamu', 303; Albrand F., 1838, 66.
60 Alpers E.A., 1975, chapter 6.
61 PRO/FO/54/1, Owen to Palmerston, 8 April 1834.
62 See above, Chapter 2.
63 Compare the entries for 1802 and 1816/19 in Table 3 and Figure 2.
64 See the first section of Chapter 2.
65 Burj = Fort; al-Siyabi, 1965, 79–80; IOR/V/23/40, Miles S.B., 1880–1,

'Notes on the Tribes of Oman', in 'Muscat Administration Report, 1880–1';
cf. Krapf J.L., 1860, 'Travels, Researches and Missionary Labours in
Eastern Africa', 119, where he says that the Mazaria are of Persian origin.

66 Kashf, 95; Tuhfa II, 2–3.
67 Sayf b Sultan's (I) army commander against the Portuguese in Mombasa
was a Baluchi by the name of Shahdâd b Shâdî al-Bulûshî, Kitab al-Zunuj,
241; Juhaina, 106.
68 Bathurst R.D., 1967, 121; Strandes J., 1899, 'The Portuguese Period in East
Africa', 229; Mombasa Chronicle in SD, 213; Pate Chronicle in SD, 261;
Stigand C.H., 1913, 55.
69 Juhaina, 108 and 118; Mombasa Chronicle, 214; on Qayd al-ard see
Chapter 8.
70 Mombasa Chronicle, 214–16; Miles S.B., 1919, 221.
71 Mombasa Chronicle, 216.
72 IOR/V/23/45, Miles S.B., 1883–4, 27; Bathurst R.D., 1967, 266–8.
73 Cashmore T.H., 1961, 'A note on the chronology of the Wanyika of the
Kenya coast', in TNR, vol. 57, 153–72; the Mijikenda or nine tribes are
also known as Wanyika or Wanika, people of the Nyika; see also Berg
F.J., 1968, 'The Swahili Community of Mombasa, 1500–1900', in JAH,
vol. 9, 35–56.
74 Juhaina, 118; Mombasa Chronicle, 217; but cf. Guillain-Documents I, 535
where he says that Muhammad was appointed in 1739.
75 Juhaina, ibid.; Kitab al-Zunuj, 243.
76 Kitab al-Zunuj, 242, which gives the reasons of drinking wine, smoking
tobacco and womanising by Sayf as the main reasons for him alienating the
ulama!
77 See the first section of Chapter 2.
78 Mombasa Chronicle, 217.
79 Juhaina, 119; Kitab al-Zunuj, 313.
80 IOR/V/23/45, Miles S.B., 1883–4, 28; Juhaina, 119 and Mombasa Chronicle, 217; Bhacker M.R., 1988, 309.
81 Juhaina, 30; IOR/ibid.
82 Bathurst R.D., 1967, 266–8; Strandes J., 1899, 278–9.
83 Stigand C.H., 1913, 60; Guillain-Documents, I, 550.
84 Juhaina, 119; Stigand C.H., 1913, 57.
85 IOR/L/P&S/5/501, Rigby to Anderson, 4 April 1859; Pate Chronicle, 269;
Khabari Lamu, 18–19; Stigand C.H., 1913, 67.
86 IOR/V/23/53, Miles S.B., 1887–8, 31; Guillain-Documents, I, 367.
87 Juhaina, 121; Pate Chronicle, 266–72; Stigand C.H., 1913, 66–7; Guillain-
Documents, I, 567–9.
88 Tarikh al-Mazari', 31; Khabari Lamu, 20–1; IOR/ibid.
89 Ylvisaker M., 1979, 70.
90 Kitab al-Zunuj, 245; Guillain-Documents, I, 568–9. A contemporary
account of the battle of Shela is given by Bwana Bakari in Stigand C.H.,
1913, 76–7; see also Abdulaziz M.H., 1979, 'Muyaka, 19th Century
Swahili Popular Poetry', 117.
91 Kitab al-Zunuj, 345; cf. Guillain-Documents, I, 567 where he names the
envoy of Lamu as 'Abd-al-Raḥmân Nûr al-Dîn.
92 IOR/V/23/217, BS, 182–3; see the second section of Chapter 4.
93 See Table 4.

94 See the first section of Chapter 5.
95 Juhaina, 120; Tarikh al-Mazari', 37; Khabar al-Lamu, 28–9; Guillain-Documents, I, 368–9; Albrand F., 1838, 84.
96 Juhaina, 121; Guillain-Documents, I, 624; see Figure 2.
97 Juhaina, ibid.
98 Kitab al-Zunuj, 244–5.
99 IOR/V/23/45, Miles S.B., 1883–4, 28; Guillain-Documents, I, 569.
100 Text of the letter is in Juhaina, 123–4; see also Knappert J., 1979, 'Four Centuries of Swahili Verse', 151.
101 Abdulaziz M.H., 1979, 121; Guillain-Documents, I, 569; Knappert J., 1979, 152.
102 Muyaka al-Ghassani quoted in Knappert J., 1979, 151–2.
103 See the second section of Chapter 4.
104 IOR/V/23/45, Miles S.B., 1883–4, op. cit.; IOR/V/23/217, BS, 307.
105 IOR/V/23/217, BS, 308.
106 Miles S.B., 1919, 318; Kelly J.B., 1968, 131.
107 IOR/V/23/217, BS, 308.
108 Said-Ruete E., 1886, 10; IOR/V/23/45, Miles S.B., 1883–4, op. cit.
109 The alienation between the two took place when Said forcefully seized the forts of Bidbid and Sumayil belonging to al-Jabri, see above, Chapter 4.
110 al-Adnaniya, 134; al-Qahtaniya, 474; al-Fath, 470.
111 Tuhfa II, 186; al-Fath, ibid.
112 al-Fath, 512. The following account is based primarily on Ibn Ruzaiq's three works al-Fath, al-Adnaniya and al-Qahtaniya, and Tuhfa II, 186–200 and IOR/V/23/45, Miles S.B., 1883–4, op. cit.
113 Tuhfa II, 190–3; cf. al-Fath, 525.
114 al-Fath, 525–6.
115 Details in al-Fath, 500–30.
116 al-Fath, 530.
117 ibid.
118 See the first section of Chapter 6.

6 THE SUPPRESSION OF OMANI INTERESTS IN THE GULF AND THE ALBUSAIDI MOVE TO ZANZIBAR

1 al-Fath, 530; IOR/V/23/45, Miles S.B., 1883–4, 25; IOR/V/23/217, BS, 125.
2 IOR/V/23/217, BS, 371–2.
3 IOR/ibid.; IOR/V/23/45, Miles S.B., ibid.; al-Fath, 530.
4 IOR/V/23/217, BS, ibid.; for exchange rates see Lambton A.K.S., 1970, 'Persian Trade under the Early Qajars', in Richards D.S., [ed.], 1970, op. cit., 221; Milburn W., 1813, I, 116 and 173–4.
5 IOR/V/23/45, Miles S.B., ibid.
6 It seems that after the death of the Harthi *tamima*, Sa'îd b Mâjid, during the campaign against Bahrain in 1816, Isa b Salih I became the new *tamima* of this influential tribe.
7 al-Fath, 530–1.
8 PRO/Adm 1/189, King to Croker, 5 March 1817. Considering that the Qasimis were now joined by the Utbis, the figure of 8,000 men seems very

low when compared with the figure given for 1809 of 25,000 men at a time when the Qasimis are said to have only had 60 vessels, see IOR/P/383/8, Manesty to Duncan, 8 July 1809.

9 IOR/V/23/217, BS, 132 and 310–12.

10 For the defeat of the Marathas see Wolpert S., 1977, 204; Spear P., 1965, chap. 8; for that of the Wahhabis see Ibn Bishr, n.d.; al-Rashid Z.M., 1981 and Winder R.B., 1965, 'Saudi Arabia in the Nineteenth Century'.

11 IOR/P/41/29, Sadlier to Bombay, 15 May 1819.

12 IOR/V/23/217, BS, 314.

13 IOR/idem, 313.

14 IOR/V/23/45, Miles S.B., 1883–4, 26.

15 IOR/P/42/40, Keir to Bombay, 1 December 1819.

16 See the second section of Chapter 5.

17 IOR/G/40/34, Keir to Tehran, 2 February 1820.

18 IOR/P/45/6, Warden to Keir, 16 February 1820.

19 For details connected with the treaty see Dubuisson P., 1978, op. cit.; Kelly J.B., 1968, 149–59.

20 IOR/V/23/217, BS., 373.

21 Sheriff A.M.H., 1987, 202; Alpers E.A, 1969, 45–7; Nicholls C.S., 1971, 101–2; Gray J.M., 1962a, 111; Coupland R., 1938, 151–3; Cooper F., 1977, 30; Pouwels R.L., 1987, 99; Berg F.J., 1971, 76; Ylvisaker M., 1979, 'Lamu in the nineteenth century, Land, Trade and Politics', 77.

22 IOR/P/386/61, Agent at Muscat to PRPG, 21 December 1829.

23 Guillain-Documents, I, 589; for a contemporary drawing of the palace at Mtoni see Guillain C., 1851, 'Voyage à la côte orientale d'Afrique exécuté pendant les années 1846, 1847 et 1848', plate 5 entitled 'Vue de Mtony, Residence de Campagne du Sultan'.

24 For details of the Bani Bu Ali 'expeditions' see IOR/V/23/217, BS, 189–91; Lorimer J.G., 1908–15, IA, 462–5; Kelly J.B., 1968, chap. 5; Moyse-Bartlett H., 1966, 'The Pirates of Trucial Oman', chap. 6; see also al-Fath, 532–6; Tuhfa II, 187–9; Juhaina, 141.

25 See, for example, Nicholls C.S., 1971, 117.

26 al-Fath, 533.

27 IOR/15/6/65, Murphy G.P., 1928, 'Report on Sur', 9 October 1928.

28 IOR/P/381/33, Seton to Bombay, 9 July 1802.

29 Int. Madame Collette Le Cour Grandmaison, Muscat, 26 January 1985; see also her 'The Harthy Migration to Central Africa', MNHC, Muscat, 1986.

30 Juhaina, 19; Int. with Shaykh 'Alî b Nâṣir b Muhammad al-Ismâ'îlî in Wete, Pemba, 29 July 1986; Bhacker M.R., 1988, 312.

31 The Albusaidi rulers appointed many of the Barwanis to important positions in East Africa, see Saadi, Kadhi Amur Umar, 1941, 'Mafia–History and Traditions', in TNR, vol. 12.

32 Juhaina, 93–4; Gray J.M., 1962a, 22; Baxter C.H., 'Pangani – the Trade Centre of Ancient History', in TNR, vol. 17, 1944.

33 Berg F.G., 1971, 50.

34 Juhaina, 19–23 and 33–6; Gray J.M., 1947, 'Ahmed b. Ibrahim – the first Arab to reach Buganda', in *Uganda Journal*, vol. 11, 80–97; Gray J.M, 1961, 'The Diaries of Emin Pasha', in *Uganda Journal*, vol. 25, 8–10; Burton R.F., 1860, 'The Lake Regions of Central Africa', I, 392–3 and II, 193; Stanley H.M., 1878, 'Through the Dark Continent', I, 453; Stanley R.

and Neame A., [eds], 1961, 'The Exploration Diaries of H.M. Stanley', 117; int. Shaykh 'Ali b Nasir al-Ismâ'ili, Wete, Pemba 29 July 1986 – see note 30 of this chapter; int. Shaykh Sâlim b Badr b Nâsir al-Mazrû'î and Shaykh Mas'ûd b Hamad al-Mazrû'î in the Sunni/Ibadi mosque in Zanzibar, 24 July 1986; int. Jum'a b Sâlim b Khamîs al-Mughairî, the grandson, on his mother's side, of the author of 'Juhaina', at his home in Zanzibar, 24 July 1986.

35 Juhaina, 145, passim; Lambert H.E., 1958, 'The Arab Community and the Twelve Tribes of Mombasa', in Wilson G., [ed.], 1958, 'Mombasa – Social Survey', I, 25–80 quoted in Berg F.J., 1971, 74–5; Guillain C., 1851, plate 10; int. Shaykh Sâlih b Sâlim b Sâlih al-Hadramî, a prominent merchant in Wete, Pemba, 28 and 29 July 1986; also interviews in preceding note.

36 Bennett N.R., 1978, 22; Kelly J.B., 1968, 224–7; Lorimer J.G., 1908–15, IA, 450–2.

37 See the second section of Chapter 5.

38 Tarikh al-Mazari', 45–56; Ylvisaker M., 1975.

39 For a description of the bounties of Pemba see Juhaina, 25–33; see also Owen W.F., 1833, 'Narrative of Voyages to Explore the Shores of Africa, Arabia and Madagascar, I, 314–15 passim.

40 For further discussion of the economic expansion see below, Parts III and IV; for the Somali coast see Cassenelli. V., 1973, 'The Benadir Past: Essays in Southern Somali History', Ph.D. Dissn., Uni. of Wisconsin.

41 See the first section of Chapter 5.

42 PRO/Adm/52/3940, Emery J.B., 1824–6, op. cit.; Boteler T, 1835, 'Narrative of a Voyage of Discovery to Africa and Arabia', II, 206.

43 PRO/ibid.

44 IOR/V/23/45, Miles S.B., 1883–4, 26.

45 For a discussion of these events based on French Archives, see Nicholls C.S., 1971, chapter 6.

46 Juhaina, 138;

47 Nicholls C.S., 1971, 131.

48 Bennett N.R., 1986, 'Arab versus European: Diplomacy and War in nineteenth century East Central Africa', 33, al-Murjibi-Bontinck, 60; Martin B.G., 1976, 'Muslim Brotherhoods in Nineteenth Century Africa', 169; Albrand F., 1838, op. cit.

49 IOR/P/386/3, PRPG to Bombay, 11 December 1825.

50 Juhaina, 121–3; Stigand C.H., 1913, 86; Pate Chronicle, 284–5.

51 Juhaina, ibid.; Guillain-Documents, I, 575.

52 Boteler T., 1835, II, 1–2.

53 For detailed discussions of the way the Albusaidi managed to take control of the Lamu Archipelago see Ylvisaker M., 1975, chap. 5 and Nicholls C.S., 1971, chaps 5 and 6.

54 Bennett N.R., 1978, 18.

55 For writers holding such views see note 21 of this chapter.

56 Nicholls C.S., 1971, 144.

57 IOR/V/23/217, BS, 194–5; ZA/CA4/1, 'Copies of Sir John Gray's Papers'; Burton R.F., 1872, I, 302–3; Bhacker M.R., 1988, 314.

58 See the third section of Chapter 3.

59 IOR/V/23/45, Miles S.B., 1883–4, 27.

60 al-Fath, 537.

61 IOR/V/23/217, BS, 197.
62 IOR/V/23/45, Miles S.B., 1883–4, op. cit.; al-Fath, 537–8.
63 IOR/ibid.
64 Eilts H.F., 1973, 'Sayyid Muhammad bin 'Aqil of Dhufar: malevolent or maligned?', in EIHC, vol. 109, 179–230.
65 IOR/ibid.; al-Fath, 539.
66 al-Fath, ibid.
67 IOR/ibid.
68 IOR/P/387/43, Said b Sultan to Agent in Bombay, n.d., received 5 March 1833.
69 See, for example, Nicholls C.S., 1971, 249.
70 IOR/V/23/217, BS, 633; see Table 2.
71 IOR/L/P&S/5/48, Hamerton to Bombay, 29 May 1842.
72 Int. Ahmad b 'Abd al-Nabî Makkî, Undersecretary to the Ministry of Trade and Industry, Qurum, Oman, 3 February 1985; int. Ja'afar b Muhammad b Sa'îd, London (during a visit), 18 June 1987. According to these informants, the firm of Khimji Ramdas not only provided the Albusaidi household with groceries but also supplied foodstuffs to the army in Masira in Said b Taymur's time. Dharamsi Nansi of the same firm supplied the Qabus b Said household with groceries in the 1980s.
73 This information, which seems to be common knowledge among the mercantile communities of Matrah and Muscat, was repeated in many interviews.
74 IOR/L/P&S/5/422, Christopher to Hines, 10 May 1843. For an Arabic version of such a *barwa* see Juhaina, 175; ZA/AA5/3, Rigby to Bombay, 18 September 1860; Burton R.F., 1872, I, 270.
75 This is clear from the layout of the buildings around the Albusaidi palaces both in Zanzibar and in Muscat.
76 For the 1859 troubles see below, Chapter 12; for the 1895 rebellion, see IOR/V/23/67–70 and PRO/FOCP/6805, 6849, 6861 and 6913.

7 THE RE-EMERGENCE OF BRITISH POLICY TOWARDS OMAN: POST-1833

1 See above, Chapter 3.
2 For the text of the Morseby Treaty see IOR/V/23/217, BS, 654–7.
3 IOR/P/385/55, Said b Sultan to Bombay n.d.; Owen W.F., 1833, I, 343.
4 Details of this episode are in the files IOR/P/385/53 and IOR/P/385/55; see also Gray J.M., 1957, 'The British in Mombasa, 1824–1826'.
5 Pouwels R.L., 1987, 99.
6 IOR/P/386/12, Bourbon to Bombay, 5 September 1826.
7 See above, Chapter 4.
8 al-Fath, 540.
9 IOR/V/23/45, Miles S.B., 1883–4, 29.
10 IOR/P/386/63, Muhammad b Salim to Bombay, 13 March 1830; IOR/P/386/63, Aga Mohammad Shoostry to Bombay, 2 April 1830.
11 al-Fath, 541.
12 IOR/F/4/1398/55441, Norris to Wilson, 9 April 1830.
13 Guillain-Documents, I, 585; Juhaina, 141; for the terms of the 1828 agreement see Juhaina, 127–8.

14 Tarikh al-Mazari', 66; Guillain-Documents, I, 595–8.
15 Guillain-Documents, I, 594 but cf. Juhaina, 130 where al-Mughairi says that Nasir al-Maskari was killed later after escaping to Pemba.
16 IOR/V/23/217, BS, 200–2.
17 IOR/ibid.; IOR/V/23/45, Miles S.B., 1883–4, 29.
18 al-Fath, 541.
19 For Badr b Sayf, see above, Chapter 4.
20 IOR/V/23/217, BS, 203–4; al-Fath, 542–3.
21 IOR/V/23/217, BS, 329; IOR/V/23/45, Miles S.B., 1883–4, 29.
22 al-Fath, 542.
23 ibid.
24 Said-Ruete E., 1886, 8; Guillain-Documents, II, 224.
25 Said-Ruete E., ibid.
26 IOR/F/4/1435/56726, Sayyida Moza bint Ahmad to Bombay, 8 April 1832; IOR/P/387/27, Sayyida Moza to PRPG, 9 April 1832.
27 al-Fath, 542.
28 IOR/V/23/217, BS, 203–5.
29 al-Fath, ibid.
30 ibid.; IOR/V/23/45, Miles S.B., 1883–4, 30.
31 Guillain-Documents, I, 597–9.
32 See Table 4.
33 Tuhfa, II, 206; al-Fath, 542–3; IOR/V/23/45, Miles, ibid.
34 IOR/P/387/4, Commander of cruiser *Tigris* to Bombay, 15 June 1830.
35 IOR/P/387/3, Said b Sultan to Bombay, 24 August 1830.
36 IOR/P/387/2, Wilson to Hamud b Azzan, 24 May 1830.
37 IOR/V/23/45, Miles, ibid.; IOR/V/23/217, BS, 205.
38 For the Wahhabi revival see Ibn Bishr, n.d., II, 38–44; Kelly J.B., 1968, 227–30; al-Rashid, Z.M. 1981, chap. 5; Winder R.B., 1965, chap. 4.
39 Ibn Bishr, II, 40; IOR/F/4/1435, PRPG to Bombay, 28 January 1833.
40 IOR/P/387/55, Calcutta to Bombay, 25 June 1833.
41 IOR/F/4/1435, PRPG to Bombay, 25 June 1833.
42 See above, Table 4.
43 Guillain-Documents, I, 597–9.
44 IOR/V/23/45, Miles S.B., 1883–4, 31.
45 al-Fath, 543–4; Ibn Ruzaiq calls the fort (*ḥiṣn banî Mazrû'*) but this is more commonly known as (*burg al-Mazâri'a*), see al-Siyabi, 1965, 79–80.
46 For these events, see al-Fath, 539–48.
47 ibid.
48 Ibn Bishr, II, 57; Winder R.B., 1965, 94.
49 According to Ibn Ruzaiq, the phrase was coined by Sayyida Moza bint Ahmad, see al-Fath, 540.
50 al-Fath, 548.
51 IOR/F/4/1516, Blane to Hamud b Azzan, 3 July 1834; IOR/V/23/45, Miles S.B., 1883–4, 31.
52 al-Fath, 548.
53 For Turki b Abdallah's relations with the British, see IOR/F/44/1435, correspondence of April 1834.
54 For these developments see Yapp M.E., 1960, 'British Policy in Central Asia, 1830–1843', Ph.D. Dissn., Uni. of London, 51–2 et passim.
55 ZA/BA98/2, 'Treaties with Muscat and Zanzibar', compiled in 1900, 3–6;

IOR/P/387/59, 'The American Treaty', 27 May 1834; Aitchison C.U., 1892, vol. 11, Appendix. 5. For Edmund Roberts's account of events leading up to the treaty see his 1837, 'Embassy to the Eastern Courts of Cochin-China, Siam and Muscat in the U.S. Sloop-of-War Peacock...' and US/Arch/NEMA, E. Robert's Correspondence, chap. 9.

56 IOR/V/23/45, Miles S.B., 1883–4, 30.

57 For the changed situation in Arabia since 1819 and for Muhammad Ali's ambitions in Arabia and his relations with France see Kelly J.B., 1968, chap. 7.

58 IOR/V/23/217, BS, 440–3.

59 For early American commercial connections with East Africa see Gray J.M., 1946, 'Early Connections between the United States and East Africa', in TNR, vol. 22, 55–86; Northway P.H., 1954, 'Salem and Zanzibar – East African Trade', in EIHC, vol. 90; Bennett N.R., 1959, 'Americans in Zanzibar, 1825–1845', in EIHC, vol. 95, reprinted in TNR, vol. 56, 1961; Bennett N.R., 1961, 'Americans in Zanzibar, 1845–1865', in EIHC, vol. 97, reprinted in TNR, vol. 57, 1961 (pages quoted here are from the TNR version).

60 Bennett N.R., 1959, op. cit.

61 Roberts to Woodbury, 26 December 1828, quoted in Bennett NR, 1959 and in Eilts H.F., 1962, 'Ahmad bin Na'aman's Mission to the United States in 1840. The Voyage of Al-Sultanah to New York City', in EIHC, vol. 98.

62 The agreement was signed on 28 March 1828 according to Portuguese archives quoted in Alpers E.A., 1975, 236.

63 IOR/V/23/45, Miles S.B., 1883–4, 26; Guillain-Documents, II, 529.

64 For connections between the Albusaid and rulers of the Comoro Islands as early as the 1750s, see ZA/PMMR/55, Sultan Ahmad b Salih to Ahmad b Said Albusaidi, 12 jamad al-awwal 1163 = 19 April 1750 – for the text of this document see Appendix 1.

65 IOR/P/387/58, Report by Capt. Hart, 10 February 1834.

66 IOR/V/23/45, Miles S.B., 1883–4, 30.

67 Article 2 of the treaty, see above, note 55 of this chapter.

68 For the Omani-British 1798 Treaty, see above, Chapter 3.

69 IOR/V/23/45, Miles S.B., 1883–4, 30.

70 IOR/P/387/58, Report by Capt. Hart, 10 February 1834.

71 ibid.

72 ibid.

73 ibid.

74 The Omani-French Treaty, due partly to frequent changes in officials at Bourbon, did not get signed until 1844, see below, Chapter 11.

75 IOR/P/387/59, Bentinck to Gore, 13 April 1834.

76 For Mazrui lineages, see above, Figure 3.

77 Omari bin Stamboul, 1951, 'An Early History of Mombasa and Tanga', tr. by Baker E.C., in TNR, vol. 31; Guillain-Documents, I, 602;

78 IOR/V/23/45, Miles S.B., 1883–4, 32.

79 Krapf J.L., 1860, 536.

80 Juhaina, 144–50.

81 Guillain-Documents, I, 604.

82 IOR/V/23/45, Miles, ibid.; Krapf J.L., 1860, 537.

83 Juhaina, 127–8; Krapf J.L., 1860, 534–6.

84 IOR/ibid.; Guillain-Documents, I, 605; unfortunately no *nisba* is given in the sources for this Ali b Mansur.
85 Krapf J.L., 1860, 537.
86 For the Mazrui governors of Mombasa see Figure 3.
87 On Sulayman b Hamad see below, note 91 of chapter 8.
88 PRO/FOCP/401/210, Kirk to Anderson, 28 September 1895; IOR/ibid.; Juhaina, 135; Guillain-Documents, I, 606–9; Krapf J.L., 1860, 536; Tarikh al-Mazari', 72.
89 Berg F.J., 1971, 81; Koffsky P.L., 1977, 'History of Takaungu, East Africa, 1830–1896', Ph.D. Dissn., Uni. of Wisconsin, 12.
90 Burton R.F., 1872, II, 105; Guillain-Documents, III, 262–3.

8 THE 'OMANI' AND THE 'INDIAN' ROLES IN THE NINETEENTH CENTURY COMMERCIAL EXPANSION

1 IOR/L/P&S/501, Rigby to Anderson, 4 April 1859.
2 For a discussion of the origins of the 'Swahili' culture, see Chapter 1.
3 Cooper F., 1977, 118.
4 Nicholls C.S., 1968, 402; idem., 1971, 375.
5 Sheriff A.M.H., 1987, 105.
6 ibid., 37.
7 US/Arch/NEMA, Roberts to Mclane, 14 May 1834, 157.
8 Guillain C., 1841, 'Côte de Zanguebar et Mascate' in RC, vol. 1, 1843, 536.
9 IOR/L/MAR/C/586, Hardy, 1811, op. cit.
10 IOR/P/381/33, Seton to Bombay, 9 July 1802.
11 Bird J., 1839–40, op. cit.
12 IOR/P/381/33, ibid.
13 Burton R.F., 1860, passim.
14 For the development of trade routes in the African interior see below, this chapter.
15 Burton R.F., 1860, II, 223–5.
16 al-Murjibi-Bontinck, 22.
17 ibid., 44.
18 ibid.; Burton R.F., 1860, I, 324; Bennett N.R., 1986, 35.
19 Macqueen J., 1845, 'The Visit of Leif bin Said to the Great African Lake' in JRGS, vol. 15, 372; Cooley W.D., 1845, 'The Geography of the N'yassi' in JRGS, vol. 15, 185–235.
20 al-Murjibi-Bontinck, 49, n. 68; Burton R.F., 1860, II, 228.
21 al-Murjibi-Bontinck, 49, n. 69; Burton R.F., 1860, II, 149–51; Livingstone D., 1874, 'Last Journals', I, 277.
22 Guillain-Documents II, 50; Albrand F., 1838, 78; for the spelling of the name see Juhaina, 143.
23 Burton R.F., 1860, II, 223–4; for full name see IOR/V/23/45, Miles S.B., 1883–4, 30.
24 ZA/AA12/1E, Accounts and Receipts dated 17 dhu al-hijja = 2 October 1852; Sheriff A.M.H., 1971, 339–42; idem, 1987, 104, 177; Bennett N.R., 1986, 92; Gray J.M., 1947, op. cit.; Albrand F., 1838, 78; Burton R.F., 1860, II, 149–51.
25 Morice-Projet, 119.

26 ibid., 137.
27 SD, 'History of Sudi', 231.
28 Morice-Projet, 137.
29 Morice-Projet, 82.
30 Bennett N.R., 1975, 'Africa and Europe: From Roman Times to National Independence', 30.
31 Roberts A.D., 1970, 'Nyamwezi Trade' in Gray R. and Birmingham D., [eds], 1970, 'Pre-Colonial African Trade', 39–74; Oliver R., 1963, 'Discernible Developments in the Interior, c.1500–1850', in Oliver R. and Mathew G., [eds], 'History of East Africa', I, 169–211; Tosh J., 1970, 'The Northern Inter-lacustrine Region', in Gray R. and Birmingham D. [eds], 1970, 103–18.
32 IOR/L/MAR/C/586, Hardy, 1811, op. cit.
33 Baxter H.C., 1944, 'Pangani: the Trade Centre of Ancient History' in TNR, vol. 17, 15–25.
34 Roberts A.D., 1970, op. cit.
35 Lamphear J., 1970, 'The Kamba and the northern Mrima Coast', in Gray R. and Birmingham D., [eds], 1970, 75–101; Jackson K.A., 1972, 'An ethnohistorical study of the oral traditions of the Akamba of Kenya', Ph.D. Dissn., UCLA, 215–45.
36 Sheriff A.M.H., 1987, 168.
37 For the contemporary development of Kilwa, see Morice-Projet, 62; Burton R.F., 1872, II, 341–67; Karpf J.L., 1860, 344, 423; Albrand F., 1838, 78–80.
38 For the central route see Roberts A.D., 1968, 'The Nyamwezi' in Roberts A.D., [ed.], 1968, 'Tanzania Before 1900', 117–47; idem, 1970, op. cit.; Oliver R., 1963, op. cit.; Tosh J., 1970, op. cit.; Unomah A.C., 1973, 'Economic expansion and political change in Unyanyembe', Ph.D. Dissn., Uni. of Ibadan; Brown W.T., 1970, 'Bagamoyo: an Historical Introduction', in TNR, vol. 71; Brown W.T., 1971, 'The Politics of Business; relations between Zanzibar and Bagamoyo in the late nineteenth century', in AHJ, vol. 4; Brown B. and Brown W.T., 1976, 'East African Trade Towns: A Shared Growth', in Arens W., [ed.], 1976, 'A Century of Change in East Africa'.
39 For the northern route see Ylvisaker M., 1975; idem, 1979; Berg F.J., 1971; Lamphear J., 1970; Jackson K.A., 1972; Cassanelli L.V., 1973.
40 Bennett N.R., 1978, 34–5.
41 Bennett N.R., 1971, 'Mirambo of Tanzania, 1840?-1884', 25; emphasis is mine.
42 Albrand F., 1838, 75.
43 al-Murjibi-Bontinck, 21–2, 60, passim.
44 Bontinck's introduction to ibid., 22; Roberts A.D., 1968, 136.
45 PRO/FO/84/2150/293, Portal to Salisbury, 28 November 1891.
46 Burton R.F., 1872, I, 261.
47 IOR/L/MAR/C/586, Smee T., 6 April 1811, op. cit.
48 IOR/ibid.; Morice-Projet, 181; Albrand F., 1838, 75.
49 Ly-Tio-Fane M., 1958, 'Mauritius and the Spice Trade: the Odessy of Pierre Poivre', 1–18; Ridley H.N., 1912, 'Spices', 157–62.
50 French archives quoted in Nicholls C.S., 1968, n. 3, 196.
51 For a discussion of the eighteenth century East African slave trade see Sheriff A.M.H., 1971, Chapter 4; idem, 1987, chap. 2.

52 IOR/L/MAR/C/586, Smee T., 6 April 1811, op. cit.
53 Indian archives quoted in Sheriff A.M.H., 1987, 48.
54 Ruschenberger W., 1838, 'Narrative of a Voyage around the World', I, 73–5; Crofton R.H., 1936, 'A Pageant of the Spice Islands', 80.
55 Juhaina, 143; Al-Farsi S.F., 1942, 29; Guillain-Documents, II, 49; Albrand F., 1838, 69–70; Burton R.F., 1872, I, 363–4; Gray J.M., 1964a, 'The Recovery of Kilwa by the Arabs in 1785', in TNR, vol. 62, 21–3.
56 Albrand F., 1838, 69.
57 Tidbury G.E., 1949, 'The Clove Tree', 108, passim.
58 IOR/in Sheriff A.M.H., 1971, Appendix A.
59 Bird J., 1839–40, op. cit.
60 ibid.; Burton R.F., 1872, I, 364–5.
61 ibid.; Robert's papers quoted in Sheriff A.M.H., 1987, 50; the first figure is quoted in MT$ but the value of the two currencies was the same at the time according to US/Arch/NEMA, Hines to Seward, 25 October 1864, 535.
62 Ruschenberger W.S., 1838, I, 51; Northway P.H., 1954, 384; Guillain-Documents II, 50–1; Said-Ruete E., 1886, 109.
63 Guillain C., 1841, 538.
64 Loarer quoted in Sheriff A.M.H., 1987, 54.
65 ZA/AL1/4, 'Protests in hand of A. O'Swald in Hurricane of 1872'; Zanzibar Museum, copy of report sent by Kirk to FO, 20 April 1872.
66 Cooper F., 1977, chap. 2.
67 See, among others, Alpers E.A., 1967; Kelly J.B., 1968; Cooper F., 1974 and 1977; Nicholls C.S., 1968 and 1971; Sheriff A.M.H., 1971 and 1987; Beachey R.W., 1976a, 'The Slave Trade of Eastern Africa'; Lovejoy P.E., 1983, 'Transformations in Slavery: a History of Slavery in Africa'; Martin E.B. and Ryan T.C., 1977, 'A Quantitative Assessment of the Arab Slave Trade of East Africa, 1770–1896' in *Kenya Historical Review*, vol. 5; Lodhi A., 1973, 'The Institution of Slavery in Zanzibar and Pemba'; Miers S., 1975, 'Britain and the Ending of the Slave Trade'.
68 Martin E.B. and Ryan T.C., 1977, 74; see also Sheriff A.M.H.1987, Table 6.4, 229.
69 See above, Chapter 1.
70 Challaye M.C. De., 1844, 'Mémoire sur l'emigration des Indiens et sur le travail libre dans les colonies de Maurice et de Bourbon', in RC, vol. 3, 557–609.
71 ibid., 560.
72 ibid., 574–5.
73 ZA/AA5/2, Said b Sultan to Palmerston, 18 December 1846.
74 ZA/AA12/2 Rigby to Bombay, 14 September 1860; ZA/AA3/1, Bombay to Hamerton, 26 February 1841; IOR/V/23/217, BS, 650; IOR/L/P&S/5/398, Hamerton to Bombay, 1 July 1841.
75 ZA/AA12/2, Ahmad b Nu'man quoted in Rigby to Wilson, 5 September 1861.
76 Int. Jum'a b Salim al-Mughairi, Zanzibar, 24 July 1986, see note. 34 of Chapter 6; int. Shaykh Ali b Nasir al-Ismaili, Pemba, 29 July 1986, see note 30 of Chapter 6; ZA/ibid.; see also IOR/15/6/5, 'Slave Trade Correspondence, 1847–1872'.
77 Malcolm J., 1827, 'Sketches of Persia by a Traveller', I, 10–26; for Malcolm's meeting with Sultan b Ahmad, see Kaye J.Y., 1856, 'The Life and Correspondence of Sir John Malcolm', I, 105–10.

78   Maurizi V., 1819, 29 and 131.
79   Heude W., 1819, 'A Voyage up the Persian Gulf', 20–34; Lumsden T., 1822, 'A Journey from Merut in India to London', 61–70.
80   Roberts E., 1837, 354.
81   Johnson J., 1818, 'A Journey from India to England', 7–15.
82   *Khawr* is a Persian word meaning salt water inlet, and is frequently used in place names in Arabia, e.g. Khawr Fakkan, Khawr al-Udayd.
83   Int. 'Abd-al-Bâqî b 'Alî b Fayd-allâh b Jamâl, Matrah, 1980; int. Anwar 'Alî b 'Abd-al-Rida b' Abd-al-Bâqî, Oxford (during a visit), 6 June 1984; Bhacker M.R., 1988, 322.
84   IOR/V/23/217, BS, 636–87.
85   Sheriff A.M.H., 1987, 38; idem., 1971, 160–4.
86   IOR/V/23/217, BS, 646; although Sheriff quotes from the Maharashtra State Archives in India, copies of the reports in question are identical to the ones in the India Office Library in London as is evident from the quotations.
87   IOR/ibid., 648–9.
88   For examples of these in Muscat, Ras al-Khayma and Bander Abbas, see IOR/ibid., 650.
89   *Qayd al-ard* literally means 'the shackler of earth' but the word Qayd in Arabic also means a 'bond' or 'registration'. Thus the sobriquet may have come about as a result of land reforms and the need to draw up a proper document to prove ownership of land during Sayf b Sultan al-Ya'rubi's reign in Oman, see refs in the next note.
90   Tuhfa II, 100; al-Shua'a, 272; al-Fath, 295; Qisas, 370–80; al-Siyabi, 1982, IV, 9–11.
91   This Sulayman b Hamad, described by Rigby – in ZA/AA12/2, Rigby to Wilson, 5 September 1861, 10, – as a cousin of Said b Sultan was in fact a more distant relation. He was Sulayman b Hamad b Said b Muhammad b Abdallah b Khalaf while the Sultan was Said b Sultan b Ahmad b Said b Mohammad b Khalaf, this last being the fifth-generation-removed common ancestor of the two, see Pullicino P., 1954, table 1 and Guillain-Documents, II, 24; for a portrait of Sulayman see Guillain, C. 1851, plate 29.
92   IOR/L/P&S/5/501, Rigby to Anderson, 25 April 1859.
93   Germain A., 1868b, 'Note sur Zanzibar et la Côte Orientale d'Afrique', in *Bulletin de la Société de Géographie*, vol. 16, 534.
94   ibid., Guillain-Documents, II, 24–6.
95   US/Arch/NEMA, Ward to Buchanan, 13 March 1847, 384; idem, Ward to Abbott, 13 March 1851, 479; idem, Ropes to Seward, 5 October 1865, 539.
96   IOR/L/P&S/5/503, Rigby to Bombay, 4 April 1859.
97   IOR/L/P&S/5/432, Hamerton to Bombay, 30 August 1841.
98   Unomah A.C., 1973, 86–96, passim.
99   ZA/AA12/2, Rigby to Bombay, 14 September 1860; PRO/FO/54/4, Norsworthy to Bombay, n.d. but during September 1841.
100 IOR/L/P&S/5/422, Christopher to Hines, 18 May 1843.
101 PRO/FO/54/4, Hamerton to Bombay, 28 September 1841.
102 Niebuhr C., 1792, [tr.], 116.
103 Int. Anwar 'Ali b 'Abd al-Rida b Abd al-Baqi, Oxford, 6 June 1984; see note 83 of this chapter; Pelly L., 1863–4, 'Remarks on the Tribes, Trade and Resources around the shore line of the Persian Gulf' in TBGS, vol. 17, 32–103.

104 Morice-Projet, passim; Sheriff A.M.H., 1987, 44.
105 Fraser J.B., 1825, 'Narrative of a Journey into Khorasan', 18.
106 Wellsted J.R., 1838, I, 32.
107 Helfer P., 1878, 'Travels of Doctor and Madame Helfer', II, 3–14; Juhaina, 139.
108 Int. as in note 103 above.
109 Int. 'Alî b Ramaḍan and 'Abd-al-Ḥusain b 'Abd-al-Riḍa, Matrah, 5 January 1984.
110 Guillain C., 1851, plates 6 and 7.
111 Burton R.F., 1872, I, 433; for Muscat cloth imports into Zanzibar see IOR/L/P&S/9/42, Playfair to Wood, 22 January 1865.
112 Burton R.F., 1860, II, 400.
113 Among others, the same interviewees as in note 109 who still practice this trade in Matrah.
114 Int. Sayf b Sâlim, Director of Culture, Ministry of Information, Culture and Sports, Zanzibar, 14 July 1986; int. 'Alî b Nâsir b Muḥammad al-Ma'walî, Zanzibar, 8 July 1986 – owns a shop selling textiles and other goods in Zanzibar town.
115 Int. as in note103 above; int 'Alî b Ibrâhîm b Hâshim al-Maymanî, Matrah, 8 January 1984.
116 al-Fath, 388–9.
117 For Imam Said b Ahmad, see above, Chapter 2.
118 Examples of these are the Khoja Dâwûd b 'Alî Khattrî and the Bulûshî 'Alî b Îsa b 'Abd-al-Rahmân Khattrî, both now merchants in Matrah.
119 Int. Mûsa b Ibrâhîm b Hâshim al-Maymanî, Matrah, 8 January 1984 – Musa, himself a *sonara*, a descendant of the early arrivals, was the leader of his community in 1984; see also Guillain C., 1841, op. cit.; Henshaw J., 1840, 'Around the World', 202–35; for Jews also involved in making silver ornaments in Muscat in the 1830s see Wellsted J.R., 1838, I, 22.
120 For references to these activities being carried out in Muscat/Matrah in 1819, see Loch F.E., quoted in Belgrave C., 1966, 60–71; see also Pelly L., 1863–4, op. cit.; Germain A., 1868a, 'Quelques mots sur l'Oman et le Sultan de Mascate', in *Bulletin de la Société de Géographie*, vol. 16, 339–64; idem, 1868b, op. cit.; Gullain C., 1841, op. cit.; Sykes Col., 1853, 'Notes on the Possessions of the Imaum of Muscat, on the Climate and Productions of Zanzibar...', in TBGS, vol. 23; Osgood J.F., 1854, 'Notes of Travel or Recollections of Majunga, Zanzibar, Muscat, Aden, Mocha and Other Eastern Ports', 90–1; Ruschenberger W., 1838, I, 85; Fraser J.B., 1825, 18; Roberts E., 1837, 354–5.
121 Roberts E., 1837, 355.
122 Int. Muhammad b 'Awaḍ al-Khabbâz, Matrah, 6 January 1984.
123 Fraser J.B., 1825, 17; Pelly L., 1863–4, op. cit.
124 Wellsted J.R., 1840, 45–59; Germain A., 1868a, 342; for similar descriptions earlier on in the century, see Heude W., 1819, 20–39 and Fraser J.B., 1825, 8.
125 Wellsted J.R., 1838, 319–20.
126 The customs master and other prominent merchants lending to the ruling family did not pay tax but are said to have adjusted their accounts accordingly.
127 Information on the date trade was obtained in several interviews with the

descendants of the early Lawatiya date traders in Oman.
128 Guillain C., 1841, 554.
129 For 1800 see Malcolm J., 1827, I, 10–26; for 1814 see Blakeney R., 1841, 'Journal of an Oriental Voyage', 199–203; for 1816 see Buckingham J.S., 1830, II, 392–430; for 1821 see Fraser J.B., 1825, 17; for the 1830s see Wellsted J.R., 1840, 45–9 and idem., 1837, 'Narrative of a Journey into the Interior of Oman', in JRGS, vol. 7, 102–13 and idem., 1838, I, 10–37 and 371–403; Roberts E., 1837, 351–63; Ruschenberger W., 1838, I, 77–158; and Fontanier V., 1844, 'Voyage dans l'Inde et dans le Golfe Persique' II, i, 22–45.
130 US/Arch, quoted in Allen C.H., 1978, 165.
131 MacMurdo J., 1820, 'An Account of the province of Cutch, and of the countries lying between Guzerat and the River Indus...', in TLSB, vol. 2, 217.
132 ibid., 218; IOR/V/23/212, Leech R., 'Memoir on the trade & c. of the port of Mandvee in Kutch', May 1837, 221; for Mandvi's trade with East Africa, see below, Chapter 10.

9 BEGINNINGS OF THE INTEGRATION OF MUSCAT AND ZANZIBAR INTO THE WORLD ECONOMY

1 al-Mas'udi, 'The Ivory Trade', in SD, 15.
2 PRO/FO/84/1146, Hamerton to Bombay, 9 October 1843.
3 IOR/V/23/212, Leech R., 1837, 212; Postans T., 1839–40, 'Some Account of the Present State of the Trade between the Port of Mandavie in Cutch, and the East Coast of Africa', in TBGS, vol. 3, 169–76.
4 See above, Introduction.
5 al-Fath, 356; Aitken E.H. [ed.], 1907, 'Gazetteer of the Province of Sind', 113; see also Allen C.H., 1978, 118–24.
6 Int. Jawâd b Ja'far al-Khâbûrî, Ruwi, 8 January 1984; int. Kamâl b 'Abd-al-Rida Sultan, Matrah, 8 January 1984
7 US Arch/Microcopy/468/1, Ward to State Dept., 7 March 1847.
8 Burton R.F., 1872, I, 328–32.
9 ZA/BA66/43, Shelswell-White G.H., 1935, 'Notes on the Hadrami and Shihri Community of Zanzibar', 3.
10 See the first section of Chapter 8.
11 ZA/AA5/1, Hamerton to Bombay, 2 January 1842; Christie J., 1876, 'Cholera Epidemics in East Africa', 328.
12 PRO/FOCP/6861, O'Sullivan, 1896, 'Report on Pemba by Vice-Consul O'Sullivan', in Hardinge to Salisbury, 18 June 1896.
13 For these early nineteenth century migrations, see IOR/V/23/212–15; Carnac J.R., 1819, 'Some Account of the Famine of Guzerat in the Years 1812 and 1813', in TLSB, vol. 1, 296–304; Jacob G.L., 1860–2, 'Extracts from a Journal kept during a Tour made in 1851 through Kutch...', in TBGS, vol. 16, 56–67.
14 Same interviewees as in note 127 of Chapter 8; for similar information obtained from Banyan oral sources, see Allen C.H., 1978, 142.
15 Christie J., 1876, 313, passim.
16 Krapf J.L., 1860, 224; Burdo A., 1886, 485 cited in Bennett N.R., 1986, 32.

17 The figures are means worked out from the annual figures given in Appendix A in Sheriff A.M.H., 1971; the exchange rate used to convert rupees into MT$ is Rs.2.13 = MT$1 as the average of the rates for the first half of the nineteenth century given in Milburn W., 1813, I, 116, 173–4 and Landen R.G., 1967, 128–31.

18 Sheriff A.M.H., 1971, Appendix C, the figures are given in US$ but in this period $1 = MT$1 according to US/Arch/NEMA, Hines to Seward, 25 October 1864, 535; see also Nicholls C.S., 1971, 364.

19 US/Arch/NEMA, Waters J. to Waters R., 15 August 1844, 246; US/Arch/NEMA, Ward to Buchanan, 13 March 1847, 385.

20 Loarer's Report quoted in Nicholls C.S., 1968, chap. 8.

21 Cochet L., 1857, quoted in Alpers E.A., 1975, 234.

22 PRO/FO/54/17 and IOR/L/P&S/9/37, Rigby to Wood, 1 May 1860.

23 Sheriff A.M.H., 1971, 273–75; idem, 1987, 102–3.

24 Berg F.J., 1971, chap. 6; Ylvisaker M., 1979, chap. 7.

25 Burton R.F., 1860, II, 404.

26 US/Arch/NEMA, Ropes to Seward, 5 October 1865, 539.

27 Guillain-Documents, II, 87; Burton R.F., 1860, II, 406; Burton R.F., 1872, I, 357.

28 Guillain C., 1841, 535.

29 US/Arch/NEMA, Instructions to Captain John L. Gallop of the Bark 'Reaper', 1843, 279; US/Arch/NEMA, Return Manifest of the Bark 'Reaper', 1844, 283.

30 US/Arch/NEMA, Bates W.B., 'Journals and Observations', 29 June 1845, 267.

31 Loarer's Report quoted in Nicholls C.S., 1968, chap. 8.

32 US/Arch/NEMA, Ward to Shepard, 5 February 1849, 438.

33 ibid.

34 Guillain C., 1841, 536.

35 Speke J.H., 1862, 'On the Commerce of Central Africa', in TBGS, vol. 15, 138–45; cf. Hamerton quoted in Burton R.F., 1860, II, 406.

36 Loarer quoted in Nicholls C.S., 1968, chap. 8 and above, Table 6.

37 Pelly L., 1863–4, 63.

38 Owen W.F., 1833, 'Narrative of Voyages to Explore the Shores of Africa, Arabia and Madagascar...', I, 340–1; Pouwels R.L., 1987, 240, n. 82.

39 PRO/FO/54/17 and IOR/L/P&S/9/37, Rigby to Wood, 1 May 1860; Burton R.F., 1860, II, 416–17; Burton R.F., 1872, I, 207–9.

40 For the differential taxation system see Sheriff A.M.H., 1971, chap. 6; idem, 1987, chap. 4.

41 ibid., 104; see also Bennett N.R., 1959, op. cit.

42 ibid.; Burton R.F., 1860, II, 4.

43 On the central route see note 38 of Chapter 8.

44 Brown B., 1971, op. cit.

45 PRO/FO/84/1344, Kirk to FO, 27 June 1871; see also Brown W.T., 1971, op. cit.

46 Speke J.H., 1863, quoted in Bennett N.R., 1986, 36.

47 al-Murjibi-Bontinck, 102; Speke J.H., 1863, 'Journal of the Discovery of the Source of the Nile', 15; Stanley H.M., 1878, 'Through the Dark Continent', II, 123.

48 On Muscat's entrepôtole between East Africa and India see Bird J.,

1839–40, op. cit. and MacMurdo J., 1820, op. cit.
49 Int. Ali al-Jamali, Qurum, 5 January 1985; int. Noor al-Din Ali Bhay Mulla Abd-al-Ali Noorani, Zanzibar, 24 July 1986, see note 24 of Chapter 5; see also Guillain C., 1841, op. cit. and Burton R.F., 1872, I, 240.
50 The adjective *merekeni* was apparently at first applied to one Jum'a b Sâlim b Raqad who purportedly introduced large quantities of the American cloth into the interior, see al-Murjibi-Bontinck, 85 and n. 232, p. 231.
51 Interviewees as in note 103 of Chapter 8; see also Guillain C., 1841, 540–1 and Burton R.F., 1860, I, 147–50 and II, 396.
52 PRO/FO/54/17 and IOR/L/P&S/9/37, Rigby to Wood, 1 May 1860; Guillain C., 1841, 541.
53 See the second section of Chapter 7.
54 PRO and IOR/ ibid.; Cochet quoted in Nicholls C.S., 1968, chap. 8.
55 For comparisons of the commerce carried out by companies of different Western nations, see Nicholls C.S., 1968, chap. 8 or idem, 1971, chap. 12; see also Bennett N.R., 1959, 1961 and 1963.

10 COMMERCIAL AND POLITICAL RIVALRY AND BRITISH ENCROACHMENTS IN EAST AFRICA

1 IOR/L/P&S/5/422, Christopher to Hines, 10 May 1843.
2 Stocqueler J.H., 1832, 'Fifteen Months Pilgrimage through untrodden tracks of Khuzistan and Persia', 3–8.
3 See the second section of Chapter 7.
4 IOR/P/387/58, Report by Capt. Hart, 10 February 1834.
5 See, for example, Chapter 11 for the British–French rapprochement in the 1840s.
6 See below, Chapter 11.
7 See the second section of Chapter 7.
8 See Yapp M.E., 1980, 'Strategies of British India: Britain, Iran and Afghanistan, 1798–1850'.
9 See above, Chapter 7.
10 The agreement was signed on 22 Safar 1255 = 7 May 1839; IOR/L/P&S/6/14, Khurshid Pasha to Hennell, 3 April 1839.
11 IOR/V/23/217, BS, 441–3; IOR/L/P&S/6/15, Governor in Council to Court, 13 April 1832; IOR/V/23/45, Miles S.B., 1883–4, 32.
12 PRO/FO/78/342, Campbell to Palmerston, 7 February 1838.
13 IOR/L/P&S/5/376, Khoja Reuben Aslam (East India Company agent in Muscat) to Hennell, 10 June 1839; IOR/F/4/1435, PRPG to Bombay, 25 June 1833.
14 IOR/L/P&S/5/377, Bombay to Secret Committee, 10 September 1839.
15 al-Fath, 543–8; IOR/L/P&S/5/13, Hennell to Bombay, 21 August 1839.
16 See the second section of Chapter 6.
17 See the third section of Chapter 7.
18 IOR/L/P&S/5/385, Hennell to Reid, 4 August 1840.
19 IOR/L/P&S/5/388, Supreme Govt. to Bombay, 14 September 1840.
20 IOR quoted in Kelly J.B., 1968, 342.
21 Nicholls C.S., 1968, 214; idem, 1971, 155–6.
22 IOR/L/P&S/5/381, Reuben Aslam to Bombay, 29 September 1838.

23 PRO/FO/54/4, Said b Sultan to Palmerston, 1 May 1841; Guillain C., 1845, 'Documents sur l'Histoire, la Géographie, et le Commerce de la Partie Occidentale de Madagascar', 134–6.
24 Guillain C., 1845, ibid.; Decary R., 1960, 'L'Ile Nosy Be de Madagascar', 14.
25 IOR/L/P&S/5/385, Hennell to Bombay, 5 August 1840.
26 PRO/FO/54/3, Hennell to Bombay, 31 July 1840.
27 ibid.
28 See the third section of Chapter 3.
29 IOR/L/P&S/5/385, Hennell to Bombay, 5 August 1840.
30 PRO/FO/54/3, Said b Sultan to Palmerston, 30 July 1840.
31 PRO/FO/54/4, Said b Sultan to Governor of Bourbon, n.d., in Hennell to Secret Committee, 3 November 1841.
32 PRO/FO/78/373, Campbell to Palmerston, 26 January 1839.
33 ZA/AA5/1 and PRO/FO/54/3, Palmerston to Said b Sultan, 30 September 1840.
34 IOR/L/P&S/5/392, Bombay to Secret Committee, 30 December 1840.
35 For the 1839 Omani-British Treaty, see PRO/FO/54/2; IOR/V/23/217, BS, 250–6; and Aitchison C.U., 1892, vol. 11, 292–8.
36 For the 1798 Omani-British Treaty, see above, Chapter 3.
37 For the 1833 Omani-American Treaty, see above, Chapter 7.
38 Bennett N.R., 1959, 96.
39 Sheriff A.M.H., 1987, 93–4, passim.
40 Nicholls C.S., 1971, 160.
41 USArch/Microcopy/468/1, Forsyth to Waters, 7 April 1836; US/Arch/NEMA, Waters's Jnl, 17 March 1837, 194.
42 US/Arch/NEMA, Waters's Jnl for 1837, 189–206; US/Arch/NEMA, Botsford to Marshall, 24 September 1842, 237–8.
43 Bennett N.R., 1959, 101.
44 Quoted in Bennett N.R., 1961, 127.
45 US/Arch/NEMA, Botsford to Webster, 10 November 1842, 240.
46 Bennett N.R., ibid.
47 US/Arch/NEMA, Waters W. to Waters R., 1 October 1841, 232.
48 US/Arch/NEMA, Waters R. to Waters W., 17 December 1839, 223.
49 US/Arch/NEMA, Waters's Jnl, 3 September 1844, 257.
50 Misra B.B., 1961, 'The Indian Middle Classes; Their Growth in Modern Times', 98–9; Kucchall S.C., 1963, 'The Industrial Economy of India', 421.
51 Kucchall S.C., 1963, ibid.; Anstey V., 1952, 'The Economic Development of India', 134–8.
52 Kucchall S.C., 1963, 433–6.
53 For the Joint Family organisation, see above, Chapter 5.
54 Int. Dr Garang Mehta and Mr Shirali Mohammed Ali Champsi, Zanzibar, 8 July 1986; information obtained from Chandrasen Narutum, Mandvi, 1986.
55 Postans T., 1839–40, op. cit.; MacMurdo J., 1820, op. cit.
56 IOR/V/23/212, Leech R., 1837, 'Memoir on the Trade & c. of the port of Mandvee in Kutch'; Postans, ibid.; MacMurdo, ibid.; Sheriff A.M.H., 1971, Appendix A.
57 MacMurdo J., 1820, 217.
58 ibid., 218; see also Leech R., 1837, in IOR/ibid.
59 Bird J., 1839–40, op. cit.

60 Carnac J.R., 1819, op. cit; Jacob G.L., 1860–2.
61 Jacob G.L., 1860–2, op. cit.
62 Sheriff A.M.H., 1987, 107.
63 ZA/CA4/1, Said b Sultan to Newman, Hunt and Christopher, 10 March 1845; PRO/FO/84/425, Norsworthy to Newman, Hunt and Christopher, 27 June 1834.
64 PRO/FO/54/1, Newman, Hunt and Christopher to Palmerston, 10 July 1834; PRO/FO/54/4, Norsworthy to Richard, 12 September 1841.
65 PRO/FO/54/4, ibid.
66 ZA/CA4/1, Said b Sultan to Newman and Hunt, 10 March 1845 and Newman and Hunt to Aberdeen, 11 July 1845; Sheriff A.M.H., 1987, 91.
67 PRO/FO/54/2, FO to India Board, 6 June 1838.
68 IOR/P/387/58, Report by Capt. Hart, 21 May 1834.
69 PRO/FO/54/2, FO to India Board, 6 June 1838; Cogan to India Board, 16 June 1838 and Cogan's Memo., in Carnac to Hobhouse, 3 February 1838.
70 ZA/AA5/1, Hamerton to Said b Sultan, 25 Ramadan 1256 = 20 November 1840.
71 PRO/FO/54/4, Queen Seneko to Said b Sultan, 21 March 1841.
72 ZA/AA5/1 and PRO/FO/54/3, Palmerston to Said b Sultan, 30 September 1840.
73 ZA/CA4/1 and PRO/FO/54/4, Said b Sultan to Palmerston, 1 May 1841.
74 PRO/FO/54/4, Palmerston to Said b Sultan, 13 August 1841.

11 THE SUBORDINATION OF MUSCAT'S RULERS AND THEIR ASSOCIATES FROM INDIA

1 IOR/P/387/58, Report by Capt. Hart, 21 May 1834; IOR/V/23/217, BS, 276.
2 ZA/AA5/1, Hamerton to Said b Sultan, 21 May 1841.
3 PRO/FO/54/5, Cogan to Forbes, 28 October 1842.
4 ZA/AA3/1, Hamerton to the Governor of Mauritius, 17 August 1841.
5 ZA/AA3/1, Hamerton to Bombay, 13 July 1841.
6 ZA/AA1/3, W. Henderson and Co. to Aberdeen, 27 May 1846; IOR/L/P&S/ 5/393, Agent in Muscat to Bombay, 4 April 1841.
7 Guillain-Documents, II, 4, n.1.
8 PRO/FO/54/7, Hamerton to FO, 24 March 1845.
9 ZA/AA3/1, Hamerton to Bombay, 30 August 1841.
10 IOR/F/4/2034, Hamerton to Bombay, 9 December 1843.
11 ZA/AA1/2, Said b Sultan to Aberdeen, 8 April 1844.
12 ZA/CA4/1/3 and PRO/FO/54/7, Said b Sultan to Aberdeen, n.d., in Said b Sultan to Cogan, 28 September 1845.
13 ZA/CA4/1/3, ibid.
14 ZA/AA3/1, Hamerton to Bombay, 3 January 1842.
15 Rushbrook Williams L.F., 1958, 'The Black Hills – Kutch in History and Legend', 203.
16 IOR/15/6/8, Miles to Ross, 16 January 1875.
17 ZA/AA3/1, Hamerton to Bombay, 13 July 1841.
18 Consul Ward quoted in Bennett N.R., 1961, 123–4.
19 IOR/L/P&S/5/407, Bombay to Secret Committee, 23 May 1842.

20 On these events and on Ali b Nasir's mission, see ZA/AA1/2 and PRO/FO/54/4–9.
21 ZA/AA3/6, Hamerton to Bombay, 19 March 1844.
22 IOR/F/4/2014, Agent at Muscat to Bombay, 8 May 1843.
23 PRO/FO/84/647, Palmerston to Hamerton, 6 December 1846; IOR/L/P&S/9/38, Rigby to Russell, 5 October 1861.
24 PRO/FO/54/5, Aberdeen to Hamerton, 11 July 1843; for the 1844 Omani-French Treaty, see ZA/BA98/2, 6–10 for the French version; IOR/V/23/217, BS, 266–71 and Aitchison C.U., 1892, vol. 11, 29–34 of the Appendices for the version in English.
25 ZA/AA12/2, Sunley to Malmesbury, 7 October 1852; Newitt M., 1984, 'The Comoro Islands – Struggle against Dependency in the Indian Ocean', 28–32.
26 Newitt M., 1984, 34.
27 Juhaina, 151; al-Fath, 547; ZA/AA3/6, Hamerton to Bombay, 14 April 1845; IOR/V/23/45, Miles S.B., 1883–4, 33; IOR/V/23/217, BS, 217.
28 Juhaina, 151; al-Fath, 547; Guillain-Documents, III, 99–102; Stigand C.H., 1913, 91–3; IOR/ibid.; ZA/ibid.
29 IOR/V/23/45, Miles S.B., 1883–4, 33.
30 IOR/V/23/217, BS, 217.
31 IOR/V/23/45, Miles, ibid.
32 IOR/P/387/55, Calcutta to Bombay, 25 June 1833.
33 PRO/FO/84/647, Palmerston to Hamerton, 6 December 1846.
34 ZA/AA3/6, Hamerton to Bombay, 7 March 1848; for the text of the 1845 Treaty, see IOR/V/23/217, BS, 660–2.
35 U.S.Arch/quoted in Nicholls C.S., 1971, 187.
36 For details of the war in Bander Abbas, see al-Fath, 552–3.
37 ZA/AA1/6, Clarendon to Hamerton, 30 December 1854; deed of cession in Aitchison C.U., 1892, vol. 11, 302.
38 IOR/P/381/33, Seton to Bombay, 9 July 1802; Miles in IOR/ibid.; Kelly, ibid.; at that time 2 tomans = £1 = MT$4.7 according to Milburn W., 1813, I, 116, 173–4; US/Arch/NEMA, Mansfield to Marcy, 31 January 1856; Lambton A.K.S., 1970, op. cit. and Pelly L., 1863–4, op. cit.
39 See the first section of Chapter 12.
40 IOR/V/23/45, Miles S.B., 1883–4, 36; Kelly J.B., 1968, 532; Burton R.F., 1872, II, 303.
41 Inscription on Said b Sultan's grave in Zanzibar; al-Fath, 460; Juhaina 158.
42 ZA/AA5/3, Majid b Said to Rigby, 23 Shawwal 1277 = 4 May 1861, and Rigby to Bombay, 1 February 1860.
43 ZA/ibid.; see also Russell C.E.B., 1935, 'General Rigby, Zanzibar and the Slave Trade', chap. 5.
44 ZA/AA5/3, Majid b Said to Rigby, 24 Dhu al-Hijja 1277 = 3 July 1861.
45 The title 'Sultan' was formally applied after the separation of Oman into two 'Sultanates', of 'Muscat and Oman' and of 'Zanzibar', see Chapter 12.
46 ZA/AA5/3, Majid b Said to Rigby, 6 Muharram 1278 = 14 July 1861.
47 ZA/AA5/3, Rigby's handwritten notes on the margin of the above letter.
48 IOR/L/P&S/9/38, Rigby to Forbes, 12 July 1861.
49 IOR/L/P&S/9/38, Majid b Said to Rigby, 17 Muharram 1278 = 25 July 1861.
50 IOR/L/P&S/9/38, Rigby to Forbes, 5 September 1861.

51 ZA/AA12/2, Biographical note on C.P. Rigby, n.d.; Russell C.E.B., 1935, 94.
52 ZA/AA5/3, Rigby to Bombay, 4 September 1860; Russell C.E.B., 1935, 95.
53 US/Arch/NEMA, Jablonski to Thuvenel, 7 September 1861, 518, n. 142.
54 PRO/FO/84/1292, Churchill to Bombay, 14 August 1868.
55 ZA/AA5/6, Decree by Majid b Said, 28 Dhu al-Qa'ada 1281 = 24 April 1865.
56 IOR/15/6/8, Agreement between Captain Jones and Thuwayni b Said dated 14 Shawwal 1274 = 28 May 1858, in Miles to Ross, 16 January 1875.
57 ZA/AA1/7, Clarendon to Kirk, 20 October 1869; PRO/FOCP/2314, Proclamation of the Rao of Kutch, 24 April 1869.
58 ZA/AA5/7, Kirk to Majid b Said, 28 December 1869.
59 IOR/L/P&S/3/84, Rao Pragmalgi Bahadur to Kutchis in Muscat and Zanzibar, 15 December 1872.
60 US/Arch/NEMA, Ward to Clayton, 20 July 1850, 464.
61 PRO/FO/54/22, Playfair to Bombay, 18 November 1865.
62 IOR/L/P&S/9/37 and PRO/FO/54/17, Rigby to Wood, 1 May 1860.
63 IOR and PRO/ibid., Rigby C., 1863–4, 'Extracts from the Administration Report of the Political Agent in Zanzibar', in TBGS, vol. 17.
64 ZA/AA12/2 and IOR/L/P&S/9/38, Rigby to Bombay and Rigby to Forbes, 12 July 1861.
65 PRO/FO/84/1391, 'Memorandum regarding Banians or natives of India in East Africa', in Frere to Granville, 7 May 1873.
66 ZA/AA1/57, O'Neill to Salisbury, 31 October 1888 quoting the *Manchester Guardian* of 25 February 1888.
67 Kimberley to Hardinge, 27 November 1894, in Hardinge A., 1928, 'A Diplomatist in the East', 351.
68 Salisbury quoted in Uzoigwe G.N., 1974, 'Britain and the Conquest of Africa – the Age of Salisbury', 156–7.
69 ZA/AA1/76, Euan Smith to Michahelles, 20 September 1890.
70 PRO/FO/84/1744, Holmwood to Salisbury, 25 July 1886; Bennett N.R., 1978, 42; Mangat J.S., 1969, 18.
71 ZA/AA5/16, Portal to Khalifa b Said, 26 June 1889; Juhaina, 227; al-Murjibi-Bontinck, 207; Mangat J.S., 1969, 18; Bennett N.R., 1978, 106; in 1889 Hansuraj Moorarjee was the commercial agent of the Shivji Topan House in Zanzibar.
72 IOR/15/6/16, Miles to Ross, 5 February 1884.
73 See the first section of Chapter 5.
74 For Topan Tajiani's business obtained through the Shivji Topan House, see US/Arch/NEMA, Emerton's Jnl, 19 July 1848, 410 and McMullan to Shepherd, 28 January 1851, 475.
75 Bennett N.R., 1978, 79.
76 PRO/FO/84/1344, Zanzibar's Admin. Rep., 18 July 1870.
77 See above, Figure 2 and Table 3.
78 Bennett N.R., 1978, 107.
79 IOR/15/6/475, Persian Gulf Admin. Rep., 1875–6; IOR/15/6/16, Miles to Ross, 5 February 1884; Landen R.G., 1967, 391.
80 ZA/AA5/3, Rigby to Bombay, 18 September 1860.
81 IOR/L/P&S/5/501, Rigby to Anderson, 4 April 1859.
82 See below, Chapter 12.

83 ZA/AA12/2, Sulayman b Hamad to Rigby, 23 October 1859; ZA/AA3/18, Rigby to Anderson, 18 September 1860; IOR/ibid.; IOR/L/P&S/9/38, Rigby to Forbes, 5 September 1861; see also Bennett N.R., 1978, 80; Sheriff A.M.H., 1987, 109; Mangat J.S., 1969, 17; on Said b Sultan's will see Chapter 12. and Appendix 3.

84 PRO/FO/84/1357, Kirk to Bombay, 10 April 1872.

85 For these later connections between Banyans and the Zanzibar Sultans, see ZA/AA5/14, Ratansi Purshotam to Hamud b Mohammad, 17 Sha'aban 1315 = 11 January 1898 and other correspondence in the same series; for Muscat, see above, Chapter 6.

86 PRO/FO/54/4, Hamerton to Bombay, 28 September 1841.

87 IOR/15/6/38, Dhavji Jivandas, Virji Ratansi and others to Wilson, 4 November 1895; emphasis is mine.

12 POST-1856 SUCCESSION DISPUTE AND BRITISH INTERVENTION

1 al-Farsi, 1942, 15; Guillain-Documents, II, 224; Hilal's dispute with his father had originated when he had been disinherited by Said for drinking alcohol and not for having violated his father's harim as is often alleged, see also Bhacker, M.R., 1991, 'Family strife ...'; Said-Ruete E., 1886, 139–40; Guillain-Documents, II, 224–8; al-Farsi, 1942, 15–6; cf. Nicholls C.S,, 1971, 274; Kelly J.B., 1968, 534.

2 al-Farsi, ibid.; Guillain-Documents, II, 228.

3 PRO/FO/54/6 and IOR/L/P&S/5/501, Said b Sultan to Aberdeen, 6 Rajab 1260 = 23 July 1844; for the full text of the letter see Appendix 2.

4 al-Farsi, 1942, 17; Germain A., 1868b, op. cit.

5 ZA/AA12/2, Rigby to Bombay, 17 February 1859; ZA/AA3/11, Hamerton to Bombay, 15 November 1854; IOR/L/P&S/5/501, Rigby to Anderson, 4 April 1859; PRO/FO/54/16, Hamerton to FO, 26 June 1854; Said-Ruete E., 1886, 108.

6 al-Farsi, 1942, 16; Guillain-Documents, II, 229.

7 al-Farsi, ibid.; PRO/FO/54/16, Hamerton to FO, 26 June 1854.

8 al-Farsi, 17; PRO/ibid.; ZA/AA3/11, Hamerton to Bombay, 18 April 1854; Pullicino P., 1954, table 7.

9 Said-Ruete E., 1886, 108.

10 Three of the most prominent examples are Coupland R., 1939, Part 1; Kelly J.B., 1968, chap. 12; Sheriff A.M.H., 1987, chap. 6.

11 For Hilal's visit to London see PRO/FO/54/7–10.

12 ZA/AA3/18 and IOR/L/P&S/507, Coghlan to Anderson, 4 December 1860; the full name given to the Commission was: 'Commission appointed by Government to Investigate and Report on the Disputes between the Rulers of Muscat and Zanzibar'.

13 IOR/L/P&S/5/501, Hilal b Muhammad quoted in Rigby to Anderson, 4 April 1859.

14 On the Barawina, see above, Chapter 6.

15 ZA/AA3/18 and IOR/L/P&S/507, Coghlan to Anderson, 4 December 1860.

16 ZA/AA12/2, Hamerton to Clarendon, 10 November 1856; IOR/L/P&S/ 5/501, Rigby to Anderson, 4 April 1859.

17 ZA/AA3/11, Hamerton to Bombay, 15 November 1854.
18 Juhaina, 199.
19 ibid.; according to al-Mughairi, Barghash was undoubtedly on board but Abdallah b Salim's presence can only be inferred from the fact that he was a constant companion of Said b Sultan, was in Muscat with Barghash prior to Said's death and in Zanzibar after his death.
20 Said-Ruete E., 1886, 40; al-Farsi, 1942, 17; ZA/AA12/2, Barghash b Said to Elphinstone, 31 March 1860.
21 al-Farsi, 1942, 85; Said-Ruete E., 1886, 108.
22 ZA/AA12/2, Hamerton to Clarendon, 10 November 1856; Said-Ruete E., ibid.
23 ZA/ibid.
24 ibid.
25 ZA/AA12/2, Rigby to Bombay, 17 February 1859; al-Farsi, 1942, 37 and 85.
26 al-Farsi, 1942, 17.
27 ZA/AA12/2, Hamerton to Clarendon, 10 November 1856.
28 Barghash b Said quoted in al-Farsi, 1942, 85.
29 ZA/AA12/2, Majid b Said to Coghlan, 14 October 1860; IOR/L/P&S/5/501, Rigby to Anderson, 4 April 1859.
30 ZA/AA12/2, Rigby to Bombay, 14 April 1859.
31 For Majid's debts and finances see above, Chapter 11.
32 ZA/AA12/2, Majid b Said to Jairam Shivji House, Bombay, n.d. but sometime after April 1857.
33 IOR/L/P&S/9/38, Rigby to Forbes, 5 September 1861.
34 ZA/AA12/2, Rigby to Bombay, 14 January 1859.
35 For examples of these agreements, see Juhaina, 200.
36 The Mutiny broke out at Meerut on 10 May 1857 and continued until the end of June 1858, see Spear P., 1965, chap. 11.
37 IOR/L/P&S/9/38, Rigby to Russell, 1 July 1861.
38 ZA/AA12/2, Rigby to Bombay, 17 February 1859; Juhaina, 200.
39 ZA/AA12/2, Rigby to Bombay, 1 August 1858.
40 ZA/AA2/2, Jones to Jenkins, 25 February 1859.
41 Juhaina, 200–1.
42 ZA/AA12/2, Rigby to Bombay, 22 March 1859.
43 ZA/AA12/2, Rigby to Bombay, 4 April 1859; IOR/L/P&S/5/446, Rigby to Anderson, 4 April 1859.
44 ZA/ibid.
45 ZA/AA12/2, Barghash b Said to Elphinstone, 31 March 1860 and Bombay to Rigby, 29 September 1859.
46 ZA/AA2/2, Jones to Jenkins, 25 February 1859.
47 ZA/AA2/2, 'H.H.Syed Soweynee, Imam of Muscat [sic] to Captain Felix Jones', 24 Safar 1276 = 22 September 1859.
48 ZA/AA2/2, PRPG to Bombay, 11 April 1859.
49 ZA/AA12/2, Rigby to Bombay, 4 April 1859.
50 ibid.; Juhaina, 197.
51 Juhaina, 201; IOR/L/P&S/5/501, Rigby to Anderson, 19 April 1859.
52 ZA/ibid.
53 ZA/AA12/2, Majid b Said to Coghlan, 14 October 1860.
54 Juhaina, 201; IOR/ibid.

55 IOR/L/P&S/5/501, Thuwayni b Said to Sulayman b Hamad quoted in Rigby to Anderson, 25 April 1859.
56 IOR/L/P&S/5/501, Rigby to Anderson, 25 April 1859.
57 IOR/ibid.; ZA/AA12/2, Majid b Said to Coghlan, 14 October 1860.
58 Juhaina, 203; IOR/L/P&S/5/501, Rigby to Anderson, 14 April 1859; IOR/ 15/6/233, 'Biographical Sketches of Saleh bin Ali and his son Isa bin Saleh', – [hereafter Hirth-Sketch] –, n.d. but compiled in 1930; IOR/ 15/1/186, 'Biographical Histories of Noteworthy Persons' by Surgeon Major Jayakar – [hereafter Jayakar Biography of...] –, in Ross to PAM, 29 September 1882.
59 ZA/AA12/2, Barghash b Said to Elphinstone, 31 March 1860; Juhaina, 205; al-Farsi, 1942, 50.
60 ZA/ibid.; ZA/AA12/2, Rigby to FO, 26 July 1859; ZA/AA12/2, Rigby to Coghlan, 5 October 1860; al-Farsi, 50; Juhaina 200–5. The Masakira were under Sayf b Sulayman al-Maskari who, according to al-Farsi, was the leader of the Ghafiris in Zanzibar; for the names of other leaders involved, see Bhacker M.R., 1988, 338.
61 Pouwels R., 1987, 152 and 180.
62 For a first-hand inside account of these divisions, see Said-Ruete E., 1886, chap. 26.
63 IOR/L/P&S/5/501, Rigby to Bombay, 9 April 1859.
64 ZA/AA12/2, Rigby to Bombay, 26 July 1859 and 21 October 1859.
65 Juhaina, 204.
66 ZA/AA12/2, Rigby to Bombay, 12 September 1859; Juhaina, 202.
67 ZA/ibid.
68 Said-Ruete E., 1886, 239.
69 IOR/15/1/186, Jayakar Biography of Salih b Ali al-Harthi, 1882; IOR/ 15/6/233, Hirth-Sketch, 1930; ZA/AA12/2, Rigby to Bombay, 9 October 1859.
70 ZA/ibid.; ZA/AA5/9, al-Hajj Sharif b Dewji Jamal to Ali b Hamud, 30 Shaban 1316 = 3 January 1899; Said-Ruete E., 1886, 137; al-Farsi, 1942, 49; and interviews at Zanzibar, 1986; 'Marseilles' was the name given to the plantation formerly known as 'Machui' by Khalid b Said for his 'predilection for France and for everything French'; the *shamba* now forms part of an experimental farm known as Kizimbani, see Map 3.
71 Said-Ruete E., 1886, 238–43
72 ZA/AA12/2, Rigby to Bombay, 9 October 1859.
73 ZA/AA12/2, Rigby to Bombay, 21 October 1859.
74 ZA/AA12/2, Rigby to Bombay, 29 October 1859.
75 ZA/ibid.; Juhaina 198–9.
76 ZA/ibid.; IOR/L/P&S/5/501, Rigby to Anderson, 4 April 1859.
77 IOR/L/P&S/5/507, Barghash b Said quoted in Coghlan to Bombay, 4 December 1860.
78 IOR/L/P&S/9/38, Rigby to Forbes, 29 June 1861.
79 US/Arch/NEMA, Jablonski to Thuvenel, 7 September 1861, 518, n. 142.
80 IOR/L/P&S/5/507, Coghlan to Bombay, 4 December 1860.
81 ibid., the emphasis is in the original; ZA/AA2/2, PRPG to Thuwayni, 28 October 1859.
82 ibid.

83 Juhaina, 204.
84 IOR/L/P&S/5/447, Cruttenden to Anderson, 24 September 1859; ZA/AA2/2, Thuwayni b Said to Jones, 24 Safar 1276 = 22 September 1859.
85 For the text of the Canning Award see IOR/L/P&S/5/507.
86 ZA/AA2/4 and IOR/L/P&S/5/507, Thuwayni b Said to Lord Canning, 15 May 1861 and Majid b Said to Rigby, 29 June 1861.
87 See, for example, Sheriff A.M.H., 1987, 216–17.
88 Kieran A.J., 1968, 'The Origins of the Zanzibar Guarantee of 1862', in *Canadian Journal of African Studies*, vol. 2, 147–66.
89 IOR/L/P&S/5/507, Napoleon III to Majid b Said, 4 June 1859.
90 ZA/AA5/3, Majid b Said to Rigby, 13 Jumada al-Akhir 1277 = 27 December 1860; IOR/L/P&S/9/38, Rigby to Russell, 1 July 1861.
91 Kieran A.J., 1968, op. cit.
92 IOR/L/P&S/9/38, Rigby to Russell, 1 July 1861.
93 Text is in Aitchison C.U., 1892, vol. 11, 304–5.

Bibliography

OMANI, IBADI, AND PRIMARY ARABIC AND SWAHILI SOURCES

al-'Ânî, 'Abd-al-Raḥmân, 'Dawr al-'Umâniyîn fî al-milâḥat wa al-tijârat al-Islamîya ḥatta al-qarn al-râb'i al-hijrî', MNHC, Muscat, 1981.

Anon. Ms, 'Anonymous titleless history of Oman', BL Add Ms. 23,343, probably a continuation of al-Ma'walî's 'Qisas' (q.v.).

Anon., 'Lam' al-Shihâb fî sîrat Muhammad b 'Abd-al-Wahhâb', probably written by al-Rîkî, Ḥasan b Jamâl, 1233/1817.

al-Buhry, Hemedi bin Abdallah, 'Utenzi wa Vita vya Wadachi Kutamalaki Mrima', 1307/1889–90, tr. Allen J.W.T., EALB, 1971.

Fadl Al-lâh, Rashîd al-Dîn, 'Jâmi' al-Tawârîkh', 1960 edn, Tehran.

al-Fârsî,'Abd-allâh b Ṣâliḥ, 'Âlbûsa'îdîyûn, ḥukkâm Zanjbâr', MNHC, Muscat, 1982; English translation of the original Kiswahili, published as 'Seyyid Said bin Sultan, the Joint Ruler of Oman and Zanzibar', Lancers Books, New Delhi, 1986.

al-Ḥârthî, Sâlim b Ḥamad b Sulaymân, 'al-'Uqûd al-fiddîya fî `Uṣûl al-Ibâḍiyâ', Beirut, n.d., MNHC, Muscat, 1983.

Hâshim, Mahdî Ṭâlib, 'al-Ḥarakat al-Ibâḍîya fî al-Mashriq al-'Arabî', Baghdad, 1981.

al-Hinâ`î,Mubârak b 'Alî'al-'Umâniyûn wa Qal'at Mumbâsa', MNHC, Muscat, 1980.

Ibn Bishr, 'Uthmân b 'Abd-allâh, ''Unwân al-Majd fî ta`rîkh Najd', 2 vols, Cairo and Beirut 2 vols in one but both n.d.

Ibn Qaysar, 'Abd-allâh b Khalfân, 'Sîrat al-Imâm Nâṣir bin Murshid', BL MS Add. 23,343, part 2, printed MNHC, Muscat, 1983.

Ibn Ruzaiq, Ḥumayd b Muhammad b Ruzaiq b Bakhît al-Nakhlî,
    a) 'al-Fatḥ al-Mubîn fî sîrat al-Sâdat al-Âlbûsa'îdîyûn', Ms Cambridge Uni. Lib. Add. 2892, printed MNHC, Muscat, 1977, Eng. tr., Badger G.P., 1871.
    b) 'al-Saḥîfat al-Qaḥtânîya', Rhodes House, Oxford Uni., Ms Afr. S.3, dated 1269/1852.
    c) 'al-Saḥîfat al-'Adnânîya', BL Or. 6569, Ms dated 1258/1842.
    d) 'al-Qaṣîdat al-Qudsîya al-Nûrânîya fî Manâqib al-'Adnânîya', BM Or. 6565 (vol. 2 only).

248   *Bibliography*

e) 'al-Shu'â` al-Shâ`'i bi al-Lam'ân fî dhikr A`immat 'Umân', copy based on Ms in Cambridge Uni. Lib., printed MNHC, Muscat, 1978.

f) 'Dîwân Sabâ`ik al-Lujain', BL Or. 6563, dated 1243/1827.

al-Idrîsî, al-Sharîf, 'Nuzhat al-Mushtâq', extracts in Elliot H.M. and Dowson J., [eds], 1867–77 (q.v.).

Ismâ'îl Kâshif, Sayyida, 'Umân fî fajr al-Islâm', MNHC, Muscat, 1979.

al-Istakhrî, Abû Ishâq, 'Kitâb al-Masâlik wa al-Mamâlik', 1927 edn, Brill, Leiden.

'Kashf al-Ghumma al-jâmi' li akhbâr al-`umma', attributed to its copier, Sirhân b Sa'îd al-Izkawî, BM Ms Or. 8076, selections printed by MNHC, Muscat, 1980 (see also Ross E.C., 1874 and Klein H., 1938).

Khalîfât, ' Awad Muhammad,

a) 'Nash `at al-Harakat al-Ibâdîya', Amman, 1978.

b) 'al-'Usûl al-târîkhîya li al-firqat al-Ibâdîya', MNHC, Muscat, 1982.

'Kitâb al-Salwa fî akhbâr Kilwa', BL Ms Or. 2666, printed MNHC, 1985, (see also Strong S.A., 1895).

'Kitâb al-Zunûj', text and Italian translation in Cerulli E., 1957, in 'Somalia, Scritti vari editi ed inediti', vol. 1, 233–92.

al-Lamuy, Shaikhu Faraji bin Hamed al-Bakari, 1938, 'Khabari Lamu', in *Bantu Studies*, vol. 12, 3–33.

al-Marhûbî, 'Âmir b 'Umayr, 'al-Hadârat al-'Umânîya al-Qadîma', MNHC, Muscat, 1986.

al-Mas'ûdî,'Alî b al-Husain (Abû al-Hasan), 'Murûj al-dhahab wa Ma'âdin al-Jawhar', Beirut, 1368/1948.

al-Ma'walî, Muhammad b Âmir b Râshid (Abû Sulaymân), 'Qisas wa akhbâr jarat bi 'Umân', printed MNHC, Muscat, 1979; another version published under the title of 'Târîkh ahl 'Umân' but unattributed, MNHC, Muscat, 1980.

al-Mazrû'î, al-Amîn b 'Alî, 'Tâ`rîkh wilâyat al-Mazâri'a fî Ifrîqya al-Sharqîya', Ms in MNHC, mimeographed copy of English translation by Ritchie J.M., entitled 'The History of the Mazrui Dynasty of Mombasa', in Fort Jesus, Mombasa.

'Mombasa Chronicle', in Guillain-Documents, I, 614–22; Owen W.F., 1833, I, 414–22 and Freeman-Grenville G.S.P., 1962a, 213–19.

al-Mughairî, Sa'îd b 'Alî,'Juhainat al-akhbâr fî ta`rîkh Zanjbâr', printed MNHC, Muscat, 1979.

al-Murjibî, Hamad b Muhammad (Tippu Tip), 'Maisha ya Hamed bin Muhammed al-Murjebi yaani Tippu Tip', Swahili text in Whiteley W.H., 1958/9, (see also Brode H., 1907 and Bontinck F., 1974).

al-Nu'mân, al-Qâdî Abû Hanîfa, 'Risâlat Iftitâh al-Da'wa', 1970 edn, Beirut.

Omari bin Stamboul, 'An Early History of Mombasa and Tanga', tr., Baker E.C., 1951, in TNR, vol. 31. 32–6.

'Pate Chronicle', several versions (see Stigand C.H., 1913; Werner A., 1914–16; Freeman-Grenville G.S.P., 1962a).

Saadi, Kadhi Amur Omar, 1941, 'Mafia – History and Traditions', in TNR, vol. 12, 23–7.

al-Sâlimî, 'Abd-allâh b Humayd,

a) 'Tuhfat al-a'yân bi sîrat ahl 'Umân', 2 vols [ed. Ibrâhîm b Atfayyish (Abû Ishâq)], Cairo, 1380/1961

b) 'al-Lam'at al-mardîya min 'ashi'at al-Ibâdîya', MNHC, Muscat, 1981.

al-Sâlimî, Muhammad b 'Abd-allâh,

a) 'Nahdat al-a'yân bi ḥurriyat 'Umân', Cairo, n.d.
b) Nâjî 'Assâf, "Umân, tâ`rîkh yatakallam', Damascus, 1963.
al-Siyâbî,Sâlim b Ḥamûd,
   a) 1965, 'Is'âf al-a'yân fî ansâb ahl 'Umân', Beirut.
b) 1966, 'al-'Unwân 'an tâ`rîkh 'Umân', Beirut.
c) 1979, 'Aṣdaq al-manâhij fî tamyîz al-Ibâdîya min al-khawârij', (Cairo Uni. edn by Sayyida Ismâ'îl Kâshif), MNHC, Muscat.
d) 1980, 'al-Haqîqat wa al-Mujâz fî ta rîkh al-Ibâdîya bi al-Yaman wa al-Hijâz', MNHC, Muscat.
e) 1982, "Umân 'abr al-tâ`rîkh', 4 vols, MNHC, Muscat.
al-Ṭabarî, 'Tâ`rîkh al-Ṭabarî', 1879 edn, Brill, Leiden.
al-Tâzî, "Abd-al-Hâdî, al-Ṣilât 'al-tâ`rîkhîya bayna al-Maghrib wa 'Umân', MNHC, Muscat, 1981.
al-'Uqailî, Muḥammad Rashîd, 'al-Ibâdîya fî 'Umân wa 'alâqâtuhâ ma'a al-dawlat al-'Abbâsiya fî 'aṣrihâ al-awwal', MNHC, Muscat, 1984.
Wizârat al-Dâkhilîya (Ministry of the Interior, Oman), 'al-Murshid al-'Âmm li al-wilâyât wa al-Qabâ`il fî salṭanat 'Umân', 1982.
Zâhir b Sa'îd, 'Tanzîh al-absâr wa al-afkâr fî riḥlat sulṭân Zanjbâr', MNHC, Muscat, 1981.

ARCHIVAL SOURCES

India Office Library and Records, London

Muscat Records [begin 1800]

R/15/6, Political Agency, Muscat and, from 1841, also Political Agency, Zanzibar.

Residency Records [begin 1763]

R/15/1, Political Residency at Bushire.

Bombay Records [begin 1702]

P/series, Proceedings of the Government of India and of the Presidencies and Provinces. The most relevant are Bombay Public Proceedings, Bombay Political and Secret Proceedings, Bombay Commercial Reports and Bombay Commercial Proceedings.

Board of Control Records [begin 1784]

F/4, Board's Collections, 1796–1858.

250   *Bibliography*

Factory Records [begin 1608]

G/29, Persia and the Persian Gulf, 1790–1800.

Home Miscellaneous Records [begin c.1600]

H/478, 1801.

Political and Secret Department Records [begin 1756]

L/P&S/3, Home Correspondence, vols 83–7, for correspondence on Frere's Mission, 1873.

L/P&S/5, vols 259–77, Secret Letters and Enclosures from India, 1866–74.
L/P&S/5, vols 321–58, Secret Letters from Bombay, 1798–1873.
L/P&S/5, vols 363–509, Enclosures to Secret Letters from Bombay, 1802–69.

L/P&S/9, Secret Letters from Aden, Zanzibar and Muscat, vols 37–51, 1859–83.

L/P&S/C, Précis of correspondence and compilations by Saldanha J.A., numerous volumes.

Marine Department Records [begin 1600]

L/MAR/A/14, on the earliest British contacts with the East African coast.

L/MAR/C, Miscellaneous Records, vol. 586, contains journals and papers on Smee's and Hardy's visit to East Africa, 1811.

Official Publications [begin c.1800]

V/23, includes selections from the Records, Parliamentary Papers and Annual Reports.

Public Record Office, London

Muscat

FO/54, vols 1–36, 1834–1905, contain correspondence also on Zanzibar, particularly vols 1–24 for the period up to the 1870s.

Slave Trade

FO/84, vols 425–2059, 1842–90.

Confidential Prints

FOCP, vols 401, 403, 2314, 6805, 6827, 6849, 6861 and 6913, 1819–95/6.

Admirality Records

Adm/52/3940, Journal of Lt. J.B. Emery, 1824–6.

Zanzibar Archives

British Consular Records

AA1, Foreign Office, General Correspondence, vols 1–77, 1846–90.

AA2, General Series, vols 1–58, 1853–90.

AA3, General Correspondence, Government of Bombay, vols 1–45, 1840–90.

AA4, General Correspondence, Government of India, vols 1–20, 1874–87.

AA5, Correspondence of the Albusaidi Rulers, vols 1–20, 1841–90.

AA12, Miscellanea, contains duplicates of despatches, slave trade reports and agreements from Gvt of Bombay, in English, Arabic and occasionally in Gujerati, vols 1–15, 1843–90.

Zanzibar Government Records

AC series, Zanzibar Protectorate Records, 1890–1913.

AC3, General Correspondence, Zanzibar Government, vols 1–24, contains correspondence of the Sultans, 1890–1911.

AC10, General Correspondence, Imperial British East Africa Company, vols 1–11, 1888–93.

AV and AW series, Photographs, Maps and Plans, contains photographs of the ruling family, officials, buildings, ceremonies, plans and maps, 1804–1964.

German Consular Records

AL series, divided into various sections, 1869–1914.

Miscellaneous Records

AD5/17, 'Publication of History by Sir Said bin Ali al-Mughairi, ...entitled Juhainat al-Akhbar', 1946–62; publication history but no copy of the book itself.

BA66/43, Shelswell-White G.H., 1935, 'Notes on the Hadrami and Shihri community in Zanzibar'.

BA98/2, 'Treaties etc. with Muscat and Zanzibar', compiled in 1900.

BZ1/1, Copies of Documents from the USA, 1847–51.

BZ2/1, contains photocopy of Morice, 1777 (q.v.).

CA4/1, Sir John Gray Papers, mainly duplicates from the London

FO/54/8 series.

CA4/1/3, Correspondence of Said b Sultan, 1843–56.

HC7, HBM Civil Court Cases.

United States Archives

Despatches from US Consuls in Zanzibar, Microcopy 468, Rolls 1–5, 1836–1906.

Despatches from US Consuls in Muscat, Microcopy T-638, Rolls 1–2, 1880–1906.

For published archival material see Bennett N.R. and Brooks G.E., [eds], 1965; and Porter J.D., 1982.

OTHER PRIMARY AND SECONDARY SOURCES

Abdulaziz M.H., 1979, 'Muyaka, 19th Century Swahili Popular Poetry', London.
Abdul Qadir K., 1968, 'Waqâ`i'-i manâzil-i Rûm: A Diary of a Journey to Constantinople', ed. Hasan M., Aligarh Muslim Uni.
Abu Hakima A.M., 1965, 'History of Eastern Arabia, 1750–1800', Beirut, Khayats.
Abu Hakima A.M., 1970, 'Ta`rîkh al-Kuwayt', 2 vols, Kuwait.
Aitchison C.U., 1892, 'A Collection of Treaties, Engagements and Sanads Relating to India and Neighbouring Countries', vol. 11, Calcutta.
Aitken E.H., 1907, [ed.], 'Gazetteer of the Province of Sind', Karachi.
al-'Ajlânî, Munîr, n.d., 'Tâ`rîkh al-Bilâd al-'Arabîya al-Sa'ûdîya: al-Dawlat al-Sa'ûdîya al-`Ûlâ', Beirut.
Akinola G.A., 1972, 'Slavery and slave revolts in the Sultanate of Zanzibar in the nineteenth century', *Journal of the Historical Society of Nigeria*, vol. 6, 215–28.
Albaharna H.M., 1968, 'The Legal Status of the Arabian Gulf States', Manchester Uni. Pr.
Albrand F., 1838, 'Extrait d'une memoire sur Zanzibar et sur Quiloa', *Bulletin de la Société de Géographie*, vol. 10, 65–84.
Algar H., 1969, 'The Revolt of Agha Khan Mahallati and the Transference of the Ismaili Imamate to India', *Studia Islamica*, vol. 29, 55–81.

Allen C.H., 1978, 'Sayyids, Shets and Sultans: Politics and Trade in Masqat under the Al Bu Said, 1785–1914', Ph.D. Dissn., Uni. of Washington, DC.
——1981, 'The Indian Merchant Community of Masqat', BSOAS, vol. 44, 39–53.
——1982, 'The State of Masqat in the Gulf and East Africa', IJMES, vol. 14, 117–27.
Allen J. de V., 1974, 'Swahili Culture Reconsidered: Some Historical Implications of the Material Culture of the Northern Kenya Coast in the Eighteenth and Nineteenth Centuries', *Azania*, vol. 9, 105–38.
——1981, 'Swahili Culture and the Nature of East Coast Settlement', IJAHS, vol. 14, 306–35.
——1982, 'The 'Shirazi' Problem in East African Coastal History', in Allen J. de V. and Wilson T.H., [eds], 1982, 'From Zinj to Zanzibar, In Honour of James Kirkman', *Paideuma*, vol. 28, 9–29, Wiesbaden.
——1985, 'Habash, Habshi, Sidi, Sayyid', in Stone J.C., [ed.], 1985, 'Africa and the Sea', *Proceedings of a Colloquium at the University of Aberdeen*, Aberdeen Uni. African Studies Group, 131–52.
——n.d., 'Lamu', Nairobi, Kenya National Museum.
——n.d., 'Lamu Town, A Guide', Nairobi, Kenya National Museum.
——and Wilson T.H., [eds], 1982, 'From Zinj to Zanzibar, In Honour of James Kirkman', *Paideuma*, vol. 28, Wiesbaden.
Alpers E.A., 1967, 'The East African Slave Trade', Historical Association of Tanzania, Paper no. 3, Nairobi.
——1969, 'The Coast and the Development of the Caravan Trade', in Kimambo I.N. and Temu A.J., [eds], 1969, 'A History of Tanzania', Nairobi EAPH, 35–56.
——1970, 'The French slave trade in East Africa (1721–1810)', *Cahiers d'Etudes Africaines*, vol. 10, 80–127.
——1975, 'Ivory and Slaves in East Central Africa', Nairobi, Heinemann.
——1976, 'Gujarat and the trade of East Africa, c.1500–1800', IJAHS, vol. 9, 22–44.
——1983, 'Muqdisho in the nineteenth century: a regional perspective', JAH, vol. 24, 441–59.
Amiji H.M., 1971, 'Some notes on religious dissent in nineteenth-century East Africa', AHS, vol. 4, 603–16.
Amin A.A., 1967, 'British Interests in the Persian Gulf', Leiden, Brill.
Anderson J.N., 1964, 'The Ismaili Khojas of East Africa', in MES, vol. 1, 21–39.
Anderson-Moreshead, A.E., 1897, 'The History of the Universities Mission to Central Africa', London.
Anstey V., 1952, 'The Economic Development of India', London.
al-'Aqqâd, Salâh, 1974, 'al-Tayyârât al-Siyâsîya fî al-Khalîj al-'Arabî', Cairo.
Arens W., [ed.], 1976, 'A Century of Change in East Africa', London.
Aubin J., 1971, 'Cojeatar et Albuquerque', *Mare Luso Indicum*, vol. 1, 99–134.
——1972, 'Le Royaume d'Ormuz au dedut de XVIe siecle', *Mare Luso Indicum*, vol. 2, 77–179.
Badger G.P., [ed. and tr.], 1871, 'History of the Imams and Seyyids of Oman', translation of Ibn Ruzaiq's 'al-Fath al-Mubîn...' (q.v.), London, Hakluyt.
Barth F., 1983, 'Sohar: Culture and Society in an Omani Town', Johns Hopkins Uni. Pr.

——1987, 'Complications of Geography, Ethnology and Tribalism', in Pridham B.R., [ed.], 1987, 'Oman: Economic, Social and Strategic Developments', London, Croom Helm, 17–31.

Bathurst R.D., 1967, 'The Ya'rubi Dynasty of Oman', D. Phil. th., Uni. of Oxford.

——1972, 'Maritime Trade and Imamate Government: Two Principal Themes in the History of Oman to 1728', in Hopwood D., [ed.], 1972, 'The Arabian Peninsula, Society and Politics', London, Allen & Unwin, 98–106.

Battacharya D.K., 1973, 'Indians of African Origin', *Cahiers d'Etudes Africaines*, vol. 40, 579–82.

Baxter H.C., 1944, 'Pangani: the trade centre of Ancient History', TNR, no. 17, 15–25.

Beachey R.W., 1967, 'The East African ivory trade in the nineteenth century', JAH, vol. 8, 269–90.

——1976a, 'The Slave Trade of Eastern Africa', London, Collings.

——1976b, 'A Collection of Documents on the Slave Trade of Eastern Africa', London, Collings.

Becker C.H., 1911, tr. Martin B.G., 1968, 'Materials for the understanding of Islam in German East Africa', TNR, no. 68, 31–61.

Beckingham C.F., 'Bahr Faris', in EI2.

——1941, 'The reign of Ahmad b Said, Imam of Oman', JRAS, vol. 18, 257–60.

——1983, 'Some Notes on the Portuguese in Oman', JOS, vol. 6, 13–19.

Belgrave C., 1966, 'The Pirate Coast', London.

Bennett N.R., 1959, 'Americans in Zanzibar, 1825–45', in both EIHC, vol. 95, 239–62 and TNR, vol 56 (March 1961), 93–108.

——1961, 'Americans in Zanzibar, 1845–1865', in both EIHC, vol. 97, 31–56 and TNR, vol. 57 (July 1961), 121–38.

——1963, 'Studies in East African History', Boston Uni. Pr.

——[ed.], 1968, 'Leadership in Eastern Africa: Six Political Biographies', Boston, African Studies Center.

——1971, 'Mirambo of Tanzania, ca. 1840–1884', New York, Oxford Uni. Pr.

——1973, 'The Arab Impact', in Ogot B., [ed.], 1973, 'Zamani: A Survey of East African History', Nairobi, EAPH, 210–28.

——1975, 'Africa and Europe, from Roman Times to National Independence', New York, Africana Publishing Co.

——1978, 'A History of the Arab State of Zanzibar', London, Methuen.

——1986, 'Arab versus European, Diplomacy and War in nineteenth century East Central Africa', New York, Africana Publishing Co.

——and Brooks G.E., [eds], 1965, 'New England Merchants in Africa', Boston Uni. Pr.

Berg F.J., 1968, 'The Swahili community of Mombasa, 1500–1900', JAH, vol. 9, 35–56.

——1971, 'Mombasa under the Busaidi Sultanate: the city and its hinterland in the nineteenth century', Ph.D. Dissn., Uni of Wisconsin.

——1973, 'The coast from the Portuguese invasion', in Ogot B., [ed.], 'Zamani: A Survey of East Africa History', Nairobi, EAPH, 115–34.

Bhacker M.R., 1981, 'British Role in the Conflict between the Imamate and the Sultanate of Oman: The Treaty of Seeb, 1920', MA th., SOAS, Uni. of London.

——1988, 'Roots of domination and dependency: British reaction towards the development of Omani commerce at Muscat and Zanzibar in the nineteenth century', D.Phil th., Uni. of Oxford.

——1991, 'Family strife and foreign intervention: causes in the separation of Zanzibar from Oman: a reappraisal', BSOAS, vol. 54, 269–80.

Bidwell R., 1978, 'Bibliographical Notes on European Accounts of Muscat, 1500–1900', *Arabian Studies*, vol. 4, 123–60.

Bird J., 1839–40, 'Commercial and Geographical View of East Africa', TBGS, vol. 3, 112–22.

Blakeney R., 1841, 'Journey of an Oriental Voyage', London.

Bonnenfant P. [ed.], 1982, 'Le Péninsule Arabique d'aujourd'hui', 2 vols, CNRS, Paris.

Bontinck F., 1974, 'L'Autobiographie de Hamed ben Mohammed el-Murjebi Tippo Tip (ca. 1840–1905)', Kon. Acad. voor Overzeese Wetenschappen, Brussels.

Boteler T., 1835, 'Narrative of a Voyage of Discovery to Africa and Arabia', 2 vols, London, Bentley.

Boxer C.R., 1969, 'The Portuguese Seaborne Empire', London, Hutchison & Co. Ltd.

——1983, 'New light on the relations between the Portuguese and the Omanis, 1613–1633', JOS, vol. 6, 35–9.

——and Azevedo C., 1960, 'Fort Jesus and the Portuguese in Mombasa, 1593–1729', London, Hollis & Carter.

Braudel F., 1973, 'The Mediterranean and the Mediterranean World in the Age of Philip II', tr. Reynolds S., 2 vols, London.

Brode H., 1907, 'Tippoo Tib: The Story of His Career in Central Africa, narrated from his own accounts', tr. Havelock H., London.

——1911, 'British and German East Africa', London, Arnold.

Brown B., 1971, 'Muslim influence on trade and politics in the Lake Tanganyika region', AHS, vol. 4, 617–29.

——and Brown W.T., 1976, 'East African Trade Towns: A Shared Growth', in Arens W., [ed.], 1976, 'A Century of Change in East Africa', London.

Brown W.T., 1978, 'Bagamoyo: an historical introduction', in TNR, vol. 71, 69–83.

——1971, 'The Politics of Business: relations between Zanzibar and Bagamoyo in the late nineteenth century', AHS, vol. 4, 631–43.

Brunschvig R., 'Abd', in EI2.

Buckingham J.S., 1830, 'Travels in Assyria, Media, and Persia', 2 vols, London.

Burnes A., 1836, 'On the maritime communications of India, as carried on by the natives, particularly from Kutch at the mouth of the Indus', JRGS, vol. 6, 23–9.

Burton R.F., 1856 'First Footsteps in East Africa or an exploration of Harar', 2 vols, London, Tylston and Edwards.

——1859, 'The Lake Regions of Central Equatorial Africa', JRGS, vol. 29, 1–464.

——1860, 'The Lake Regions of Central Africa', 2 vols, London, Longman.

——1872, 'Zanzibar: City, Island and Coast', 2 vols, London, Tinsley Brothers.

——1873, 'The Lands of Cazembe', London, Murray.

Carnac J.R., 1819, 'Some Account of the Famine of Guzerat in the Years 1812 and 1813', TLSB, vol. 1, 296–304.

Carter J.R., 1982, 'Tribes in Oman', London, Peninsular Publishing.

Cashmore T.H., 1961, 'A note on the chronology of the Wanyika of the Kenya coast', TNR, no. 57, 153–72.

——1968, 'Sheikh Mbaruk bin Salim al-Mazrui', in Bennett N.R., [ed.], 1968, 'Leadership in Eastern Africa: Six Political Biographies', Boston, African Studies Center.

Cassanelli L.V., 1973, 'The Benadir Past: Essays in Southern Somali History', Ph.D. Dissn., Uni. of Wisconsin.

Challaye M.C. De, 1844, 'Mémoire sur l'emigration des Indiens et sur le travail libre dans les colonies de Maurice et de Bourbon', *Revue Coloniale*, vol. 3, 557–609.

Chaudhuri K.N., 1965, 'The English East India Company: The Study of an Early Joint-Stock Company, 1600–1640', London.

——1978, 'The trading world of Asia and the English East India Company, 1660–1760', Cambridge Uni. Pr.

——1985, 'Trade and Civilisation in the Indian Ocean', Cambridge Uni. Pr.

Chittick H.N., 1959, 'Notes on Kilwa', TNR, no. 53, 179–203.

——1965, 'The Shirazi Colonization of East Africa', JAH, vol. 6, 275–94.

——1969, 'A new look at the history of Pate', JAH, vol. 10, 375–91.

——1974, 'Kilwa: An Islamic Trading City on the East African Coast', 2 vols, Nairobi.

——1975, 'The Peopling of the East African Coast', in Chittick H.N. and Rotberg R.I., [eds], 1975, 'East Africa and the Orient', New York, Africana Publishing, 16–43.

——1980, 'East Africa and the Orient: Ports and trade before the arrival of the Portuguese', in 'Historical Relations across the Indian Ocean', UNESCO.

——and Rotberg R.I., [eds], 1975, 'East Africa and the Orient', New York, Africana Publishing.

Chopra P.N., 1982, 'Religions and Communities in India', London, East-West Publications.

Christie J., 1876, 'Cholera Epidemics in East Africa', London, Macmillan.

Clerc De, 1864, 'Réceuil des Traités de la France', vol. 1, Paris.

Colomb P.H., 1873, 'Slave Catching in the Indian Ocean', London, Longman.

Cooley W.D., 1845, 'The Geography of N'yassi', JRGS, vol. 15, 185–235.

——1854, 'Notice of a caravan journey from the east to the west coast of Africa', JRGS, vol. 24, 269–70.

Cooper F., 1974, 'Plantation slavery on the east coast of Africa in the nineteenth century', Ph.D. Dissn., Yale Uni.

——1977, 'Plantation Slavery on the East Coast of Africa', Yale Uni. Pr.

——1979, 'The Problem of Slavery in African Studies', JAH, vol. 20, 103–25.

——1981, 'Islam and Cultural Hegemony: The Ideology of Slaveowners on the East African Coast', in Lovejoy P.E., [ed.], 1981, 'The Ideology of Slavery in Africa', London, Sage, 271–309. 271–309.

Corancez L.A., 1810, 'Histoire des Wahabis depuis leur origine jusqu'a la fin de 1809', Paris.

Coupland R., 1938, 'East Africa and Its Invaders', Oxford, Clarendon Pr.

——1939, 'The Exploitation of East Africa, 1856–1928', London, Faber.

Craster J.E., 1913, 'Pemba, The Spice Island of Zanzibar', London, Unwin.

Crofton R.H., 1936, 'A Pageant of the Spice Islands', London, Bale & Danielson.

Cruttenden C.J., 1836–8, 'Journal of an excursion from Morebet to Dyreez, the principal towns of Dofar', TBGS, vol. 1, 184–8.

——1848, 'On Eastern Africa', JRGS, vol. 18. 136–9.

Curzon G.N., 1892, 'Persia and the Persian Question', 2 vols, London.

Dale G., 1920, 'The Peoples of Zanzibar', London.

Danvers F.C., 1984, 'The Portuguese in India', 2 vols, London.

Darwish, Madîha Ahmad, 1982, 'Saltanat 'Umân fî al-qarnayn al-thâmin 'ashar wa al-tâsi' 'ashar', Jeddah, Dar al-Shuruq.

Das Gupta A., 1967a, 'Malabar in Asian Trade, 1740–1800', Cambridge Uni. Pr.

——1967b, 'The Crisis at Surat, 1730–32', *Bengal Past and Present*, special issue, 148–62.

——1970, 'Trade and Politics in 18th century India', in Richards D.S., [ed.], 1970, 'Islam and the Trade of Asia', Oxford, Cassirer, 97–104.

——1979, 'Indian Merchants and the Decline of Surat', Wiesbaden, Steiner.

Datoo B.A., 1970, 'Misconceptions about the use of monsoons by dhows in East African waters', *East African Geographical Review*, vol. 8, 1–10.

——1974, 'Influence of the monsoons on the movement of dhows along the East African coast', *East African Geographical Review*, vol. 12, 23–33.

——1975, 'Port Development in East Africa: Spatial patterns from the ninth to the sixteenth centuries', Nairobi, EALB.

Decary R., 1960, 'L'Ile Nosy Be de Madagascar', Paris.

Devereux W.C., 1869, 'A Cruise in the "Gorgon" ', London, Bell & Daldy.

Digby S., 1971, 'War Horse and Elephant in the Delhi Sultanate: A Study of Military Supplies', Oxford, Orient Monographs.

Dubuisson P.R., 1978, 'Qasimi piracy and the General Treaty of Peace (1820)', *Arabian Studies*, vol. 4, 47–58.

Eastman C., 1971, 'Who are the Waswahili?', *Africa*, vol. 41, 228–35.

Eccles G.J., 1928, 'The Sultanate of Muscat and Oman', *Asiatic Review*, vol. 24, 571–5.

Eickelman D.F., 1985, 'From Theocracy to Monarchy: Authority and Legitimacy in inner Oman, 1935–1957', IJMES, vol. 17, 3–24.

——1987, 'Ibadism and the Sectarian Perspective', in Pridham B.R., [ed.], 1987, 'Oman: Economic, Social and Strategic Developments', London, Croom Helm, 31–50.

Eilts H.F., 1962, 'Ahmed bin Na'man's mission to the United States in 1840. The Voyage of Al-Sultanah to New York', EIHC, vol. 98, 219–77.

——1973, 'Sayyid Muhammad bin 'Aqil of Dhufar: malevolent or maligned?', EIHC, vol. 109, 179–230.

Elliot H.M. and Dowson J., [eds], 1867–77, 'The History of India as Told by its Own Historians', 8 vols, London, reprint, Allahabad, 1972.

Emery J.B., 1833, 'A short account of Mombasa and the neighbouring coast of Africa', JRGS, vol. 3, 280–3.

Ennami A.K., 1971, 'Studies in Ibadism', Ph.D. th., Uni. of Cambridge.

Enthoven R.E., 1920, 'The Tribes and Castes of Bombay', vol. 1, Bombay.

Esmail A.A., 1972, 'Satpanth Ismailis and Modern Changes within it with special reference to East Africa', Ph.D. th., Uni. of Edinburgh.

——and Nanji A., 1977, 'The Ismailis in History', in Nasr S.H., [ed.], 1977, 'Isma'ili Contributions to Islamic Culture', Tehran, Imperial Iranian Academy of Philosophy, 225–60.

Farrant L., 1975, 'Tippu Tip and the East African Slave Trade', London, Hamilton.

Fernandes P., 1969, 'Storm over Seringapatam, The Incredible Story of Hyder Ali and Tippu Sultan', Bombay.

Ferrier R.W., 1970, 'The trade between India and the Persian Gulf and the East India Company in the 17th century', *Bengal Past and Present*, vol. 89, 189–99.

Fitzgerald W.W., 1898, 'Travels in the Coastlands of British East Africa and the Islands of Zanzibar and Pemba', London, Chapman & Hill.

Floor W.M., 1979, 'A description of the Persian Gulf and its inhabitants in 1756', *Persica*, vol. 8, 163–86.

——1982, 'First Contacts between the Netherlands and Masqat or A Report on the Discovery of the Coast of Oman in 1666: Translation and Introduction', *Zeitschrift der Deutschen Morgenlandischen*, vol. 132, 289–307.

——1985, 'A Description of Masqat and Oman Anno 1673 A.D./1084 Q', *Moyen Orient et Océan Indien*, vol. 2, 1–69.

Fontanier V., 1844, 'Voyage dans l'Inde et dans le Golfe Persique', 2 vols, Paris.

Forrest D., 1970, 'Tiger of Mysore. The Life and Death of Tipu Sultan', London, Chatto & Windus.

Foster W., 1906–27, 'The English Factories in India', 13 vols, Oxford.

Fraser H.A., 1860–2, 'Memoranda and Extracts...relative to the Capabilities of the River Juba in East Africa for navigation; and the Resources of the countries adjoining it', TBGS, vol. 16, 78–87.

Fraser J.B., 1825, 'Narrative of a Journey into Khorasan', London.

Freeman-Grenville G.S.P., 1960, 'The Historiography of the East African Coast', TNR, no. 55, 279–89.

——1962a, [ed.], 'The East African Coast: Select Documents', Oxford, Clarendon Pr.

——1962b, 'The Medieval History of the Coast of Tanganyika', Oxford Uni. Pr.

——1965, [translation of Morice, 1777] (q.v.), 'The French at Kilwa Island', Oxford, Clarendon Pr.

——1978, 'Shi'i Rulers at Kilwa', *Numismatic Chronicle*, vol. 8, 187–90.

Froelich J.-C., 1968, 'Les Arabes en Afrique de l'Est', *Revue Française d'Etudes Politiques Africaines*, 26–40.

Fyzee A.A., 1966, 'Cases in the Muhammadan Law of India and Pakistan', Oxford Uni. Pr.

Gardane A., 1865, 'La Mission du General Gardane en Perse sous le Première Empire', Paris.

Garlake P.S., 1966, 'The Early Islamic Architecture of the East African Coast', Oxford Uni. Pr.

Gavin R.J., 1962, 'The Bartle Frere Expedition and Zanzibar, 1873', *Historical Journal*, vol. 5, 122–48.

——1965, 'Sayyid Said', *Tarikh*, vol. 1, 16–29.

Germain A., 1868a, 'Quelques mots sur l'Oman et le Sultan de Maskate', *Bulletin de la Société de Géographie*, vol. 16, 339–64.

——1868b, 'Note sur Zanzibar et la côte orientale d'Afrique', *Bulletin de la Société de Géographie*, vol. 16, 530–59.

Gobineau A. de, 1859, 'Trois Ans en Asie (de 1855 a 1858)', Paris, Hachette.

Goiten S.D., 1954, 'From the Mediterranean to India: Documents on the Trade to India, South Arabia, and East Africa from the Eleventh and Twelfth Centuries', *Speculum*, vol. 29, 181–97.

——1980, 'From Aden to India – specimens of the Correspondence of India

Traders of the Twelfth Century', *Journal of the Economic and Social History of the Orient*, vol. 23, 43–66.

Gopal M.H., 1971, 'Tipu Sultan's Mysore: an economic study', Bombay.

Graham G.S., 1967, 'Great Britain in the Indian Ocean', Oxford, Clarendon Pr.

Grant D.K., 1938, 'Mangrove woods of Tanganyika Territory, their siviculture and dependent industries', TNR, no. 5, 5–16.

Gray J.M., 1946, 'Early Connections between the United States and East Africa', TNR, no. 22, 55–86.

——1947, 'Ahmed b. Ibrahim – the First Arab to reach Buganda', *Uganda Journal*, vol. 11, 80–97.

——1951–2, 'A History of Kilwa', part 1 in TNR, no. 31, 1–24; part 2 in TNR, no. 32, 11–37.

——1955, 'The Hadimu and Tumbatu of Zanzibar', published posthumously, TNR, 1977, nos 81 and 82, 135–53.

——1956, 'The French at Kilwa, 1776–1784', TNR, no. 44, 28–49.

——1957, 'The British in Mombasa, 1824–1826', London, Macmillan.

——1958, 'Trading Expeditions from the coast to lakes Tanganyika and Victoria before 1857', TNR, no. 49, 226–46.

——1961, 'The Diaries of Emin Pasha', *Uganda Journal*, vol. 25, 8–10.

——1962a, 'History of Zanzibar from the Middle Ages to 1856', Oxford Uni. Pr.

——1962b, 'The French at Kilwa in 1797', TNR, nos 58 and 59, 172–3.

——1964a, 'The Recovery of Kilwa by the Arabs in 1785', TNR, no. 62, 20–4.

——1964b, 'A French Account of Kilwa at the end of the eighteenth century', TNR, no. 63, 222–8.

Gray R. and Birmingham D., [eds], 1970, 'Precolonial African Trade', Oxford Uni. Pr.

Gregory R.G., 1971, 'India and East Africa. A History of Race Relations within the British Empire, 1890–1939', Oxford Uni. Pr.

Guillain C., 1841, 'Côte de Zanguebar et Mascate', *Revue Coloniale*, vol. 1, 1943, 520–71.

——1845, 'Documents sur l'Histoire, la Géographie, et le Commerce de la Partie Occidentale de Madagascar', Paris.

——1851, 'Voyage à la côte orientale d'Afrique exécuté pendant les années 1846, 1847 et 1848', in India Office Lib.

——1856, 'Documents sur l'Histoire, la Géographie et le Commerce de la Côte Orientale d'Afrique', 3 vols and album.

al-Hamdani A., 1956, 'Beginnings of the Ismaili Da'wa in northern India', Cairo, Sirovic.

——1967, 'The Fatimid-Abbasid Conflict in India', *Islamic Culture*, vol. 41, 185–91.

Hamilton A., 1727, 'A New Account of the East Indies', 2 vols, Edinburgh.

Hardinge A., 1928, 'A Diplomatist in the East', London, Cape.

Hasan M., 1971, 'History of Tipu Sultan', Calcutta, World Pr.

Helfer P., 1878 'Travels of Doctor and Madame Helfer in Syria, Mesopotamia, Burmah and other lands'. London, Bentley.

Henshaw J., 1840, 'Around the World', New York.

Heude W., 1819, 'A Voyage up the Persian Gulf and a Journey Overland from India to England in 1817', London.

Hodgson M.G., 1974, 'The Venture of Islam', 3 vols, Uni. of Chicago Pr.

Hollingsworth L.W., 1953, 'Zanzibar under the Foreign Office, 1890–1913', London, Macmillan.

Hollister J.N., 1953, 'The Shia of India', London, Luzac.

Holt P.M., 1966, 'Egypt and the Fertile Crescent, 1516–1922', Cornell Uni. Pr.

Hopwood D., [ed.], 1972, 'The Arabian Peninsula, Society and Politics', London, Allen & Unwin.

Horton M.C., 1984, 'The Early Settlement of the Northern Swahili Coast', Ph.D. th., Uni. of Cambridge.

Hourani G.F., 1951, 'Arab Seafaring in the Indian Ocean in Ancient and Early Medieval Times', Princeton Uni. Pr.

Hoyle B.S., 1967, 'The Seaports of East Africa', Nairobi, EAPH.

al-Humaydân, 'Abd-al-latîf Nâsir, 1981, 'Nufûdh al-Jubûr fî sharq al-Jazîrat al-'Arabîya..., 933/1525–1288/1871', *Majalla Kulliyat al-Âdâb*, Basra, vol. 18, 211–40.

Ingham K., 1962, 'A History of East Africa', London, Longman.

Ingrams W.H., 1931, 'Zanzibar, Its History and Its People', London, Witherby.

Irwing G.W., 1977, 'Africans Abroad: A Documentary History', Columbia Uni. Pr.

Isaacs N., 1936, 'Travels and Adventures in Eastern Africa', 2 vols, Cape Town.

Issawi C., 1970, 'The Decline of Middle Eastern Trade', in Richards D.S., [ed.], 1970, 'Islam and the Trade of Asia', Oxford, Cassirer, 245–66.

Jackson K.A., 1972, 'An ethnohistorical study of the oral traditions of the Akamba of Kenya', Ph.D. Dissn., UCLA.

Jacob G.L., 1860–2, 'Extracts from a Journal kept during a tour made in 1851 through Kutch ...', TBGS, vol. 16, 56–67.

Jameson J.F., 1923, 'Privateering and Piracy', London.

Jehangir B.H., 1973, 'The Arabs in Sind', Ph.D. Dissn., Uni. of Utah.

Jiddawi A.M., 1951, 'Extracts from an Arab account book, 1840–1854', TNR, no. 31, 25–31.

Johnson J., 1818, 'A Journey from India to England', London.

Jun-Yan Z., 1983, 'Relations between China and the Arabs in early times', JOS, vol. 6, 91–109.

Kajare F., 1914, 'Le Sultanat d'Oman: La Question de Mascate', Paris.

Kaniki M.H., [ed.], 1980, 'Tanzania Under Colonial Rule', London, Longman.

Kaye J.Y., 1856, 'The Life and Correspondence of Major-General Sir John Malcolm, G.C.B', 2 vols, London.

Kelly J.B., 1959, 'Sultanate and Imamate in Oman', Chatham House Memorandum.

——1965, 'Mehmet Ali's Expedition to the Persian Gulf, 1837–1840', MES, vol. 1, 350–81, vol. 2, 31–65.

——1968, 'Britain and the Persian Gulf, 1795–1880', Oxford, Clarendon Pr.

——1972, 'A Prevalence of Furies: Tribes, Politics and Religion in Oman and Trucial Oman', in Hopwood D., [ed.], 1972, 'The Arabian Peninsula, Society and Politics', London, Allen & Unwin.

Keppel G., 1837, 'Narrative of a Journey from India to England', London.

Kevran M., 1984, 'A la recherche du Suhar...', *Arabie Orientale, Mésopotamie et Iran Méridional*, no. 37, Paris.

Khazanov A.M., 1983, [English translation], 'Nomads and the Outside World', Cambridge Uni. Pr.

Kieran A.J., 1968, 'The Origins of the Zanzibar Guarantee of 1862', *Canadian Journal of African Studies*, vol. 2, 147–66.

Kilson M.L. and Rotberg R., [eds], 1976, 'The African Diaspora: Interpretative Essays', Cambridge Uni. Pr.

Kimambo I.N. and Temu A.J., [eds], 1969, 'A History of Tanzania', Nairobi, EAPH.

Kirk W., 1962, 'The north-east monsoon and some aspects of African history', JAH, vol. 3, 263–7.

Kirkman J., 1983, 'The Early History of Oman in East Africa', JOS, vol. 6, 41–5.

Kirkpatrick W., 1811, 'Select Letters of Tippoo Sultan', London.

Klein H., 1938, 'Kapitel XXXIII der anonymen arabischen Chronik Kashf al-ghumma al-jami li-akbar al-umma...', translation of parts of 'Kashf al-Ghumma', (q.v.), Hamburg.

Knappert J., 1979, 'Four Centuries of Swahili Verse', Nairobi, Heinemann.

——1985, 'East Africa and the Indian Ocean', in Stone J.C., [ed.], 'Africa and the Sea', Proceedings of a Colloquium at the University of Aberdeen, Aberdeen Uni. African Studies Group, 117–31.

Koffsky P.L., 1977, 'History of Takaungu, East Africa, 1830–1896', Ph.D. Dissn., Uni. of Wisconsin.

Krapf J.L., 1860, 'Travels, Researches and Missionary Labours in Eastern Africa', London.

Kroell A., 1977, 'Louis XIV, la Perse et Mascate', *Le Monde Iranien et l'Islam*, vol. 4, 1–78.

Kucchall S.C., 1963, 'The Industrial Economy of India', Allahabad.

Kumar R., 1962, 'British Attitudes towards the Ibadiyya Revivalist Movement in East Arabia', *International Studies*, vol. 3, 443–50.

——1965, 'India and the Persian Gulf Region, 1858–1907: A Study in British Imperial Policy', London, Asia Publishing House.

Lambton A.K.S., 1970, 'Persian Trade under the Early Qajars', in Richards D.S., [ed.], 1970, 'Islam and the Trade of Asia', Oxford, Cassirer, 215–44.

Lamphear J., 1970, 'The Kamba and the northern Mrima coast', in Gray R. and Birmingham D., [eds], 1970, 'Precolonial African Trade', Oxford Uni. Pr.

Landen R.G., 1967, 'Oman since 1856: Disruptive Modernization in a Traditional Arab Society', Princeton Uni. Pr.

Le Cour Grandmaison C., 1977, 'Spatial organisation, tribal groupings and kinship in Ibra', JOS, vol. 3, 95–106.

——1985, 'The Harthy Migration to Central Africa', published in Arabic under the title, 'Hijrât al-Hirth ilâ Awâsit al-Qârrat al-Ifriqîya', MNHC, 1985.

Leigh J.S., 1836–7, [Kirkman J.S., ed., 1980], 'The Zanzibar Diary of John Studdy Leigh', IJAHS, vol. 13, 281–312 and 492–507.

Levtzion N., 1986, 'Eighteenth century renewal and reform movements in Islam', *Proceedings of the British Society for Middle East Studies*, 185–94.

Lewicki T., 'Ibadiyya', in EI2.

——1935, 'Les premiers commerçants arabes en Chine', *Rocznik Oriental-istyczny*, vol. 11. 173–86.

——1959, 'Les Ibadites dans l'Arabie du Sud au Moyen Age', *Folia Orientalia*, vol. 1, 3–17.

——1971, 'The Ibadites in Arabia and Africa', *Journal of World History*, vol. 13, 3–81.

Lewis B., 1949/50, 'The Fatimids and the Route to India', *Revue de la Faculté des Sciences de l'Université d'Istanbul*, vols 1–4, 50–4.
——1976, 'The African Diaspora and the Civilization of Islam', in Kilson M.L. and Rotberg R., [eds], 1976, 'The African Diaspora: Interpretative Essays', Cambridge Uni. Pr., 37–57.
Livingstone D., 1857, 'Missionary Travels and Researches in South Africa', London, Murray.
——1874, [Waller H., ed.], 'Last Journals', 2 vols, London, Murray.
Loarer Capitaine, 1851, 'L'Ile de Zanzibar', *Revue de l'Orient*, vol. 9, 240–99.
Lockhart L., 1935–7, 'Nadir Shah's Campaigns in Oman, 1737–44', BSOAS, vol. 8 , 157–71.
——1946, 'The Menace of Muscat and its consequences in the late seventeenth and early eighteenth centuries', *Asiatic Review*, vol. 42, 363–9.
Lodhi A., 1973, 'The Institution of Slavery in Zanzibar and Pemba', Uppsala.
Lofchie M.F., 1965, 'Zanzibar, Background to Revolution', Princeton Uni. Pr.
Lombard M., 1971, 'L'Islam dans sa Première Grandeur', Paris, [Eng. translation], 1975, 'The Golden Age of Islam', Amsterdam.
Lorimer J.G., 1908–15, 'Gazetteer of the Persian Gulf, 'Oman and Central Arabia', 5 parts in 2 vols, Calcutta.
Lovejoy P.E., [ed.], 1981, 'The Ideology of Slavery in Africa', London, Sage.
——1983, 'Transformations in Slavery: A history of slavery in Africa', London, Sage.
Low C.R., 1877, 'History of the Indian Navy', 2 vols, London.
Lumsden T., 1822, 'A Journey from Merut in India to London', London.
Lyne R.N., 1905, 'Zanzibar in Contemporary Times', London, Hurst & Blackett.
Ly-Tio-Fane M., 1958, 'Mauritius and the Spice Trade: The Odyssey of Pierre Poivre', Port Louis, Mauritius, Esclapon.
Mckay W.F., 1975, 'A Precolonial History of the Southern Kenya Coast', Ph.D. Dissn., Boston Uni.
McMaster D.N., 1966, 'The Ocean-going dhow trade to East Africa', *East African Geographical Review*, vol. 4, 13–24.
MacMurdo J., 1820, 'An Account of the province of Cutch', TLSB, vol. 2, 205–41.
Macqueen J., 1845, 'Notes on African Geography: visit of Leif Ben Saed to the Great African Lake', JRGS, vol. 15, 371–6.
Malcolm J., 1827, 'Sketches of Persia by a Traveller', London.
Mangat J.S., 1969, 'A History of the Asians in East Africa', Oxford.
Martin B.G., [tr.] 1968, 'Materials for the understanding of Islam in German East Africa', Becker C.H., 1911, TNR, no. 68, 31–61.
——1969, 'Muslim politics and resistance to colonial rule. Shaykh Uways B. Muhammad al-Barawi and the Qadiriya brotherhood in East Africa', JAH, vol. 10, 471–86.
——1971, 'Notes on some members of the learned classes of Zanzibar and East Africa in the nineteenth century', AHS, vol. 4, 525–46.
——1974, 'Arab migrations to East Africa in medieval times', IJAHS, vol. 7, 367–90.
——1976, 'Muslim Brotherhoods in nineteenth century Africa', Cambridge Uni. Pr.
Martin E.B., 1978, 'Zanzibar, Tradition and Revolution', London.

——and Ryan T.C., 1977, 'A quantitative assessment of the Arab slave trade of East Africa, 1770–1896', *Kenya Historical Review*, vol. 5, 71–91.

Marx E., 1977, 'The tribe as a unit of subsistence: nomadic pastoralism in the Middle East', *American Anthropologist*, vol. 79, 343–63.

Mathew G., 1963, 'The East African coast until the coming of the Portuguese', in Oliver R. and Mathew J., [eds], 1963, 'History of East Africa', vol. 1, Oxford, Clarendon Pr., 94–127.

Maurizi V., (Shaikh Mansur), 1819, 'History of Seyd Said, Sultan of Muscat...', London, Booth.

Michaud J., 1801, 'Histoire des Progrès et da la chute de l'Empire de Mysore...', 2 vols, Paris.

Middleton J., 1961, 'Land Tenure in Zanzibar', London, HMSO.

——and Campbell J., 1965, 'Zanzibar, its Society and its Politics', Oxford Uni. Pr.

Miège J.-L., 1982, 'L'Oman et l'Afrique Orientale au XIX siecle', in Bonnenfant P. [ed.], 1982, 'Le Péninsule Arabique d'aujord'hui', 2 vols, CNRS, Paris.

Miers S., 1975, 'Britain and the Ending of the Slave Trade', London, Longman.

Milburn W., 1813, 'Oriental Commerce', 2 vols, London.

Miles S.B., 1877, 'On the Route Between Sohar and el-Bereymi in Oman...', *Journal of the Asiatic Society of Bengal*, vol. 46, 41–60.

——1919, 'The Countries and Tribes of the Persian Gulf', 2 vols, London (1966 reprint).

Misra B.B., 1961, 'The Indian Middle Classes; Their Growth in Modern Times', Delhi, Oxford Uni. Pr.

Misra S.C., 1964, 'Muslim Communities in Gujarat: Preliminary studies in their history and social organisation', Bombay.

Mollat M., [ed.], 1970, 'Sociétés et Compagnies de Commerce en Orient et dans l'Océan Indien', Paris.

Morice, 1777, 'Projet d'un Etablissement sur la côte orientale d'Afrique', Rhodes House Lib., Uni. of Oxford, MSS Afr. r. 6; photocopy of this version also in ZA/BZ2/1; Eng. translation by Freeman-Grenville G.S.P., 1965.

Morsy Abdullah M., 1970, 'The First Sa'udi Dynasty and Uman, 1795–1818', *Proceedings of the Seminar of Arabian Studies*, no. 4, 34–41.

——1978, 'Imârât al-Sâḥil wa 'Umân wa al-Dawlat al-Sa'ûdiyya al-ʿûlâ, 1793–1818', Cairo.

Mookerji R.K., 1912, 'Indian Shipping: A History of the Seaborne Trade of the Indians from the Earliest Times', Bombay, Longman.

Moyse-Bartlett H., 1966, 'The Pirates of Trucial Oman', London, Macdonald.

al-Nadvî, Muhammad Ismâ'îl, n.d. 'Tâʾrîkh al-ṣilât bayna al-Hind wa al-Bilad al-'Arabiya', Beirut.

al-Nadvi S.S., 1930, 'Arab-o-Hind ki Ta'alluqat', Allahabad.

——1966, 'Arab Navigation', Lahore.

Naff T. and Owen R., [eds], 1977, 'Studies in Eighteenth-Century Islamic History', Carbondale, Southern Illinois Uni. Pr.

Nanji A., 1978, 'The Nizari Isma'ili Tradition in the Indo–Pakistan Sub-continent', New York, Caravan Books.

Nasr S.H., [ed.], 1977, 'Isma'ili Contributions to Islamic Culture', Tehran, Imperial Iranian Academy of Philosophy.

New C., 1873, 'Life, Wanderings and Labours in Eastern Africa', London, Hodder & Stoughton.

Newitt M., 1984 'The Comoro Islands – Struggle against Dependency in the Indian Ocean', London, Westview.

Nicholls C.S., 1968, 'European and Arab Activities on the East African Coast, 1798–1856, and the local reaction to them', D.Phil. th., Uni. of Oxford.

——1971, 'The Swahili Coast – Politics, Diplomacy and Trade on the East African Littoral, 1798–1856', London, Allen & Unwin.

Niebuhr C., [tr.], 1792, 'Travels through Arabia', 2 vols, Edinburgh.

Nightingale P., 1970, 'Trade and Empire in Western India, 1784–1806', Cambridge Uni. Pr.

Northway P.H., 1954, 'Salem and the Zanzibar East African trade, 1825–1845', EIHC, vol. 90, 123–53, 261–73 and 361–88.

Nurse D. and Spear T., 1984, 'The Swahili: Reconstructing the History and Language of an African Society, 800–1500', Uni. of Pennsylvania Pr.

Ogot B., [ed.], 1973, 'Zamani: A Survey of East African History', Nairobi, EAPH.

Oliver R., 1963, 'Discernible developments in the interior, c. 1500–1840', in Oliver R. and Mathew J., [eds], 1963, 'History of East Africa', vol. 1, Oxford, Clarendon Pr., 169–211.

——and Mathew G., [eds], 1963, 'History of East Africa', vol. 1, Oxford, Clarendon Pr.

Osgood J.F., 1854, 'Notes on Travel; or Recollections of Majunga, Zanzibar, Muscat, Aden, Mocha and other Eastern Ports', Salem.

Owen W.F., 1833, 'Narrative of Voyages to Explore the Shores of Africa, Arabia and Madagascar', 2 vols, London, Bentley.

Ozbaran S, 1972, 'The Ottoman Turks and the Portuguese in the Persian Gulf, 1534–1581', *Journal of Asian History*, vol. 6, 45–87.

Palgrave W.G., 1865, 'Narrative of a Year's Journey through Central and Eastern Arabia', London, Macmillan.

Parsons A., 1808, 'Travels in Asia and Africa', London.

Pearce F.B., 1920, 'Zanzibar, the Island Metropolis of Eastern Africa', London, Unwin.

Pearson M.N., 1976, 'Merchants and Rulers in Gujarat: the response to the Portuguese in the sixteenth century', Uni. of California Pr.

Pelly L., 1863–4, 'Remarks on the tribes and resources around the shore line of the Persian Gulf', TBGS, vol. 17, 32–103.

——1864, 'Remarks on the Port of Lingah, the Island of Kishm, and the Port of Bunder Abbas, and its neighbourhood', TBGS, vol. 17, 237–55.

——1865, 'Report on a journey to Riyadh in Central Arabia', Cambridge, Oleander Pr.

——1865–7, 'Remarks on the Pearl Oyster Beds in the Persian Gulf', TBGS, vol. 18, 32–6.

Pengelley W.M., 1860–2, 'Remarks on a portion of the Eastern coast of Arabia between Muscat and Sohar', TBGS, vol. 16, 30–40.

Perry J.R., 1973, 'Mir Muhanna and the Dutch: Patterns of Piracy in the Persian Gulf', *Studia Iranica*, vol. 2, 79–95.

Peterson J.E., 1978, 'Oman in the Twentieth Century: Political Foundations of an Emerging State', London, Croom Helm.

Picklay A.S., 1940, 'History of the Ismailis', Bombay.

Pocock D.F., 1955, 'Indians in East Africa, with special reference to their Social and Economic Situation and Relationship', D.Phil. th., Uni. of Oxford.

Porter J.D., [ed.], 1982, 'U.S. Documents on Oman and the Persian Gulf, 1835–1949', USA Documentary Publications.

Postans T., 1839–40, 'Some Account of the present state of the trade between the port of Mandvie in Cutch, and the East Coast of Africa', TBGS, vol. 3, 169–76.

Pouwels R.L., 1974, 'Tenth Century Settlement of the East African Coast: the case for Qarmatian/Ismaili connection', in *Azania*, vol. 9, 65–74.

——1978, 'The Medieval Foundations of East African Islam', IJAHS, vol. 11, 201–27 and 393–409.

——1987, 'Horn and Crescent, Cultural Change and Traditional Islam on the East African Coast, 800–1900', Cambridge Uni. Pr.

Pridham B.R. [ed.], 1987, 'Oman: Economic, Social and Strategic Developments', London, Croom Helm.

Prins A.H., 1958, 'On Swahili Historiography', *Journal of the East African Swahili Committee*, vol. 28, 26–41.

——1961, 'The Swahili-speaking Peoples of Zanzibar and the East African Coast', London, International East African Institute.

——1965, 'Sailing from Lamu', Assen, Van Gorcum.

Pullicino P., 1954, 'Aulad el-Imam', Zanzibar.

al-Qasimi S.M., 1986, 'The Myth of Arab Piracy in the Gulf', London, Routledge.

Qasim J.Z., 1968, 'Dawlat Bû Sa'îd fî 'Umân wa Sharq Ifrîqiya, 1741–1861', Cairo.

al-Rashid Z.M., 1981, 'Su'udi Relations with Eastern Arabia and 'Uman (1800–1871)', London, Luzac.

Ravenstein E.G., 1898, 'A Journal of the First Voyage of Vasco De Gama, 1497–99', London.

Renault F., 1971, 'Lavigerie l'esclavage africain et l'Europe, 1868–1892', D. es Lettres, published th., Paris, 2 vols

Reusch R., 1954, 'History of East Africa', Stuttgart.

Richards D.S., [ed.], 1970, 'Islam and the Trade of Asia', Oxford, Cassirer.

Ricks T.M., 1970, 'Persian Gulf Seafaring and East Africa: Ninth to Twelfth Centuries', AHS, vol. 3, 339–57.

Ridley H.N., 1912, 'Spices', London, Macmillan.

Risso P., 1986, 'Oman & Muscat, An Early Modern History', London, Croom Helm.

Rivoyre D. De, 1883, 'Obock, Mascate, Bouchire, Bassorah', Paris, Plon.

Rizvi S.A. and King S.Q., 1973, 'Some East African Ithna'ashari Jamaats (1840–1967)', *Journal of Religion in Africa*, vol. 5, 12–22.

——1974, 'The Khoja Shia Ithna-ashariya Community in East Africa', *The Muslim World*, vol. 64, 194–204.

Roberts A.D., 1967, 'The History of Abdullah ibn Suliman', *African Social Research*, vol. 4, 241–70.

——[ed.], 1968, 'Tanzania before 1900', Nairobi, EAPH.

——1970, 'Nyamwezi Trade', in Gray R. and Birmingham D., [eds], 1970, 'Precolonial African Trade', Oxford Uni. Pr., 39–74.

Roberts E., 1837, 'Embassy to the Eastern Courts of Cochin-China, Siam and Muscat in the U.S. Sloop-of-War Peacock,...1832–34', New York, Harper.

Rodney W., 1972, 'How Europe Underdeveloped Africa', London.
Ross E.C., 1866, 'Memorandum of notes on Mekran...', TBGS, vol. 18, 36–78.
——1873, 'Memorandum on the Tribal Divisions in the Principality of Oman', TBGS, vol. 19, 187–98.
——1874, 'Annals of Oman', a partial translation of 'Kashf al-Ghumma' (q.v.), *Journal of the Asiatic Society of Bengal*, vol. 43, 111–96.
Ross R., [tr. and ed.], 1986, 'The Dutch on the Swahili Coast, 1776–1778: Two Slaving Journals', IJAHS, part 1, 305–60; part 2, 479–506.
Ruschenberger W.S., 1838, 'Narrative of a Voyage round the World', 2 vols, London, Bentley.
Rushbrook Williams L.F., 1985, 'The Black Hills: Kutch in history and legend', London.
Russell C.E.B., 1935, 'General Rigby, Zanzibar and the Slave Trade', London, Allen & Unwin.
Sadlier G.F., 1819, 'Diary of a Journey Across Arabia', Bombay.
Said-Ruete E., [tr.], 1886, 'Memoirs of an Arabian Princess', London.
Said-Ruete R., 1929, 'Said bin Sultan (1791–1856), Ruler of Oman and Zanzibar', London.
Salibi K., 1980, 'A History of Arabia', Beirut, Caravan Books.
Schacht J., 1956, 'Bibiothèques et Manuscrits abadites', *Revue Africaine*, vol. 100, 376–98.
——1965, 'Notes on Islam in East Africa', *Studia Islamica*, vol. 23, 91–133.
Serjeant R.B., 1963, 'The Portuguese off the South Arabian Coast', Oxford Uni. Pr.
Shepherd G., 1982, 'The Making of the Swahili: A View from the Southern End of the East African Coast', *Paideuma*, vol. 28, 129–49.
Sheriff A.M.H., 1971, 'The rise of a commercial empire: an aspect of the economic history of Zanzibar, 1770–1873', Ph.D. th., Uni. of London.
——1987, 'Slaves, Spices & Ivory in Zanzibar', London, Currey.
Skeet I., 1974, 'Muscat and Oman: the end of an era', London, Faber.
Smith G.R., 1978, 'Omani Manuscript Collection at Muscat – Part 1. A General Description of the MSS', *Arabian Studies*, vol. 4, 161–90.
Spear P., 1965, 'A History of India', vol. 2, London, Penguin.
Spear T., 1974, 'The Kaya complex: a history of the Mijikenda peoples of the Kenya coast to 1900', Ph.D. dissn., uni. of Wisconsin.
——1981, 'Oral Traditions: Whose History?', *History in Africa*, vol. 8, 165–81.
Speke J.H., 1862, 'On the commerce of Central Africa', TBGS, vol. 15, 145–8.
——1863, 'Journal of the Discovery of the Sources of the Nile', London.
——1864, 'What led to the Discovery of the Sources of the Nile', London.
Stanley H.M., 1872, 'How I Found Livingstone', London, 2nd edn.
——1878, 'Through the Dark Continent', 2 vols, London.
——1961, [ed. Stanley R. and Neame A.], 'The Exploration Diaries of H.M. Stanley', London, Kimber.
Steensgaard N., 1972, 'Carracks, Caravans and Companies: The Structural Crisis in the European–Asian Trade in the Early Seventeenth Century', Scandinavian Institute of Asian Studies, Monograph no. 17, Copenhagen.
Stern S.M., 1949, 'Ismaili Propaganda and Fatimid Rule in Sind', *Islamic Culture*, vol. 23, 298–307.
——1960, 'The Early Ismaili Missionaries in North-West Persia and in Kurasan and Transoxania', BSOAS, vol. 23, 56–90.

Stiffe A., 1860, 'A visit to the hot springs of Bosher', TBGS, vol. 15, 123–8.

Stigand C.H., 1913, 'The Land of Zinj', London, Constable.

Stocqueler J.H., 1832, 'Fifteen Months Pilgrimage through untrodden tracks of Kuzistan and Persia', London.

Stone J.C., [ed.], 1985, 'Africa and the Sea', *Proceedings of a Colloquium at the University of Aberdeen*, Aberdeen Uni. African Studies Group.

Strandes J., 1899, [tr. by Wallwork J.F.], 'The Portuguese Period in East Africa', Nairobi, 1961.

Strong S.A., [ed.], 1895, 'History of Kilwa', JRAS, vol. 54, 385–430.

al-Sudairan Nasser, 1973, 'La France et Mascate', Thèse de troisième cycle, Université de Bordeaux III.

Sulivan G.L., 1873, 'Dhow Chasing in Zanzibar Waters', London.

Sutton J.E., [ed.], 1969, 'Dar es Salaam: City, Port and Region', TNR, no. 71, special issue.

Sykes Colonel, 1853, 'Notes on the possessions of the Imaum of Muskat, on the climate and production of Zanzibar, and the prospects of African Discovery', JRGS, vol. 23, 101–19.

al-Tabuki S.B., 'Tribal Structures in South Oman', *Arabian Studies*, vol. 6, 51–6.

Thooti N.A., 1935, 'The Vaishanava of Gujerat', New Delhi.

Tibbetts G.R., 1974, 'Arabia in the fifteenth century navigational texts', *Arabian Studies*, vol. 1, 86–101.

Tidbury G.E., 1949, 'The Clove Tree', London, Lockwood.

al-Tirâzî, 'Abd-allâh, 1983, 'Mawsû'at al-tâˋrîkh al-Islâmî wa al-Hadârat al-Islâmîya li bilâd al-Sind wa al-Panjâb fî 'ahd al-'Arab', 2 vols, 'Ãlam al-Ma'rifa, Jeddah.

Tirmidhi, B.A., 1947, 'The Contribution of the Scholars of Gujarat to Arabic Language and Literature', Ph.D., Uni. of Bombay.

Tolmacheva M., 1976, 'The Origin of the Name Swahili', TNR, nos 77–8, 27–37.

——1986, 'Towards a definition of the term Zanj', *Azania*, vol. 21, 105–13.

Topan M.T., 1962–3, 'Biography of Sir Tharia Topan Knight', Manuscript in private possession.

Tosh J., 1970, 'The northern inter-lacustrine region', in Gray R. and Birmingham D., [eds], 1970, 'Precolonial African Trade, Oxford Uni. Pr., 103–18.

Toussaint A., 1972, 'Histoire des iles mascareignes', Paris.

Townsend J., 1977, 'Oman: The making of the modern state', London, Croom Helm.

Trimingham J.S., 1964, 'Islam in East Africa', Oxford, Clarendon Pr.

——1965, 'Islam in Ethiopia', Oxford Uni. Pr.

——1975a, 'The Arab Geographers and the East African Coast', in Chittick H.N. and Rotberg R.I., [eds], 1975, 'East Africa and the Orient', New York, Africana Publishing, 115–47.

——1975b, 'Notes on Arabic Sources of Information on East Africa', in Chittick H.N. and Rotberg R.I., [eds], 1975, 'East Africa and the Orient', New York, Africana Publishing, 248–72.

Tuson P., 1979, 'The Records of the British Residency and Agencies in the Persian Gulf', London, BL.

Unomah A.C., 1973, 'Economic expansion and political change in Unyanyembe, c. 1840–1900', Ph.D. th., Uni. of Ibadan.

Uzoigwe G.N., 1974, 'Britain and the Conquest of Africa. The Age of Salisbury', Uni. of Michigan Pr.

Vatikiotis P.J., 1969, 'The History of Egypt, from Muhammad Ali to Sadat', London, Weidenfeld & Nicolson.

Villiers A., 1940, 'Sons of Sindbad', New York.

——1948, 'Some Aspects of the Arab dhow trade', *Middle East Journal*, vol. 11, 398–416.

Voll J.O., 1982, 'Islam: Continuity and Change in the Modern World', London, Westview.

Wadia R.A., 1955, 'The Bombay Dockyard and the Wadia Master Builders', Bombay.

Walji S.R., 1974, 'A History of the Ismaili Community in Tanzania', Ph.D. Dissn., Uni. of Wisconsin.

Weisgerber G., 1979, 'Muscat in 1688: Engelbert Kaempfer's Report and Engravings', JOS, vol. 5, 95–101.

Wellsted J.R., 1837, 'Narrative of a Journey into the Interior of Oman', JRGS, vol. 7, 102–13.

——1838, 'Travels in Arabia', 2 vols, London, Murray.

——1840, 'Travels to the City of the Caliphs, along the Shores of the Persian Gulf and the Mediterranean', 2 vols, London.

Werner A., 1914–16, 'A Swahili History of Pate', *Journal of the African Society*, vol. 14–16, 148–66, 278–97 and 392–413.

Whitehouse D., 1979, 'Maritime trade in the Arabian Sea. The 9th and 10th centuries A.D.', *South Asian Archeology, 1977*, 865–85, Naples.

——and Williamson A., 1973, 'Sasanian maritime trade', *Iran*, vol. 11, 29–49.

Whiteley W.H., [ed.], 1958/9, 'Maisha ya Hamed bin Muhammed el Murjebi yaani Tippu Tip', in *Swahili*, vol. 28–9, supplement.

Wilkinson J.C., 1969, 'Arab Settlement in Oman: The Origins and Development of the Tribal Pattern and its Relationship to the Imamate', D. Phil. th., Uni. of Oxford.

——1972, 'The Origins of the Omani State', in Hopwood D., [ed.], 1972, 'The Arabian Peninsula, Society and Politics', London, Allen & Unwin, 67–88.

——1973, 'Arab–Persian land relationships in Late Sasanid Oman', *Proceedings of the Seminar for Arabian Studies*, no. 6, 40–51.

——1974, 'Bayasira and Bayadir', *Arabian Studies*, vol. 1, 75–85.

——1975, 'The Julanda of Oman', JOS, vol. 1, 97–109.

——1976, 'The Ibadi Imama', BSOAS, vol. 39, 535–51.

——1977, 'Water and Tribal Settlement in South-East Arabia: A Study of the Aflaj of Oman', Oxford, Clarendon Pr.

——1978, 'Omani Manuscript Collection at Muscat – Part II: Early Ibadi Fiqh Works', *Arabian Studies*, vol. 6, 191–208.

——1979, 'Ṣuḥâr (Sohar) in the Early Islamic period: the written evidence', *South Asian Archeology, 1977*, 887–907, Naples.

——1981, 'Oman and East Africa. New light on early Kilwan history from the Omani sources', IJAHS, vol. 6, 272–305.

——1983, 'Traditional concepts of territory in South East Arabia', *Geographical Journal*, vol. 169, 301–15.

——1987, 'The Imamate Tradition of Oman', Cambridge Uni. Pr.

Williamson A., 1973a, 'Sohar and Omani Seafaring in the Indian Ocean', Muscat.

——1973b, 'Hurmuz and the trade of the Gulf in the 14th and the 15th centuries A.D.', *Proceedings of the Seminar for Arabian Studies*, no. 6, 52–68.

Winder R.B., 1965, 'Saudi Arabia in the Nineteenth Century', London, Macmillan.

Wolpert S., 1977, 'A New History of India', Oxford Uni. Pr.

Yapp M.E., 1960, 'British Policy in Central Asia, 1830–1843', Ph.D. th., Uni. of London.

——1980, 'Strategies of British India: Britain, Iran and Afghanistan, 1798–1850', Oxford Uni. Pr.

——1987, 'The Making of the Modern Near East, 1792–1923', London, Longman.

Ylvisaker M., 1975, 'The Political and Economic Relationship of the Lamu Archipelago to the Adjacent Kenya Coast in the nineteenth century', Ph.D. Dissn., Boston Uni.

——1979, 'Lamu in the Nineteenth Century: Land, Trade and Politics', Boston, African Studies Center.

——1982, 'The Ivory trade in the Lamu area, 1600–1870', *Paideuma*, vol. 28, 221–31.

Yule H., [ed.], 1871, 'The Book of Marco Polo', London.

Zaehner R.C., [ed.], 1959, 'The Concise Encyclopedia of Living Faiths', London, Hutchinson.

Index

1 Non-Western individuals are classified under their first names, thus Sa' îd b Sulṭân Âlbûsa'îdî is shown under Sa'îd. Westerners will be found under their surnames.
2 Tribal and family names are normally classified under the main name, thus Âl-Khalîfa is under Khalîfa; Banû Nabhân under Nabhân; Alwâd Qays under Qays.
3 Entries with the Arabic article *al* are under the main noun, thus al-Ya'rubî will be found under Y.